50 YEARS OF BRITISH GRAND PRIX DRIVERS

By Peter Scherer

tfm Publishing Limited

Published by:-

t/m Publishing Limited
Brimstree View
Kemberton
Nr. Shifnal
Shropshire
TF11 9LL

Tel: 01952 586408
Fax: 01952 587654
E-mail: nikki@tfmpub.freeserve.co.uk

Design and layout: Nikki Bramhill

First Edition   December 1999

ISBN 0 9530052 8 3

Contents

Part One

Drivers who started their Grand Prix careers in the 1950s

Part Two

Drivers who started their Grand Prix careers in the 1960s

Part Three

Drivers who started their Grand Prix careers in the 1970s

Part Four

Drivers who started their Grand Prix careers in the 1980s

Part Five

Drivers who started their Grand Prix careers in the 1990s

Part Six

Statistics and alphabetic index

M y first glimpse of a real life Grand Prix car came at the qualifying day for the Mallory Park 2000 Guineas in 1962, when I was seven years old. I was lucky enough to see John Surtees in his Bowmaker Lola as well as Graham Hill, but many of the other facts from that day sadly passed me by.

Although my enthusiasm continued to build, it was the 1967 British Grand Prix at Silverstone that really fired my interest. It was Jim Clark's last British Grand Prix win, the last year before sponsorship and my first chance to obtain some of the drivers autographs. Having seen the finish of the race from the pit balcony, I raced down the steps to greet Pedro Rodriguez who had just finished the 80-lap race with his Cooper Maserati in fifth place. As he climbed from the car I thrust my autograph book to the fore, and he kindly obliged by signing it. Since that day I have visited most of Europe's Grand Prix circuits and at some time met most of the drivers, but that day has a lasting place in my memories.

As the Millennium approached I decided to update my own archive of British Grand Prix drivers' careers. A number of my colleagues suggested that it would a good idea to put it in print, and the seeds for this book were then sown. Whether a gentleman racer of the early fifties or a career-minded professional of the nineties, they are all included. Where possible we have included the driver's autograph and a photograph.

Over the last two years I have painstakingly researched every British Grand Prix driver's career, provided that they actually started a World Championship Grand Prix since 1950. Everyone knows what they achieved during their Grand Prix careers, but I have attempted to trace the story of how they got there and in some cases what they did after. None of this would have been possible without the co-operation of the BRDC Archive at Silverstone, where I have scoured copies of Speed & Motorsport from the mid-thirties to the mid-fifties, and every copy of Autosport ever published.

Most of the photographs have been supplied by the BRDC, along with Ted Walker at Ferret Fotographics and a selection from the drivers themselves. Steve Small's book 'The Grand Prix Who's Who' has also been invaluable in pointing me in the right direction and confirming or denying some of the vaguer facts.

I would also like to thank Paul Lawrence and Nikki Bramhill at TFM Publishing Ltd for helping put this project together and some of the drivers and their families for their encouragement. Last but by no means least, my wife Lynda and the BRDC's James Beckett for plying me with coffee as I ploughed through the seemingly endless notes.

Peter Scherer
Derby
December 1999

50 years of British Grand Prix drivers

Part One
1950s

CHAPTER 1

GEORGE ABECASSIS
Born March 21st 1913
Died December 18th 1991

George Abecassis (left).
Photo: BRDC Archive.

Abecassis was a driver whose career spanned both sides of the war years. He started racing in 1935 and enjoyed considerable success before the war put racing on hold for seven long years. When the sport resumed in late 1946, Abecassis was one of the first competitors.

After a number of years racing a Bugatti, he helped develop the Alta Grand Prix car. Most of the fifties however, were spent in partnership with John Heath, for whom he made his two Grand Prix starts in the HWM. Both attempts were at the Swiss Grands Prix of 1951 and 1952, but he retired from both races.

He was also part of the works David Brown Aston Martin sports car team and after marrying Brown's daughter Angela, he retired from the sport at the end of 1956 at the age of 43. With Aston Martin he twice finished fifth at Le Mans, but through the mid-50s,

most of his success was at national level. During his career, like so many of his contemporaries, he regularly competed in speed events but contesting several ice racing events in Sweden was rather more unusual.

GRAND PRIX RECORD	
Starts	2
Wins	0
Poles	0
Fastest laps	0
WC points	0
Best finish	DNF

1935 Raced at Brooklands and Donington Park in an Austin Seven, taking a 3rd place at Donington in an 850 scratch race.

1936 Finished 3rd in a Brooklands Handicap with an Alta.

1937 Continued to race his Alta with varying success.

1938 Won the Imperial and Crystal Palace Trophies with the Alta, and led the Sydenham Trophy until spinning into the lake. He also won the Brooklands British Trophy and Easter Handicap, had a sports car victory at Crystal Palace, three class wins at the Lewes Speed Trials and took the outright record during one of two Prescott Hillclimb victories. There was also a 2nd place in the Coronation Trophy at Crystal Palace, 2nd and 3rd in classes at Brighton Speed Trials, 2nd at Prescott (three times) and in the Brooklands October Handicap, 4th in the London Grand Prix, 14th in the JCC Donington International Trophy and 19th at Shelsley Walsh.

1939 Won the Imperial Trophy at Crystal Palace again in his Alta Sports.

1946 Continued to race an Alta, but also won the Invitation race at Gransden Lodge in a Bugatti.

1947 Started the year ice racing in Sweden and finished 3rd in the Vinter Grand Prix. Driving his ERA he finished 2nd in the Swedish Grand Prix and 3rd in the Ulster Trophy. An outing in a Cisitalia netted 2nd place from the Caracalla race in Rome, but success came mainly with his Bugatti. Finished 2nd in the Gransden Trophy, but most results were in hillclimbs including 2nd overall at Prescott and Bouley Bay, a class win at Bo'ness, 5th on a second visit to Prescott, 7th and a class win at Shelsley Walsh, and 3rd in class at the Poole Speed Trials. The Alta also made occasional appearances, and took 11th at Prescott.

1948 Although the Alta appeared in the Empire Trophy, he took 2nd place in the Jersey Road Race at the wheel of a Maserati.

1949 The Grand Prix Alta was taken to 7th in the British Grand Prix and 6th in the Richmond Trophy at Goodwood, while other results included 3rd in the Goodwood Easter Handicap with a Cooper and 4th in the Madgwick Cup with an HWM Alta.

1950 His HWM secured 6th at Roubaix, 7th in the Goodwood Chichester Cup, and 9th in the Prix de Berne. But as part of the Aston Martin team he finished 5th in the TT and Le Mans, sharing his DB2 with Lance Macklin. The DB2 also claimed 12th in the Sports class at Shelsley Walsh, and he finished 3rd in a Goodwood Handicap with a Healey.

1951 A one-off World Championship outing ended with the HWM retiring at the Swiss Grand Prix. The car was used to better effect on home soil, with a victory and 3rd place at Castle Combe, 2nd at Winfield, 3rd in the Madgwick Cup at Goodwood 4th in the Daily Mirror Trophy at Boreham and 7th in the Daily Graphic Trophy at Goodwood. A further continental foray clinched 5th in the Columbus Centenary Grand Prix in Genoa, while continuing as part of the Aston Martin team he took 5th at Le Mans with Shawe-Taylor.

1952 A return to the Swiss Grand Prix for his second and final World Championship outing, resulted in a broken hub causing his HWM to crash out of the race. He finished 4th in the Goodwood Richmond Trophy and 2nd at Ibsley and in the Goodwood Easter Handicap. Having moved up to an Aston Martin DB3 he finished 2nd in the Jersey Road Race, 3rd in the International Trophy Production race at Silverstone and 3rd at Snetterton.

1953 After taking 2nd in the Sebring 12hrs with Parnell in an Aston Martin DB3, he raced in the Mille Miglia, Le Mans and Goodwood 9hrs without recording a finish. Sports Car success did come however with an HWM Jaguar, with two wins at Goodwood and Snetterton, a class win at Shelsley Walsh, 3rd and 4th in classes at Prescott and 7th at Caen. He was also heading for 4th with Frere at the Reims 12hrs, when retirement struck.

1954 Concentrated on the HWM in mostly national races, winning at Davidstow, taking 2nd in the International Trophy Sports Car race at Silverstone, 2nd and 3rd at Goodwood, 3rd in both Libre and Sports at Castle Combe, 4th in the Goodwood Easter Handicap, 8th in the Empire Trophy and 14th in the TT. After taking 2nd at Hedemora, he was heading for similar result at the Hyeres 12hrs until crashing out. He also drove a Daimler to 6th place in the International Trophy Production Touring Race.

1955 Won the Redex Trophy at Castle Combe, the USAF Trophy and Sports at Oulton Park and two scratch wins and a handicap win at Goodwood in the HWM. There was also 2nd in class at the Brighton Golden Jubilee Speed Trials, 3rd in a Goodwood Handicap, 6th at Oulton Park and Goodwood and 8th in the British Grand Prix Sports Car race. Driving a Healey 100S he took 11th in the Mille Miglia and finished 2nd at Snetterton in a Jaguar D-Type.

1956 Had a win at Goodwood, 2nd and 3rd at Snetterton, a class win at Shelsley Walsh, 2nd in class at Brighton Speed Trials and 6th in class in the Lake Freden Ice race in Sweden, all with the HWM. Retired from racing at the end of the season.

❖

CLIFF ALLISON
Born February 8th 1932

Cliff Allison.

A 500cc Formula 3 graduate who also became one of Colin Chapman's first works drivers at Lotus, partnering Chapman himself in a Lotus XI. Success in sports cars and Formula 2 led to his entry into Grand Prix racing with Lotus in 1958, firstly with the Lotus 12 and then with the superb 16. Some impressive performances throughout that season led to him joining Ferrari the following year, with the chance to race both Formula 1 and sports cars.

Two years at Maranello brought moderate success in Grand Prix and a victory with sports cars in the Buenos Aires 1000km. His best Grand Prix result was second in Argentina at the start of the season, but his potential was never to be fully realised for an accident at Monaco left him with a badly broken arm and dropped by Ferrari. After returning to the UK to race for UDT Laystall, he crashed during qualifying for the Belgian Grand Prix and seriously injured his legs after being thrown from the car, which prompted his retirement.

GRAND PRIX RECORD

Starts	16
Wins	0
Poles	0
Fastest laps	0
WC points	11
Best finish	2nd

1952 Made his racing debut with an F3 Cooper JAP at Charterhall.

1953 Raced in F3 again and finished 3rd at Brough.

1954 Won at Cadwell Park, finished 2nd at Charterhall and in the Redex Trophy at Crystal Palace, 3rd at Brough, 4th and 5th at Crystal Palace, 5th at Snetterton, 6th at Aintree and scored a class win at the Barbon Hillclimb with his Cooper JAP.

1955 Finished 4th in the F3 Championship, winning twice at Charterhall and Brough, plus Olivers Mount and Cadwell Park. Finished 2nd at Brands Hatch, two 2nds and a 3rd at Snetterton, 3rd twice at both Crystal Palace and Oulton Park, 3rd and 5th at Aintree, 4th at the International Trophy support race and a 2nd in class at Barbon. He also raced a Lotus XI to 11th place in the TT, sharing with Colin Chapman.

1956 Joined the fledgling Team Lotus and took his F2 car to 3rd in the Madgwick Cup, Sporting Life Trophy at Oulton Park and F2 race at Brands Hatch, 4th in the British Grand Prix F2 race, 6th in the Sussex Trophy and 7th in the Oulton Park Gold Cup. With the Lotus XI he won sports car races at Aintree and Brands Hatch, finished 2nd in the Crystal Palace August Trophy, the Coupe Deboutteville and at Brands Hatch, 4th at Whitsun Goodwood and 5th at Crystal Palace. In F3 he was 4th at

the International Trophy, 5th at Oulton Park and 6th at Aintree.

1957 His successes with the Lotus XI began to outweigh his F2 results, with 14th overall and victory in the Index of Performance at Le Mans, sharing with Keith Hall. He also won at Roskilde, and twice at Brands Hatch, with 5th in the Coupe Deboutteville at Rouen, 9th at Karlskoga and took a class win at Spa. He raced the Lotus 12 F2 car to 2nd in the Oulton Park Gold Cup and 3rd at Goodwood.

1958 A full year of Grand Prix racing with Lotus started with 6th place in both Monaco and the Dutch Grand Prix, before taking 4th in Belgium. His only retirement came in the French GP, but at the British he practiced the new Lotus 16. He elected to race the older 12 having qualified an amazing 5th, only to retire with low oil pressure. He raced the 16 in Germany to 5th place, but crashed during qualifying in Portugal and hired a 250F Maserati from Centro Sud for the race. Electing to stay with the older car, he rounded off his year with 7th in Italy and 10th in Morocco. He won the F2 section of the International Trophy with 6th overall, took 3rd in the Lavant Cup, 4th in the Glover Trophy and Kentish 100 and 5th in the Aintree 200. At Le Mans he retired the works Lotus 15 he was sharing with Graham Hill, but came 6th at Sebring with Chapman. In the British Grand Prix sports car race he finished 3rd and 14th in the similar German race.

1959 Following successful tests at Modena, he joined the Ferrari team. On his Grand Prix debut for the team in Monaco, he retired after colliding with Von Trips and Halford. Moving to the newer 246 Dino, he had a 5th in the Italian and 9th in the Dutch, but retired from the German and US races. As part of the sports car squad he was 2nd at the Sebring 12hrs with Behra, 3rd in the TT with Hill and Gendebien and 5th in the Nurburgring 1000km with Gurney.

1960 A crash during qualifying for the Monaco Grand Prix brought a premature end to his season and his Ferrari career, badly breaking his arm after being thrown from the car. He had previously taken a career best 2nd place in Argentina, as well as 8th at the International Trophy, winning the Buenos Aires 1000km and coming 3rd in the Nurburgring 1000km with Hill and Mairesse.

1961 Having signed for the UDT Laystall team, he took its Lotus 18 to 8th at the Monaco Grand Prix. At the Belgian Grand Prix there was only one car to share with Henry Taylor, but another serious accident in practice caused severe leg injuries and forced his retirement from racing. Prior to this he had finished 2nd in the Lombank Trophy at Snetterton and 5th in the Brussels Grand Prix with the Lotus 18. With the Lotus 19 sports car he took 3rd at the International Trophy at Silverstone, at Snetterton and at Aintree, but retired at Le Mans.

PETER ASHDOWN
Born October 16th 1934

1956 Started the year with the MK9, but after winning at Karlskoga, a crash at Montlhery twisted the chassis. Moving on to a Lotus XI he had a win, three 2nds and two

Peter Ashdown in the Lola Mk1.

A works sports car driver for both Lotus and Lola, Ashdown was virtually unbeatable in the late fifties and early sixties, before proving his worth in Formula Junior. His one and only Grand Prix start came in the F2 class of the 1959 British, but the highlight of his career came with three successive Autosport Sports Car Championships. He also raced sports cars at international level and class wins at Sebring and the Nurburgring were highlights. After leaving Lola at the end of 1961, he raced for one further year but despite offers to return he stayed in retirement.

1953 and 1954 Drove a Dellow in trials, hillclimbs and driving tests.

1955 Raced a Lotus Mk9 and took three 3rd places at Silverstone, 2nd in class at the Stapleford Hillclimb and 3rd in class at Charterhall.

3rds at Silverstone, a win, 3rd and 4th at Goodwood, 2nd at Snetterton and 3rd in class in the Eastern Counties Trophy, 2nd and 3rd at both Aintree and Oulton Park, and a 3rd, 4th and two 5ths at Brands Hatch. He collected the John Coombs Trophy as top privateer.

1957 As part of the Lotus works sports car team, he took his XI to victory in the Kanonloppet Karlskoga race again, with a further win at Snetterton, 2nd at Brands Hatch (twice) and Goodwood, 3rd in class at the Empire Trophy and 2nd overall at the Stapleford Hillclimb.

1958 Further success in the works XI included a win and 2nd at Mallory, victory in the Sid Greene Trophy at Brands Hatch, plus two 2nd places at Brands Hatch, 3rd at Roskilde and Snetterton, 5th at Oulton Park and a class win in the TT. His season ended prematurely when he crashed and was injured at Rouen. The ambulance carrying him was then hit by Flockhart's car and caught fire.

1959 His only Grand Prix outing came with Alan Brown's F2 Cooper T45 at the British, finishing 12th overall and 3rd in class. He also drove the same car to 4th in the John Davy Trophy at Brands Hatch. As a works Lola driver he won the Autosport Sports Car Championship in a MkI, winning the Wrotham Trophy at Brands Hatch, at Snetterton, Silverstone, Aintree, the Auvergne Trophy at Clermont Ferrand, the Chichester Cup at Goodwood, the International Trophy Sports and his class with 2nd overall at the Empire Trophy. Further 2nd places came at Crystal Palace, the Rochester Trophy at Brands Hatch, Snetterton, Oulton Park and the Brands Hatch August Trophy, along with 3rd at Snetterton and

GRAND PRIX RECORD	
Starts	1
Wins	0
Poles	0
Fastest laps	0
WC points	0
Best finish	12th

6th overall with a class win at the TT. His Formula Junior debut brought a 2nd place at Goodwood with the Lola, despite an off, followed by a further 2nd at Boxing Day Brands Hatch.

1960 Became Autosport Sports Car Champion again in the Lola MKI, winning at Silverstone (twice), Crystal Palace and Brands Hatch, finished 2nd at Oulton Park, 3rd at the Empire Trophy and British Grand Prix meeting and took class wins at the Nurburgring 1000km and Sebring 12hrs sharing with Charles Voegele. Success also came in Formula Junior, winning the Eastern Counties Trophy at Snetterton, as well as a win, 2nd and 5th at Brands Hatch, 3rd at Snetterton and 2nd at both Monaco and Nurburgring.

1961 Autosport Sports Car Champion for the third successive year in his Lola which he shared with Voegele at Nurburgring once more to take 3rd in class. Apart from 3rd in the Chichester Cup, the Lola Formula Junior car provided little success. With a Lotus however he was 2nd at Mallory, 3rd and 4th at Snetterton and 3rd at both Brands Hatch and Crystal Palace, as well as 3rd at Snetterton with a Gemini.

1962 After taking the Lola Formula Junior to 3rd in the London Trophy, he left the team. He rolled his new Lotus 20 on its debut at the International Trophy meeting, but came back to win at Snetterton and take 2nd at Goodwood and 6th at Crystal Palace. He shared a Lotus 23 with Ian Walker to a class win at the Nurburgring 1000km and had a couple of drives in a Superspeed Ford Anglia, winning his class at Snetterton and taking 2nd at Crystal Palace. His final race was at Brands Hatch on Boxing Day, taking 2nd in a Lotus Cortina.

❖

BILL ASTON
Born March 29th 1900
Died March 4th 1974

A former test pilot for Vickers and motorcycle racer who turned to Formula 3 cars in the late forties, with a reasonable amount of success. He decided to graduate to Formula 1 in 1952 with his self-built air-cooled Aston Butterworth, running both himself and Robin Montgomerie-Charrington with little in the way of results and failed to finish in his only Grand Prix, the 1952 German. After a few years out he returned to national racing with a Jaguar saloon and Aston Martin sports car.

1949 Scored a number of UK F3 wins, as well as taking a victory in Brussels, 2nd in Zandvoort, 3rd in the British Grand Prix support and Silverstone, and 7th in a Goodwood Handicap.

Bill Aston.
Photo: Ferret Fotographics.

1950 Won the Lavant and Madgwick Cups at Goodwood and an Easter Handicap in his Cooper JAP, and finished 2nd in the Grand Prix of Mons, 5th in the British Grand Prix support race and 15th at the International Trophy F3 race.

GRAND PRIX RECORD	
Starts	1
Wins	0
Poles	0
Fastest laps	0
WC points	0
Best finish	DNF

1951 Led the F3 race at Chimay until the carburettor broke and seized his engine. He took 3rd in the Lavant Cup, but turned his back on F3 at the end of the year.

1952 Attempted to make his Grand Prix debut at the British at the age of 52, but his Aston Butterworth was deemed too slow to start. He did make the grid for the German, retiring with no oil pressure after qualifying 21st, but failed to qualify again in Italy. He retired from the International Trophy at Silverstone and also contested the non-championship Monza Grand Prix.

1953 Continued to race the Aston Butterworth without success.

1960 Raced a 3.4 Jaguar in saloons, and had wins at Silverstone (twice), Snetterton and Brands Hatch. He also finished 2nd and 3rd at Brands Hatch, 3rd in a Mallory Handicap, 3rd in class at a Brands Hatch Sprint and at Silverstone and 5th in the British Grand Prix Saloon Car race. He also campaigned an Aston Martin DBR2 taking four wins at Silverstone, and an MGA in which he secured a victory and 3rd at Silverstone.

1961 Took his Jaguar to a class win at the International Trophy Saloon Car race, and 3rd at Brands Hatch. He also claimed a win and 3rd place at Brands Hatch and 3rd at Silverstone in a Mini.

1962 As well as continuing with his Jaguar, with which he recorded a 2nd in class at Brands Hatch, outings in a Vauxhall VX4/90 netted 2nd in class at Brands and 10th overall with Dizzy Addicott in the Brands 6hrs.

1963 Collected two wins at Silverstone and one each at Brands and Snetterton, as well as a 3rd in class at Snetterton with his Jaguar.

1965 Raced his Mini to 2nd places at Brands Hatch (twice) and Lydden.

JOHN BARBER
Born 1929

A Formula 3 racer from the early fifties who graduated to a Cooper Bristol, mainly in national Libre races. His one and only Grand Prix was in Argentina in 1953 when he finished eighth, but after becoming involved in a fatal sports car accident the same year on the Isle of Man, he made only spasmodic appearances thereafter.

1951 Racing a Cooper JAP F3 car he finished 2nd at Ibsley and 2nd in class at Prescott Hillclimb.

1952 Moving up to a Cooper Bristol he had a win at Snetterton, 6th at Prescott, 7th in the British Grand Prix Libre and 24th in the Silverstone International Trophy. However the car was crashed and destroyed before the end of the season. He also raced his Cooper JAP and results included 3rd in a Snetterton Libre race.

1953 With the use of a semi-works Cooper Bristol he finished 8th in Argentina on his one and only Grand Prix appearance, after qualifying last. He also drove the car to 12th in the Buenos Aires Libre race and raced a Golding Cooper sports to 3rd at Snetterton, before becoming involved in the aftermath of a fatal accident during the Empire Trophy on the Isle of Man.

1955 After a year out he returned to national racing with a C-Type Jaguar, taking 3rd at Silverstone and a class win on the Rest and be Thankful Hillclimb.

1956 Further outings with his Jaguar C-Type brought few results.

1957 Came out of virtual retirement to take a Frazer Nash to two handicap wins at Silverstone.

GRAND PRIX RECORD	
Starts	1
Wins	0
Poles	0
Fastest laps	0
WC points	0
Best finish	8th

DON BEAUMAN
Born July 26th 1928
Killed July 9th 1955

After starting his career in F3, he raced an ex-Hawthorn Riley with considerable verve during 1953, collecting numerous national race wins. From 1954 his racing was supported by Sir Jeremy Boles who purchased a Connaught mainly for Libre racing, but it also allowed a Grand Prix debut at the British. After continuing with car the following year and becoming a member of the works Jaguar team, he crashed fatally during the Leinster Trophy.

1950 Raced an F3 Cooper with little in the way of results.

1951 Continued in F3 he won the April Handicap at Brands Hatch, and finished 3rd at the same circuit later in the year.

1952 Finished 2nd in the Ards F3 race with his Cooper JAP, but otherwise had little success.

1953 Changing to the ex-Hawthorn Pre-War Riley TT Sprite kick started his racing career, winning at Thruxton, Goodwood and Ibsley. He also took 2nd at Castle Combe and Goodwood, 3rd at Goodwood and in the Leinster Trophy, 4th at Snetterton and Castle Combe and 5th at Crystal Palace, which gave him 5th overall in the Performance Cars 1500 Trophy Championship. He also went to the Nurburgring 1000km with a Frazer Nash and won his class.

1954 His Grand Prix debut came at the British in Sir Jeremy Boles' Connaught A-Type, qualifying 17th and finishing 11th. The car was used extensively in national Libre and F1 races, winning the Chester Trophy at Oulton Park, at Brands Hatch (twice), plus 2nd in the Rochester Cup at Brands Hatch, Snetterton Libre, London Trophy at Crystal Palace, Madgwick Cup at Goodwood and Brands Hatch Libre. He finished 3rd in Snetterton Libre and the

Crystal Palace Trophy, 4th in the Oulton Park Gold Cup, 5th in the Goodwood Trophy, 6th in the Daily Telegraph Trophy at Aintree, 9th in the Silverstone International Trophy and 3rd at Chimay in the Grand Prix des Frontieres. He also won the Dutch Sports Grand Prix in an Aston Martin DB3 and finished 7th in the TT in a Gordini.

GRAND PRIX RECORD	
Starts	1
Wins	0
Poles	0
Fastest laps	0
WC points	0
Best finish	11th

Eric Brandon after winning the 500cc F3 race at Silverstone on August 20th 1949.
Photo: BRDC Archive.

1955 Continuing to race the Boles Connaughts in F2 and sports, he collected 3rd in the Lavant Cup and Glover Trophy, 4th in the Easter Handicap and 5th in the Chichester Cup, all at Goodwood. He was also 2nd in the Farningham Trophy at Brands Hatch with the Connaught, but drove a Leonard MG to 13th in the Empire Trophy. He had raced for Jaguar at Le Mans and tested for Aston Martin, but it was in the Connaught sports that he crashed fatally during the Leinster Trophy race.

ERIC BRANDON
Born July 18th 1920
Died August 8th 1982

One of the stars of 500cc F3 racing who never realised his potential in other categories. His early career ran in parallel with his good friend John Cooper, but it was after the formation of Ecurie Richmond with Alan Brown that he tried his hand with an F2 Cooper Bristol. He finally turned to Sports Cars in the mid-fifties, and retired from racing at the end of 1956.

1946 Contested his first event as passenger to John Cooper in an MGTC at the Aldershot Trial, and later shared the debut of the first ever Cooper.

1947 He continued to share the Cooper MKI in speed events, and contested the first ever 500cc F3 race at Gransden Lodge. Won his class on four occasions at Prescott Hillclimbs, had a 2nd at Prescott, a win, 2nd and 3rd at Brighton, and a win and 2nd at Southsea.

1948 Took 2nd place in the F3 race at the inaugural Goodwood meeting, won his class at both Shelsley Walsh and Prescott Hillclimbs, and had 2nd in class at Luton Hoo, Stanmer Park and Burghfield Common Speed Trials and Prescott in his Cooper. He also had a 4th overall at Boscombe Speed Trial, a 3rd at Prescott and

took 3rd in class at Brighton with an MG and 7th with a Cooper Sports.

1949 Became a regular front runner in his F3 Cooper, with wins at the International Trophy and Brough, plus three class wins at Prescott, Shelsley Walsh and Great Auclum Hillclimbs and overall victory at the Gosport Speed Trials. He was 2nd in the Madgwick Cup at Goodwood, and had a 2nd in class at Prescott.

1950 Continuing to set the pace with his Cooper, he recorded 2nd overall at Prescott (twice), 2nd in the Lavant Cup at Goodwood, 2nd in the F3 race at the inaugural Brands Hatch meeting, 3rd at Rouen and both Goodwood and Brands Hatch (twice). He took 6th in the Coupe du Monde at Ostend and finished 7th in the F3 race at the British Grand Prix. He also won the Maidstone and Mid Kent Navigational Trial, the Exeter Trial and the 750MC Inter Club driving test.

1951 Became almost unbeatable in F3 on his way to the Autosport Championship title. He won the International Trophy support race, had three wins each at Brands Hatch and Boreham, plus Madrid, Silverstone and Nurburgring. He was 2nd in the Lavant Cup at Goodwood, at Brands Hatch (twice), Brough, Silverstone, Dragvignon and Grenzlandring, 3rd at Brands Hatch (twice), plus Ibsley and Silverstone and finished 5th at both Goodwood and the British Grand Prix support.

GRAND PRIX RECORD	
Starts	5
Wins	0
Poles	0
Fastest laps	0
WC points	0
Best finish	8th

1952 His partnership with Alan Brown took him into Grand Prix racing with a Cooper Bristol, debuting the car with 8th in the Swiss, followed by 9th in Belgium, 20th in the British and 13th in the Italian. Away from the Grand Prix scene he took the car to 3rd in the Lavant Cup, 5th at Boreham and in the non-championship Monza Grand Prix and 11th at Reims. Also racing in F3 he scored wins at Nurburgring and Charterhall, with 2nd at the British Grand Prix meeting and Grenzlandring.

1953 Finished 4th at Syracuse in the Cooper Bristol and won a Sports Car race at Davidstow in a Tojeiro. Back in F3 came victory at Agen, 2nd at Snetterton, the British Grand Prix meeting, Davidstow and the Eifelrennen, 3rd at the International Trophy and 4th at Crystal Palace.

1954 His final Grand Prix came with a one-off return at the British, ending in retirement for the Cooper Bristol. Apart from 5th with a Cooper Alta in the Lavant Cup, he once again concentrated on F3. A win at Hedemora, was followed by 2nd at Bressuine, 3rd at Davidstow, 4th at Snetterton (twice) and Falkenberg and 6th at Goodwood and Brands Hatch.

1955 Had two F3 wins at Brands Hatch, took 2nd at Davidstow, 3rd at Silverstone, 4th in the Earl of March Trophy at Goodwood and at Brands Hatch. He also raced a Halseylec Climax Sports, taking a double victory and a 2nd at Davidstow, 5th at Goodwood and 6th in the Empire Trophy.

1956 Further outings in the Halseylec failed to bring any notable success, and he retired at the end of the season.

TOMMY BRIDGER
Born June 24th 1934
Died July 3rd 1991

A fairly successful F3 racer who seemed almost reluctant to leave the formula, racing in F3 from 1953 through to 1957. He did move on to F2 in 1958, during which time he made his one and only Grand Prix appearance in Morocco, only to return to F3 the following year. He dabbled with sports and saloon cars, before retiring at the end of the 1960 season.

1953 Began racing with an F3 Cooper JAP.

1954 Took 2nd places at both Brands Hatch and Castle Combe in an F3 Kieft Norton.

1955 Finished 3rd in the Clubmans F3 Championship, with two wins, a 2nd and a 3rd at Silverstone, 3rd at Crystal Palace and Boxing Day Brands Hatch, and 13th in the International Trophy support race at Silverstone.

1956 Became a front runner with a new F3 Cooper, regularly challenging champion Jim Russell. He won at Snetterton and Oulton Park, with a 2nd, 3rd, 4th and 5th at Brands Hatch, two 2nds and a 3rd at Snetterton, 3rd at

Aintree and the British Grand Prix support race, and 6th at Goodwood.

GRAND PRIX RECORD	
Starts	1
Wins	0
Poles	0
Fastest laps	0
WC points	0
Best finish	DNF

1957 Continuing rivalry with Russell brought two wins at Brands Hatch and the BARC Trophy at Crystal Palace. He also scored three 2nd places and a 3rd at Snetterton, 2nd at Silverstone and the Sporting Record Trophy at Brands Hatch, 3rd in the Redex Trophy at Crystal Palace, and Oulton Park. He raced a Borgward Isabella to 3rd in class at the International Trophy Saloon Car race.

1958 Finally made the move to F2 with a BRP Cooper, he came 2nd in the Crystal Palace Trophy, 8th in the Coupe de Vitesse at Reims, but crashed out of the Glover Trophy and his one and only Grand Prix outing in Morocco. He went to Le Mans where his Tojeiro retired but finished 3rd in class and 14th overall with Alan Foster in an MGA TC at the TT. Further outings in the Borgward Isabella brought two wins at Brands Hatch, one at Silverstone, with 2nd at Mallory Park and 3rd in class at the International Trophy. He continued to race in F3 winning at Crystal Palace, Goodwood, at Oulton Park (twice) and at Brands Hatch (three times), with 2nd at Snetterton, 3rd at Brands Hatch and the British Grand Prix meeting, 3rd at Brands and 4th at Crystal Palace.

1959 Returned to race winning form with his F3 Cooper Norton, taking the Commander Yorke and Lewis-Evans Trophies at Brands Hatch, plus two victories at Snetterton, Crystal Palace, Mallory Park and Brands Hatch.

1960 With the virtual disappearance of F3, he changed to sports cars with an MGA. He had a 2nd place in the Wrotham Trophy at Brands Hatch and Snetterton 3hrs, and had another 2nd and three 3rds at Snetterton. At Oulton Park he collected two 6th places, and went to the Zandvoort World Cup and was 6th again. At the TT he was 27th overall and he also raced the third works Formula Junior Lotus at the British Grand Prix meeting.

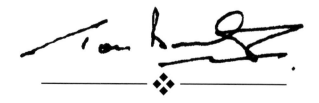

CHRIS BRISTOW
Born December 2nd 1937
Killed June 19th 1960

One of the rising stars of the late fifties, he died at Spa before he could establish himself as a Grand Prix ace. Bristow quickly made the transition from a club sports car racer to International Formula 2 and then up to Grand Prix racing in only his fourth season of racing. Having collected numerous podium finishes, he made his Grand Prix debut with a BRP Cooper at the British in 1959. The following year he joined the Yeoman Credit Grand Prix team, but in only his third Grand Prix with the team he crashed into a perimeter fence at the Belgian circuit and suffered fatal head injuries.

1956 Raced his own MG Special and took his first win at Crystal Palace, having retired the same car earlier in the day at Brands Hatch.

1957 Starting the year in a Cooper Sports, he had a win and 2nd at Silverstone, a win, two 2nds and a 4th at Goodwood, with 3rd and 4th at Brands Hatch. Other outings included 4th at Silverstone in a Lotus Climax Sports and 4th at Brands Hatch in an F2 Cooper.

1958 He won the Chequered Flag Sports Car race at Brands Hatch in a Hume Climax, but spent most of the year racing an Elva. Two wins and two 2nds were taken at Silverstone, with 3rd, 4th and 6th in the Chichester Cup at Goodwood.

1959 Made his Grand Prix debut at the British, taking a BRP Cooper Borgward to 10th overall and a class victory despite almost running out of fuel. His F1 debut came at Oulton Park, where he took a Cooper to 3rd place.

Victories came at Snetterton and the Brands Hatch John Davy Trophy in an F2 Hume Cooper, at Brands Hatch in a F2 Cooper and at Crystal Palace in a Cooper Monaco Sports. He also took the Hume to 3rd in the London Trophy, the Cooper Monaco to 3rd at Snetterton and 2nd in class at the Kingsdown Trophy and the F2 Cooper Borgward to 5th at Rouen and in the Snetterton Silver City Trophy.

1960 Having joined Yeoman Credit for the Grand Prix season, he qualified 3rd in Monaco but retired with a broken gearbox. In the Dutch he qualified 7th but blew the engine, while in Belgium he qualified 9th before his fatal crash in the race. He had also won the False Bay 100 in Capetown and taken 3rd in the Glover Trophy, 4th at Goodwood and Oulton Park and 6th in the Aintree 200 with his Cooper Borgward.

GRAND PRIX RECORD	
Starts	4
Wins	0
Poles	0
Fastest laps	0
WC points	0
Best finish	10th

Chris Bristow racing at Brands, April 10th 1960.

Photo: BRDC Archive.

TONY BROOKS
Born February 25th 1932

History was made in 1955 when this 23 year-old dental student, who was still a relative novice in motorsport, became the first British driver to win a continental race since Sir Henry Segrave when he took his works Connaught to victory at Syracuse. After a rapid rise to fame in sports cars, he drove works BRMs, Vanwalls and Ferraris in Grands Prix, and took his first win, albeit sharing with Moss, on only his third Grand Prix appearance. He won the Nurburgring 1000km and TT with Aston Martin, but increasingly aware of the risks, he retired from racing to concentrate on his family and his business before his 30th birthday. In 1959 he finished runner-up to Jack Brabham in the World Championship.

1952 Began racing with his mother's Healey Silverstone, with 10 outings at Goodwood, taking two wins, 3rd, 4th, 6th (twice), 9th, 10th and 12th (twice).

1953 After two outings at Goodwood with the Healey Silverstone netted a 3rd and 4th place, a change to a Frazer Nash brought continued success. Apart from a 3rd place at Crystal Palace, all of his races were again at Goodwood, scoring one victory, three 3rds and a 5th.

1954 Once again most of the year was spent racing at Goodwood, where he collected a win, a 2nd, two 5ths and two 6ths. He ventured to Crystal Palace and finished 2nd in the Norbury Trophy, as well as a further 2nd and 3rd and made his Snetterton debut with a 3rd place finish, all at the wheel of his Frazer Nash. Other successes included a win in an Aintree Saloon race in a Porsche, a class win at the International Trophy Saloon car race in a DKW, a win at Brands Hatch in a Connaught Sports and 14th place in the sports car race supporting the British Grand Prix with his Frazer Nash.

1955 His single-seater debut came with a fine 4th place at Crystal Palace driving John Riseley-Prichard's Connaught. Armed with a works car he went to the Syracuse Grand Prix and won. Further outings in Riseley-Prichard's car brought 4th overall and an F2 class win at the Aintree Daily Telegraph Trophy, 5th overall and an F2 class win at the Castle Combe Avon Trophy, 3rd in an Aintree Libre race and 2nd in the Air India Trophy at Boxing Day Brands Hatch. He shared an Aston Martin DB3S with Riseley-Prichard at Le Mans and finished 3rd in the Goodwood 9hrs sharing the same car with Peter Collins. He continued to be a Goodwood regular with his Frazer Nash, taking two 2nds, two 3rds and a 4th, and won his class in the International Trophy sports car race. Driving a DKW in Saloons he won his class at the International Trophy and was 3rd overall with a class win in the Sporting Life International and a further Saloon car race at Oulton Park. There was also a 2nd place at Aintree in a Connaught sports and 3rd in class at a Prescott Hillclimb.

Tony Brooks.

Photo: BRDC Archive.

1956 Joining the BRM Grand Pix team, he made his debut at the British after being forced to non-start at Monaco with valve trouble. He qualified 9th but retired after the throttle stuck open and threw him out at Abbey in the ensuing crash, which left him with a broken jaw. He retired his BRM at the Silverstone International Trophy, but was 2nd in the Aintree 200. Outings in Rob Walker's F2 Cooper brought 2nd in the Oulton Park Gold Cup and a win at Brands Hatch, and he also drove a Mercedes 3000SL to victory in a combined Saloon/GT race at Oulton Park. Continuing as a regular in the Aston Martin squad, he won the Goodwood Trophy in a DB3S, took 2nd in the Daily Herald Trophy at Oulton Park, 4th at Rouen and 5th sharing with Collins at the Nurburgring 1000km. A couple of races in a Connaught sports secured a win and 8th at Silverstone.

1957 Moved on to the Vanwall Grand Prix team and finished 4th at Monaco on his debut, after qualifying 9th. At the British he qualified joint second and shared his first victory with Moss, going on to finish 7th in Italy, 9th in Germany and retired at Pescara. Despite missing part of the year after crashing his Aston Martin at Le Mans, he still finished 5th in the World Championship. The Vanwall was also raced at the Goodwood Richmond Trophy, finishing 6th, while further races in an F2 Cooper secured the Lavant Cup at Goodwood. Apart from Le Mans his successes with Aston Martin were a victory at the Nurburgring 1000km with Noel Cunningham-Reid, two wins at Spa, 3rd at Goodwood and 4th at Silverstone.

GRAND PRIX RECORD	
Starts	38
Wins	6
Poles	3
Fastest laps	3
WC points	75
Won his 3rd Grand Prix	

1958 A second season with Vanwall brought his first pole position at Monaco, but ended in retirement. A further retirement at the Dutch preceded his first solo victory in Belgium. Further victories came in the German and Italian, along with 7th at the British and non-finishes at the French, Portuguese and Moroccan, to secure 3rd place in the World Championship. He also won the F2 class at the Aintree 200 in a Cooper, won the TT with Moss and finished 2nd in the Empire Trophy and 5th in the International Trophy sports car race with an Aston Martin DBR1.

1959 Vanwall's withdrawal from Grand Prix racing prompted a move to Ferrari and he finished 2nd on his debut with the 246 Dino in Monaco. After retiring from the Dutch again he took pole and victory in France, but returned to the 1958 Vanwall for the British and retired with a misfire. Back at the wheel of the Ferrari he took

pole and victory again in Germany, 3rd in the US Grand Prix, 9th in the Portuguese and failed to finish in Italy. He finished the year as runner-up in the World Championship behind Jack Brabham. He also took his Ferrari to 2nd in the Aintree 200, while in sports cars he was 3rd in the TT with Allison, Gendebien and Hill and 3rd in the Nurburgring 1000km with Behra.

1960 Having left Ferrari to return to the UK, he initially signed to drive the rear-engined Vanwall in a deal that failed to materialise. He found a drive with the Yeoman Credit Cooper team, but out of seven starts he only made the finish in three, with 4th in Monaco, and 5th in the British and Portuguese. For the French he had even returned to a modified Vanwall of 1958 vintage, but retired from the race. He also drove it to 7th place at Goodwood.

1961 Rejoined BRM for a full Grand Prix season, but despite qualifying well the results were less than impressive. From eight starts, he finished at all but Monaco and the German, with 5th in Italy, 9th in the Dutch and British, 13th in the Belgian and 3rd in the US in his final race before retirement. He had also finished 8th in the Silver City Trophy at Brands Hatch, 4th in Intercontinental and 6th at the International Trophy at Silverstone, 4th in the Oulton Park Gold Cup, 6th in the Modena Grand Prix and 17th in the Aintree 200.

ALAN BROWN
Born November 20th 1919

An early graduate from Formula 3 racing, a long liaison with Cooper Bristols launched his Grand Prix career in 1952, under his own Ecurie Richmond banner. Brown found great success with sports and single seaters, notably his victory in the 1954 Empire Trophy at Oulton Park. After retiring from racing in 1956, he became an entrant in most categories for a host of star name drivers.

1950 Finished 3rd at Blandford, Brands Hatch and in the Winfield Invitation Grand Prix in his F3 Cooper. He also went to Reims and finished 5th in the Coupe des Races and took 12th in the International Trophy F3 race.

1951 Further F3 victories came in the Luxembourg Grand Prix and at Grenzlandring, Dragvignon, Silverstone and Boreham. He was also 2nd five times at

GRAND PRIX RECORD	
Starts	8
Wins	0
Poles	0
Fastest laps	0
WC points	2
Best finish	5th

Woodcote Cup, 6th in the Monza Grand Prix and 19th in the International Trophy. Still active in F3 he won at Boreham and Fairwood, with 2nd in the Earl of March Trophy, the International Trophy support and Brussels Grand Prix and 5th at Zandvoort.

1953 Started the year with 9th in Argentina with a works Cooper Bristol, while later outings resulted in 12th at the Italian and retirement from both the British and German. He also took 2nd at Snetterton and Goodwood and 3rd at Goodwood and Crystal Palace with the car. Racing a Sports Cooper Bristol he collected a class win at the International Trophy and the Norbury Trophy, 2nd in class at the Nurburgring 1000km, 5th in the Coupe du Salon and 7th in the Goodwood 9 hours. In F3 he collected the Earl of March Trophy, with 3rd at Easter Goodwood and 9th at the British Grand Prix.

Brands Hatch, as well as in the International Trophy, at Boreham, Goodwood, Gamston and Nurburgring, 3rd twice at Brands Hatch and 6th in the British Grand Prix support. An outing with HWM at Winfield also netted 2nd place in F2.

1952 Entered the Grand Prix scene with his Cooper Bristol, after forming Ecurie Richmond with Eric Brandon. 5th on his debut in the Swiss, was followed by 6th in the Belgian and unclassified in the British and Italian, from 22nd and 15th. The car was also taken to 2nd at Boreham and the Lavant Cup, 3rd in the Madgwick Cup, 4th in the

1954 Having failed to start his Cooper Bristol at the British Grand Prix, his single seater exploits were more on the national scene. 3rd in the London Trophy, with his sports version he won the Dutch Sports Grand Prix, the Empire Trophy at Oulton Park, his class at the International Trophy support and Gosport Speed Trials. He was also 2nd at Crystal Palace, 3rd and 6th at Goodwood, 3rd at Silverstone (twice), 7th in the British

Alan Brown competing in the 1953 British Empire Trophy on the Isle of Man (June 18th).
Photo: BRDC Archive.

Grand Prix Sports Car race, 4th in the Goodwood Easter Handicap and 7th in Libre, 12th in the TT and his crowning glory, victory in the Empire Trophy. Back in F3 he came 4th at Bressuine and 5th in the Earl of March Trophy. There was still time for 2nd at Silverstone in a Jaguar XK120, 3rd in class at Brighton Speed Trials in a Cooper Alta and the debut of the new Vanwall at the International Trophy.

1955 He raced a Connaught at the International Trophy and took a sports version to 2nd in the Rochester Cup at Brands Hatch. He also finished 3rd at Brands in a Cooper Maserati Sports and 4th in the Wrotham Cup in a Cooper Aston Martin.

1956 His final year of racing was at the wheel of a Jaguar D-Type, with 3rd at Snetterton and 4th in the International Trophy Sports. He also took a class win at the Ramsgate Speed Trials with a Frazer Nash.

❖

IVOR BUEB
Born June 6th 1923
Killed August 1st 1959

Another graduate from 500cc Formula 3, Bueb had little to show for his early years of racing, but became a regular podium finisher after changing to a Cooper in 1954. He became a works driver with Cooper the following year, winning the 500 F3 Hillclimb Championship. The highlight of the year however came as part of the Jaguar sports car team, when he won at Le Mans sharing with Mike Hawthorn. Two years later he won again, but never had a real opportunity to show his paces on the Grand Prix scene. He was killed at Clermont Ferrand when his BRP Cooper Borgward crashed during the Circuit D'Auvergne in 1959.

1952 Began racing late in the year, and had one win at Silverstone in an IOTA F3.

1953 A full year of F3 racing in an Arnott, with a win and 2nd at Goodwood, 2nd at Silverstone, 5th in the Elizabethan Trophy at Crystal Palace and 14th in the British Grand Prix support race. He also had a class win and 2nd at Westwood Sprints.

1954 Moved on to a privately entered Cooper in F3, and won the Redex Trophy at Crystal Palace, the

Kirkistown Open Handicap, at Brands Hatch, Silverstone, Cadwell Park and the Christmas Trophy at Brands Hatch. He was 2nd at Castle Combe, Aintree and Crystal Palace, 3rd at the British Grand Prix, again at Silverstone (twice), Brands Hatch, and Crystal Palace, 4th at Fairwood, Silverstone, Beveridge Park Kirkcaldy, the International Trophy support race, and twice at Brands Hatch and Snetterton, and 7th at Brands Hatch. At Staverton Speed Trials he took two class wins and two 2nds and had a 2nd and 3rd in class at Prescott Hillclimb.

1955 As part of the works Cooper team he raced both 500 F3 and sports. He won the 500 Championship of Ireland at Kirkistown, the International Trophy support race, the Redex Trophy at Crystal Palace, Castle Combe, the Sporting Record Trophy at Brands Hatch, the Earl of March Trophy at Goodwood and Brands Hatch Yuletide Trophy. He also scored a win, three 2nds and a 3rd at Brands Hatch, 2nd at Castle Combe, Crystal Palace (twice), Oulton Park, Snetterton, Brough, Ibsley and Cadwell and 3rd at Snetterton. He was the 500 F3 Hillclimb Champion and runner-up in the National F3 Championship. With the sports car he won the Anerley Trophy at Crystal Palace, the Airkruise Trophy at Brands Hatch, the Aeroplane Co. Trophy and sports car race at Castle Combe plus three further victories at Brands Hatch. He took a 2nd at Crystal Palace, Ibsley, Snetterton and in the Lex Trophy at Brands Hatch. He was also 3rd at Goodwood and 7th in the 9 hour race sharing with Jim Russell, 10th with a class win at the TT sharing with Michael Macdowell and 9th with a class win at the International Trophy. At Prescott he had a 3rd overall and 2nd in class with his F3 Cooper, but crowned his season by winning at Le Mans for Jaguar with Hawthorn.

1956 Further races with Jaguar included sharing a D-Type to victory at the Reims 12 hours with Duncan Hamilton, 3rd in Aintree sports with a D-Type, as well as driving an XK140 to victory in the International Trophy Saloons, with 3rd at Aintree and 2nd at Oulton Park. He took a Cooper sports to 2nd at Brands Hatch (twice) with 2nd and 3rd at Snetterton and also drove a Lotus sports to 5th at the International Trophy and led at Reims with Mackay-Fraser until losing the gears. The occasional F2 outing brought 2nd at Brands Hatch, 3rd at the British Grand Prix support and 6th in the Sporting Life Trophy at Oulton Park. In F3 he won at Crystal Palace, was 3rd at Aintree (twice), four times at Brands Hatch, the International Trophy support and Commander Yorke Trophy at Silverstone. He finished 4th at Aintree, Brands

GRAND PRIX RECORD	
Starts	5
Wins	0
Poles	0
Fastest laps	0
WC points	0
Best finish	11th

Hatch and Oulton Park, 5th in the John Bull Trophy at Oulton Park and Goodwood, 6th in the Sporting Life Trophy at Brands Hatch and 7th in the British Grand Prix support.

1957 He won his 2nd Le Mans for Jaguar with Ron Flockhart, finished 3rd at the Sebring 12hrs with Hawthorn and 11th in the Nurburgring 1000km with Jock Lawrence. His F1 debut came at Syracuse with a 5th in a works Connaught, followed by 3rd at Pau. He had the same car for his Grand Prix debut at Monaco, but retired after qualifying 16th. At the British Grand Prix he handled the Gilby Engineering Maserati 250F, but failed to be classified as a finisher. He had already taken the 250F to 10th at the Reims GP, and retired it from the International Trophy, while his Cooper F2 outings brought him 4th in the GP de Paris and 6th in the Oulton Park Gold Cup. At Snetterton he was a double winner with the Lotus sports and took 3rd at Aintree, 3rd and 5th at Brands Hatch, 3rd overall and 2nd in class at the International Trophy. He was 44th on the Tulip Rally in a Ford Zephyr and won the International Trophy Saloon Car race for Jaguar.

1958 A run in Bernie Ecclestone's Connaught ended in retirement at the British Grand Prix, but his Lotus 12 did make the finish at the German Grand Prix, with 11th overall and 6th in the F2 class. His other F2 outings brought 2nd in the Circuit D'Auvergne and London Trophy, 4th in the Crystal Palace Trophy with Lotus, and 10th in the Kentish 100 at Brands Hatch with a Cooper. With a Lister Jaguar he won the Scott-Brown Memorial Snetterton, the Kingsdown Trophy at Brands Hatch, Crystal Palace, the Air India Trophy at Snetterton, plus 2nd in both the Gold Cup and International sports at Oulton Park. He raced a D-Type at Le Mans with Hamilton and took 4th in the Belgian Sports Grand Prix at Spa and Aintree, 6th at the International Trophy and 9th in the Monza 500. He also had a run in the Ecurie Ecosse Tojeiro and took 4th in the British Grand Prix support race.

1959 He failed to qualify for the Monaco Grand Prix in his BRP Cooper Climax, but took 13th overall and 4th in the F2 class with a similar Borgward-powered car. He had already taken his F2 Cooper to 2nd in the London Trophy, 4th overall and a class win at the Aintree 200, 3rd in the Empire Trophy, 2nd in class at the International Trophy and 5th at Syracuse, when he crashed fatally during the Circuit D'Auvergne. With Jaguar he had Touring wins at Silverstone (twice), Goodwood and Aintree and with the Lister he had won at Goodwood, taken 3rd at the International Trophy and 6th at the British Grand Prix. Just to confirm his versatility, he finished 3rd on the Alpine Rally and 16th on the Monte Carlo Rally, sharing a Sunbeam Rapier with Tish Ozanne.

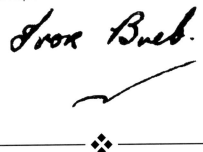

---- ❖ ----

50 years of British Grand Prix drivers

Part One
1950s

CHAPTER 2

IAN BURGESS
Born July 6th 1930

Ian Burgess.

GRAND PRIX RECORD	
Starts	16
Wins	0
Poles	0
Fastest laps	0
WC points	0
Best finish	6th

Burgess took the racing world by storm in 1951, when he won at Nurburgring and came second at Avus with his Formula 3 Cooper, in only his second season of racing. He raced a variety of cars until Cooper, his employers at the time, gave him an F2 drive in 1957. His Grand Prix debut came the following year, but although he had a fairly successful national racing career, he tended to lack competitive machinery in Grands Prix. His best result came in the 1959 German Grand Prix when he finished sixth in the Cooper Maserati of the Scuderia Centro Sud team. Having raced at Grand Prix level for six different teams over a six-year span, he retired at the end of 1963 after an unsuccessful time with the rare BRM-powered Scirocco.

1950 Began racing with an F3 Cooper, taking 2nd and 3rd at Brands Hatch, 3rd at Castle Combe and took part in the Brighton Speed Trials.

1951 He won the Eifelrennen F3 race at Nurburgring in torrential rain, beating all the recognised stars, and claimed 2nd place and fastest lap at Avus.

1953 Finished 3rd in a Crystal Palace sports car race with a Kieft Bristol and was 12th in the British Grand Prix F3 race driving a Mackson.

1954 Sharing an OSCA with Morewood he was 8th in the TT, and finished 17th in the British Grand Prix F3 race.

1955 Further outings in a Kieft Bristol brought 2nd in the Anerley Trophy and 3rd in the Norbury Trophy, both at Crystal Palace. He was also 27th in the TT sharing a Lotus Connaught with John Coombs.

1956 Working for the Cooper Car Co, he helped run its Brands Hatch-based racing school. Scored a 5th place in a Brands Hatch F2 race with a Beart-Rodger and finished 14th in the British Grand Prix F2 race in an OSCA.

1957 He finally got to race a works F2 Cooper, retiring from the International Trophy at Silverstone and taking 4th in the Oulton Park Gold Cup.

1958 His Grand Prix debut came at the British, where his works Cooper retired after qualifying 16th. Most of the year was spent racing Tommy Atkins' F2 Cooper, and it was with this car he raced at the German Grand Prix, taking 7th overall and 3rd in class. He won the Vanwall Trophy at Snetterton, the Crystal Palace Trophy, and came 4th at Reims and Montlhery, 13th at Brands Hatch, but crashed and broke his leg at Avus. An outing at the TT resulted in 20th place driving an Elva.

1959 Joined Scuderia Centro Sud for his Grand Prix campaign, retiring its Cooper Maserati in both the French and British, before taking a career best 6th in Germany and 14th in Italy. Continuing to race Atkins' F2 Cooper, he took 3rd in a Silverstone Libre race, 5th in the John Davy F2 Trophy at Brands Hatch and 8th at Rouen.

1960 A further year in the Centro Sud Cooper Maserati brought little success, failing to qualify in Monaco, retirement in the British and US Grand Prix, and 10th in the French. He also drove the car to 9th in the International Trophy and 10th at the Brands Hatch Silver City Trophy. An early season trip to New Zealand with Atkins' Cooper secured the Teretonga Trophy, as well as 3rd in the Lady Wigram Trophy. He also had a Formula Junior race at Brands Hatch, taking 3rd in a Cooper.

1961 Moving on to the Camoradi International team to race a Lotus 18, he failed to even make the grid at both the Dutch and Belgian Grand Prix, through no fault of his own. He later took 14th in both the French and British, before changing to a Cooper Climax to take 12th in the German. He also finished 4th in Naples and 8th in Brussels with the Lotus, along with 5th at Zeltweg and 6th at the Oulton Park Gold Cup in the Cooper.

1962 Three Grand Prix outings with an Anglo American Equipe Cooper Climax resulted in 11th at the German, 12th at the British and non-qualification at the Italian. Travelling around Europe to contest the non-championship races, he collected 4th at Solitude, 5th at Roskilde, Karlskoga and Naples, 7th in Brussels, 11th at Reims and 18th at the International Trophy, driving both the Cooper and a Lotus.

1963 His final year of Grand Prix racing brought two starts in the BRM-powered Scirocco, retiring from both the British and German. He also retired in most of his non-championship outings, but finished 8th at the Oulton Park Gold Cup.

PETER COLLINS
Born November 6th 1931
Killed August 3rd 1958

Peter Collins aboard his yacht 'Genie Maris' at Dartmouth.
Photo: BRDC Archive.

A potential World Champion in the making, Collins graduated from a successful F3 career to become a works Ferrari driver. His graduation to the Ferrari squad came via the HWM Grand Prix team having qualified sixth for his first Grand Prix in Switzerland in 1952. He then drove for Vanwall and BRM and raced sports cars for Aston Martin. In 1955 he shared a Mercedes with Moss to win the Targa Florio and also finished second on the Mille Miglia with Loius Klemantaski in a Ferrari. He joined Ferrari for 1956 and raced both Grand Prix and sports cars for the team, adding to his impressive tally of success in classic sports car races.

The Lancia-Ferrari took him to two Grand Prix wins and third in the World Championship in 1956 but the following season the car was put-paced by the Maseratis and Vanwalls. In 1958, equipped with the Dino 246, Collins was again a World Championship contender but tragedy was about to strike. Having won his home Grand Prix at Silverstone, Peter lost his life in the following race at Nurburgring when his car somersaulted after hitting a bank.

Peter Collins being pushed to the start of the 1956 British Grand Prix at Silverstone.
Photo: BRDC Archive.

1949 Won the Allcomers 100 mile F3 race at Silverstone, won at Goodwood and took 8th in the F3 race at the Silverstone International Trophy. He also contested speed events and took a victory, 7th and 9th in class at Prescott, 3rd at Shelsley Walsh and 8th at Weston Super Mare.

1950 Continuing in F3 with several minor race victories, as well as 2nd at Goodwood and Blandford, 3rd at the British Grand Prix and at Castle Combe. He won his class at the Brighton Speed Trials, Prescott, Shelsley Walsh and Bo'ness Hillclimbs, finished 2nd at Rest and be Thankful, 3rd at Prescott, 5th Shelsley and Bouley Bay and 6th at Prescott.

GRAND PRIX RECORD	
Starts	32
Wins	3
Poles	0
Fastest laps	0
WC points	47
Won his 15th Grand Prix	

1951 Another year of F3 brought wins at Ulster, Winfield, Silverstone, Gamston, twice at Ibsley three times at Goodwood, as well as 2nd at Boreham and 6th at Croft. On the hills he took 4th overall at Rest and be Thankful, 5th with a class win at Shelsley, and a class win at Prescott. Outings with an Allard sportscar brought wins at Ibsley, Croft and Gamston, along with a 3rd at Gamston and victory at Westwood Park Speed Trial. Other results included 21st in the International Trophy Production race at Silverstone in a DB Panhard and a class win on the Burnham Rally in a Ford Consul.

1952 Became a fully-fledged member of the HWM Grand Prix team, qualifying 6th on his debut in Switzerland, but retired after spinning off when a halfshaft broke. After retiring again in Belgium he finished 6th in the French, retired at the British and failed to qualify for either the German or Italian. In non-championship outings he finished 2nd in Les Sables D'Olonne, 3rd in the Luxembourg Grand Prix, 4th at La Baule, 6th at Rouen, 7th in the Marseilles Grand Prix and 9th in the Silverstone International Trophy. He drove a Cadillac Allard in the TT, a Ford Anglia in the Monte Carlo Rally, won the Goodwood 9hrs and took 7th in Monaco for Aston Martin and won the Luxembourg F3 Grand Prix.

1953 Continuing with HWM, his best Grand Prix result came with 8th in the Dutch. His other results were 13th in France, with retirement in both the Belgian and British. He secured 3rd in the Eifelrennen with his HWM, 5th at Sables D'Olonne and 8th in Aix les Bains. His regular Aston Martin outings with Pat Griffith brought a win in the TT, 2nd in the Goodwood 9 hours and 16th in the Mille Miglia, along with 3rd and 4th places in Silverstone Sports car races at the British Grand Prix and International Trophy.

1954 Joining the Vandervell Racing Team his duties were shared between the Thinwall and Vanwall. With the latter he contested the British Grand Prix, retiring with a blown headgasket. After taking 7th in the Italian he failed to start the Spanish due to an accident during practice. He also drove the Vanwall to 2nd in the Goodwood Trophy, but with the Thinwall he took wins in the Goodwood Whit Trophy and Libre race, the Woodcote Cup at Goodwood and Snetterton Libre race. An outing with Connaught secured 2nd in the Crystal Palace Trophy, while his Aston Martin outings brought a victory at the British Grand Prix Sports car race, 2nd at Aintree, 3rd in the Buenos Aires 1000km and 8th in the Silverstone International Trophy Sports car race. He also finished 95th with Graham Whitehead on the Monte Carlo Rally.

1955 Originally joined BRM for its Grand Prix campaign, but World Championship outings were restricted to races in a Maserati 250F in the British and Italian which both ended in retirement. Further races with the 250F produced victory in the International Trophy at Silverstone and the London Trophy at Crystal Palace. He took the awesome V16 BRM to wins in the Daily Telegraph Trophy at Aintree and Chichester Cup at Goodwood, along with 5th in a Goodwood Easter Handicap and dominated the Oulton Park Gold Cup in the BRM P25 until low oil pressure ended his challenge. He won the Targa Florio with Moss and Mercedes and took 2nd at Le Mans with Frere in an Aston Martin DB3S. He finished 2nd in the Mille Miglia with Klemantaski for Ferrari, 2nd in the Nurburgring 1000km with Hawthorn and Ferrari and 3rd in the Goodwood 9 hours with Brooks and Aston Martin. His further Aston Martin outings resulted in 2nd in the British Grand Prix Sports car race and at Snetterton, 3rd in the Daily Herald Trophy at Oulton Park and International Trophy Sports at Silverstone, 5th at Goodwood, 8th in the Empire Trophy and 95th on the Monte Carlo Rally again.

1956 Became a works Ferrari driver as team-mate to Fangio. After retiring the old 555 V8 in the Argentinian opener, Grand Prix success quickly followed with the Lancia-Ferrari D50. After sharing his car with Fangio to 2nd place in Monaco, he won the Belgian and French and shared 2nd in both the British and Italian with De Portago and Fangio respectively, to finish 3rd in the World Championship. He took his D50 to 3rd in Syracuse and in sports cars he finished 2nd in the Mille Miglia and Swedish Grand Prix, 5th in the Nurburgring 1000km and GP de Mendoza and won the Circuit of Sicily and Supercortemaggiore for Ferrari. He also found time to finish 2nd at Le Mans with Moss and Aston Martin.

1957 A second season at Ferrari proved less successful, with 3rd in the French and German Grands Prix his best results on his way to 7th in the World Championship. He did however win both the Syracuse and Naples Grands Prix and took the new 246 Dino to 4th at the Modena Grand Prix. His sports car campaign brought further success with wins in the Venezuelan Grand Prix, plus 2nd in the Swedish Grand Prix, Nurburgring 1000km and Buenos Aires 1000km, 3rd in the Buenos Aires City GP, 4th in the Cuban GP and 6th in the Sebring 12 hours. He also went to Nassau and took a Healey Special to class victory.

1958 Began the year with the new Ferrari 246 Dino and after retiring in Argentina he took 3rd at Monaco and 5th in the French, before claiming victory in the British at Silverstone. Two weeks later he crashed fatally at the German GP, sustaining severe head injuries after he was thrown from the car. He still finished fifth in the World Championship. He had also won his second Silverstone International Trophy and came 2nd in the Coupe de Vitesse at Reims. While with the Ferrari sports car team he won the Buenos Aires 1000km and Sebring 12hrs, with 2nd in the Nurburgring 1000km and Goodwood Sussex Trophy.

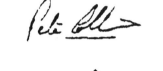

---------------- ❖ ----------------

TONY CROOK
Born February 16th 1920

Not a household name, but one of the most prolific national racers of the late forties and early fifties, mainly at the wheel of Frazer Nash or Bristol cars. Crook became chairman and managing director of the latter following his retirement from racing. Apart from his two Grands Prix outings at Silverstone in 1952 and 1953, his greatest claim to fame was winning the first post-war motor race on the British mainland at Gransden Lodge in 1946. He also won twice on the day that Castle Combe hosted its first race meeting in July 1950.

GRAND PRIX RECORD	
Starts	2
Wins	0
Poles	0
Fastest laps	0
WC points	0
Best finish	21st

Tony Crook in May 1951.

Photo: BRDC Archive.

1946 Won at Gransden Lodge in a Frazer Nash BMW.

1947 Finished 8th in the Manx Cup, was a double class winner at VSCC Prescott, had a win and 2nd in class at both Poole and Southsea Speed Trials, 2nd and 3rd in class at Brighton and two 2nds in class at Prescott.

1948 Finished in 2nd place with the Frazer Nash BMW at the inaugural Goodwood meeting. He won his class twice at Prescott in his BMW 328, took 2nd in class at the Burghfield Common Speed Trial, 5th overall with a class win and 2nd at Boscombe Speed Trials and victory plus 7th in class at Prescott. He took an Alfa Romeo to 11th at Luton Hoo and 16th at Stanmer Park Speed Trials, and was third in class at Prescott with both his BMW and Alfa Romeo. He was also a class winner with the Alfa Romeo at Brighton as well as taking 2nd in the BMW.

1949 His 2.8-litre Alfa Romeo took a win at Silverstone and 7th in a Goodwood Handicap while at the wheel of a Veritas sports car he finished 2nd in class at Gosport and 3rd at Brighton Speed Trials. He won at the Great Auclum Speed Trials in his BMW, as well as taking 2nd and 3rd in Goodwood Handicaps and 3rd at Blandford Camp.

1950 Concentrating on his Frazer Nash sports car, he took two wins at Castle Combe and one at Goodwood, 2nd at Castle Combe, 4th in the Silverstone International Trophy Production race, 6th in Goodwood's Lavant Cup and 10th in the TT. In speed events he was 2nd in the sports class at Shelsley Walsh with the Frazer Nash and 7th at Brighton in a Lagonda. He also raced a Bristol saloon to 2nd at Castle Combe.

1951 The second most successful driver of the year at Goodwood to Mike Hawthorn, with 2nd in the Sports and

Handicap at the Brooklands Trophy, a scratch race win, 2nd in Handicap, and a further 4th place all in his trusty Frazer Nash. Away from Goodwood he finished 4th in the International Trophy Production race at Silverstone, took double wins at Castle Combe and Boreham, a 2nd at Castle Combe and class wins at both Brighton and Great Auclum Speed Trials. He also won his class at Boreham Speed Trials with a Bristol Saloon.

1952 Entered his stripped down Bristol-powered Frazer Nash for the British Grand Prix and came home in 21st place. He had earlier raced to 17th in the International Trophy at Silverstone, but successes came once more from his sports car exploits. A double victory at Castle Combe, a win at Silverstone, 3rd at Monaco and Boreham, 8th in the International Trophy Production Sports and a class win at Boreham Speed Trials followed, along with a 5th place at the International Trophy meeting with his Bristol Saloon.

1953 His second and final Grand Prix outing came with a Cooper Bristol at the British and ended with a broken fuel feed on the startline. His sports car Cooper Bristol recorded 2nd at Silverstone (twice), 3rd at Snetterton (twice), 4th at Crystal Palace, 6th at Aintree and 10th in the Goodwood 9hrs. He had an F2 win and 2nd in Snetterton Libre races with a Cooper Alta, 2nd at Silverstone in the Bristol Saloon and 10th at the British Grand Prix Sports Car race with his Frazer Nash.

1954 Win after win came with the updated Cooper Sports, three at Brands, six at Silverstone (including three in one day), two at Snetterton, two at Crystal Palace (including the Norbury Trophy) and one each at Goodwood, Oulton Park and Aintree. There were also 2nd 3rd and 4th places at Goodwood, two class wins at

Snetterton, 2nd and 3rd at Oulton Park and Snetterton, 3rd in the Glade Trophy at Crystal Palace, 5th at Goodwood and 14th in the Silverstone International Trophy Sports. In speed events he won the class at Wethersfield, was a double class winner at Snetterton, twice the fastest sports car at Shelsley Walsh, a double class winner at Prescott and a class winner at Brighton. He finished 4th in an F1 race at Snetterton in the Cooper Bristol and his Bristol Saloon also collected 3rd at Snetterton Speed Trial and a class win at Stapleford. The year was rounded off with 2nd in Silverstone Libre in a Lister Bristol and victory in the Albatross Trophy at Boxing Day Brands Hatch in the Cooper Bristol sports.

1955 Continued successfully with the Cooper Bristol Sports, winning his class at Shelsley Walsh, Brighton, Hempsford CUAC Speed Trial and Prescott, plus taking 2nd in the Silverstone International Trophy Sports and 4th and 5th places at Crystal Palace. He also took his Frazer Nash to 6th in Goodwood Sports and the Bristol to class wins in the International Trophy Touring Car race and at Brighton. He retired from racing at the end of the season.

GEOFFREY CROSSLEY
Born May 11th 1921

A genuine amateur from the immediate Pre and Post War years, he had relatively little experience prior to making his Grand Prix debut in the 1949 Belgian. With only occasional appearances during the early fifties, he left the racing scene for good after an aborted comeback at Goodwood in 1955.

1937 Drove a Bentley on the RAC Hastings Rally.

1939 Took 2nd place in both the Allcomers and Handicap races at Donington Park's final Pre War meeting, driving a BMW 328.

1947 Raced an Alta in the British Empire Trophy and Gransden Trophy.

1949 Debuted his brand new Alta with 7th place in the Belgian Grand Prix at Spa. Also took a class lap record at Montlhery, 20th in the Silverstone International Trophy, and 9th in Goodwood's Easter Handicap.

GRAND PRIX RECORD	
Starts	2
Wins	0
Poles	0
Fastest laps	0
WC points	0
Best finish	9th

1950 Qualified his Alta in 17th place for the British Grand Prix, but retired with broken transmission. 9th in the Belgian Grand Prix from 12th on the grid, and 6th in the Jersey Road race.

COLIN DAVIS
Born July 29th 1933

The son of the legendary Bentley boy Sammy Davis, Colin spent most of his racing career on the continent, after an early grounding in 500cc Formula 3. His two Grands Prix were both for the Centro Sud team in uncompetitive Cooper Maseratis, but he found great success in Formula Junior winning the International title in 1960. Through the early sixties he raced works Ferraris and Porsches in the classic sports car races, winning the Targa Florio in 1964 and taking second on the same event a year later. He retired from racing at the end of 1966.

1954 Made his racing debut at Silverstone, taking 2nd with his Cooper Norton in a 100 mile F3 race. He also took 3rd place in both the Yorke Trophy and Open Challenge at Brands Hatch.

1955 His first national race win was at Brands Hatch in June. But further F3 successes came with 2nd at Oulton Park and Karlskoga, 3rd in the Earl of March Trophy at Goodwood, Oulton Park and Castle Combe, as well as at Goodwood after taking over the Beart car from Moss. In the Rochester Cup Libre race at Brands Hatch he was 4th in a Cooper JAP, and finished 6th in both the Redex F3 Trophy at Crystal Palace and the Daily Telegraph F3 Trophy at Brands Hatch.

Colin Davis.

1956 Continuing in F3 with Francis Beart, he won at Aintree, with 2nd and 3rd at Goodwood and 2nd at Silverstone. He borrowed Charles Mortimer's car to win an up to 1100cc race at Goodwood and borrowed his old Cooper to win the Gran Premio di Roma Castelfusano, witnessed by the Maserati brothers. He also shared an Austin Healey to 8th place in the Reims 12hrs and came 2nd in a Goodwood Handicap with a Lotus Climax.

1957 After testing for Maserati he was signed on a race to race contract, only for the team's season to be suspended after fatalities on the Mille Miglia. He won the Coppa d'Oro della Sicilia at Syracuse and at Vallelunga in an OSCA.

1958 Racing mainly for De Tomaso, he won the Shell Trophy at Monza despite sliding off up a bank at Parabolica in the rain. Sharing his OSCA with Alessandro

De Tomaso he was 2nd in the 12hrs of Messina and took a class win and 11th overall at Le Mans.

1959 Both of his Grand Prix starts were made in a Centro Sud Cooper Maserati, retiring in the French and taking 11th in the Italian. He was one of the stars of the new Formula Junior category with the works Taraschi, winning at Albi, Pau, Naples and Reggio Calabria. He won the 10 hours of Messina in a Centro Sud Cooper Monaco and finished 6th overall with a class win in the Targa Florio driving Virgilio Conrero's Alfa Romeo Giulietta, after the Maserati brothers withdrew his original car. He also had an outing with an F2 Porsche at Reims, finishing 9th.

1960 Became the International Formula Junior Champion driving for Taraschi and OSCA, with wins at Pau, the Monza Lotteria, Messina, Syracuse, Salerno and Reggio Calabria. He led at Pescara until a brake pipe broke and he plunged off the road, only to rejoin and finish 7th, and took 2nd at Modena. He was 5th in the Cuban Grand Prix driving a Serenissima Cooper Monaco, shared a Fiat Abarth with Sepp Liebl to 2nd and a class win in the Nurburgring 500km, and shared a Ferrari with Carlo Abate to a class win in the Nurburgring 1000km and finished 6th in the TT.

1961 Finished 4th overall and took a class win with Abate in a Ferrari, and was 5th in the Paris 1000km. With OSCA he retired at Le Mans and finished 3rd in class at Pescara.

1962 Driving for Ferrari he was 3rd in the Paris 1000km with Scarfiotti and 9th at Le Mans with Abate. He drove a new works front-engined Taraschi to 2nd in a Formula Junior race at Circuito de Garda and took 2nd at Caserta in a De Sanctis.

1963 His only race of the year brought 2nd place in the Formula Junior Lotteria, with a Wainer Ford.

1964 Won the Targa Florio with Pucci on his Porsche works debut, driving a 904GT. He took 3rd in the Paris 1000km with Edgar Barth and retired at Le Mans with Mitter.

1965 Finished 2nd in the Targa Florio with Mitter in a Porsche Spyder.

1966 Finished 4th at Le Mans with Siffert in a Porsche 906 and 7th in the Monza 1000km with Glemser in a Carrera 6.

GRAND PRIX RECORD

Starts	2
Wins	0
Poles	0
Fastest laps	0
WC points	0
Best finish	11th

❖

KEN DOWNING
Born December 5th 1917

A genuine privateer who bore allegiance to the Connaught marque for most of his career, both in sports cars and single seaters. Although Downing only made two Grand Prix starts, he was a regular podium finisher in national events. The high point of his Grand Prix outings was running as high as fourth place in the 1952 British before spinning to avoid a backmarker and dropping to ninth place. After a disappointing year with an Aston Martin DB3S in 1953 he retired from the sport.

1948 Made his competition debut on the Eastbourne Rally and won the novice award. His racing debut came at the inaugural Goodwood meeting, taking 2nd place in his Healey road car despite being left on the grid.

1949 Bought the Brooke Special with a 2-litre Riley engine and raced it mainly for fun as it was totally outclassed. He did however take 3rd and two 4ths in Goodwood Handicaps, 7th in the Lavant Cup and 8th in the Madgwick Cup.

1950 He was persuaded to put a 24-litre 12 cylinder engine into the Brooke Special, and after an all day test at Silverstone for £5 he left most of its oil on the paddock floor. The same problem plagued the car's first outing at Gamston, but he did secure a victory at the same meeting with his Connaught. Most of the year was spent sorting the Connaught, but he did take a 3rd in class at the

GRAND PRIX RECORD	
Starts	2
Wins	0
Poles	0
Fastest laps	0
WC points	0
Best finish	9th

Gravesend Speed Trials and 3rd at Silverstone despite throwing the gearstick to his mechanic as he passed the pits, finishing the race with 3rd gear only. He also raced a Healey in Standard Sports and Saloons, winning at Castle Combe, the Gamston Handicap, and finished 28th at the Silverstone International Trophy.

1951 A regular club winner in the Connaught sports with 15 victories, only unplaced once. He was also a founder of the Cheshire Car Circuit Club which started racing at Oulton Park, although he never raced there himself. His wins included Gamston, Ibsley, Silverstone and Winfield, along with many more 2nd and 3rd places. He won the Sports class at Replow Speed Trials in the Connaught and took his Healey road car to victory in a Gamston Handicap, with 2nd at Silverstone and Winfield.

1952 Graduating into single seaters with a Connaught A-Type, he oiled a plug, broke a driveshaft and blew the

Ken Downing racing his Connaught in the 1952 British Grand Prix at Silverstone.

headgasket in the Silverstone International Trophy heat, but still started the final and finished 13th. He used the same car for his British Grand Prix debut, finishing 9th after running as high as 4th until a spin to avoid a backmarker. He retired from his only other Grand Prix start in the Dutch, but did win the Madgwick Cup at Goodwood and looked set to win the GP des Frontieres at Chimay having led from the first corner. However he backed off too early in the spectator-lined streets and was pipped on the line. He also took 4th at Boreham and in a Goodwood Handicap and set an F1 hill record at Prescott that stood for five years. He also won a Boreham sports car race in his Connaught and took 2nd in the Handicap and 10th in F2, while at Silverstone he rounded his year off with 3rd in both the Allcomers and Handicap races.

1953 Changed to an Aston Martin DB3S and despite a win at Silverstone, there was little success and he retired from racing at the end of the year.

❖

PAUL EMERY
Born November 12th 1916
Died February 3rd 1992

One of the first constructor drivers, Emery built a variety of cars for a variety of formulae, under the family name of Emeryson. After briefly competing pre-war, he raced his Emeryson sports cars and 500cc Formula 3s before moving up with varying success. He only made one Grand Prix start himself, but went on to build F1 cars for the Scirocco Powell team as well as his own Emerysons. Towards the end of his career he found a niche in the world of Oval Midget racing, as well as running a successful team of Hillman Imps in the British Saloon Car Championship.

1936 Won at Brooklands in an Emeryson.

1947 Finished 2nd in class at the Burghfield Common Speed Trials in a Hudson Special and 2nd in class at Silverstone in an Emeryson.

1948 Contested the Manx Cup in an MG and the Empire Trophy with his Emeryson, with little success.

1949 On the circuits he raced a 4.5-litre Duesenberg-engined Emeryson, but claimed a 2nd in class at Great Auclum Speed Trial in his Hudson Special.

1950 Racing in 500 F3 he took his Emeryson JAP to 2nd place at the inaugural Brands Hatch meeting and also contested the Jersey Road Race, as well as national F3 races.

Paul Emery.

1951 Continuing in F3 with Norton power in his Emeryson, his best result came with 3rd place at Brands Hatch.

1952 3rd at Snetterton and 19th at the British Grand Prix were some of his better F3 results from a disappointing season.

1953 His F3 car was taken to Picardy where it finished 2nd, while on the home front his best results came with 6th in the Brands Hatch Daily Telegraph Trophy, and at Goodwood. He also drove an F2 Emeryson Alta and recorded 4th place at Snetterton, but retired from the Crystal Palace Trophy.

1954 As well as racing an Emeryson sports car in national events, his outings in the F2 Emeryson Alta brought a 4th place at Boxing Day Brands Hatch in the Silver City Trophy Libre race.

1955 Concentrating on racing his Emeryson in national Libre, brought a 3rd in the Farningham Trophy at Brands Hatch, 5th in the Crystal Palace International Trophy, 6th in the Avon Trophy at Castle Combe and 8th in the London Trophy at Crystal Palace. He also claimed FTD at both Tarrant Rushton and Stapleford Speed events. He competed at Goodwood, where he shared a Lotus to 11th place in the nine hour race.

1956 His one and only Grand Prix start came at the British, where his Emeryson Alta qualified 23rd and retired with an ignition fault. At Crystal Palace though, he took an excellent 2nd place behind Moss's Maserati 250F in the London Trophy. He won a Libre race at Mallory Park and drove his sports car to 3rd place at Brands Hatch and Goodwood Handicaps, 4th in a Brands Hatch scratch race and 2nd in class at Prescott Hillclimb.

GRAND PRIX RECORD	
Starts	1
Wins	0
Poles	0
Fastest laps	0
WC points	0
Best finish	DNF

1957 With the majority of his year spent on the national scene, he won the Raleigh Trophy Libre and took two 2nd places at Mallory Park, and finished 4th at Brands Hatch in a Parsenn sports car.

1958 Having gone to the Monaco Grand Prix with Bernie Ecclestone's Connaught B-Type, he failed to qualify. The car was used again to take 5th in the Aintree 200, while with his more familiar Emeryson he had a class win at a Shelsley Walsh Hillclimb.

1959 Apart from an outing with the Connaught at the Oulton Park Gold Cup, his own racing career had all but ended.

1964 Had a class win at Brighton Speed Trials in an Emery GT.

1971 Dominated a BRSCC-run Midget series, winning with his Dastle at White City, Walthamstow and Harringey.

1976 Shared Richard Falconer's Emeryson in the Birkett 6hrs relay at Silverstone.

❖

JACK FAIRMAN
Born March 15th 1913

Such was the demand for Fairman's test driving and development skills that his own racing career tended to take a back seat as a consequence. He was involved in the development of the Connaught Formula 1 car but his biggest successes were to come in 1959 when he won both the Tourist Trophy and Nurburgring 1000km races with Moss and Shelby in an Aston Martin DBR1. As part of works Jaguar, Aston Martin and Bristol teams, he contested all of the classic sports car races during his career. His 12 Grands Prix were spread over nine years and race outings finally tailed off in 1963, after spending a year on the sidelines with the disastrous ATS Grand Prix car.

1946 Took FTD at Elstree Speed Trials and 5th in class at Westcourt in a Bentley.

1947 Racing a Bugatti he finished 2nd in the Itala Trophy at Gransden Lodge, finished 8th at Bo'ness Hillclimb and 11th in Southsea Speed Trials.

1948 Finished 3rd in the Castletown Trophy on the Isle of Man in his Bugatti.

1949 Sharing an HRG with Eric Thompson, he took a class win and 8th overall at Le Mans, and a class win in the Spa 24hrs. Driving his own Riley in club events he was 2nd in the Blandford Trophy, 3rd in the Lavant Cup at Goodwood and 8th in the Goodwood Easter Handicap.

1950 Was due to race an Aston Martin at Le Mans but was injured in a road accident and had to withdraw. He also raced Tony Rolt's Alfa Romeo and won at Silverstone.

1951 Joined the Jaguar works team and led Le Mans with Moss in a C-Type until retiring. He also finished 3rd at Goodwood in a Frazer Nash, and had occasional outings in his Bentley.

1952 Finished 14th in the TT for Jaguar, won a Goodwood Handicap in a Jaguar, and had a couple of races in an Allard.

1953 His Grand Prix debut came with an HWM Alta at the British and ended in retirement with clutch failure. He also drove a works Connaught at the Italian but failed to be classified as a finisher. He shared the Connaught with Salvadori to finish in 3rd place at Charterhall and 4th in his heat with the HWM in the Coronation Trophy at Crystal Palace. He raced for Bristol in sports cars, taking a class win and 5th overall at Reims, but retired at Le Mans, and shared Joe Kelly's Jaguar C-Type to 8th in the TT.

1954 An absence of Grand Prix outings but a very varied year nevertheless. 10th in the TT with a Connaught, 5th in the London Trophy and 13th in the International Trophy in an F2 Turner, 2nd in class at Silverstone in a Borgward Isabella saloon and 4th in class at the Reims 12 hours sharing a Bristol with Wisdom.

1955 He failed to make the start of the British Grand Prix after his works Connaught B-Type had engine problems. He crashed out of the Daily Telegraph Trophy at Aintree and retired from the International Trophy. He raced for Bristol at Le Mans again and finished 9th, shared an MG to 20th in the TT and finished 52nd in the Monte Carlo Rally in a Sunbeam.

1956 Two Grand Prix starts with Connaught resulted in two points finishes, with 4th in the British and 5th in the Italian. He also raced the car to 5th at Brands Hatch, while his sports car outings brought 3rd with Titterington for Jaguar at the Reims 12hrs, 4th at Goodwood and 14th in the Empire Trophy in an HWM Sports.

1957 His only Grand Prix outing ended in retirement at the British with a works BRM P25. Back in the Connaught he finished 2nd at Syracuse and in the Richmond Trophy and 3rd in the Glover Trophy. He retired a Cooper from the International Trophy and raced a D-Type Jaguar to 4th at Goodwood, 8th in the Nurburgring 1000km and 10th in the Swedish Grand Prix. He finished 4th in the Monzanapolis 500 with an Ecurie Ecosse-modified D-Type.

1958 After retiring Bernie Ecclestone's Connaught at the British Grand Prix, he finished 8th in Morocco with a works Cooper Climax in his only other Grand Prix of the year. He raced a Monza Lister entered by Ecurie Ecosse to 11th in the Monzanapolis 500, and with the Jaguar D-Type he took 3rd in class at Silverstone, 7th in the Spa GP and Nurburbring 1000km, but retired from Le Mans.

1959 Two outings in Tommy Atkins' Cooper ended in retirement in both the British and Italian Grand Prix, but he took the Maserati-engined version to 4th at the Silverstone International Trophy. He also won both the TT and Nurburgring 1000km with Moss and Shelby in an Aston Martin DBR1.

GRAND PRIX RECORD	
Starts	12
Wins	0
Poles	0
Fastest laps	0
WC points	5
Best finish	4th

Tuck Cooper, retiring from what turned out to be his last Grand Prix. He retired his Aston Martin at Le Mans and took a 3rd place in a Libre race at Mallory Park in a Cooper Maserati.

Jack Fairman on the grid at Silverstone.

Photo: BRDC Archive.

1960 Another British Grand Prix ended with retirement in an Atkins' Cooper, but he had earlier taken the car to 7th in the International Trophy. He won the Rouen GP in an Aston Martin DBR1, won a sports car race at Oulton Park in a Lotus XV, took 5th in the TT with Whitehead in a Ferrari and 9th at Le Mans for Aston Martin.

1961 After debuting the Ferguson P99 in the Empire Trophy, he raced it in the British Grand Prix, but was disqualified after Moss took over the car and had a push start. He also contested the Italian Grand Prix in a Fred

1962 Finished 17th at Le Mans in a Tojeiro and failed to start the Indianapolis 500 when another driver crashed his car. Took 3rd place twice at Mallory Park Libre races in a Cooper Maserati.

1963 Became the nominated reserve driver for the ATS Grand Prix team and finished 7th in the Imola Grand Prix in a Porsche.

Jack Fairman

❖

RON FLOCKHART
Born June 16th 1923
Killed April 12th 1962

A former motorcycle racer who turned to cars in 1948, Flockhart was equally at home in hillclimbs and on race circuits. His Grand Prix record failed to do justice to his undoubted talent, with only 13 starts over a seven-year period. He did however excel in sports cars and winning at Le Mans in 1956 and 1957 with his Ecurie Ecosse Jaguar D-Type were the highlights of his career. In 1959, he started five Grands Prix with BRM, taking a best finish of sixth in France. As his interest in racing turned from cars to aeroplanes, he appeared less and less. It was his attempt to break the London-Sydney record that claimed his life, during a practice flight in Australia in April 1962.

1948 Bought an MG to prepare for his car racing debut.

1949 Began with sand races at St. Andrews and had a JP Vincent for F3 racing.

1950 He continued to race his JP and also took his MG to a class win on the Lothian February Trial.

1951 A further year with the JP brought a win at Dundrod and 3rd in a Croft Libre race. On the hills he finished 5th at both Bo'ness and Rest & be Thankful.

1952 Graduating to an ERA he concentrated on hillclimbs and libre races, with victory in a libre race at Crimond, class wins at Bo'ness and Rest & be Thankful, and 5th in the libre race at the British Grand Prix.

1953 Victories at Snetterton, Charterhall and in a Goodwood Handicap followed with the ERA. He finished 2nd and 3rd at Snetterton, 3rd in the Chichester Cup at Goodwood, 4th in the Bordeaux Grand Prix and Libre race at the British Grand Prix and 7th in the Richmond Trophy at Goodwood. There was a victory on the Bo'ness Hillclimb, along with a class win at Rest & be Thankful and 2nd in a TV Challenge Hillclimb Match race for Scotland at Bo'ness. He had a win at Snetterton in an Aston Martin DB3, and a couple of outings in an F2 Connaught brought him 3rd at Charterhall.

1954 His Grand Prix debut came at the British as deputy for the flu-stricken Prince Bira, crashing the Maserati 250F when he hit a wet

GRAND PRIX RECORD	
Starts	13
Wins	0
Poles	0
Fastest laps	0
WC points	5
Best finish	3rd

bank at Copse and was tipped out of the car. His year was mainly spent driving the awesome V16 for BRM in libre races. He took a win at Ibsley and two at Snetterton, finished 2nd in the Goodwood Whit Trophy and Hastings Trophy at Castle Combe, 3rd in the Aintree 200, Libre and Snetterton Libre and 4th in the Chichester Cup and Richmond Trophy at Goodwood. He also raced a Healey in sports car races, including the Empire Trophy.

1955 A year of promise but with little to show for it with the troublesome BRM. 2nd place in Snetterton Libre was the highlight, matched by a 2nd at Castle Combe's Empire News Trophy in a Vanwall and 2nd at Charterhall in a Healey sports.

1956 An outing with the new BRM P25 at the British Grand Pix ended with engine failure on the 3rd lap, but a trip to the Italian with a works Connaught resulted in a career best 3rd place, after qualifying only two off the back. The year was dominated by his drives in the Ecurie Ecosse Jaguar D-Type, winning at Le Mans and taking 4th in the Reims 12hrs with Ninian Sanderson. He had a win and 2nd at Snetterton, won at Charterhall, had a win, 2nd and two 3rds at Goodwood, was 6th in the Silverstone sports car race at the International Trophy and British Grand Prix, and came 7th in the Empire Trophy. He also raced a Lotus in sports car races, with 3rd in the Oulton Park Gold Cup and took a Healey to 2nd at Charterhall and an Austin A90 to 5th in an Oulton Park saloon car race.

Ron Flockhart in the Cooper Monaco, August 1960.

Photo: BRDC Archive.

Ron Flockhart winning at Ibsley in 1954 with the V16 BRM.

Photo: BRDC Archive.

1957 Two Grand Prix outings in the BRM P25 failed to produce a finish, retiring from Monaco with an engine timing problem and sustaining burns after an accident in the French. The BRM did however claim 3rd in the Glover Trophy at Goodwood, the Silverstone International Trophy and Caen GP. He won Le Mans again for Ecosse and Jaguar with Ivor Bueb, as well as at St. Etienne, and finished 8th at the Nurburgring 1000km with Jack Fairman. Further outings with Lotus brought a class win in the Empire Trophy, victory at the International Trophy Sports car race at Silverstone, a class win at Rouen and 2nd at Goodwood. He took an F2 Cooper to 5th in the Oulton Park Gold Cup, finished 2nd at Goodwood in an F2 Lotus and finished 2nd in class in the saloon car race at the International Trophy in a 2.4-litre Jaguar.

1958 After failing to qualify Rob Walker's Cooper Climax at Monaco, his only other Grand Prix opportunity came in Morocco, where his BRM P25 broke the camshaft. He had already written off a BRM at the Silverstone International Trophy and was injured again after his Lotus hit an ambulance containing Peter Ashdown, during a sports car race at Rouen. He took a D-Type Jaguar to a win and 2nd at Charterhall, retired the Ecurie Ecosse Tojeiro at Le Mans and then took it to Goodwood and won. Further outings in a Jaguar Saloon claimed 2nd places at both Aintree and the International Trophy support race.

1959 Five Grand Prix starts with BRM, provided a best finish of 6th at the French, despite driving one-eyed after a stone smashed his goggles. He was 7th in Portugal and 13th in Italy, but failed to finish at either Monaco or the British. His BRM was taken to New Zealand where it won the Lady Wigram Trophy and took 2nd at Teretonga and

Invercargill, while nearer to home he won the Silver City Trophy at Snetterton and came 3rd in the Silverstone International Trophy. In sports cars he won at Snetterton in an Ecurie Ecosse Lister Jaguar, won at Goodwood and took 4th at Aintree in the Tojeiro and brought a D-Type Jaguar home in 4th at the International Trophy.

1960 A run in a works Lotus 18 at the French Grand Prix resulted in a 6th place finish, while the final Grand Prix of his career came in US Grand Prix, and ended in retirement with a works Cooper. He raced for Alan Brown in F2 and took 2nd in the GP des Frontieres at Chimay, 4th at Pau and 11th in the Aintree 200. He won the Empire Trophy and British Grand Prix sports car races in a Cooper Monaco, but took up a new hobby of flying.

1961 Apart from retiring at Le Mans and winning at Charterhall in an Aston Martin DBR1, it was more flying than racing.

1962 After early season races in a Lotus had ended in 5th at Warwick Farm and retirement in the Lady Wigram Trophy, he was killed in an air crash when practising for a record attempt.

PHILIP FOTHERINGHAM-PARKER

Born September 22nd 1907
Died October 15th 1981

A businessman and spare time racer from both Pre and Post War, Fotheringham-Parker made one Grand Prix appearance in 1951. During the mid-fifties he became a regular on the rally scene, contesting most of the classics until the end of 1956. After virtually retiring from racing, he became a judge at major BRDC meetings until the end of 1968 and was a regular participant in the London to Brighton veteran car run.

1936 Finished 2nd in the JCC Brooklands Handicap with a Lagonda.

1937 Raced a Ford V8 at Brooklands, and took an award win in the MCC one hour trial, and 3rd in class at the JCC meeting.

1939 Had moderate success racing an Alvis Silver Eagle at Brooklands.

1947 Took part in the Gransden Handicap with an Alfa Romeo and finished 12th in class at Brighton Speed Trials with a Delage.

1948 Had intended contesting the British Grand Prix, but lost the drive to Hampshire.

1949 Sharing Hamilton's Maserati 6C he finished 11th in the British Grand Prix. He also took 2nd in the Wakefield Trophy at the Curragh, but retired from the International Trophy at Silverstone.

1950 Finished 11th in the International Trophy with Hamilton's Maserati, but took his own Alfa Romeo to a win and 2nd place in Goodwood Handicaps.

1951 A broken oil pipe ended his only Grand Prix, at the British in a Maserati 4CL. The car was taken to victory at Winfield in an Invitation Grand Prix, and also took 3rd in the Richmond Trophy and 10th in the Festival of Britain Trophy at Goodwood, but retired from the International Trophy. He drove a Jaguar to 3rd in a Goodwood Handicap and an ERA to 13th in the Ulster Trophy.

GRAND PRIX RECORD

Starts	1
Wins	0
Poles	0
Fastest laps	0
WC points	0
Best finish	DNF

1952 He crashed a Connaught out of his heat in the International Trophy, but brought a Talbot home in 3rd in the Chichester Cup at Goodwood.

1953 Contested Le Mans with Sydney Allard and finished 12th in the TT with Meyer in an Aston Martin.

1954 Finished 78th on the Monte Carlo Rally in a Sunbeam Talbot and completed the Tulip Rally in a Ford Zephyr.

1955 Took 35th on the Tulip and 89th on the Monte Carlo Rallies in a Ford Zodiac.

1956 Had a final outing on the Monte Carlo Rally.

❖

JOE (J.G.) FRY

Born 1915
Killed July 29th 1950

An expert in hillclimbs and speed events, Fry performed numerous giant-killing feats with his highly developed Freikaiserwagen Specials. His biggest claim to fame was beating Raymond Mays' Shelsley Walsh record in 1949, but by comparison his circuit racing experiences were few. His one and only Grand Prix appearance was in the 1950 British at Silverstone. He shared a Maserati with Brian Shawe-Taylor, having made a Formula One debut with a Maserati in the International Trophy race of the previous season. Less than a month after his sole Grand Prix he met his death at Blandford Camp, after losing control of the Freikaiserwagen.

1936 Debuted his self-built Freikaiserwagen in sprints and hillclimbs, sharing with cousin David.

1937 2nd in class at Bristol Speed Hillclimb, 3rd in Lewes Speed Trial and 6th overall with a class win at Shelsley Walsh with the Freikaiserwagen. Also drove a Bentley to a class win in the Inter-Varsity Speed Trial, 2nd in class at Poole Speed Trials, and at Donington Park took a Handicap win and a 2nd place in the Stanley Cup meeting.

1938 Success continued with the ever improving Freikaiserwagen. 5th overall and a class win twice, 10th overall and a 2nd in class all at Shelsley, plus a win and 2nd in class at Syston.

1939 Numerous class wins in the Freikaiserwagen, but overall victories still eluded him. A newer more powerful car was to be built over the war years, based on a GN chassis.

racing side there was a 12th place finish in the British Grand Prix F3 race with an IOTA and an F1 debut at the Silverstone International Trophy, which resulted in a 15th place finish in his Maserati. With the same car he was 7th in the Daily Graphic Trophy at Goodwood and 4th in a Goodwood Handicap.

1950 Finished 10th with the Maserati in the British Grand Prix, sharing the car with Brian Shawe-Taylor, having qualified 20th of the 21 starters. Won an F3 race at Lulsgate and finished 14th in the British Grand Prix F3 race with an Arengo, as well as racing the Freikaiserwagen. Only a few weeks after his Grand Prix appearance, Joe lost control of his home-built special during a race at Blandford Camp, with fatal consequences.

Joe Fry in the Freikaiserwagen.

1946 Debuted the new car in speed events, with no notable successes.

1947 Won the Bugatti Handicap at Gransden Lodge, and continued with the new Freikaiserwagen in speed events. Won his class at Southsea with sixth overall, won the class again at Poole, finished 2nd in class at Brighton and 11th overall at Shelsley Walsh.

1948 Started to race his car in 500 F3, but the successes continued to come from the speed events. 6th overall with 1st and 2nd in class at Prescott, 2nd in class at Bo'ness, 3rd overall and a class win on the second Prescott visit, a class win at Bouley Bay and 4th overall and 2nd in class at the final Prescott.

1949 Yet another Freikaiserwagen derivative, but this time much lighter and with more power. A regular FTD contender including the shattering of Raymond Mays' long standing Shelsley Walsh hill record. He also won at Weston Super Mare, Blandford and Shelsley, finished 3rd overall at Prescott, a class win at Brighton and both class win and 2nd with a Bugatti at Lulsgate. On the circuit

BOB GERARD
Born January 19th 1914
Died 26th January 1990

With numerous successes to his credit from his Pre War activity, Bob was one of the British trailblazers in the resurrection of motorsport in the late forties. Two British Empire Trophy victories in his ERA were among the long list of credits in a driving career that spanned almost thirty years. He raced all over Europe in a wide array of cars, mainly single-seaters and collected many national and international awards. His final Grand Prix appearance also produced his best result with sixth place in the 1957 British. After winning the Autosport GT Championship in 1959, competitive outings become less frequent. However a new career as an entrant soon took off, with drivers in mainly non-championship Formula 1 races, Formula 2 and 3 until 1980. The most challenging corner at Mallory Park is named after Bob Gerard.

1933 Made his competition debut with a Riley on the Lands End Trial.

1935 Contested sprints and speed trials in his Riley, including taking 4th in a Brooklands Handicap.

1936 Continued with the Riley and collected a class award at the Brooklands JCC meeting.

GRAND PRIX RECORD	
Starts	1
Wins	0
Poles	0
Fastest laps	0
WC points	0
Best finish	10th

1937 Finished 9th in the TT with his Riley, and won both scratch and Haemorrhagic Trophy races with an MG at Donington Park's United Hospitals raceday. Other successes with the Riley included three scratch race wins and one handicap at Donington's Stanley Cup meeting, a class win at Brooklands MCC meeting, and 3rd place with A.D.Bateman in a Brooklands 12 hour race.

1938 Another year with the Riley brought 14th in the TT, 10th in the Empire Trophy, two scratch race victories, 12th in the Nuffield Trophy, 4th in the Junior Handicap and a win, 2nd and 3rd at the United Hospitals Day, all at Donington. Also took 5th at the BRDC Brooklands and a class award at MCC Brooklands.

1939 A final year with the Riley at Brooklands, Donington and Crystal Palace, with a win and 3rd in the Brooklands March Handicap.

1945 Won the Bristol Hillclimb at Portishead in his ERA.

1946 Finished 3rd in the Ulster Trophy, took a class win at Prescott Hillclimb and took part in the first Post War mainland race at Gransden with his ERA.

1947 Won the British Empire Trophy on the Isle of Man and the Ulster Trophy at Ballyclare. Finished 3rd in the Marne Grand Prix at Reims and 4th at Spa, sharing with Cuth Harrison, took two FTDs at Prescott Hillclimb, 2nd at Prescott and Shelsley Walsh, 4th and a class win at Bo'ness Hillclimb and 4th at Shelsley Walsh with his ERA. Took both the Riley and ERA to Brighton Speed Trials and came away with a class win and three 3rds.

1948 Finished 3rd in the British Grand Prix, 2nd in the Ulster Trophy, won the Jersey Road race and took 2nd in the Goodwood Trophy with his ERA. Also found success with the same car in speed events, with victory at Luton Hoo, two wins at Prescott, plus a 2nd with class win and a 3rd with a class win. A win at Stanmer Park was followed by 2nd at Brighton, two 3rds at Shelsley Walsh and a class win at Bo'ness.

1949 Took 2nd in the British Grand Prix and won the British Empire Trophy for the second time. Finished 7th in the Silverstone International Trophy, 3rd in Goodwood's Daily Graphic Trophy and won the Jersey Road race for the second successive year, all in the faithful ERA. There was also an outing in the International Trophy Production race, bringing 20th place in a Frazer Nash.

1950 Made two World Championship Grand Prix starts in the ERA, finishing 6th in both the British and Monaco, after qualifying 13th and 16th respectively. Also won his third British Empire Trophy, took 3rd in the Goodwood Daily Graphic Trophy, 4th in the Jersey Road Race, 2nd in the Ulster Trophy, 5th in the Chichester Cup at Goodwood, 3rd and 6th in Goodwood Handicaps and won at Castle Combe. Drove the Frazer Nash in Production races and took 3rd in the TT.

1951 Apart from taking 11th in the British Grand Prix in his ERA, racing was mainly restricted to Britain. 4th in the Daily Graphic Trophy at Goodwood, a win and 2nd at

GRAND PRIX RECORD	
Starts	8
Wins	0
Poles	0
Fastest laps	0
WC points	0
Best finish	6th

Castle Combe, 4th in the Ulster Trophy, victory in the Kenning Trophy at Gamston, 15th in Silverstone's International Trophy and 2nd at Ibsley. Further outings with Frazer Nash brought 3rd overall and a class win in the TT, 2nd in the Empire Trophy and 2nd in the International Trophy Production Sports race. F3 outings brought wins at Brands Hatch and Winfield, with 2nd at Ibsley and Castle Combe and 6th at Goodwood.

1952 A year away from Grand Prix racing but took the ERA to libre wins at Castle Combe, Charterhall and Snetterton, 3rd in the Sussex International Trophy at Goodwood, 6th in the British Grand Prix Libre race at Silverstone and 10th in the Chichester Cup at Goodwood. Took 4th in the Goodwood 9hrs with David Clarke in the Frazer Nash and had F3 success with victory at Goodwood, 2nd at Silverstone, 4th at Charterhall and 8th in the British Grand Prix F3 race.

1953 Brought out a Cooper Bristol for the French Grand Prix and finished 11th, but retired from his only other World Championship outing when the suspension broke at the British. Other successes with the Cooper Bristol were a libre win at Charterhall and F2 wins at Castle Combe and Snetterton. Finished 2nd in Snetterton F2, 3rd in the London Trophy at Crystal Palace, 4th at Charterhall and the Goodwood Trophy, 5th in the Madgwick Cup at Goodwood, 6th in the Richmond Trophy at Goodwood and the International Trophy at Silverstone and 8th at Rouen. The ERA was taken to 2nd at Castle Combe (twice) and in Charterhall Formula Libre races (twice). There was an F3 win at Charterhall, 3rd at Snetterton, 5th at Castle Combe and the Frazer Nash claimed 6th in the Goodwood 9hrs with a class win, and 7th in the TT with Clarke again sharing the driving.

1954 Grand Prix activity was restricted to 10th place in the British with the Cooper Bristol. However, there was victory in the London Trophy at Crystal Palace, Castle Combe Libre, Charterhall, Oulton Park and the Madgwick Cup at Goodwood. He scored 2nd in Oulton Park Libre, 2nd in Snetterton F1, 2nd and 4th Snetterton Libre, 3rd in the Oulton Park Gold Cup, 4th in the Aintree 200 and Goodwood Trophy, 6th in the Woodcote Cup at Goodwood and 7th in Aintree Libre. In F3 there was a 5th in the British Grand Prix support race and 6th at Aintree.

1955 Another absence from the Grand Prix scene but the Cooper Bristol went on to win the Goodwood Easter Handicap, the Rochester Cup and Farningham Trophy at

Bob Gerard in his ERA in 1950.

Photo: BRDC Archive.

Brands Hatch, the Crystal Palace Club Trophy and a Silverstone Libre race. Took 2nd places in the Daily Telegraph Trophy at Aintree, the London Trophy at Crystal Palace and the Goodwood Glover Trophy and Lavant Cup. Finished 3rd in the Empire News and Avon International Trophies at Castle Combe, 6th in the Daily Dispatch Trophy and Oulton Park Gold Cup, and 10th in the Silverstone International Trophy. A couple of races at the wheel of a Maserati also brought a victory at Charterhall in the Daily Record Trophy.

1956 A return to the British Grand Prix resulted in 11th place with the Cooper Bristol in a fairly quiet year. Two wins in Mallory Libre races, 2nd in the Aintree 100, 3rd in a heat of the London Trophy, and 4th in Silverstone's International Trophy. The Maserati was brought home 10th in the International Trophy Sports Car race and there was a 5th place in a Turner in a Brands Hatch handicap.

1957 A final Grand Prix appearance at the British equalled his best ever finish in the World Championship, with a hard earned 6th.

1958 Having virtually retired from single seater racing, 3rd in class was claimed in the International Trophy Saloons and at Mallory Park, as well as 10th overall and a class win at the British Grand Prix meeting in his Austin A35. The Turner was taken to a class win and 4th at Mallory in the Autosport Championship, as well as 3rd in a Libre race.

1959 Became joint Autosport GT Champion with Dickie Stoop, after a successful year with his Turner. Won at Oulton Park and twice at Snetterton, took 2nd and 3rd at Snetterton and 2nd at Goodwood. His Austin A35 again saw action and recorded a 3rd in class at Snetterton.

1960 Started the year with a win for the Turner in the opening Autosport round at Silverstone, followed by two 2nd places at Snetterton, 2nd at Mallory and 3rd at both Snetterton and Mallory.

1961 Had further outings in the Turner GT along with a win at Mallory in a Cooper BMC F3 car.

———————— ❖ ————————

50 years of British Grand Prix drivers

50 years of British Grand Prix drivers

Part One
1950s

CHAPTER 3

DICK GIBSON
Born April 16th 1918

Dick Gibson, 1961 South African GP.

A purely amateur driver who, following a couple of years on the national scene, began to take things more seriously after acquiring a Cooper Bristol from Tony Crook in 1954. A competent racer who graced the Grand Prix stage on two occasions, he raced F2 Coopers at the German Grand Prix in 1957 and 1958. He later raced successfully in South Africa and New Zealand, winning the South African Formula 1 Championship in 1958 and 1959. However, a serious accident in 1960 at Cape Town prompted his retirement after one final comeback race in the 1961 South African Grand Prix.

1952 He raced a Jaguar XK120 in national events with moderate success.

1953 A further year with the XK120 and he was quite content until he met Tony Crook who got him interested in a Cooper Bristol.

1954 Armed with his new Cooper Bristol he achieved his first aim on the car's debut at the Easter Goodwood meeting, which was to finish. He later recorded a 2nd place at Crystal Palace, 3rd at Davidstow and a class win at the Prescott Silver Jubilee Hillclimb.

1955 Moving onto a Connaught A-Type, he was 3rd in class in the Avon Trophy at Castle Combe and 8th at the Oulton Park Gold Cup. He also raced his Bristol Saloon road car to 3rd at Brunton Hillclimb.

1956 Continuing with his Connaught, he was 2nd in class at the Empire Trophy, 5th in the Aintree 200 sharing with Bob Berry, 5th at the London Trophy, 6th at Mallory Park and in the Aintree 100, and 8th in the International Trophy at Silverstone.

1957 Moving on to a Cooper T43 Climax, he was 6th in the International Coupe de Vitesse at Reims, winning the F2 class and finished 7th in the International Trophy. He retired the car from the F2 section of the German Grand Prix after breaking his steering. He also shared Tony Crook's Cooper Bristol at the Oulton Park Gold Cup, finishing 9th.

1958 Another outing at the German Grand Prix ended in retirement, but the season had started with the Cooper in New Zealand. A class win and 6th at the New Zealand Grand Prix, was followed by 7th at Teretonga and 8th in

GRAND PRIX RECORD	
Starts	2
Wins	0
Poles	0
Fastest laps	0
WC points	0
Best finish	DNF

the Lady Wigram Trophy. He had a 10th in the French F2 Grand Prix and 8th at the Circuit D'Auvergne, before shipping the car to South Africa at the end of the season. Three wins from four races crowned him as the South African F1 Champion. He had also raced a Peerless at Le Mans with Peter Jopp, but it was, in his own words, too slow to be competitive.

1959 Retained the South African F1 title with three wins out of four races.

1960 He bought Jack Brabham's F2 Cooper and finished 7th in the South African Grand Prix. At a following meeting in Capetown he crashed and was quite badly injured. When the car was repaired he entered it for other drivers during his own recovery and had entered it for the Italian Grand. As he was still on crutches, he asked Vic Wilson to drive, but he was unable to qualify it for the race. With a special dispensation from his doctor, Gibson reclaimed his seat and successfully completed 12 laps, taking the Monza banking at 161mph. Totally exhausted from his efforts, he handed the car back to Wilson for the race. He later took 4th place in the Coupe de Salon at Montlhery.

1961 Had one last outing in the South African Grand Prix, and then retired from racing.

❖

HORACE GOULD
Born September 20th 1921
Died November 4th 1968

A large Bristolian motor dealer who, after a couple of years contesting national races in a Cooper Bristol, bought himself an ex-Prince Bira Maserati 250F and contested Grand Prix and non-championship F1 races all over Europe and even as far afield as Argentina in 1958. His best result came with with a famous fifth place in the 1956 British GP. Living mainly off his starting money from the previous race, Gould proved more than a match for many of the more affluent continentals, before calling time on his racing career after an abortive trip to the Italian Grand Prix of 1960. Sadly, he later succumbed to a heart attack at the age of 47.

1953 His Cooper Bristol provided several podium finishes, with a victory in a Silverstone Libre race, 2nd at Thruxton and Castle Combe F2, 3rd in the London Trophy and Libre at Crystal Palace, Castle Combe Libre and 4th in F2 at Snetterton. At the Libre race supporting the British Grand Prix he finished 8th and took fastest

GRAND PRIX RECORD	
Starts	14
Wins	0
Poles	0
Fastest laps	0
WC points	2
Best finish	5th

time of the day at the Tarrant Rushton Speed Trials, along with 3rd in the F2 class at Prescott Hillclimb. In sports cars he raced a Riley and a Cooper MG, taking a win at Castle Combe, 2nd at Charterhall, 4th at Snetterton and two 4ths at Silverstone.

1954 A further year in the Cooper Bristol included his Grand Prix debut at the British, where he qualified 20th, but was unclassified in the race after numerous pitstops. He won the Joe Fry Memorial Trophy at Castle Combe, finished 2nd in the New Zealand Grand Prix, Glade Trophy at Crystal Palace and a Snetterton Libre race. Also took 3rd in the London Trophy at Crystal Palace, the Hastings Trophy at Castle Combe and the Silver City Airways Trophy at Brands Hatch, 4th at Snetterton and in the Crystal Palace August Trophy and 5th in both the Madgwick Cup and Goodwood Libre. He also raced a Kieft in sports cars, taking 2nd at Aintree, 13th in the International Trophy support race at Silverstone, as well as taking part in the Empire Trophy.

1955 Having travelled to Italy to buy an ex-Bira Maserati 250F, he crashed out of his first Grand Prix of the year in Holland. Further outings in the British and the Italian both ended in retirement, but in non-championship European forays he finished 3rd at Albi and 4th at Syracuse. At home he finished 2nd in the Avon International at Castle Combe and Charterhall, 3rd in the Daily Telegraph Trophy at Aintree and had a great battle for the lead of the Crystal Palace International Trophy until retiring. He also continued to race a Bristol-powered Kieft in sports car races.

1956 The 250F was taken to four Grands Prix and came home with 5th at the British, 8th in Monaco, and retirements in Belgium and Germany. He won the Aintree 100 and finished 2nd in the Naples GP and Snetterton's Vanwall Trophy, but retired at Syracuse and broke his arm in Caen after being thrown from the car.

1957 Six attempts on the Grand Prix scene resulted in 10th place in Italy, crashes at Pescara and Monaco and rear axle failures in the French and German. He failed to start the British after his foot was run over in the pit lane as he helped extinguish a fire on Gerard's Cooper. His other outings netted 3rd at Invercargill, 4th in Naples, 5th at Caen, 6th at Reims and the Silverstone International Trophy, and 8th at Pau.

1958 Maserati's withdrawal from Grand Prix racing caused difficulties in getting any spares. He did manage 9th in Argentina, but drove a car from Centro Sud in

Horace Gould in his Cooper Bristol at Silverstone.

Photo: Ferret Fotographics.

Monaco and failed to qualify. He took his own car to the Dutch Grand Prix where it was raced by Masten Gregory, but apart from taking 4th at Syracuse his Grand Prix career was all but over.

1960 The old 250F was taken to the boycotted Italian Grand Prix for a last outing, but never even took to the track after the engine refused to start.

❖

BRUCE HALFORD
Born May 18th 1931

With only a year of national racing behind him, Halford joined the Grand Prix scene with an ex-Bira Maserati 250F at the 1956 British, but gained his successes away from the World Championship arena. He raced Lotuses, Coopers, Aston Martins and a Lister Jaguar, before bowing out at the end of 1963. He came back to racing in the mid-seventies and until 1985 he was a leading figure in the historic racing world, notably for a string of successes in a Lotus 16.

1955 Had a win at Ibsley and 2nd at Castle Combe in a Riley along with 4th at Aintree in a Cooper Bristol and 6th in the Kingsland Trophy at Brands Hatch in an HWM.

1956 His newly acquired ex-Bira 250F Maserati qualified in 20th place on his Grand Prix debut at the

British, but retired with engine problems. In Germany he qualified 9th but was disqualified for receiving a push start after spinning off, and engine problems in Italy once again forced his retirement. He had a win with the car in an Oulton Park Libre race, had two 2nd places at Mallory Park, 3rd in the Aintree 100, 6th at Brands Hatch and retired from the Caen Grand Prix.

1957 Three further Grand Prix outings resulted in 11th place in Germany and retirement at both Pescara and the Italian. The 250F was also taken to 3rd at Caen, 6th in Naples, 11th at Reims, but retired at Pau, Syracuse and the Silverstone International Trophy. He also raced a Talbot at Le Mans and retired.

1958 Apart from taking the 250F to 3rd at Caen again, the year was spent racing a Lister Jaguar mainly in national events. He won a Goodwood handicap, had a 2nd, 3rd and 4th at Snetterton, 2nd at Crystal Palace and Mallory Park, 3rd in the Kingsdown Trophy at Brands Hatch. He finished third three times at Oulton Park, including the Gold Cup, 6th in the British Grand Prix support race and 15th at Le Mans with Brian Naylor.

1959 A one-off return to Grand Prix racing came with John Fisher's Lotus 16 at Monaco, retiring after an accident with Allison and Von Trips. He also drove the Lotus at the Empire Trophy, finished 12th at Rouen, retired at Syracuse and the Aintree 200 but was hospitalised after crashing during the Auvergne Trophy at Clermont Ferrand. As a guest in the BRM team he took 2nd behind team mate Flockhart in the Silver City Trophy at Snetterton and finished 5th in the British Grand Prix sports car race with his Lister. Further Lister outings included a retirement at Oulton Park when the car landed in the lake and was found settled on an unexploded bomb.

Bruce Halford at Silverstone.

Photo: BRDC Archive.

1963 6th place with a Cooper Monaco in a Silverstone sports car race, preceded his retirement from racing.

1974 Returned to racing with occasional outings in a Lister Jaguar in Historic Sport/GT races, taking 2nd at Silverstone and 3rd in class at Thruxton.

1975 Contested the Speed Merchants/JCB Historic Championship in the Lister Jaguar, with a win at Silverstone, 2nd at Brands Hatch and 2nd and 4th at Oulton Park.

1976 Finished 3rd in class at Silverstone in a Lister Jaguar.

1960 After failing to qualify Fred Tuck's Cooper T51 at Monaco, he made his final Grand Prix appearance with a similar Yeoman Credit car in France, recording a career best 8th despite retiring with engine failure before the end. Having concentrated on the F2 Cooper he also finished 2nd in the Lombank Trophy and 4th in the Vanwall Trophy at Snetterton, 5th at Goodwood, 6th at Oulton Park, 8th in the Silver City Trophy at Brands Hatch and the Oulton Park Gold Cup. He won a Libre race at Snetterton in Naylor's JBW Maserati and had a sports car win at Brands Hatch with his Lister Jaguar. He drove an Aston Martin to victory in the Raffles Club Trophy at Brands Hatch, took 2nd at Silverstone, and 7th in the British Grand Prix support race.

1961 After winning the Whit Trophy sports car race at Brands Hatch, he wrecked the Ecurie Ecosse Cooper Monaco at Le Mans.

1962 The highlight of a fairly unproductive season came with a 2nd at class at Brands Hatch in his Lister Jaguar.

1977 Had another run with the Lister to finish 3rd in the Scott-Brown Memorial Trophy at Snetterton.

1978 A full year of historic racing was undertaken in a Lotus 16, winning an Allcomers race at Cadwell Park, the European Historic race at the TT from a 10sec start, as well as 2nd in FIA Historic at Brands Hatch and 3rd in the Empire Trophy at Donington.

1979 Won his class in the Esso Donington Historic Championship and took 3rd in class in the Lloyds & Scottish Series. He won at Donington Park (twice) and Oulton Park, took three 2nds and two 3rds at Silverstone and a 2nd and 3rd at Donington, all in the Lotus 16.

1980 Won his class again in the Donington Historic Championship, and finished 4th in class in the Lloyds & Scottish. He won twice at Donington and took the Hawthorn Memorial Trophy at Silverstone. He was also 3rd and 4th at Donington, 2nd, 3rd and 9th at Brands Hatch and 6th at Silverstone.

1981 Another successful year with his Lotus 16 brought 2nd in class in the Lloyds & Scottish Championship, with two 2nds and a 3rd at Silverstone. He also won the Swedish Airforce Historic Trophy at Knutsdorp, came 2nd in the HGPCA Race of the Year and Baltex Plastics Trophy at Donington, and was unable to take up pole for the Oulton Park Gold Cup when the car refused to start.

1982 Scored two victories at Montlhery, plus Nurburgring, Monaco and the Cheshire Building Society Trophy at Oulton Park, added to 4th place in the Lloyds &

GRAND PRIX RECORD	
Starts	8
Wins	0
Poles	0
Fastest laps	0
WC points	0
Best finish	8th

Scottish series, which was achieved with two wins at Silverstone, and a win and two 2nds at Brands Hatch.

1983 Continuing success with the Lotus 16 resulted in victories at the Silverstone Newgate Construction Trophy, the Brands Hatch Mail on Sunday Trophy and at Cadwell Park, as well as 3rd at Donington Park and 4th in the Oulton Park Cheshire Building Society Trophy.

1984 Despite only a handful of outings, he was still victorious in the Hawthorn Trophy at Silverstone and at Ingliston, with 2nd at Cadwell Park in the Lotus 16.

1985 Returned to his roots with a Maserati 250F and took a win and 6th at Silverstone and 5th in the Historic race supporting the British Grand Prix at Brands Hatch.

———————— ❖ ————————

DUNCAN HAMILTON
Born April 30th 1920
Died May 13th 1994

Despite starting his racing career in single seaters and contesting Grands Prix in works Talbot Lagos and HWMs, this colourful character reached the peak of his career driving works Jaguar sports cars. Victory at Le Mans with Rolt in 1953 was followed by wins in the Reims 12 hours and a Coupe de Paris double. Famous for his exploits both on and off the track, Hamilton lived life to the full and, having survived the war, raced with verve all over the world. He spent the closing years of his career racing Jaguar D Types to great effect before retiring at the end of 1958. He passed away peacefully at the age of 74.

1946 Contested Shelsley Walsh and Prescott hillclimbs.

1947 Drove an MG and a Bugatti in speed events.

1948 Graduated to a Maserati 6C and retired from the British Grand Prix with low oil pressure. Also raced the car in the Empire Trophy and finished 9th in the Goodwood Trophy.

1949 Continuing to race his Maserati, he finished 11th in the British Grand Prix sharing with Fotheringham-Parker, took 2nd in a Goodwood handicap, 9th in the Daily Graphic Trophy at Goodwood, took a class win at Luton Hoo Speed Trials, but retired from the International Trophy at Silverstone.

1950 A further year with the Maserati brought a victory at the Curragh in the Wakefield Trophy and a Goodwood handicap and 8th in the Chichester Cup. At Le Mans he shared a Healey with Rolt to 4th place, and drove the same car to 8th and a

Duncan Hamilton.

Photo: BRDC Archive.

class win in the Production Race at the International Trophy meeting at Silverstone.

1951 He qualified his works Talbot Lago 11th for the British Grand Prix on his World Championship debut, and brought the car home 12th. A further outing in Germany ended in retirement with no oil pressure, but he had already taken 2nd place in the International Trophy at Silverstone and 5th in the Dutch Grand Prix and Festival of Britain Trophy at Goodwood. With an HWM he secured 2nd in the Wakefield Trophy at the Curragh and 3rd in an F2 race at Winfield. He took an ERA to 3rd in the Richmond Trophy at Goodwood, picked up a double victory at Boreham and 3rd in the International Trophy Production Race with a Jaguar XK120. Sharing his Nash Healey with Rolt once more, they brought the car home 6th overall at Le Mans.

1952 Formula changes forced a move from Talbot to drive works HWMs. Engine failure led to retirement from the British GP, but he finished 7th in the Dutch on the only other World Championship outing of the year. 3rd at Ibsley, 4th in the Eifelrennen and 5th at Zandvoort followed with the HWM, while the Talbot made a couple of appearances and collected 3rd in the Richmond Trophy and Chichester Cup at Goodwood. He took his Jaguar C-Type to 2nd place in sports car races at Turnberry and Boreham, won the Goodwood Easter Handicap and finished 2nd in a Snetterton Libre race with an XK120.

1953 His final Grand Prix ended in retirement from the British when the HWM suffered engine failure, but the season was highlighted by victory at Le Mans with Rolt in the C-Type Jaguar. There was also a 4th place with the Jaguar at Goodwood, while the HWM took 6th in the Crystal Palace and Ulster Trophies.

1954 A return to Le Mans to debut the D-Type Jaguar with Rolt, resulted in 2nd place. There were victories in the Coupe de Paris at Montlhery and Aintree, 2nd place in the Wakefield Trophy and 2nd with Rolt in the Reims 12 hours. He also took two 2nds at Silverstone, 3rd at Hedemora, 4th at La Baule and the Empire Trophy, 5th in the O'Boyle Trophy, 6th in the International Trophy Sports and Portuguese Grand Prix. Still at the wheel of an HWM Jaguar, he also collected 5th in an Oulton Park Libre race.

1955 Two victories at Snetterton, plus Goodwood and Silverstone kept the D-Type to the fore. He took 2nd in the Coupe de Paris, 3rd in the Dakar Grand Prix, 5th at the International Trophy Sports, 6th in Silverstone Libre, 7th in the Empire Trophy and a class win in the Epsom Downs Trophy at Silverstone.

GRAND PRIX RECORD	
Starts	5
Wins	0
Poles	0
Fastest laps	0
WC points	0
Best finish	7th

1956 Won the Coupe de Paris and Reims 12 hours with Bueb and Jaguar, and finished 2nd at Chimay, 2nd in the Coupe du Salon and 10th in the British Grand Prix Sports Car race. He also shared a works Ferrari with Hawthorn and de Portago to 3rd in the Swedish Grand Prix and took a 2.4 Jaguar to 3rd in the Silverstone Production Touring Car race.

1957 Continuing to race his D-Type, he collected 3rd in St. Etienne and at Aintree, 4th at Goodwood, 5th at Spa and 6th at Le Mans with Gregory. In the Production Touring Cars he brought his 3.4 Jaguar home 2nd at Silverstone.

1958 Still relying on the D-Type for the most part, he came 2nd in the Goodwood Whit Trophy, 2nd and 3rd in the Sussex Trophy and Goodwood Handicaps, 4th in the Empire Trophy, 6th at Aintree and in the TT, and 7th in the International Trophy Sports. With the saloons he won at Goodwood (twice), and decided to retire from racing at the end of the year.

❖

DAVID HAMPSHIRE
Born December 29th 1917
Died August 25th 1990

Hampshire was a Pre-War racer who came to prominence in the late forties and early fifties, highlighted by fourth place in the 1949 British Grand Prix, sharing Billy Cotton's ERA. His only World Championship outings were in 1950 with a Maserati 4CLT in the British and French races. After a couple of seasons out of racing, he came back for one more year in 1955, contesting sports car races in a Lister Bristol.

1938 Won the Reilly Cup and took 2nd in class at Syston Speed Trials, three 2nd in class finishes at Prescott Hillclimb, 2nd and 3rd in United Hospitals Donington Park Handicaps, all driving a Bugatti.

1939 Took 2nd in the handicap at Donington Park's final Pre-War meeting, with a Maserati. Finished 5th and 8th at the Syston Speed Trials with his Bugatti and a BHW.

1946 Raced a Maserati and Delage at Gransden Lodge on the relaunching of British motorsport.

1947 Retired an ERA from the Lausanne and Geneva Grand Prix and raced Reg Parnell's Challenger at Gransden and in the Empire Trophy.

1948 2nd in the British Empire Trophy, 7th in the British Grand Prix, took a class win at Bo'ness Hillclimb and 3rd

David Hampshire

Photo: BRDC Archive.

the Silverstone International Trophy, all Maserati mounted.

1951 The Ambrosiana Maserati was used again for 10th in the Ulster Trophy and 20th in the Silverstone International Trophy. There were a few minor outings in the ERA and a works Aston Martin DB2 was shared with Parnell on the way to 7th at Le Mans.

1955 Won the Aintree Sports car race, finished 6th at Goodwood, 9th and a class win with Peter Scott-Russell in the Goodwood 9 hours and 10th with a class win at the British Grand Prix Sports Car race driving a Lister Bristol.

in the Goodwood Trophy with an ERA. Won at Gransden Lodge and retired from the Jersey Road Race in a Delage.

GRAND PRIX RECORD

Starts	2
Wins	0
Poles	0
Fastest laps	0
WC points	0
Best finish	9th

1949 Shared an ERA to 4th place in the British Grand Prix, also drove the car to 7th in the Empire Trophy, 11th in the Silverstone International Trophy, retired at Albi and took class wins at Bo'ness Hillclimb and Weston Speed Trials. At the wheel of a Maserati he finished 8th in the Jersey Road race, 3rd in a Goodwood handicap and 4th in the Daily Graphic Trophy and Woodcote Cup at Goodwood.

1950 The Scuderia Ambrosiana Maserati 4CLT was used at the British Grand Prix, finishing 9th from 16th on the grid. A second Grand Prix outing with the car came in the French Grand Prix, which turned out to be his only other World Championship appearance. After qualifying 18th, his race ended prematurely with engine failure. Won the Nottingham Trophy at Gamston and took 2nd in the Libre and Racing Car races, 2nd in the Ulster Trophy, 4th in the Jersey Road Race, 5th in the Empire Trophy, 9th in

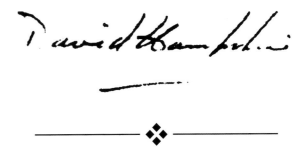

❖

T.C. (CUTH) HARRISON
Born July 6th 1906
Died January 21st 1981

Successful in reliability trials and speed events in the late thirties, Harrison was a front-runner with his ERA in the immediate Post-War years until semi-retirement after the 1950 season. His three World Championship outings were in 1950 at the wheel of an ERA and he was one of the drivers caught up in the famous multiple accident at Monaco that year. That was his last season of racing, but racing's loss was trialing's gain, and he took two RAC Trials titles and victories galore. To confirm his all round ability, Cuth was a member of the Ford works rally team until the early 1960s and was still competing successfully in trials until close to his 60th birthday.

1938 Finished 9th in the TT and 5th in the Coronation Trophy at Donington in his Riley.

GRAND PRIX RECORD	
Starts	3
Wins	0
Poles	0
Fastest laps	0
WC points	0
Best finish	7th

1946 Raced his ex-Dixon Riley at Gransden Lodge.

1947 Shared an ERA with Bob Gerard to 3rd in the Marne Grand Prix at Reims and 4th in the European Grand Prix at Spa. Took the car to 4th in the Ulster Trophy and 9th in the Empire Trophy as well as bringing the Riley out to finish 2nd in the Manx Cup. There was also a class win with Ford on the Blackpool Rally.

1948 Retired the ERA from the British Grand Prix with a broken valve and from Monaco with engine failure. Finished 3rd in the Ulster Trophy, 4th in the Empire and Goodwood Trophies, 5th at Penya Rhin and retired on Jersey. Took the Riley back to the Manx Cup and retired, won the Sheffield and Hallam Trial, his own Harrison Trial, the NMMC and Jeans Gold Cup Trials, and 2nd in the Bisley Trial.

1949 6th in the Italian Grand Prix in the ERA, but retired from the British when the engine failed again. Finished 3rd in the Richmond Trophy and Woodcote Cup at Goodwood, 4th in the Empire Trophy, 6th in the Daily Graphic Trophy at Goodwood and 9th in the Silverstone International Trophy with his ERA. Among the trialing successes were 2nd on the High Peak and 3rd on the Sheffield and Hallamshire.

1950 Contested three World Championship Grands Prix in his ERA, finishing 7th in the British from 15th on the grid but got caught up in the multiple accident at Monaco after starting 14th. His final outing ended with another engine failure in the Italian Grand Prix. He also took the car to 3rd in the Ulster Trophy, 4th in the Silverstone International Trophy and 8th in Goodwood Easter Handicaps. As well as 2nd place in the RAC Trials Championship, there were wins in the Kitching, Yorkshire Trophy, Wilson Trophy, Thomas Cup and the Gloucester Trial. He also took 2nd at the North Midlands Autumn, 6th on the High Peak and 9th on the Derbyshire Sporting Trial.

1951 RAC Trials Champion with wins on the Kitching, High Peak and Gloucester Trials, plus 2nd on the Yorkshire. Was RAC Trials Champion again and won the TV Wendover Trial.

1952 Continued taking both individual and team prizes, trialing with his two sons. Finished as runner-up in the BTRDA Series with his Harford. Also finished 12th on the Monte Carlo Rally in a works Ford Zephyr.

Cuth Harrison.

Photo: BRDC Archive.

1953 As part of the works Ford rally team, finished 3rd on the RAC Rally in a Zephyr and took the team prize and class win. He also finished 13th on the Monte Carlo Rally, but retired on the Alpine and Tulip. There was still time for trialing, winning the Davis Trophy and finishing 14th in the RAC Championship.

1954 Collected Class wins on the RAC and Tulip Rallies in a Zephyr and yet more trailing awards.

1955 After finishing 18th on the Monte Carlo Rally in his works Ford, a broken leg sustained while winter sporting in Switzerland shortened his season. There was still 7th in class on the Rally of the Midnight Sun, 7th overall and a class win on the Criterium des Alpes, as well as taking the Harford trials car to class victory in the Sandtoft Sprint.

1956 Finished 11th in the RAC Trials Championship and took 10th overall and 2nd in class with his Zephyr on the Tulip Rally.

1958 Won overall on the White Rose Trial, and with sons Edward and John completing the top three, they also claimed the team prize. Became RAC Trials Champion again and took 10th in the BTRDA Championship. Contested the Monte Carlo Rally again with his Zephyr, finishing 45th.

1959 Finished 2nd in class on both the RAC and Alpine Rallies and collected the team prize on the Tulip and took 34th overall on the Monte Carlo Rally with his Zephyr. Finished 8th in the RAC Trials Championship.

1960 Part of the team prize winning Zephyr squad on the Safari Rally and 20th on the Monte Carlo Rally. He also took 17th in the BTRDA Trials Championship.

1961 Finished 7th on the Safari Rally in a Zephyr and collected even more trialing success, including victory on the Stone Trough Trial.

1962 Collected 1st class awards on the Rotherham Centenary and Derbyshire Trials, and 2nd class on Clee Hill.

1963 11th in the RAC Trials Championship.

1965 4th in the Chase Cup, 5th in the Yorkshire Sporting and 6th in the Stone Trough Trials.

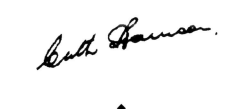

❖

MIKE HAWTHORN
Born April 10th 1929
Killed January 22nd 1959

The first British World Champion who spent most of his career at the wheel of works Ferraris. He won the hearts of the British public by being the first British driver to really reach the top in the sport. Having competed on two wheels as a schoolboy, he started racing in 1950 and made his Grand Prix debut just two years later. His first victory came with Ferrari in the 1953 French but his world championship came when he returned to Ferrari and raced the 246 Dino in 1958. Hawthorn's Grand Prix results showed more consistency than overall victories, taking only one win in his championship season. He also had numerous victories in worldwide sports car races, notably victory at Le Mans in 1955 with Ivor Bueb and Jaguar. Cruelly, having announced his retirement at the end of '58, he lost his life in a road accident a matter of weeks later on the infamous Hog's Back road near Guildford in January 1959. He was three months short of his 30th birthday.

Mike Hawthorn.
Photo: BRDC Archive.

GRAND PRIX RECORD	
Starts	45
Wins	3
Poles	4
Fastest laps	6
WC points	127.64
Won his 9th Grand Prix	

Mike Hawthorn in his Ferrari.

Photo: BRDC Archive.

1950 Won his class with a Riley at Brighton Speed Trials, with father Leslie 2nd.

1951 Continuing to race his Riley TT Sprite, he won the Leinster Trophy at Wicklow, the Ulster Handicap at Dundrod, Boreham Sports, Goodwood scratch and handicap. He had two wins and a 3rd at Castle Combe, a win and 2nd at Gamston, and with further top three finishes at Goodwood he took the Brooklands Trophy for his overall performances at the circuit.

1952 Having quickly progressed to a Cooper Bristol run by his father, he made his Grand Prix debut in Belgium, qualifying 6th and finishing 4th. Having retired in the French, he collected 3rd in the British, 4th in the Dutch but was unclassified in Italy. Overall he finished joint 4th in the World Championship from only five starts. His Cooper Bristol also won the Sussex Trophy, Lavant and Chichester Cups at Goodwood, Libre and F2 at Ibsley, the Daily Mail F2 Trophy and Libre at Boreham. He finished 2nd in the Goodwood Richmond Trophy and Ulster Trophy, 4th at Zandvoort, 7th at Reims and 18th in the Silverstone International Trophy. He had also taken his Riley to an early season win at Goodwood and had an F2 win at Turnberry in a Connaught. He won an Alpine Cup after rallying a Sunbeam Talbot, took 3rd in the British Empire Trophy with a Frazer Nash and received an invitation to drive for Ferrari as he lay in a hospital bed recovering from a crash at the Modena Grand Prix.

1953 His first year with Ferrari resulted in a 100% finishing record, with the crowning glory being his first Grand Prix victory at the French. He took 3rd in the German and Swiss, 4th in the Argentinian, Dutch and Italian, 5th in the British and 6th in Belgium to finish 4th in

the title race for the 2nd successive year. Away from the championship he won the Ulster and Silverstone International Trophies and took the Thinwall Special Ferrari to wins in both the Woodcote Cup and Goodwood Trophy. His works car was also 2nd at Rouen and Pau and 4th in the Buenos Aires City GP, while with sports cars he was a winner at the Spa 24 hours with Farina, the Pescara 12 hours with Maglioli and 4th at Monza.

1954 An early season crash at Syracuse and the death of his father were followed by Mike being disqualified from the opening World Championship Grand Prix in Argentina. After being overcome by fumes in Belgium he handed his car to Gonzalez who brought it home in 3rd place. He retired in the French but 2nd place in the British gave his season the boost it needed. 2nd places in both the German and Italian preceded victory in the seasonal finale in Spain, and secured 4th in the championship with his Ferrari. He continued to excel in sports cars, winning the Supercortemaggiore with Maglioli and took 2nd at the Nurburgring 1000km with Collins, 2nd in the Portuguese Grand Prix and 2nd in the TT with Trintignant. A couple of outings in the Vanwall also brought success, with 2nd in the Daily Telegraph Trophy at Oulton Park and 4th in the Woodcote Cup at Goodwood.

1955 Having started the year developing the Vanwall, retirement in both Monte Carlo and Belgium brought a return to the Ferrari Grand Prix team. His only classified finishes came with 6th at the British, where he handed his car to Castellotti after feeling unwell, and then 7th in the Dutch. His Ferrari also finished 2nd in the Oulton Park Daily Herald Trophy and Gold Cup and 4th in the Silverstone International Trophy. He won the Crystal Palace Trophy with a Maserati 250F and raced a Lancia Aurelia Saloon in a handicap race at Ibsley. As well as his Ferrari sports car outings which brought 2nd places in the Supercortemaggiore and at Monza, he was a regular member of the works Jaguar squad. Victory at Le Mans and the Sebring 12 hours, were complimented by 5th in the British Grand Prix sports and a Production Car victory at Silverstone in a Jaguar MKVII.

1956 Only three Grand Prix starts, with 3rd in the Owen Organisation Maserati 250F in Argentina and 10th with Harry Schell in a Vanwall at the French his sole results. He continued to race Jaguars and took 2nd at Reims and 6th at Le Mans. For Ferrari he won the Supercortemaggiore with Collins and was 3rd in Sweden. Outings in a Lotus Mk6 also brought a win at Aintree, two 2nd places at Goodwood and 4th in the Empire Trophy.

1957 Back into the Ferrari fold with the Lancia-Ferrari, retirement in Argentina was followed by a shared 7th in

Monaco after taking over Von Trips' car. 4th in the French, 3rd in the British, 2nd in the German and 6th in the Italian brought 4th overall in his quest for the world title. He also took 2nd in the Naples GP and 4th in the Buenos Aires City GP, while his sports car successes with Ferrari came with 2nd in Venezuela and Sweden, 3rd in the Nurburgring 1000km and 4th at Le Mans. Sharing his Jaguar with Bueb he was 3rd at the Sebring 12 hours and won the International Trophy Touring Car race at Silverstone for Jaguar.

1958 The Ferrari 246 Dino proved competitive from the start and despite only taking one win at the French Grand Prix, 2nd places in the Belgian, British, Portuguese, Italian and Moroccan were enough to crown him as World Champion driver. He also won the Glover Trophy at Goodwood in the 246 and shared a car with Phil Hill and Luigi Musso to 3rd in the Two Worlds Trophy at Monza. He won the Monza 1000km with Hill, took 2nd in the Nurburgring 1000km with Collins and 3rd in the Targa Florio with Von Trips. He continued to race a Jaguar 3.4 successfully in saloon car races, before announcing his retirement at the end of the season.

❖

GRAHAM HILL
Born February 15th 1929
Killed November 29th 1975

One of the legends of British motorsport despite making a relatively late start in the sport, Hill became one of the most popular racing drivers in British history. He was 25 before he competed in his first race at Brands Hatch. World Champion in both 1962 and 1968, and with victories at both Le Mans and Indianapolis, Hill holds a proud record that is unlikely to be beaten. He contested 176 Grands Prix and won the Monaco race an incredible five times. Most of his successes came during his periods with Lotus and BRM, but he also drove Grands Prix for Brabham and his own Embassy Hill Racing Team. Having broken both legs in an accident at Watkins Glen at the end of 1969, he battled back to fitness to resume his career.

He was equally successful in sports cars, saloons and F2, retiring from racing during the 1975 season to concentrate on running his own Grand Prix team. Tragically, he lost his life along with protege Tony Brise and a number of other team members in a plane crash when returning from testing in France. His London rowing club helmet colours later returned to Grand Prix racing, with son and fellow World Champion Damon.

GRAND PRIX RECORD	
Starts	176
Wins	14
Poles	13
Fastest laps	10
WC points	289
Won his 33rd Grand Prix	

1953 After competing in the occasional motorcycle scramble, his first taste of racing cars came with four laps for £1 in a Cooper JAP F3 car at Brands Hatch.

1954 Had two F3 races at Brands Hatch, and took a 4th place.

1955 Toured Europe as a riding mechanic for Dan Margulies' Jaguar C-Type. He got to drive the car at Castle Combe and during the Cagliari to Sassari race across Sardinia. At the Goodwood 9 hours he also had his first run in a Lotus.

1956 Working as a Lotus mechanic, he was loaned the parts to build a Lotus XI. He led the Autosport Championship until breaking a con rod in the Oulton Park finale, but won at Brands Hatch, Mallory Park, Silverstone and Aintree, with 2nd at Brands Hatch twice, 3rd in the

Graham Hill.

Photo: BRDC Archive.

Graham Hill after finishing second in the 1964 International Trophy.

Photo: BRDC Archive.

Anerley and Norbury Trophies at Crystal Palace and 3rd in class at Prescott Hillclimb. He drove the same car in F2 races at Brands Hatch and Silverstone, taking 5th and 7th respectively, while with an Equipe Endeavour Cooper he was 3rd in the Farningham Trophy and 6th in the Wrotham Cup at Brands Hatch.

1957 Continued success with a Lotus XI brought four wins at Brands Hatch, plus Oulton Park and a class win at the Empire Trophy. He was 2nd at Goodwood, 4th in the Chichester Cup at Goodwood and Crystal Palace's Anerley Trophy, plus 5th in Vanwall Libre Trophy at Snetterton. At the Kingsdown Trophy Brands Hatch he was 2nd in a Tojeiro, drove Tommy Atkins' Aston Martin DB3S to 3rd at Brands Hatch and 9th at Goodwood, with 2nd at Brands in a Willment sports. His first big single seater race was with Atkins' F2 Cooper at Easter Goodwood, taking 5th after stalling on the grid. He finished 13th at the International Trophy in the Cooper and later joined Lotus as a driver rather than a mechanic, taking 5th in the Woodcote Cup and 11th in the Oulton Park Gold Cup with his Lotus 12.

1958 His first season of Grand Prix racing featured a string of retirements in the fragile Lotus, only finishing twice from nine attempts with 6th in Italy and 16th in Morocco. His F2 Lotus took 2nd in the Lavant Cup, 4th in the Aintree 200 and 8th at the International Trophy, plus a Libre win at the Christmas Brands Hatch meeting. With

the Lotus 15 sports car he won the International Trophy support race, won at Snetterton, had 2nd at Rouen and in the Farningham Trophy, 6th in the Empire Trophy, but retired at Le Mans. He took a double Christmas win at Brands Hatch in a Lotus 7 and had a class win at Silverstone with an Austin A35.

1959 Despite qualifying well, the reliability of the Lotus again kept his Grand Prix finishes down to two, from seven starts. He was 7th at the Dutch and 9th in the British, and took 2nd in the Kentish Trophy, 5th in the Aintree 200 and Oulton Park Gold Cup. In F2 he was 4th in the Lavant Cup and Goodwood 100, 6th at the Circuit D'Auvergne and 7th at Rouen, while the Lotus 15 sports car collected wins at Aintree and Mallory Park. The newer Lotus 17 sports car won the Kingsdown and Farningham Trophies at Brands Hatch, won at Aintree and was 2nd at Aintree and Crystal Palace, 3rd in the Rochester and Wrotham Trophies and 4th at Oulton Park. Other results included a win at Brands and 3rd at Mallory Park in his Lotus XI, and a saloon car win at Brands in the Austin A35.

1960 Moving to BRM for the Grand Prix season he took 3rd at the Dutch and 7th at Monaco, retiring from his other six attempts despite qualifying in the top six on all but one occasion. He was 2nd in the Silver City Trophy at Brands Hatch, 3rd in the Oulton Park Gold Cup and International Trophy and 5th at the Goodwood International with his

BRM. He became a regular Porsche driver with 3rd in the Aintree 200, 4th at Solitude, the Kentish 100 and German F2 Grand Prix with the F2 car. He took 3rd overall and a class win with Bonnier in the Buenos Aires 1000km and 5th in the Targa Florio with Barth in an RSK. He shared a Carrera to 4th overall and a class win with Barth at the TT and was 7th with Von Hanstein in the Paris 1000k. His numerous other outings brought 2nd at the Copenhagen Grand Prix in a Lotus 18, 2nd in class at Rouen in a Speedwell Sprite and 3rd with a Jaguar in the International Trophy Saloons.

1961 In a second year with BRM, Grand Prix results continued to prove elusive. The now Climax-powered car took him to 5th in the US, 6th in France and 8th in the Dutch along with five retirements. He did however claim 2nd in the Glover Trophy, 3rd in the Lavant Cup, Aintree 200, Empire Trophy and Brands Hatch Guards Trophy and 7th at Modena. The BRM also made an early season trip to New Zealand, taking 2nd in the Ballarat Libre race and 3rd in the New Zealand Grand Prix. He gave the Jaguar E-Type a debut win in the Oulton Park Trophy, with 2nd at Oulton Park, 3rd at Silverstone and in the Peco Trophy at Brands Hatch. With a Jaguar Mk2 he won the International Trophy Saloon car race, with 2nd at the Empire Trophy, Silverstone and the Goodwood St. Mary's Trophy. At the TT he was 6th overall with a class win in a Porsche Abarth, 8th in the Nurburgring 1000km for Porsche, had a Christmas win at Brands Hatch and 5th at Nassau in a Ferrari Testa Rossa and finished 2nd at Oulton Park in a Lotus 19.

1962 Victory in the opening Grand Prix of the year set the pattern for the remainder, winning the German, Italian and South African, with 2nd in the Belgian and US, 4th in the British, 6th in Monaco, 9th in France and no retirements, to clinch the World Championship for BRM. He also won the International and Glover Trophies, with 2nd in the Lombank Trophy at Snetterton, Oulton Park Gold Cup and Marne GP at Reims. An outing in Rob Walker's Lotus 18/21 brought 3rd in the Mallory Park 2000 guineas and he led Le Mans in the Aston Martin 212 until retiring. Racing an E-Type Jaguar for John Coombs he was 2nd at Mallory Park and Oulton Park, 3rd at Silverstone and 4th at Brands Hatch. In a Coombs Ferrari 250 GTO he won at Aintree, Snetterton, Oulton Park and Silverstone, with 2nd in the TT and with a Jaguar 3.8 Saloon he won the Goodwood St. Mary's Trophy, with a 3rd at Snetterton. He shared a Porsche to 5th in the Nurburgring 1000km with Herrman and shared a Sunbeam Rapier to 10th in the Monte Carlo Rally.

1963 Victories in Monaco and the US, plus 3rd in the French, British and South African and 4th in the Mexican Grand Prix took his BRM to 2nd in the World Championship behind Clark. He won the Lombank Trophy at Snetterton again, along with the Aintree 200 and was 3rd in the Oulton Park Gold Cup. In the Tasman series he took Rob Walker's Ferguson P99 to 2nd at Lakeside and 6th in the Australian Grand Prix, and won the TT with a Maranello Concessionaires Ferrari 250 GTO. He shared a NART Ferrari 330LM to take 3rd in the Sebring 12 hours with Rodriguez and drove Ian Walker's

Lotus 23B to 2nd place in the Canadian Sports GP, with 10th at Riverside and 12th at Monterrey. He won the 2-litre class of the British Saloon Car Championship in the Coombs Jaguar, winning at Oulton Park, Aintree and the Goodwood St. Marys Trophy, with 2nd at Snetterton, 3rd at Crystal Palace, plus a further 2nd at Oulton Park in a Willment Ford Galaxie. He also took the E-Type to victories at Silverstone, Snetterton, Mallory Park and Goodwood.

1964 Runner-up again in the World Championship with the new P261 BRM, winning both the Monaco and US Grands Prix, 2nd in the French, British and German, and 4th in the Dutch. He was 2nd with the BRM at the International Trophy and Aintree 200, won the Rand Grand Prix with a Willment Brabham BRM and drove a Scuderia Veloce Brabham BT3 to a win in the South Pacific Trophy at Longford, with 4th at Warwick Farm during the Tasman Series. Driving Ferraris in GT he won the Reims 12 hours, the Paris 1000km, Nurburgring 1000km, Sussex Trophy and International Trophy support race, as well as taking 2nd at Le Mans. In F2 he drove a Cooper and Brabham, with 2nd at Crystal Palace and 3rd in the British Eagle Trophy at Brands Hatch. He also shared a Ford Falcon with Ian Walker on the Monte Carlo Rally.

1965 For the 3rd successive year he was World Championship runner-up in his BRM, winning at both the Monaco and US Grands Prix, with only his engine failure in Mexico stopping a 100% season of points finishes. He was 2nd in the London, Glover and Daily Mirror Trophies and returned to the Tasman Series to win the New Zealand and Australian Grand Prix and Longford. Driving a Lotus and a Brabham-BRM in F2 he won the Autocar Trophy at Snetterton, with 2nd at Rouen and Crystal Palace, 3rd in the Oulton Park Gold Cup and 4th in the British Eagle Trophy at Brands Hatch. He also finished 4th in the Targa Florio, sharing his Porsche with Bonnier.

1966 His final year with BRM featured points finishes with 2nd in the Dutch, 3rd in Monaco and the British and 4th in the German Grand Prix. He won the New Zealand and Australian Grand Prix again, with 2nd at Warwick Farm and twice at Longford in the BRM. While in the US he won the Indianapolis 500 with Mecom's Red Bull Lola, taking the same car to 5th at Mount Fuji. His best F2 result of the year came with 3rd at Pau and he raced in CanAm with a Surtees Lola T70.

1967 Joined Lotus as Clark's team mate, finishing 2nd in the Monaco and US Grands Prix, and 4th in the Canadian, with eight retirements. He took 2nd in the non-championship Spanish Grand Prix and 4th at the International Trophy, while a season of F2 brought 2nd places in the Oulton Park Gold Cup, Reims GP and the Guards 100 at Snetterton. He won the Lombank Saloon Car Trophy at Snetterton in a Lotus Cortina and returned to the Indy 500, where he retired his Lotus 42F.

1968 Jim Clark's death in Germany provided the launching pad to Hill's second World Championship. His Lotus won the Spanish, Monaco and Mexican Grands Prix, and finished 2nd in South Africa, Germany and the

US Grands Prix. He went to the Tasman races again and came 2nd at both Surfers Paradise and Warwick Farm, while the highlight of his F2 season was a 4th at Reims. The Lotus 56 Turbine retired on his visit to the Indy 500 and he also had a one-off race in an Alan Mann-entered Ford Escort at Oulton Park.

1969 His final year as a works Lotus driver brought three points finishes, notably his fifth Monaco Grand Prix victory, with 2nd in South Africa, 4th in Germany and 6th in France. The season ended however with a crash at the US Grand Prix in which he broke both legs. Another Tasman visit secured 5th in the championship, winning at Christchurch, with 2nd in the Lady Wigram Trophy and at Invercargill. He finished 2nd at the Race of Champions, while his F2 season was highlighted by a win at Albi and 3rd at Tulln Langenlebarn.

1970 Returning from the leg injuries, he raced a Lotus 49C for Rob Walker, finishing 4th in the Spanish Grand Prix, took 5th at Monaco and 6th in the British and South African. He was 4th in the Race of Champions and took his F2 Lotus 69 to 2nd in the Oulton Park Gold Cup.

1971 Moving on to the Brabham Grand Prix team, his only points finish came with a 5th in Austria, although he won the International Trophy at Silverstone. In his F2 Lotus he won the Rindt Memorial at Thruxton and had 2nd at Hockenheim, Brands Hatch and in the Colombian Grand Prix.

1972 A second and final year with Brabham brought a 5th place in Italy and 6th in both South Africa and Germany. But the highlight of the year came with victory at Le Mans, sharing a Matra with Pescarolo. He also raced a Brabham in F2, winning at Monza.

1973 Driving a Shadow for his own Embassy Team, his best Grand Prix result came with 9th in Belgium.

1974 Changing to a Lola chassis his Embassy Team collected its first championship point with his 6th place in Sweden, and had a further five top ten finishes.

1975 Having started the year with the Lola taking 10th and 12th in Argentina and Brazil, he debuted his own Hill GH1 at Monaco and failed to qualify. He decided to hang up his helmet and go into management, but was killed later the same year when his plane crashed returning from a test session in France.

❖

INNES IRELAND
Born June 12th 1930
Died October 22nd 1993

Innes Ireland.

Photo: BRDC Archive.

One of the great characters of Grand Prix racing in the sixties, Ireland graduated to the works Lotus F1 team in 1959 after a fairly successful apprenticeship in sports cars. His Grand Prix career spanned eight years and took him to a victory in the 1961 US Grand Prix, his last race for Lotus before moving to UDT Laystall as Colin Chapman wanted to sign the young Jim Clark. Continuing success in sports cars and non-championship F1 races tended to be abbreviated by a number of accidents from which he had a knack of escaping largely unscathed. Following his semi-retirement from racing at the end of 1966, he went into journalism and later became sports editor of Autocar. He played a leading role in the British Racing Drivers' Club until he lost his battle against cancer in 1993.

1952 Made his race debut with 4th place at Boreham in the Tim Birkin Memorial Trophy, driving a Bentley. He also won a Snetterton handicap race.

1953-1954 Joined the army.

1955 Restarted his racing career in club events, winning a Goodwood handicap in a Riley.

1956 Raced his own Lotus XI towards the end of the year, finishing 2nd and 4th at Goodwood, and 2nd twice at Aintree.

GRAND PRIX RECORD

Starts	50
Wins	1
Poles	0
Fastest laps	1
WC points	47
Won his 20th Grand Prix	

1957 After crashing his own new Lotus XI practising at Snetterton, he went on to collect the Brooklands Memorial Trophy, with 6th at Goodwood (twice), 5th in class at the Empire Trophy and 9th at Karlskoga. He also drove a Cooper to victories at Goodwood, Brands Hatch and Silverstone, with 2nd in the Brands Hatch Christmas Libre race.

1958 Spent the year racing both his own and works Lotus and a Ecurie Ecosse Jaguar D-Type. His Lotus XI won its class at the Reims 12 hours, the Trophee D'Auvergne, three out of six races in one day at Full Sutton and won at Snetterton three times. He was 2nd at Brands Hatch, 2nd in the Sid Greene Trophy at Brands Hatch, 2nd at Crystal Palace, 2nd and 3rd at Mallory Park and 2nd at Oulton Park and Snetterton. He took 4th at Rouen, 5th in the Chichester Cup and the TT, 6th in Mallory Park Libre, 7th with a class win at Oulton Park, 8th at the International Trophy and 9th at the British Grand Prix meeting. At Charterhall he also drove the Ecurie Ecosse Tojeiro to a double victory.

1959 His Grand Prix debut came in the Dutch with a Lotus 16, qualifying 9th and finishing 4th. Retirement then followed in the French, German, Portuguese and Italian, before ending the year with 5th in the US GP. He had also finished 4th in the International Trophy, while in sports cars he took 3rd in class at Aintree and 3rd at Rouen. He raced in F2 and after taking 7th at Reims, he had a huge crash at Rouen, which took him through a 150ft flight into the surrounding forest, escaping unhurt after losing his brakes.

1960 Apart from his retirement in the Belgian Grand Prix, he was a top 10 finisher in every other Grand Prix with the new Lotus 18. 2nd in the Dutch and US, 3rd in the British, 6th in Argentina and Portugal, 7th in France and 9th in Monaco, to finish 4th in the World Championship. He also won the Glover Trophy and Lavant Cup at Goodwood, the Silverstone International Trophy, the Snetterton Lombank Trophy and Oulton Park Trophy, with 4th at Syracuse, 6th at Solitude and 9th in the Aintree 200 in a mixture of F1 and 2 Lotus 18s. He also raced an Aston Martin DB4GT and took 3rd in the TT and 6th in the Paris 1000km.

1961 His final year with Lotus started with an accident during qualifying at Monaco, putting him out of the first two Grands Prix. He then retired in Belgium, took 4th in France, 10th in the British and retired again in Germany and Italy. In the US GP however he qualified his Lotus 21 8th and took his only Grand Prix victory to secure 5th in the World Championship. He also won the Solitude Grand Prix, the Flugplatzrennen at Zeltweg, with 5th in the Goodwood 100 and 6th in the Brussels Grand Prix. He continued to race an Aston Martin, taking 3rd in the Molyslip Trophy at Snetterton in a DB4 Zagato, plus 2nd in the Fordwater Trophy at Goodwood and at Snetterton, 5th in the TT and 6th in the Paris 1000km in a DB4GT. His other results included 9th in the Empire Trophy in a Lotus XVII and 4th in the Oulton Park Trophy with a Ferrari 250GT.

1962 Joining UDT Laystall to drive a Lotus 24 in Grands Prix, poor reliability restricted him to three classified finishes from 8 starts, with 5th in South Africa, 8th in the US and 16th in the British. He won the London and Crystal Palace Trophies, took 3rd in the Brussels Grand Prix, Mexican, Reims, Roskilde and Glover Trophy and 4th at Karlskoga and the International Trophy. With his Lotus 19 he took successive wins at Oulton Park, Goodwood, Silverstone International Trophy and Oulton Park Gold Cup, followed by the Nassau Trophy, Aintree and the Sussex Trophy, plus 2nd in the Guards Trophy and 5th in the Times Grand Prix. He won the TT and at Brands Hatch with a Ferrari GTO, with 3rd in the Peco Trophy at Brands Hatch and the Nassau TT, 4th at Oulton Park and 13th at Le Mans. He also finished 2nd in the Circuit of Garda with an Abarth 1000 and won his class in a Silverstone saloon car race in a Ford Zodiac.

1963 The Grand Prix season was spent with BRP in a Lotus 24 and later a BRP BRM. Apart from 4th in the Dutch and Italian and 9th in the French, the remaining four Grands Prix ended with three retirements and disqualification at the British after a push start. He won the Glover Trophy, with 2nd in the Aintree 200, 3rd in the Lombank Trophy, Solitude, Marne Grand Prix and Vic Hudson Memorial Trophy at Teretonga, and 4th in the International Trophy. With the Lotus sports he was 2nd at Aintree and in the International Trophy support race and 3rd in class at the Lavant Cup. He drove the Ferrari GTO to 6th at Sebring, the Aston Martin DB4GT to 6th in the Guards Trophy, but failed to finish with the 4wd Ferguson on a trip to New Zealand.

1964 Stayed with BRP and started the Grand Prix season with a practice accident at Monaco. 10th place in the Belgian and British races were split by another accident in the French, but the season recovered with 5th at both the Austrian and Italian, and 12th in Mexico. He won the Daily Mirror Trophy at Snetterton, the Glover Trophy at Goodwood and was 3rd in the Mediterranean Grand Prix and 12th in the International Trophy. At the TT and Le Mans he finished 6th with a Ferrari GTO and won his class at the International Trophy GT race in a Porsche and took 4th in the saloons with a Lotus Cortina.

1965 BRP's withdrawal left him without a Grand Prix drive until joining Parnell's team from the Belgian. 13th on his debut for the team, was improved on by 10th in the Dutch and 9th in the Italian, but he was dropped from the team in Mexico after turning up late. He also took 5th in the Mediterranean Grand Prix and 6th in the Rand Grand

Prix. Other results included 2nd in the Rand 9 hours with Sutcliffe in a Ford GT40, 6th in the Austrian Grand Prix in an AC Cobra and 6th in the Monza 1000km with Salmon in a Ferrari 250LM.

1966 After contesting the non-championship South African Grand Prix with Parnell's team, he drove a Bernard White entered BRM P261 in the US and Mexican Grand Prix, retiring from both. He drove the same car to 4th at the Oulton Park Gold Cup and also raced a Ford GT40 to 5th in the Spa 1000km with Amon, took 4th in the British Eagle Trophy and 10th in the Austrian Grand Prix.

1968 Contested the London-Sydney Marathon with Mike Taylor and Andrew Hedges, winning the first to Bombay private entrant award.

---------- ❖ ----------

JOHN JAMES
Born May 10th 1914

Having briefly raced Pre War, James' stable of cars was stored during the war and later saw action mainly in national speed events and races. He made a one-off appearance at the 1951 British Grand Prix in a Maserati 4CLT. After completing the 1952 season he decided he was getting too old for Formula 1, and with a change of formula he decided to retire from racing.

1938/39 Raced nationally with an Alfa Romeo Monza, Bugatti and a pair of Sunbeams.

GRAND PRIX RECORD	
Starts	1
Wins	0
Poles	0
Fastest laps	0
WC points	0
Best finish	DNF

John James.

1947 Finished 3rd in class with the Bugatti at Prescott Hillclimb and used the same car at Brighton Speed Trials. He also used both the Sunbeam Tiger and Tigress and Alfa at Shelsley Walsh, Prescott and the Itala Trophy at Gransden Lodge.

1948 The Bugatti recorded 3rd in class at both Prescott Hillclimb and Brighton Speed Trials.

1949 Mostly successful with his Bugatti again, taking 2nd in the Itala Trophy, 2nd and 3rd in class and 2nd in an all-Bugatti race at Lulsgate. He added 2nd in class at Prescott, 2nd in a Scratch race and the Itala Trophy at Silverstone, 3rd in class at Brighton and 4th in the Wakefield Trophy at the Curragh. He also ran the V12 Sunbeam at Prescott and took a 7th in class at Brighton and 8th at the Lydstep Hillclimb.

1950 Continued racing his Pre War cars, but with less success. But took the Bugatti to 3rd in class at Prescott.

1951 His one and only Grand Prix ended when the radiator split on his Maserati 4CLT at the British. The same car was retired in the International Trophy at Silverstone, but finished 8th in the Daily Graphic Trophy at Goodwood.

1952 After finishing 8th in the Chichester Cup at Goodwood and 11th in the British Grand Prix Libre race with the Maserati, he retired from racing.

---------- ❖ ----------

LESLIE JOHNSON
Born 1911
Died June 8th 1959

A relative latecomer to the sport, Johnson only dabbled in single seater racing, but excelled in sports cars. A win and a second at the Spa 24 hours in consecutive years at the wheel of his works Aston Martin, were matched by top finishes in the Mille Miglia, TT, Le Mans and the Reims 12 hours. His solitary Grand Prix was the 1950 British and his career ended rather abruptly in 1954 due to ill health.

1946 Competed in reliability trials with a 328 BMW and a Darraq.

1947 Began racing the Darraq and finished 6th in the Jersey Road Race, 7th in the European Grand Prix at Spa, 9th and a class win at Prescott Hillclimb and raced in the Empire Trophy and at Gransden Lodge.

1948 Retired on the first lap of the British Grand Prix, when his ERA broke a driveshaft. Won the Spa 24 hours sharing an Aston Martin with St. John Horsfall and took 3rd in the Manx Cup with an Alvis.

1949 Shared an Aston Martin with Charles Brackenberry to 2nd in the Spa 24 hours, but retired from Le Mans. Won the Silverstone International Trophy Production Race in a Jaguar XK120 and took his ERA to 3rd in the Chichester Cup and 5th in the Richmond Trophy at Goodwood.

1950 Made his one and only World Championship Grand Prix appearance, with TASO Mathieson's ERA E-Type at the British. Qualified in 12th place but retired with a broken supercharger. Other outings in the car failed to bring any notable results. Also raced a Jaguar XK120 at home and abroad, with 4th in the Palm Beach Grand Prix on the car's US debut, took 5th in the Mille Miglia and 7th in the TT, but retired from Le Mans when the car he shared with Hadley suffered clutch failure. Collected a 2nd place in a Goodwood handicap driving a Bentley.

1951 Continued to race works Jaguars, taking 4th with Tony Rolt in C-Type in both the Mille Miglia and TT. Also finished 5th in the Silverstone International Trophy Production Race, but retired from Le Mans again when sharing with Clemente Biondetti due to lack of oil pressure.

GRAND PRIX RECORD	
Starts	1
Wins	0
Poles	0
Fastest laps	0
WC points	0
Best finish	DNF

1952 Finally made the finish at Le Mans sharing a Nash Healey with Tommy Wisdom to 3rd place, and took 7th overall and 4th in class in the Mille Miglia.

Leslie Johnson (ERA).

Photo: BRDC Archive.

Leslie Johnson.

Photo: BRDC Archive.

1953 Finished 3rd in class at the Reims 12 hours with Briggs Cunningham in a Cunningham and was 11th at Le Mans with Hadley in the Nash Healey.

1954 Finished 50th on the Monte Carlo Rally in a Sunbeam Talbot, before retiring from the sport.

1960 Driving for Volvo in the British Saloon Car Championship, he finished 9th overall at the British Grand Prix meeting, won his class at Silverstone (twice) and at Brands Hatch, had a 2nd and 3rd at Goodwood and 3rd in the Farningham Trophy at Brands Hatch. He drove the Riley to a class win at Silverstone, and finished 18th at Le Mans for Triumph and 92nd on the Monte Carlo in a Sunbeam.

1961 He won the Peco GT Championship in a Lotus Elite, with three class wins and two 2nds at Brands Hatch, plus wins in the British Grand Prix support race and at Snetterton, and took 7th overall with a class win at the TT. He shared a Triumph with Slotemaker to finish 11th at Le Mans.

1962 A further season racing his Elite brought class wins at Snetterton, Brands Hatch and the Silverstone International Trophy, with 2nd at Brands Hatch, 3rd at Mallory Park and 19th overall in the TT.

1963 Racing mainly in saloon cars he took a Jaguar to 2nd in class at Brands Hatch and 3rd at Aintree, plus a Sunbeam to 3rd in class in the St.Mary's Trophy at Goodwood.

1970 Made a brief return to race a Royale in Formula F100, taking 3rd at Oulton Park and Mallory Park, plus 3rd and two 4ths at Snetterton.

1973 Raced a Chevrolet Camaro in Production Saloons, winning at Snetterton and Brands Hatch, with three 2nd places at Oulton Park, 2nd at Mallory Park and 3rd at Snetterton.

❖

STUART LEWIS-EVANS
Born April 20th 1930
Killed October 25th 1958

After nearly six years of following in his father's footsteps at the top of the 500cc F3 tree, Lewis-Evans joined Connaught at the end of 1956. He made his Grand Prix debut for the team the next year at Monaco and finished 4th. From the following race he became part of the Vanwall team alongside Moss and Brooks and was a regular points finisher, helping the team take the 1958 manufacturers' crown. Tragically, a crash in the final race of the season in Morocco left him severely burned. Although he was flown back to England, he later died from his injuries at 28 years of age and before his full potential had been realised.

GRAND PRIX RECORD	
Starts	14
Wins	0
Poles	2
Fastest laps	0
WC points	16
Best finish	3rd

1951 Began his F3 career with a Cooper, taking a win at Brands Hatch and 2nd in class at Great Auclum Speed Trials.

1952 His Cooper won the F3 race supporting the International Trophy at Silverstone, plus two wins, three 2nds and a 3rd at Brands Hatch, a victory at Chimay and 2nd at Orleans.

1953 Three F3 victories were recorded at Crystal Palace, including the Elizabethan Trophy. He also won at Orleans, took 2nd at Agen, Crystal Palace, Goodwood, at Brands Hatch (twice) and Silverstone, 3rd at Crystal Palace, in the British Grand Prix support and Davidstow, 5th at the International Trophy, and 6th in 100 milers at Goodwood and Silverstone. Two class wins and the FTD were taken at Great Auclum Hillclimb followed by a class win at Brighton Speed Trials in Coopers, and a 2nd place in a Snetterton saloon car race with a Morris Minor.

1954 Continuing success in F3 brought victories at Brands Hatch (twice), Brough, Orleans, Senigallia and Castello, with 2nd at Kirkistown, Brough and at Brands Hatch (twice). He finished 3rd at Nurburgring, Fairwood, Castle Combe, Brands Hatch and at Crystal Palace (twice), with 4th, 5th and 6th on further Brands outings.

1955 He was 3rd overall in the National F3 Championship, winning Orleans for the third successive time. He also won the John Bull Trophy at Oulton Park, the Circuit of Castello Terano, and at Brands Hatch and Charterhall. He finished 2nd and 6th at Aintree, 3rd at Ibsley, 4th in the Francis Beart and Sporting Record Trophies at Brands Hatch, 5th at Oulton Park and twice at Crystal Palace, and 6th in the Earl of March Trophy at Goodwood.

1956 For the second successive year he won the John Bull F3 Trophy at Oulton Park and the Sporting Record Trophy at Brands, with other wins at Crystal Palace, Brands Hatch, Goodwood, Aintree and scored a dead heat with Jim Russell at Mallory Park. He had 2nd places at Oulton Park (twice) and at Brands Hatch (three times), plus Crystal Palace, Mallory Park, Snetterton and Aintree. After joining Connaught towards the end of the year he collected the FTD at a Brands Hatch Speed Trial and had 2nd places racing at Brands and Oulton Park.

Stuart Lewis-Evans in a Cooper 500 at Silverstone.

Photo: BRDC Archive.

1957 Monaco provided his entry into the Grand Prix arena, qualifying his works Connaught B-Type in 13th place, and finishing 4th in the race. From thereon he raced for the Vanwall Grand Prix team, finishing 5th at Pescara, 7th in the British and retiring in France, Germany and Italy, having taken his first pole position at Monza. Earlier in the year he had won the Glover Trophy at Goodwood and taken 3rd at Pau with Connaught, while other outings in the Vanwall brought 3rd in the Marne Grand Prix at Reims and the non-championship race in Morocco. Sharing a Ferrari with Severi he took 5th at Le Mans, and driving a Willment Sports he recorded 3rd in the Brands Hatch Christmas Libre race and Oulton Park Gold Cup. He also found time to continue racing in F3, winning the Redex Trophy at Crystal Palace, the International Trophy support race, at Brands Hatch and Goodwood, with 2nd places at Oulton Park and Brands Hatch.

1958 Retirements out-numbered finishes in his second year with Vanwall, 3rd places in both the Belgian and Portuguese Grand Prix, and 4th in the British his only successes. In the final Grand Prix of the year in Morocco, his Vanwall crashed when the transmission locked and burst into flames, the luckless driver succumbing a few days later from severe burns. He had raced for Connaught again earlier in the year, with 3rd in the Lady

Wigram Trophy and 5th in the Glover Trophy. With a BRP F2 Cooper he won the Kent Trophy at Brands Hatch, with 2nd in class at the Aintree 200, 3rd in the Circuit D'Auvergne and Kentish 100, 4th in the Lavant Cup, 5th in the Caen GP and 7th in the International Trophy. He raced for Aston Martin and shared a DBR1 to 3rd in the TT with Carroll Shelby, but crashed at Le Mans where he partnered Salvadori. In F3 he won the support races at both the British Grand Prix and International Trophy meetings, as well as the Earl of March Trophy at Goodwood, the World Sports Trophy at Brands Hatch, and had various other podium finishes.

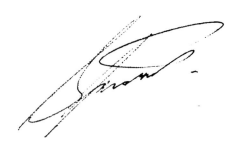

KEN McALPINE
Born September 21st 1920

Having cut his teeth in the competitive world of speed trials and hillclimbs, McAlpine came to the fore as part of the Connaught syndicate. He successfully kept the marque to the fore in both sports cars and single-seaters on the national racing scene. Probably his greatest success came in his final season of racing, taking his Connaught sports to second in the Empire Trophy.

GRAND PRIX RECORD	
Starts	7
Wins	0
Poles	0
Fastest laps	0
WC points	0
Best finish	13th

1947 Driving his Maserati mainly in speed events, he was 2nd and 10th at Prescott, 5th at Southsea and 13th at Shelsley Walsh. He also raced at Gransden Lodge and contested sporting trials.

1948 Continuing with his Maserati he won the Weston Super Mare Speed Trial, took 3rd at Stanmer Park, 4th and 6th at Prescott, 6th overall and 2nd in class at Luton Hoo, 3rd in class at Brighton and Shelsley Walsh and raced the car in the Leinster Trophy.

1949 Having turned towards circuit racing he took his Connaught sports to 2nd place in two Goodwood handicaps and scored a win at Blandford. His Maserati won at Silverstone and was 6th in the Chichester Cup at Goodwood. Success in speed events continued with the Maserati, with a class win and 3rd at Prescott, 2nd and 3rd in class at Shelsley Walsh, 2nd in class at Brighton and a second successive win at Weston Super Mare.

1950 As a member of the Connaught Racing Syndicate, he raced both sports and F2 cars. He took a scratch race win at Goodwood, plus 3rd in a handicap, 2nd at Castle Combe, 3rd at Silverstone and 4th in the Grand Prix des Frontieres at Chimay. His Maserati again saw service with 3rd at Brighton and 4th at Shelsley Walsh.

1951 Apart from a handful of Formula 3 outings, which resulted in a 3rd place at Boreham, the year was spent entirely at the wheel of his Connaughts. In the F2 A-Type he took a victory and 2nd at Ibsley, 2nd and 5th at Castle Combe and two 2nd places at Ibsley.

1952 His Grand Prix debut came at the British, qualifying 17th and finishing 16th. His only other Grand Prix outing of the year ended in retirement, when his rear suspension collapsed in Italy. He had a Formula Libre win at Snetterton and was 2nd at Charterhall, 2nd and 5th at Boreham and 10th in the Silverstone International Trophy.

Ken McAlpine (Connaught) in the pits at Silverstone.

Photo: BRDC Archive.

1953 After retiring from the Dutch Grand Prix, his British Grand Prix lasted only yards when a hose split. His A-Type survived to finish 13th in Germany, but was unclassified in the Italian GP after numerous pit stops. A trip to the non-championship Modena GP resulted in 8th place, while at home there came an F2 victory at Snetterton, plus 2nd in Libre, and 4th in the Lavant Cup at Goodwood.

1954 Although there were no Grands Prix in his schedule for the year, his newer Connaught succeded in taking 2nd in the Glover Trophy and 3rd in the Lavant Cup at Goodwood, 6th in the Aintree 200 and 15th in the Silverstone International Trophy. The sports version collected a win at Aintree, 5th at the British GP, 10th sharing with Jack Fairman at the TT, 13th in the Berlin GP and 21st at the International Trophy.

1955 He drove the streamlined B-Type Connaught at the British Grand Prix, but left the race and Grand Prix racing altogether with failing oil pressure. He took 2nd in the Empire Trophy at Oulton Park with the Connaught sports along with 2nd, 3rd and 5th at Goodwood, 3rd in class at Silverstone and 11th at the British Grand Prix. Sharing with Eric Thompson he retired at Le Mans and was 16th in the Goodwood 9 hours after the car was pushed to the finish. He retired from racing at the end of the year to concentrate on business interests.

MICHAEL MACDOWEL
Born September 13th 1932

Mike MacDowel in his F2 Cooper in 1957.

MacDowel was of the top hillclimbers of the 1970s, taking two championship titles and finishing three times runner-up over a five-year period. During his earlier spell as a works Cooper driver in sports cars and single-seaters, he made his one and only Grand Prix start in France. In the 1957 race he recorded a shared 7th place after the car was taken over by Jack Brabham. He stopped racing in 1964, but then returned to compete in speed events in 1968. This second phase of his motorsport career ended when he retired at the conclusion of the 1979 season. He also had a spell as Jaguar's competitions manager during the development of the lightweight E-Type and is currently a director of the BRDC and Silverstone Circuits.

1954 Began racing with a Lotus in sports cars, winning twice at Ibsley, with a 2nd and two 3rds at Silverstone and 4th at Crystal Palace.

1955 Secured 10 victories on his way to the 1172 Sports Car Championship, with six at Silverstone alone, plus three 2nds and a 3rd. Other victories included Ibsley and Oulton Park, with a 4th at Brands Hatch, all at the wheel of his Lotus. He also shared a Cooper with Ivor Bueb in the TT, taking a class win and 10th overall.

1956 As a works Cooper driver he had a sports car win and a 2nd at Oulton Park. He took 2nd in the Madgwick Cup, a class win and a 3rd at Aintree, 5th at Goodwood, 7th in the Oulton Park Sporting Life Trophy, 10th in the International Trophy sports car race, 11th in the Coupe de lamare Deboutteville and 3rd in class at Prescott. He also raced an F2 car and took 6th in the Woodcote Cup.

1957 His Grand Prix debut came in France, with a shared 7th place after the car was taken over by Brabham. He also had a 2nd place in the GP de Paris at Montlhery and 3rd at Brands Hatch in his Lotus XI.

1958-1960 Spent the period out of racing on a short service commission with the RAF.

1961 Became Jaguar's competition manager.

1963 Finished 2nd in the Goodwood Whitsun Trophy with a Ferrari 250GTO and was 3rd in the British Grand Prix saloon car race in John Coombs Jaguar MKII. Had a class win at Loton Park Hillclimb and 2nd in a Goodwood

GRAND PRIX RECORD	
Starts	1
Wins	0
Poles	0
Fastest laps	0
WC points	0
Best finish	7th

GT race with an E-Type Jaguar, and won the Oulton Park 5 hour saloon car race as part of the Red Rose Team.

1964 Came 2nd in the Oulton Park 5 hours with the Red Rose Jaguar Team.

1968 Began hillclimbing with an E-Type Jaguar and took class wins at Castle Howard, Prescott, Woburn and twice at Gurston Down. Changed to a Chevron B10 F2 car towards the end of the year, winning a Silverstone sprint, finishing 3rd overall with a class win at Castle Howard and taking a further class win at Gurston.

1969 Finished 5th in the British Hillclimb Championship with a Brabham BT30. His first victory came at Bouley Bay, with 2nd places at Doune, Rest & be Thankful and Craigantlet, 5th at Wiscombe, Great Auclum and Prescott, 6th at Shelsley Walsh and Tholt y Will, 7th at Barbon, 8th at Loton Park and Harewood and 9th at Shelsley Walsh. Further outings in the BARC Championship brought two 4th places and a 7th at Harewood.

1970 3rd in the British Hillclimb Championship, with victory at Doune, 2nd at Prescott and Bouley Bay, 3rd at Wiscombe and Harewood, 4th at Prescott and Craigantlet, 5th at Shelsley Walsh and Great Auclum, 7th at Barbon and 4th at Harewood in the Brabham BT30X.

1971 Runner-up in the British Hillclimb Championship, with a 4.2 litre Repco-powered Palliser. Won at Doune again, with 2nd at Prescott, Shelsley Walsh, Craigantlet, Harewood and Wiscombe, 3rd at Gurston, 4th at Prescott, and 5th at Shelsley Walsh, Bouley Bay and Great Auclum.

1972 British Hillclimb Championship runner-up again, with a 5-litre Brabham BT36X Repco. Won at Harewood, Shelsley Walsh and twice at Gurston, with 2nd at Barbon and Great Auclum, 3rd at Wiscombe and Bouley Bay, 4th at Doune and Prescott twice, 5th at Shelsley Walsh, 6th at Loton Park and crashed in the finale at Doune.

1973 Won the British Hillclimb Championship title in his Brabham Repco, winning at Shelsley Walsh (twice), Gurston Down, Doune (twice), Prescott, Wiscombe, Harewood and Bouley Bay, with 2nd at Wiscombe and Prescott, 3rd at Loton Park, Great Auclum and Barbon, and 6th at Val de Terres. He also had two wins at Harewood and one at Shelsley Walsh in the BARC Series, with 2nd at Pontypool and 3rd at Prescott.

1974 Retained his British Hillclimb title in the Brabham, winning at Loton Park, Barbon, Shelsley Walsh (twice), Doune, Wiscombe, Harewood and Pontypool, with 2nd at Prescott (twice), Wiscombe and Great Auclum. He also had BARC Series wins at Gurston, Harewood and Prescott, and a 3rd at Harewood.

1975 Changing to a Chevron B19 Alpina BMW, he took a 9th plus class wins in the British Championship rounds at Wiscombe and Prescott, and 10th with a class win at Shelsley Walsh. At the BARC's Prescott event he brought the B19 home with 5th overall and a class win. While at

Harewood he had a Chevrolet-powered Chevron B32, taking 6th overall and his class.

1976 Changed to a Ralt RT1 Hart and finished 5th in the British Hillclimb Championship, with 2nd at Doune and Pontypool, 5th at Prescott and Harewood, 6th at Gurston Down and 6th and 7th at Shelsley Walsh.

1977 Took his Ralt to 6th in the British Championship, with 3rd at Bouley Bay and Prescott, 4th at Wiscombe, Doune (twice), Shelsley Walsh and Craigantlet. Finished 5th at Prescott, 6th at Shelsley Walsh, 7th at Loton Park and Gurston, 8th at Prescott and Harewood, 9th at Pontypool and Val des Terres and 8th at a BARC Shelsley Walsh.

1978 Finished 6th in the championship with a Coogar Ralt DFV, with 2nd at Shelsley Walsh, 4th at Doune, Craigantlet and Shelsley Walsh, 5th at Loton Park, Harewood, Doune, Val des Terres and Prescott, 6th at Bouley Bay, Gurston and Prescott, 7th at Wiscombe and 9th at Barbon. In the BARC series he won at Shelsley Walsh, with 2nd at Wiscombe, 3rd at Harewood and Wiscombe and 7th at Prescott.

1979 His Coogar took 8th in the Hillclimb Championship, with 3rd at Bouley Bay, 6th at Shelsley Walsh, Doune and Val de Terres, 8th at Wiscombe (twice), 9th at Shelsley Walsh and Prescott and 10th at Doune. In the BARC series he was 2nd at Shelsley Walsh, 5th at Prescott and 6th at Gurston and Loton Park, retiring from the competitive side of the sport at the end of the season.

[signature]

--- ❖ ---

LANCE MACKLIN
Born September 2nd 1919

Most of Macklin's career was spent globetrotting with the HWM team, but there was very little to show from his World Championship Grand Prix outings. In 1953, for instance, six starts with an HWM failed to net a single finish. His best single-seater result came with victory at Silverstone in the 1952 International Trophy, but he proved himself more than accomplished in long distance sports car races. Having narrowly avoided a fatal accident in the 1955 Tourist Trophy at Dundrod, he hung his helmet up for good.

1948 Began racing an Invicta built by his father's company and also raced an ex-Barnato Hassan Bentley in the Belgian 24 hours at Spa.

GRAND PRIX RECORD	
Starts	13
Wins	0
Poles	0
Fastest laps	0
WC points	0
Best finish	8th

1949 He made his Le Mans debut sharing an Aston Martin with Marechal and took a Maserati 6CL to 2nd at Chimay.

1950 As part of the HWM team he contested non-championship races far and wide, with 2nd in Naples and the Circuit of Posillips, 3rd at Mettet and Periguex, 5th at Reims in the Couple de Petites Cylindres and 6th in Geneva. As part of the Aston Martin team he was 4th in the Coppa Europa at Monza, 5th at Le Mans with Abecassis, 8th in the TT and 2nd in class at Monza with a Lagonda.

1951 Continuing with HWM he recorded 2nd in the Circuit des Ramparts Angouleme and Madgwick Cup at Goodwood. He finished 3rd in the Modena, Columbus Centenary and Genoa Grand Prix, 5th at Erlen, 6th in the Goodwood Richmond Trophy and Marseilles GP, and 7th in the San Remo GP. He shared an Aston Martin DB2 with Eric Thompson to 3rd at Le Mans and gave the DB3 its debut in the TT.

1952 He stepped up the World Championship scene with HWM, retiring on his debut in the Swiss Grand Prix when his suspension collapsed. After taking 11th in the Belgian, he recorded 9th in the French, 15th in the British and 8th in the Dutch, but failed to qualify in Italy. He won the Silverstone International Trophy, was 2nd at Aix les Bains, 5th in the Paris GP, 7th at Pau and 9th at Rouen. He also took 4th in the International Trophy sports car race for Aston Martin.

1953 He suffered a disastrous year with the Grand Prix circus with six retirements from six starts in his HWM, all as a result of mechanical nature. He did however manage to take 3rd at Aix les Bains, 4th in the Coronation and Crystal Palace Trophies and 6th in the Sables D'Olonne. He also had outings in an HWM Jaguar Sports.

1954 His one Grand Prix start ended in retirement at the French when the engine failed. On home soil he recorded finishes at Goodwood with 4th in the Lavant Cup, 5th in the Chichester Cup and 6th in the Easter Handicap. But a trip to the Sebring 12 hours netted 3rd place with Ray Huntoon in an Austin Healey, followed later in the year by 5th in class in the Mille Miglia.

1955 His last year of attempting to progress in the World Championship, was restricted to two outings in Stirling Moss's Maserati 250F. He failed to qualify in Monaco and ended his Grand Prix career with 8th at the British. Back in sports cars he shared an HWM with Bill Smith to 4th in the Goodwood 9 hours, shared a Healey with Moss to 6th in the Sebring 12 hours, was 8th in class on the Mille Miglia, 12th in the Oulton Park Daily Herald Trophy and 14th at Silverstone. It was at the wheel of the Healey that he became involved in the tragic spectator deaths at Le Mans, after being hit by Pierre Levegh's

Lance Macklin (HWM) at Goodwood, Easter 1954.

Photo: Ferret Fotographics.

Mercedes. After a huge crash in the TT from which he escaped unscathed, he retired from racing.

❖

LESLIE MARR
Born August 14th 1922

GRAND PRIX RECORD	
Starts	2
Wins	0
Poles	0
Fastest laps	0
WC points	0
Best finish	13th

Leslie Marr.

An artist by profession, **Marr** was a successful spare time national racer nevertheless. His career was mainly tied to the Connaught marque, with which he made his two appearances at the British Grand Prix in 1954 and 1955. His career spanned little more than five seasons and ended after a foray to New Zealand in 1956.

1952 Raced a Connaught A-Type in national Libre races and an Aston Martin in sports cars.

1953 Formula Libre victories were taken twice at Snetterton and once at Silverstone. He took 2nd in the Goodwood Easter and September Handicaps, the USAF Trophy at Snetterton, 3rd in Snetterton F2, Silverstone handicap and scratch race, and 4th in the Castle Combe F2 race.

1954 His Connaught A-Type qualified 22nd on its British Grand Prix debut and finished 13th. He also claimed 3rd in the Glover Trophy at Goodwood, the F2 class at the Aintree 200, the Libre race at the Oulton Park Gold Cup and in a Snetterton Libre race. Further trips to Goodwood brought 2nd in the September Handicap, 4th in the Easter Handicap, 9th in the Trophy race and 10th in Libre. He finished 2nd in an F2 race at Davidstow, and in speed events took a win and 2nd in class at Prescott, FTD twice at Wethersfield and once at Braintree, and class wins at both Brands Hatch and Stapleford.

1955 Moving up to a newer B-Type Connaught, he qualified in 19th place for the British Grand Prix, but retired with brake problems. He won F1 races at Davidstow, had a 5th at Charterhall, but proved more successful on the speed scene once more. He was 3rd overall and a class winner at Brighton, took FTD at Hempsford CUAC, won his class at Shelsley Walsh and finished 2nd in class at Prescott.

1956 A trip to New Zealand with the Connaught brought 3rd in the Lady Wigram Trophy and 4th in the New Zealand Grand Prix, despite starting at the very back of the grid. His antipodean journey proved to be his racing finale, retiring on his return to the UK.

❖

TONY MARSH
Born July 20th 1931

Surely one of the sport's greatest all-round competitors with a motorsport career spanning nearly 40 years. Marsh was British Hillclimb champion six times, British Formula 2 Champion, a trials winner and a sports car racer. He started his motorsport career in 1952, and was still competing in speed events during 1999. With numerous victories in all the disciplines he tackled, Grand Prix racing barely got a look in. From his four starts, two were in the F2 section of the German Grand Prix, although he did find the time to contest most of the national F1 races. All of this was achieved despite taking 20 years out of motorsport to contest other forms of sport.

Tony Marsh.

GRAND PRIX RECORD	
Starts	4
Wins	0
Poles	0
Fastest laps	0
WC points	0
Best finish	8th

1952 Made his competition debut at the Clee Hill Trial with a Dellow.

1953 Began circuit racing with a Connaught at Crystal Palace and Aintree, but had two 2nd places at Silverstone with a Cooper JAP. He won the Westwood Park Sprint and took 2nd in class at Shelsley Walsh in the same car, also winning the SUNBAC Trial and taking 2nd in class at Prescott with his Dellow

1954 He finished 5th in the British Hillclimb Championship with victory at Lydstep, and 3rd and 6th at Shelsley Walsh is his Cooper JAP, class wins at Prescott and Bo'ness. He also set FTD and had a 2nd in class at Gosport Speed Trials. His Dellow took an FTD at Lydstep, and a class win at Prescott. On the race tracks he won at Brands Hatch and Silverstone in his Cooper JAP, had two 3rd places at Crystal Palace and came 2nd in the Silver City Airways Libre race at the Boxing Day Brands Hatch meeting. He shared a Connaught to 10th in the TT with Jack Fairman and 3rd in the Anerley Trophy, finished 17th in the Goodwood 9 hours with Bertie Bradnack in a Cooper Jaguar. He drove a Lotus in sports car races to finish 2nd at Brands Hatch, 3rd at Goodwood and Aintree, and a class win at the Wethersfield Speed Trials. As well as all that he won the North versus Midlands driving test in his Dellow.

1955 Collected the first of his British Hillclimb titles with his Cooper JAP, with two victories at Shelsley Walsh, plus Great Auclum, Prescott, Westbrook Hay, Rhydymwyn and 2nd at Bouley Bay. He had a double class win at Rest & be Thankful, 2nd in class at Prescott (twice), as well as a further 2nd with a Cooper in the sports car class. FTD was claimed in the Gosport Speed Trials, along with a win in his Dellow on the Chase Trial. His circuit racing activity

brought a win at Silverstone in the F3 Cooper, 2nd in Silverstone sports, 3rd in the Lex Trophy, 4th in the Farningham Trophy and 5th in the Rochester Cup, all at Brands Hatch with his selection of Coopers.

1956 Won the British Hillclimb Champion again, and became the first man to break both the overall and sports car records at Prescott in one day. He won at Shelsley (three times), Rest & be Thankful, Prescott again, Great Auclum, Westbrook Hay, with 2nd at Bouley Bay and Prescott and a host of class wins with both sports and single seater Coopers. He won two classes at the Staverton Speed Trials and drove an ERA S-Type to 3rd at Brighton. His Cooper sports had a win, three 2nds and a 3rd at Mallory Park, two 2nds at Oulton Park, a win, 2nd, 4th and 6th at Silverstone and 4th at Aintree. At the British Grand Prix he drove an F2 Cooper in the support race and finished 10th.

1957 His hillclimb title was retained, along with the Autocar British F2 crown and 3rd in the RAC Trials Championship. His F2 Cooper gave him a Grand Prix debut in Germany, finishing 15th overall and 4th in class. He won at Silverstone, Oulton Park and Charterhall, had five wins and a 2nd at Mallory Park, 2nd, 3rd and 4th at Brands Hatch. He finished 3rd in the Coupe de Vitesse, GP de Paris and Oulton Park Gold Cup, 7th in the Woodcote Cup and 11th in the International Trophy with his F2 Cooper in a mixture of F2 and Libre races. His hillclimb victories came at Prescott (three times), Rest & be Thankful, Rhydymwyn (twice) and Bouley Bay, with 2nd at Shelsley Walsh and another host of class wins. He also won the Chateau Impney Sprint and came 3rd at Brighton Speed Trials.

1958 At the German Grand Prix his F2 Cooper finished 8th overall and 4th in class. He won the Daily Mirror Trophy at Oulton Park, took 4th in the Trophee D'Auvergne 5th in the Lavant Cup and Prix de Paris. He finished 6th at Brands Hatch, 7th in the Glover Trophy and at Crystal Palace, 10th in the Berlin GP and 14th at both Reims and the International Trophy. He had a Libre victory at Silverstone and won at both Snetterton and Brands Hatch in his Lotus sports. On the hills he secured 5th in the championship with two wins at Shelsley Walsh, two 2nds at Prescott and the usual selection of sports and single seater class wins. He secured FTD at Chateau Impney again, was a double class winner at Brighton, and finished 12th in the RAC Trials Championship after victories on the Clee Hill and Roy Wilshire Trials, along with numerous class awards.

1959 Most of the season was spent racing his F2 Cooper, winning at Zeltweg. He took 2nd in the Empire Trophy and at Mallory Park, 2nd in class and 10th overall at the International Trophy, 4th at Pau, 6th in the Oulton Park Gold Cup, 7th in the Lavant Cup and 12th at Reims. In Libre racing he won the Daily Mirror Trophy at Oulton Park, and scored a win and 2nd at Mallory Park. He was 3rd in the British Hillclimb Championship with FTD at Lydstep, a class win at Prescott and 2nd in class at Shelsley Walsh and finished 2nd on the Kitching Trial.

1960 His F2 Cooper was replaced by a Lotus 18 later in the year and the tally for the season included a win at Brands Hatch, 4th at Innsbruck, 5th at Pau and Zeltweg. He finished 5th at Snetterton, 6th at Brands Hatch, 7th at Modena, 10th at the German Grand Prix and 15th overall with 2nd in class at the International Trophy. At Le Mans he won the performance index award with John Wagstaff in a Lotus Elite. Other results included a Formula Junior win at Silverstone with a Lotus, a win at Mallory Park, 2nd at Oulton Park and Snetterton, and 3rd at Aintree in a Cooper Monaco sports, and class wins at Prescott in both the Cooper and Elite.

1961 A dispute over start money prevented him racing the Lotus 18 at the Belgian Grand Prix, the car being taken over by Willy Mairesse. He retired from the British Grand Prix and took 15th in Germany, while in non-championship races he collected 3rd in the London Trophy and Brussels Grand Prix, 6th in the Silver City Trophy at Brands Hatch and 7th at Aintree. He changed to a BRM later in the season and won the Lewis-Evans Trophy at Brands Hatch, with a further 6th place and 7th at Goodwood and the Oulton Park Gold Cup. On the hills he drove his Lotus, Cooper and BRM to finish 3rd in the championship, winning at Prescott, Rest & be Thankful and twice at Shelsley Walsh, with 2nd at Bouley Bay and a win at the Chateau Impney Speed Trials. His Lotus 18 took a pair of wins at Oulton Park in Formula Junior trim, along with 2nd in the International Trophy support race.

1962 Plans to run a semi-works BRM ended when the uncompetitive car was returned to the factory. He had a 4th at Pau and 7th in the International Trophy, but concentrated on hillclimbs for the rest of the year. Wins at Shelsley Walsh, twice at Bo'ness, Rest & be Thankful plus FTDs at Wiscombe secured 4th in the championship. He also finished joint 2nd in the Autosport Sprint Series, winning at Debden and finishing 2nd at Brighton.

1963 Apart from a Libre victory at Mallory Park and 2nd at Silverstone with the BRM, almost the entire year was given over to speed events, with 2nd place in the Hillclimb Championship and 3rd in the Autosport Sprint Series. Using both the BRM and his Marsh Climax, victories came at Wiscombe, Shelsley Walsh, Barbon, Loton Park, Bo'ness, Long Marston and Dyrham Park, with two further FTDs at Prescott.

1964 Finished 4th in the Hillclimb Championship, winning at Brunton, Longleat, Dyrham Park, Wiscombe, Harewood and Prescott, with 2nd at Loton, Prescott, Bouley Bay, Barbon and twice at Shelsley Walsh. He also won the Debden Sprint and collected numerous 3rd places and class wins.

1965 Became British Hillclimb Champion for the 4th time, proving almost unbeatable in his 4.2 litre Marsh Buick V8. He won at Loton Park, twice at Prescott, Shelsley Walsh and Wiscombe, plus Bo'ness, Bouley Bay and Longleat.

1966 His 5th British Hillclimb Championship title brought wins at Bouley Bay, Barbon, Prescott, Loton, Shelsley Walsh and twice at Wiscombe, with the Buick-powered Marsh.

1967 Brought four wheel drive to the hills in his Marsh Buick and won the championship again. His victories were at Harewood, Prescott, Shelsley Walsh, Gurston Down, Bouley Bay, Wiscombe and Rest & Be Thankful, along with now familiar 2nds and 3rds. He also won a BBC televised Gurston event at the end of the year.

1968 After taking 2nd at Prescott, Wiscombe and Shelsley Walsh in his Marsh Buick, he went sailing and ski-bobbing to World Championship standards until 1988.

1989 Returned to the hillclimb and sprinting scene with a Rovercraft, and finished 7th at Weston Super Mare.

1990 Finished 9th at Brighton Speed Trials with his Rovercraft.

1991 Won at Curborough, and had 7th at Weston Super Mare, 8th at Knockhill and Brighton in the Rovercraft.

1992 Another season of sprinting with the Rovercraft brought 3rd at Blackpool, 4th at Three Sisters, 5th at Knockhill, Pembrey and Weston Super Mare.

1993 Changed from his Rovercraft to a Toleman, and collected 2nd and 3rd at Aintree, 3rd at Colerne and 5th at New Brighton.

1994 Finished 4th in the British Sprint Championship, winning at New Brighton, and taking 3rd at Jurby and Three Sisters, 4th at Ingliston with 4th and 5th at both Curborough and Aintree.

1995 Took 3rd in the British Sprint Championship, with 3rd at Ingliston, 4th at Three Sisters and 5th at Aintree.

1996 7th in the British Sprint Championship with his Toleman.

1997 Won the Gurston Down Hillclimb with his newly acquired Roman DFL and finished 7th again in the British Sprint Championship.

1998 6th in the British Sprint Championship with a Gould Ralt. He finished 2nd at Gurston Down on his debut with the car, and took a further 7th at the same venue and an 8th at Shelsley Walsh. He had a 3rd and a 4th at Aintree, two 4th places at Pembrey and 5th at Ty Croes and Nutts Corner. There was also a return to trialing in a Kincraft.

1999 Early season outings in the Gould Ralt were restricted due to health problems, but on his seasonal debut at Curborough, he was 10th, and spent the rest of the season with appearances in both the British Hillclimb and Sprint Championships.

❖

ROBIN MONTGOMERIE-CHARRINGTON
Born June 22nd 1915

A Formula 3 racer from the early fifties, Montgomerie-Charrington had moderate success mainly in continental races during his brief career. When fellow F3 exponent Bill Aston decided to build his own Grand Prix car, 'Monty' decided to purchase one and chance his arm. However, it made but a single appearance at Spa in 1952. Neither car proved to be reliable and before the season's end, he had not only turned his back on racing, but had emigrated to the United States.

1950 Raced his Cooper in both F3 and Libre, with 3rd place in a Brands Hatch F3 race his best finish of the year.

1951 His Cooper JAP went further afield and picked up 3rd place at Pau, 4th at Madrid and Nurburgring, and 3rd in the Vue des Alpes Hillclimb.

1952 His Aston Butterworth Grand Prix car made the grid for the Belgian Grand Prix, having qualified in 15th place. A chronic misfire put him out of his only Grand Prix, having already retired from the Silverstone International Trophy and non-championship Monza Grand Prix. The only taste of success came at the Grand Prix des

GRAND PRIX RECORD

Starts	1
Wins	0
Poles	0
Fastest laps	0
WC points	0
Best finish	DNF

Frontieres at Chimay, where he took 3rd place despite coasting over the finishing line out of fuel. He left the racing scene without completing the season.

❖

STIRLING MOSS
Born September 17th 1929

Probably the most famous British racing driver ever, with 16 Grand Prix victories but never a World Championship. Still active in the sport on his 70th birthday, Moss continues to be the best-known British driver, nearly 30 years after a dreadful accident at Goodwood in 1962 which ended his Grand Prix career.

He started competing in 1947 at the tender age of 18 and then took many Formula 3 successes as he rose to rapid prominence. His first major victory was in the 1950 Tourist Trophy for Jaguar and he made his Grand Prix debut the following season for HWM. With Maserati and Mercedes he finished runner-up in the World Championship in 1955 and 1956 and then switched to Vanwall for 1957 and 1958 to finish runner-up twice more. During his time as a works Mercedes driver he famously won the Mille Miglia, co-driven by Denis Jenkinson.

His patriotic desire to race British cars led him to Rob Walker's team for the next three seasons, and in each season he was third in the World Championship. But in 1962, his career effectively ended with a terrible accident at Goodwood on Easter Monday. In seven consecutive seasons, he had finished second or third in the World Championship but was destined never to win the sport's biggest prize.

After a long recovery period, he returned to the sport in the 1970s and even raced for the works Audi touring car team in 1980 and 1981. He then switched his focus to racing in classic events and continued to draw crowds wherever he competed.

1947 Drove a BMW 328 in Speed Trials.

1948 Won F3 races at Goodwood, Brough and Dunholme Lodge, along with class wins at Prescott (twice), Bouley Bay, Burghfield Common, Shelsley Walsh and Blandford Hillclimbs in an F3 Cooper.

1949 Continuing in F3 he took victories in the British Grand Prix support race, the Madgwick Cup, at Zandvoort and Blandford.

1950 F3 wins in the International Trophy and British Grand Prix supports and the Belgian 500 Grand Prix, quickly led to greater things. He scored a TT win for

GRAND PRIX RECORD

Starts	66
Wins	16
Poles	16
Fastest laps	19
WC points	186.64

Won his 21st Grand Prix

Jaguar on his debut with the team, and finished 3rd in Bari, Reims, Perigeux and Castle Combe with an HWM. He also took a sports win at Castle Combe in a Frazer Nash.

1951 His Grand Prix debut with HWM resulted in 8th in the Swiss GP, but he also collected victories in the Madgwick and Lavant Cups at Goodwood, the Wakefield and O'Boyle Trophies at the Curragh and Winfield F2. He added 2nd at Goodwood and Aix les Bains and 3rd in the Dutch, Marseilles and Monza Grand Prix. A second successive TT victory came with Jaguar, as well as two wins at Goodwood, the British Empire Trophy was clinched with a Frazer Nash and there were F3 wins in the Monaco, British and Dutch Grand Prix supports. Other victories included Brands and Goodwood F3, a class win at Freiburg Hillclimb and a Production Car victory for Jaguar at Silverstone.

1952 Five Grand Prix starts failed to provide a single finish, with HWM, Connaught and an ERA G-Type. With

Jaguar he won the Reims Grand Prix and at Boreham, Turnberry, the International Trophy (both Sports and Production Cars), and a match race at Silverstone's Nations' Trophy, along with 2nd at Charterhall and Goodwood. F3 success continued with two wins at Castle Combe, the British Grand Prix support, Comme (France), Zandvoort and twice at Goodwood. His rallying exploits netted 2nd on the Monte and a class win on the Alpine with a Sunbeam Talbot, and class wins on the MCC and Daily Express Rallies in a Jaguar XK120. He drove the HWM to 2nd in the Eifelrennen and managed 5th with the ERA in the Daily Graphic Trophy.

1953 After taking 9th in the Dutch Grand Prix with Connaught, he had three further outings in a Cooper Alta, with retirement in the French, followed by 6th in the German and 13th in the Italian. He took the same car to victories in the London and Crystal Palace Trophies, 2nd in the Madgwick Cup and 3rd in the Sables D'Olonne. F3 wins followed at the Eifelrennen, British Grand Prix, Charterhall, Crystal Palace and Prescott Hillclimb. He won the Reims 12 hours for Jaguar with Peter Whitehead, took 2nd at Le Mans with Walker, 2nd in the Portuguese Grand Prix and 4th in both the Empire Trophy and TT, and won the International Trophy Production race at Silverstone in a MKVII. With his Sunbeam he also collected a second Alpine Cup and was 6th in Monte Carlo.

1954 Started the Grand Prix season with his own Maserati 250F, picking up 3rd in Belgium and retiring from the British and German. A move to the works team brought little change, with no classified finishes from three starts. In other F1 races he won the Goodwood Trophy, the Daily Telegraph Trophy, Libre and 200 race at

Stirling Moss on his way to winning the 1961 German Grand Prix.

Photo: BRDC Archive.

Aintree, the Oulton Park Gold Cup and Libre race. He finished 2nd at the Brands Hatch Daily Telegraph Trophy and Caen Grand Prix, 3rd in the Woodcote Cup, 4th in Bordeaux and 6th in Rome. He also shared an OSCA with William Lloyd to win the Sebring 12 hours and won the Coupe du Salon at Montlhery in a Connaught Sports. He took F3 wins at Aintree and Silverstone (twice), Nurburgring and Oulton Park, won a third Alpine Cup and came 15th on the Monte Carlo Rally with his Sunbeam.

1955 Joined the Mercedes Grand Prix team alongside Fangio, and finished runner-up in the World Championship. Having shared a car with Herrman and Kling to 4th in Argentina, he took 2nd in the Belgian and Dutch before taking his first pole, fastest lap and victory in the British Grand Prix at Aintree. He also won the Mille Miglia with Jenkinson, the Targa Florio with Collins and the TT with Fitch for Mercedes, as well as taking 2nd in the Buenos Aires City and Swedish Grand Prix and the Eifelrennen. He also won his second Oulton Park Gold Cup, took 3rd at the Chichester Cup and Snetterton and 4th in Bordeaux with his Maserati. He won the Governors Cup in Lisbon in a Porsche Spyder, took 2nd in class in the Sporting Life Saloons at Oulton Park in a Standard and 6th at Sebring sharing a Healey with Macklin.

1956 Returned to Maserati after Mercedes withdrew from racing, and was once again runner-up for the World title, after victories in Monaco and Italy, 2nd in Germany and 3rd in Belgium. The 250F collected wins in the Aintree 200, Richmond Trophy, London Trophy, Bari, New Zealand and Australian Grand Prix. He took a Vanwall to victory at Silverstone in the International Trophy, drove a Cooper Sports to victories in the Empire and Sporting Life Trophies at Oulton Park, the Norbury

Trophy and 2nd in the Anerley Trophy. An Aston Martin DB3S brought wins in the Daily Herald Trophy at Oulton Park, the Goodwood and BRDC Silverstone Trophies, 2nd at Le Mans with Collins, and 2nd at Rouen, Aintree and Silverstone. His Maserati 300S secured wins in the Nassau Trophy, Venezuelan Grand Prix, Nurburgring and Buenos Aires 1000km race and Australian TT and 2nd at the British Grand Prix support. He also won the Ardmore Handicap with a Porsche Spyder and came 2nd with a Mercedes in the Tour de France.

1957 For the third successive year he was runner-up in the World Championship. Having started off with 8th for Maserati in Argentina, he changed to Vanwall, winning the British, Italian and Pescara races. The Vanwall also secured 3rd at Syracuse, but there was victory in New Zealand with the Maserati 250F and the 450S took victory in the Swedish Grand Prix, 2nd in the Buenos Aires 1000km and Sebring 12 hours. He won the Nassau Trophy again in a Ferrari 290MM and drove a Mercedes to 5th in the Tour de France and Nurburgring 1000km.

1958 Victory in Argentina with a Rob Walker Cooper preceded another season with Vanwall and runner-up spot in the World Championship for the 4th successive year. He won the Dutch, Portuguese and Moroccan and was 2nd in the French. He drove an Aston Martin to his second Empire Trophy victory and his third TT win and also won the Nurburgring 1000km. He won at Kristianstad and at Vila Real in the Maserati 300S, and the Cuban Grand Prix in a Ferrari 412MI. Cooper mounted, he collected his third Aintree 200 win, the Kentish Trophy, Caen and Melbourne Grand Prix. He also won at Silverstone in a Lister and took 7th at the Monza 500 in the Eldorado.

Stirling Moss and his Mercedes at Spa, 1955.

Photo: BRDC Archive.

Moss and Jenkinson prepare to start the 1955 Mille Miglia.

Photo: BRDC Archive.

1959 Most of the year was spent driving Rob Walker's Cooper, taking four poles and victory in Portugal and Italy. A couple of outings with a BRP BRM secured 2nd in the British, resulting in 3rd place in the World Championship. He won his third Oulton Park Gold Cup, the Glover Trophy, the Coupe de Vitesse at Reims, Rouen, Syracuse and New Zealand Grand Prix, the Circuit D'Auvergne, the Kentish 100, the Goodwood 100, Melbourne Grand Prix and Watkins Glen Libre race in a variety of Coopers. He was the Autocar British F2 Champion, drove Aston Martins to a fourth TT win, took victory at Silverstone, the Governors Cup in Nassau and the Nurburgring 1000km He won at Rouen in a Maserati Sports and took a Cooper Monaco to victory at Roskilde and Karlskoga.

1960 Alternated between Rob Walker's Lotus and Cooper in Grands Prix, finishing 3rd in the World Championship with wins in Monaco and USA. He won the Oulton Park Gold Cup again, drove an F2 Porsche to victory in the Aintree 200, at Zeltweg, Brussels, Cape and South African Grand Prix. He won the Watkins Glen Libre in a Lotus 18, won the Pacific Grand Prix and at Karskoga in a Lotus 19, the TT again in a Ferrari 250 GT and the Nurburgring 1000km and Cuban Grand Prix in a Maserati Tipo 61.

1961 3rd again in the World Championship with Rob Walker, taking the Lotus to wins in Monaco and Germany. His F1 car also won the Silver City Trophy at Brands Hatch, at Modena, Roskilde, Karskoga, Aspern and Warwick Farm, while the older Cooper picked up the Empire and International Trophies at Silverstone, and the

Lavant Cup at Goodwood. A fifth Oulton Park Gold Cup win came at the wheel of the Ferguson P99 4WD. There was a sixth TT win driving a Ferrari 250GT and other wins in the Nassau TT, Pacific Grand Prix, Players 200 at Mosport, Sussex Trophy and Brands Hatch GT.

1962 Started the year with wins at the New Zealand Grand Prix, Lady Wigram Trophy and Warwick Farm in his Lotus 18. He took a Ferrari 250GT to a class win in the Daytona 3 hours, but his Grand Prix career ended in a near-fatal crash at Goodwood on Easter Monday.

1968 Contested the London-Sydney Marathon with Mike Taylor, and broke down in the Sahara.

1974 Took part in the World Cup Rally.

1976 Shared a Holden with Jack Brabham at Bathurst, but retired after a startline shunt.

1977 Finished 3rd in the British Grand Prix Historic race in a Maserati 250F.

1978 Won the Sebring Golden Oldies race in a Maserati T61 and the FIA Coupe d'Europe in a 250F Maserati.

1979 Contested the Lloyds and Scottish Historic Series with a Maserati 250F, taking 2nd at Brand Hatch and 6th at Silverstone. He also took 2nd in a Pukekohe Production Saloon Classic Race sharing a VW Golf GTi with Denny Hulme.

1980 After racing a Maserati Birdcage at Sebring, he joined the Audi team in the British Saloon Car Championship. Finished joint 5th in the championship, with 2nd in class at Mallory Park, Brands Hatch and Thruxton. He also raced a Ferrari 246 Dino in the Lloyds and Scottish Series, finishing joint 2nd in class, with two 2nd places at Silverstone and one at Oulton Park, and joined a VW Golf team for the Willhire 24 hours at Snetterton.

1981 Finished 5th in class in the British Saloon Car Championship for Audi, with 2nd at Oulton Park and 3rd at Mallory Park and Silverstone. Took 3rd with the Mayfair VW Scirocco Team in the Willhire 24 hours and 8th in the Oulton Park Gold Cup in a Cooper Climax.

1982 Won the Air Hanson Historic Sports Enduro in a Chevron B19, and took his B8 to victory at Phoenix Park, 4th at Zandvoort and 7th at Nurburgring.

1983-1999 Continued to race his Chevron in Supersports events, as well as being a regular participant in historic races, rallies and all things motorsport. Was awarded a BRDC Gold Medal in 1999.

❖

DAVID MURRAY
Born December 28th 1909
Died April 5th 1973

Murray was a successful businessman who tasted success at home and abroad, with a Scuderia Ambrosiana Maserati 4CLT in the late forties and early fifties. However his driving career became overshadowed by his part in the formation of the Ecurie Ecosse team. As team manager to the ultra-successful semi-works Jaguar squad, he placed the St. Andrews cross at the forefront of sports car racing, with victories at Le Mans in 1956 and 1957. Four Grand Prix starts failed to net a finish after mechanical problems intervened and he retired from competition at the end of 1952.

1948 Won his class at Brighton Speed Trials and finished 10th in the Supercharged race at the inaugural Goodwood meeting, driving his Maserati.

1949 Retired his Maserati from the British Grand Prix after engine failure, but took 4th in class at Weston Speed Trials and 6th in class at Brighton Speed Trials. Finished 5th in the Goodwood Easter Handicap, 9th at the Lausanne Grand Prix, 10th in the Jersey Road Race, 18th in the Silverstone International Trophy, and retired from the Albi Grand Prix.

1950 Started the Ambrosiana Maserati in the British and Italian Grand Prix, but failed to make the finish in either after engine and gearbox maladies. He also practiced the car at the French Grand Prix, before David Hampshire took it over for the race. Victory came in the Invitation Grand Prix at Winfield along with 9th at the Penya Rhin Barcelona Grand Prix. As well as taking the Maserati to Jersey and Zandvoort, there was a retirement in the Silverstone International Trophy, plus 4th in class with a Frazer Nash in the TT, and two class wins at Bo'ness Hillclimb in an ERA.

David Murray racing in the Manx Cup at Castletown, June 14 1951.

Photo: BRDC Archive.

GRAND PRIX RECORD	
Starts	4
Wins	0
Poles	0
Fastest laps	0
WC points	0
Best finish	DNF

1951 The only Grand Prix start of the year came in the British, when after qualifying the Maserati in 15th, it retired with broken valve springs. He also qualified for the German Grand Prix, but failed to start after an accident during practice. Finished 2nd in the Isle of Man Castletown Trophy, 6th in the Ulster Trophy, 21st in the Silverstone International Trophy and retired from the Chichester Cup at Goodwood with the Maserati. There were also Production race outings in a Jaguar, and class wins at Bo'ness with the Frazer Nash and ERA.

1952 Founder of Ecurie Ecosse and drove the team's Cooper Bristol at the British Grand Prix, retiring with engine problems. He shared an Ecosse Ford Anglia with Peter Collins in the Monte Carlo Rally, took 3rd with a Ferrari in an F2 race at Ibsley, 7th with the Cooper Bristol in F2 at Boreham and had various outings in an Ecosse C-Type Jaguar. Virtually retired from competition at the end of the year.

❖

BRIAN NAYLOR
Born March 24th 1923
Died August 8th 1989

A very successful national racer who built his own cars to race in both single-seater and sports cars, under the JBW name. Although he dabbled with Grand Prix racing, his cars were outpaced, but in Libre racing particularly at his local Oulton Park circuit, he was the man to beat. His cars also won several non-championship Formula 1 races in the late 1950s. He retired from racing during the 1962 season, due to ill health.

1953 Raced in F3, had a 2nd at Snetterton in an MG TD and finished 4th with an F2 Alta Bristol at the inaugural Oulton Park meeting.

1954 Continuing in F3 he took 2nd at Brands Hatch, 3rd at Snetterton, 4th at Silverstone and two 5th places at

Brands Hatch. His MG-engined Cooper had wins and a 2nd in Snetterton sports car races, two wins and a 2nd at Silverstone and 3rd at Oulton Park. His Cooper also took a double class win at the Queensferry Sprint, while other results included a 5th at Boxing Day Brands Hatch sports in a Lotus MG, and a Stock Car victory at Odsal Stadium.

1955 Successes continued with the Lotus MG, two wins and a 3rd at Silverstone, plus a win and 2nd at Oulton Park. He also raced his Lotus Sports with Connaught power, with three wins and three 2nds at Oulton Park. He added two wins and a 3rd at Aintree, three wins at Silverstone, 2nd in class at Snetterton in the Eastern Counties 100, 3rd in the Fawkham Trophy at Brands Hatch, and two further 4th places at Snetterton. At Silverstone and Oulton Park he had Production car wins in a Porsche, and took 3rd in an Aintree handicap, and was also 2nd in class in the Sporting Life Trophy with a Ford Consul.

1956 Racing in Libre and sports the length of Britain, his Lotus XI now with a Maserati engine won the Leinster Trophy at Wicklow. He had a win and a 2nd at Charterhall, a win and 2nd at Crimond, four wins and a 2nd at Snetterton. He took a win at Aintree, a win, two 2nds and a 3rd at Mallory Park, three wins and a 4th at Silverstone and two wins and two 3rds at Oulton Park. He also took a Maserati to a double win at Charterhall, a win at Silverstone and 12th in the International Trophy support race. He drove the MG-powered Lotus to victory and 2nd at Snetterton and two 2nds at Oulton Park. An overseas trip to the Rome GP was equally successful, finishing 2nd.

1957 His Grand Prix debut came with an F2 Cooper in Germany, qualifying 17th and finishing 13th overall and 2nd in class. He took the same car to 2nd in the Vanwall Trophy, F2 and Libre races at Snetterton. He journeyed to Spa and finished 5th with a Jaguar, but spent the rest of the year adding to the successes of his Lotus Maserati. Four wins at Silverstone, two at Oulton Park, plus Snetterton and class wins at the International Trophy and Spa, with 6th in the Forez 6 hours at St. Etienne.

1958 Another outing at the German Grand Prix resulted in retirement, when the fuel pump failed on his F2 Cooper, the car later taking a 2nd place in a Snetterton Libre race. His Lotus Maserati won the sports car race at

GRAND PRIX RECORD	
Starts	7
Wins	0
Poles	0
Fastest laps	0
WC points	0
Best finish	13th

Brian Naylor racing a Cooper MG at Silverstone, October 1954.

Photo: Ferret Fotographics.

Kristianstad, while his own JBW Maserati won at Monthlery, Snetterton and four times at Silverstone. He also claimed 2nd at Snetterton, two 2nds and two 4th places at Oulton Park in Libre and sports, 5th in the Empire Trophy and 8th in the British Grand Prix support race. He went to Le Mans to share a Lister Jaguar with Bruce Halford and finished in 15th place.

1959 His F1 JBW Maserati qualified 14th for the British Grand Prix, but retired with transmission failure. The F1 car won the Vanwall Trophy at Snetterton and a Mallory Park Libre race, while both the F1 and sports car versions had continuing success. Four Libre wins at Snetterton, plus the Scott-Brown Memorial Trophy, one more at Mallory Park and a sports car win at Goodwood. He raced his F2 Cooper to 5th in both the Aintree 200 and Empire Trophy, had a 2nd place at Snetterton in a Ferrari sports, and shared Graham Whitehead's Aston Martin at Le Mans.

1960 The JBW Maserati was taken to four Grands Prix, failing to qualify in Monaco, taking 13th in the British, retiring in Italy after qualifying 7th, and retiring again in the US Grand Prix. He was 11th in the International Trophy and Brands Hatch Silver City Trophy with his F1 car. Alternating with his sports version in Libre he won the Hawthorn Memorial Handicap and Libre race at Kirkistown, the National Benzole Trophy at Snetterton, plus a win and 3rd at Mallory Park. In sports cars he was

3rd at the International Trophy and Mallory Park and also drove a Ferrari and Maserati-engined Cooper Monaco to three sports car wins at Mallory Park, with one each at Silverstone, Snetterton and Oulton Park, and 2nd in the Raffles Club Trophy at Brands Hatch.

1961 His final Grand Prix ended in retirement in Italy, after his Coventry Climax-powered JBW suffered engine failure. He took the same car to 9th in the Oulton Park Gold Cup, and took the JBW Maserati to victory in a Libre race at Mallory Park. The Cooper Ferrari collected two sports car wins at Oulton Park and one at Snetterton.

1962 Shared a Jaguar with Roy Pierpoint to 21st place in the Brands Hatch 6 hour saloon car race, before retiring from racing.

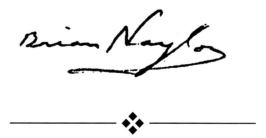

❖

50 years of British Grand Prix drivers

Part One
1950s

CHAPTER 5

RODNEY NUCKEY
Born June 26th 1929

Nuckey was a Formula 3 graduate of the early fifties who also tasted reasonable success in his privately owned Cooper Bristol. His one and only Grand Prix start came in the 1953 German, where he finished 11th. After one further year shared between the Cooper Bristol and an F3 Cooper, he disappeared from the racing scene for good.

1952 Raced an F3 Cooper Norton, taking a win at Skarpnack, a win and second at Falkenburg, and a 2nd and 3rd at Silverstone.

1953 Having graduated to a Cooper Bristol, he made his Grand Prix debut in Germany and finished 11th after qualifying 20th. He won the Finnish Grand Prix in Helsinki, finished 2nd in a Libre race at Silverstone, 3rd in

GRAND PRIX RECORD	
Starts	1
Wins	0
Poles	0
Fastest laps	0
WC points	0
Best finish	11th

both F2 and Formula Libre at Snetterton, 4th in the London Trophy at Crystal Palace, 5th in the Eifelrennen and tied with Jimmy Stewart's Connaught for victory in a Snetterton Libre race. He also had a sports car win at Silverstone in a Lotus and continued to race in F3, with wins at Brands Hatch, Silverstone and Stockholm, 2nd at Avus and Snetterton, 4th and 5th at Brands Hatch and 5th at Crystal Palace and Goodwood.

1954 He had been due to drive the Ecurie Richmond Cooper Bristol at the British Grand Prix, but the car was taken over by Eric Brandon. He did however race to 2nd in a Snetterton Libre race, 5th in the Crystal Palace Trophy, Oulton Park Gold Cup and at Snetterton. He collected F3

Rodney Nuckey at Crystal Palace.

wins at Falkenburg, Bressuine and Davidstow, with 4th at Aintree and 6th in the Earl of March Trophy at Goodwood. He also drove a Warrior sports car to 9th in the British Grand Prix support race.

REG PARNELL
Born July 2nd 1911
Died January 7th 1964

Having already made a name for himself with his Pre War exploits, Parnell was one of the men responsible for shaping motorsport in the immediate Post War years. His foresight and the Ashmore family's connections allowed them to assemble a mouthwatering stable of machinery, which became readily available at the end of the war.

He finished 3rd in the inaugural World Championship British Grand Prix at Silverstone in July 1950, having been invited to join the works Alfa Romeo team for the occasion. He won most of the prestigious trophy races at some time, many on more than one occasion. Once his own driving career ended in 1957, he took the works Aston Martin team to worldwide success, and also managed the Yeoman Credit and Bowmaker Lola Grand Prix teams, before setting up his own Parnell Racing outfit. However, he died tragically following routine surgery in 1964.

GRAND PRIX RECORD	
Starts	6
Wins	0
Poles	0
Fastest laps	0
WC points	9
Best finish	3rd

1934 Bought an old Bugatti from a local scrapyard for £25 and took it to its first meeting where it broke in the paddock!

1935 Retired his MG Magnette on its debut in a Donington Park handicap, won a 10-lap handicap, but retired again in the Nuffield Trophy.

1936 Continuing to race the MG brought retirement from the Donington Park Grand Prix, when sharing with Wilkie Wilkinson, retirement from the Empire Trophy, a crash in the Nuffield Trophy, but 3rd and 5th in a couple of Donington handicaps. In trips down to Brooklands he took a 2nd place in a handicap race, but more retirements in the Locke King Trophy and BRDC 500.

1937 Finished 3rd in the Grand Composite and Crystal Palace Cups, 4th in the London Grand Prix and 5th in

Reg Parnell (Thinwall Special) in the Silverstone International Trophy, May 1951.
Photo: BRDC Archive.

Reg Parnell and his wife in the paddock.

Photo: BRDC Archive.

class at Donington in the JCC200. He finished 11th in the Empire Trophy, 12th in the RAC Light Car Race in Douglas and took both handicap and national class wins on the Brooklands Campbell circuit. The second of two Brooklands retirements brought a licence suspension from the RAC, after a collision with Kay Petre left the lady driver in hospital.

1938 The MG was entered for other drivers during his suspension.

1939 Raced a BHW and collected two 2nds and two 3rds in Brooklands handicaps, 6th in the Empire Trophy and dominated the final Donington Pre-War meeting with one scratch and two handicaps victories. He also drove an ERA to 5th in the Imperial Trophy at Crystal Palace and had planned to use his self-built Challenger in the Nuffield Trophy, but the car wasn't ready and only made one appearance at a Prescott Hillclimb.

1946 Chose a Maserati 4CL from his collection and finished 2nd in the Ulster Trophy, 3rd at the Elstree Speed Trials, 7th at the Albi Grand Prix and took a class win in the Gransden Trophy. He also claimed 4th in a heat in Geneva but retired at Penya Rhin. His ERA proved less successful with retirements in the GP del Valentino in Turin, the Cicuito Milano, after taking 4th in his heat, and on the Bois de Boulogne where the rear axle broke before the start.

1947 After a couple of early wins in the ERA at the KAK Vinter Grand Prix and the SMK Stockholm Grand Prix,

victories followed in the Swedish Grand Prix and the Cofton Hackett sprint. At the wheel of the Maserati 4CL there was victory in the Jersey Road Race and 3rd in Nimes, but after retiring the Maserati in Nice Reg took over Fred Ashmore's seat in the old ERA, and brought it home 3rd.

1948 His Maserati 4CLT failed to make a lap in the British Grand Prix, after a runway light punctured the fuel tank. Victory came in the Goodwood and Leinster Trophies, along with 2nd at Penya Rhin, 3rd in the Jersey Road Race, 3rd at Zandvoort, 5th in the GP D'Italia Turin and 7th in the GP du Salon at Montlhery. The ERA was retired in both the Monaco and Italian Grands Prix, but it took 4th in the Bouley Bay and Bo'ness Hillclimbs. A rare trialing outing also picked up 2nd place in the Sheffield and Hallam Trial.

1949 The Maserati continued to see service and collected wins in the Daily Graphic Trophy, Chichester Cup, Richmond Trophy, Woodcote Cup and Easter Handicap at Goodwood. Continued success at Goodwood brought 2nd in both the Goodwood Trophy and a further handicap, along with 3rd in the Silverstone International Trophy. There was also 6th in the Zandvoort GP and 8th in the Swiss.

1950 Had a works Alfa Romeo for the inaugural World Championship British Grand Prix, qualifying 4th and finishing 3rd. The old Maserati 4CLT was retired from the French Grand Prix after engine failure, but won the

Richmond Trophy again at Goodwood and a Gamston Libre race. He also took 2nd in the Jersey Road Race, Gamston and Nottingham Trophies, 4th at Rosario and in the Chichester Cup and Goodwood Handicap, 8th in the Eva Peron Cup at Buenos Aires and 9th at Mar de Plata. Regular outings in the awesome BRM V16 netted victory in the Goodwood Trophy and Woodcote Cup at Goodwood, along with 2nd in the Invitation Grand Prix at Winfield. Having joined Aston Martin as a works driver, he finished 4th in the TT with a class win, 6th at Le Mans and 12th in the International Production race at Silverstone with a DB2.

1951 4th place in the French Grand Prix with the Vandervell Thinwall Special Ferrari, was followed by 5th in the British with the BRM V16. However a further outing in Italy failed when the engine expired during qualifying. Further races in the Thinwall netted the Silverstone International Trophy, as well as a Libre win at Ibsley, and 2nd in the Ulster and Goodwood Daily Graphic Trophies and Woodcote Cup. His ERA won the Goodwood Chichester Cup and Percy Andrews' Trophy at Gamston along with an Ibsley Libre race, while the Maserati 4CLT won the Castletown Trophy on the Isle of Man, the Festival of Britain Trophy at Goodwood and finished 3rd at Boreham. Further success followed with Aston Martin, taking 7th with Hampshire at Le Mans and 7th in the International Trophy Production Race.

1952 Qualified 6th and finished 7th at the British Grand Prix at the wheel of a Cooper Bristol in his only World Championship outing of the year. He won the Scottish Express National Trophy at Turnberry, took 2nd in the Daily Graphic Trophy and 3rd in the Woodcote Cup at Goodwood in the BRM V16. He raced the Cooper Bristol to an F2 victory at Boreham and the Maserati to 3rd in a Libre race at the same venue. The rest of the year was spent with Aston Martin and results included 2nd in the International Trophy Production Race and 2nd overall and class victory in the British Grand Production Race. He also took 3rd in the Jersey Road Race, 3rd overall and a class win at Boreham, 4th overall and 2nd in class in the Mille Miglia, and 8th in the Prix de Berne.

1953 Apart from taking the BRM V16 to 4th in the Chichester Cup, the year was spent almost entirely with Aston Martin. Victories came in the Empire Trophy, the BARC 9 hours, and in the British Grand Prix sports car race, Snetterton (twice), Castle Combe and at Charterhall with the debut of the DB3S. There was 2nd at the Sebring 12 hours, 3rd in the International Trophy sports car race and 5th in the Mille Miglia.

1954 Retired from his final Grand Prix when his Ferrari 500 expired in the British. The car did however win the Crystal Palace and August Trophies, the Lavant Cup, the Snetterton Redex Trophy and the BARC Goodwood F1 race. He also took 2nd in the Oulton Park Gold Cup and Aintree 200, 3rd in the Chichester Cup and Goodwood Handicap and 5th in the Goodwood Whitsun Trophy. He won with a Ferrari sports at Goodwood and took his Aston Martin to victory in the Horsfall Trophy and 3rd at Aintree. Other results included 5th in the International Trophy

sports car race debuting a Lagonda and 4th overall with a class win in a Production Saloon Daimler. He also took 4th in the British Grand Prix sports car race with the Lagonda and finished 153rd with an Aston Martin DB2 in the Monte Carlo Rally.

1955 A couple of outings in a Connaught brought 3rd in the Oulton Park Gold Cup and 6th in the Daily Telegraph Trophy at Aintree. With Aston Martin he recorded wins at Oulton Park, Charterhall and twice at Silverstone, plus 3rd in the Empire Trophy and British Grand Prix sports car race, 6th at Charterhall and 7th in the TT. There were a couple of 2nd places at Goodwood and Snetterton in a Cooper sports car.

1956 He started the year in New Zealand, with 2nd in Dunedin, 4th in the Wigram Trophy and 5th in the Grand Prix at Ardmore. Other results included 5th in the Glover Trophy and a Goodwood handicap win with a Connaught, an Aintree saloon car victory with a Mercedes 300SL and a class win with a Borgward Saloon at the International Trophy. 2nd at Spa and 3rd at Oulton Park were his best results for Aston Martin, ending the year with 6th in the Australian Grand Prix.

1957 Won the New Zealand, South Island and Dunedin Grands Prix in a Ferrari Super Squalo, before retiring from driving.

❖

DAVID PIPER
Born December 2nd 1930

Best known for his globe-trotting sports car exploits, Piper was a competent single-seater racer too in the late fifties and early sixties. His two Grand Prix starts were both at the British with a Lotus 16, but it was his first association with Ferrari in 1962 that began his run of sports car success. One of his most prominent victories was in the Rand nine hours sports car race in South Africa, which he won four times.

An accident during filming for the Le Mans feature film in 1970 left him seriously injured, losing the lower part of a leg when his Porsche 917 crashed. He was out of the sport for eight years, but returned at the end of the 1970s. He continues to this day racing his Ferraris, Lola T70, Porsche 917 and other exotic machinery in classic and Supersports races around the world.

David Piper

Photo: Ferret Fotographics.

1953 Began his motorsport career in speed events with an ex-Dennis Poore MG J4.

1954 Continuing with his MG he took 2nd in class at both the Wethersfield Sprint and Stapleford Hillclimb, along with 6th in the Albatross Trophy at Boxing Day Brands Hatch on his circuit racing debut.

1955 The MG made way for a Lotus Mk6, with victories in the Leinster Trophy at Wicklow, twice at Castle Combe and Snetterton, plus Goodwood and a class win at Wormingford Speed Trial. He was 2nd at Silverstone, along with 4th at Brands Hatch and twice at Snetterton.

1956 Stepping up to a Lotus XI he tasted success abroad, with 2nd in the Double 12 Trophy at Snetterton his only domestic podium visit. He won at Sables D'Olonne and the Coppa della Silla at Cosenza and took 2nd in the Rome Grand Prix. Other results included a class win with 11th overall in the Coupe du Salon, 3rd in class and 11th overall at the Nurburgring, 6th in class at Pescar and 13th overall in the Coupe Delamere Deboutteville at Rouen. Sharing a C-Type Jaguar with Dan Margulies, he took 4th in class on the Mille Miglia and shared an Alfa Romeo to 4th in class at Messina.

1957 Further continental travels with the Lotus brought 3rd in the Coupe de Vitesse at Montlhery, 5th in class at Spa, 7th in class at the Nurburgring 1000km. He also took 4th in class in the British Empire Trophy but the season was curtailed after his car overturned and caught fire in St.Etienne.

1958 Another year with the rebuilt Lotus XI collected 2nd in a Goodwood handicap, 3rd at Brands Hatch and Snetterton, a class win and 5th overall at Vila Real, 5th in class at the Nurburgring 1000km and 9th in the German Grand Prix support race.

1959 Moving into single seaters with a Lotus 16, his Grand Prix debut came at the British, qualifying 22nd but retiring with a blown headgasket. He won a Libre race at Brands Hatch and F2 races at Snetterton and Whitchurch. Other results included 2nd in the Farningham Trophy at Brands Hatch and at Snetterton, 4th in the Snetterton Silver City Trophy, 8th at Syracuse and 2nd in class in the British Grand Prix sports car race.

1960 His Lotus failed to start the French Grand Prix after its engine blew during qualifying, but he did bring the car home in 12th place at the British. He also won a Libre race at Snetterton and came 2nd in the Lady Wigram Trophy on a trip to New Zealand. With a Lotus XV he had sports car success with a win and 3rd at Brands Hatch, and 3rd at both Oulton Park and Snetterton. There were also occasional races in a Formula Junior Elva.

1961 He raced in non-championship F1 races with a Gilby Climax, taking 11th in the Oulton Park Gold Cup. In Formula Junior he had a Lotus 20, which collected its best finish with 2nd in Cesenatico.

1962 Continued to race a Lotus in national F1 races, with 6th in the London Trophy at Crystal Palace and 17th in the Silverstone International Trophy. Beginning his long association with Ferrari, he won the Rand 9 hours sharing with Bruce Johnstone in a 250GT and took 5th in the TT and 7th in the Tour de France with Dan Margulies. He also shared a Lancia Flaminia to 16th in the Brands Hatch 6 hour saloon car race.

1963 He won the Rand 9 hours again with Tony Maggs and took 2nd in the British Grand Prix support race with his GTO. Elsewhere, he took 4th in the Coppa Europa at Monza, 5th in the TT and Grovewood Trophy at Mallory Park, 7th in the Guards Trophy at Brands Hatch, 9th in the Auvergne Trophy, 10th in the Canadian Sports GP and 14th at Sebring. He also shared a 330LM with Gregory to 6th at Le Mans.

GRAND PRIX RECORD

Starts	2
Wins	0
Poles	0
Fastest laps	0
WC points	0
Best finish	12th

1964 For the third successive year he won the Rand 9 hours. He also took his GTO to 2nd at Daytona with Bianchi, 2nd in Angola, 3rd at Monza and in the Sussex Trophy, 4th at the Silverstone International Trophy, at Reims and at Brands Hatch. He finished 5th in the Paris 1000km, 7th in the Nurburgring 1000km with Maggs and 7th at Sebring with Rodriguez. He also drove a 250LM to 8th at Brands Hatch.

1965 Concentrating on the 250LM, victories came with Parkes in the Paris 1000km, plus the Norbury Trophy at Crystal Palace and Angola GP. He was 2nd in the Enna City Cup, at Mont Tremblant and in the Spa 500km, 3rd in the TT, Sebring 12 hours and at Silverstone and 4th in the Reims 12 hours. The GTO had a win at Brands Hatch and a 365 P2 was used to take 7th in the Guards Trophy at Brands Hatch and win another Rand 9 hours.

1966 The 365 P2/3 collected yet another Rand 9 hours victory with Attwood sharing the driving, along with the Cape 3 hours. He also won the Trophee D'Auvergne and Paris 1000km with Parkes. On home soil he finished 3rd in the Autosport Championship, having won at Oulton Park, Silverstone, the British Eagle Trophy, Crystal Palace and Castle Combe. He finished 3rd in the Mallory Park Grovewood Trophy, 5th in the Scott-Brown Memorial at Snetterton and 10th at the British Grand Prix meeting, all with a 275LM. He drove his P2/3 to 9th in the TT, shared an AC Cobra with Bob Bondurant to victory in the Ilford Films 500 at Brands Hatch, and came 12th at Le Mans in Richard Bond's Ford GT40.

1967 He shared a Ferrari 412P with Jo Siffert to 2nd in the Reims 12 hours and 5th in the Paris 1000km. With Attwood he took 2nd in the Cape 3 hours, 7th in the BOAC 500 at Brands Hatch and 9th in the Rand 9 hours. His 250/275LMs were used again in the Autosport Championship, winning at Silverstone and Brands Hatch, with 2nd at Oulton Park and 3rd at Crystal Palace. He drove his P3 to 3rd in the Wills Trophy at Croft, shared the 250LM with David Skailes to 4th in the Austrian GP and finished 9th in the Monza 1000km with a Mirage.

1968 Victories at the Norisring, Vila Real, Karlskoga and Hockenheim in the P3/4 highlighted the year, with a further 2nd at Hockenheim. On the home front Attwood shared the car to 2nd in the TT, Hobbs shared the car to 2nd in the Oulton Park Spring Cup and 8th in the Gold Cup. The 250LM took 7th at Le Mans with Attwood, and had a 4th and 5th at Silverstone as well as 7th at Mallory Park. Sharing a Ford GT40 with Mike Salmon he was 14th in the Nurburgring 1000km, while the season ended in South Africa sharing the P3/4 with Attwood. Results included 3rd in the Roy Hesketh and Cape 3 hours and 14th in the Kyalami 9 hours.

1969 Virtually a year away from Ferrari brought a win at Vila Real, 2nd in the Barcelona 12 hours and 3rd in the Paris 1000km sharing a Porsche 908 with Chris Craft. He also took 2nd at Keimola in the same car. He won the Kyalami 9 hours with Attwood in a Porsche 917 and also finished 3rd at Hockenheim. He drove a Lola T70 to 2nd in the TT, the Dunes Trophy at Zandvoort and Prix de Salzburg, 3rd at Dijon, Magny Cours and the Silverstone

Martini Trophy. Other results with the Lola included 4th at Thruxton, 5th at Silverstone and 17th in the BOAC 500 at Brands Hatch, sharing with Roy Pierpoint. His Ferrari outings netted 8th at the Norisring in his P3/4 and 2nd at the Spa 1000km sharing a works 312P with Pedro Rodriguez.

1970 The season began with a 5th place at Daytona sharing a Ferrari 312P with Adamowicz, followed by 2nd at Dijon, 3rd at Magny Cours, 4th in a Hockenheim Interserie race and 6th in the Swedish Grand Prix in a Porsche 917. He drove a Chevrolet Camaro in the British Saloon Car championship, with 2nd at Crystal Palace and 7th at Snetterton and had a 15th at Thruxton in his Lola T70. But the season ended abruptly when he was seriously injured after his 917 crashed during filming at Le Mans.

1978 Drove a Triumph Dolomite at Mallory Park's British Saloon Car round, crashing out at the hairpin.

1979 Raced regularly on the Historic GT scene with his Ferrari 330 P4.

1981 Finished 3rd at Silverstone and Falkenburg with his P4 and 4th at Phoenix Park in his 275LM.

1982 - 1999 Travelled the world as co-founder of the Supersports Series, racing his classic Porsches, Ferraris, Lola and Mirage, as well as entering cars for many others.

❖

DENNIS POORE
Born August 19th 1916
Died February 12th 1987

Poore was a champion hillclimber who had started competing before the War. In the early 1950s he had a spell with the Connaught Syndicate, with whom he made his two Grand Prix appearances in 1952. In the British, he finished fourth in his debut Grand Prix. Towards the latter part of his career he tasted success as part of the Aston Martin team, winning the BARC nine hours at Goodwood in 1955, his final year of racing.

1936 Finished 3rd in class at the Poole Speed Trials with a Ford.

GRAND PRIX RECORD

Starts	2
Wins	0
Poles	0
Fastest laps	0
WC points	3
Best finish	4th

1937 Racing an MG Midget he won the Reilly and Jackson Cup for overall victory at Syston Inter Varsity Speed Trial, won two classes at the Bristol Speed Hillclimb, 2nd in two classes at Brighton and took 2nd in a Donington Park scratch race. He was an award winner at a JCC Brooklands in a Talbot and drove the same car in the RAC Hastings Rally.

1938 Won his class at the Backwell Hillclimb with his MG, and took 1st and 2nd in Brooklands sports car races.

1947 Had a win at the Southsea Speed Trials in his Alfa Romeo 8C, and was 2nd in class at Poole, 3rd in class at Prescott, and had a race win in the Gransden Trophy at Gransden Lodge.

1948 Continued success with his Alfa Romeo brought an overall win at Prescott, class wins at Bo'ness, Bouley Bay, Shelsley Walsh and Brighton. He took 2nd at Prescott, Luton Hoo, Stanmer Park and Shelsley Walsh, 3rd at Weston Super Mare and 4th in class at Prescott. On the race circuits he won the Woodcote Cup and a race for supercharged cars at Goodwood, and was 3rd in the Castletown Trophy on the Isle of Man.

1949 Took class wins at Blandford, Prescott and Shelsley Walsh, and overall wins at Luton Hoo and Shelsley Walsh kept his Alfa Romeo to the fore in speed events. He added 2nd at Rest and be Thankful, 2nd in class and 5th overall at Prescott, and 3rd in class at Brighton. He also continued to race his Alfa and finished 2nd in the Chichester Cup and 5th in the Woodcote Cup at Goodwood, and took a Veritas sports to 2nd place in a Goodwood handicap and 5th in the Madgwick Cup.

1950 Became British Hillclimb Champion with his Alfa, after three wins at Prescott, plus Rest and be Thankful and Val des Terres. He was also 2nd at Shelsley Walsh, Bo'ness and Bouley Bay, along with 2nd in class at Blandford and 2nd in class at Shelsley Walsh in the Cromard Special. Apart from 3rd in the Chichester Cup at Goodwood in the Alfa, his racing activities were fairly restricted, but before the end of the year he had joined Connaught.

1951 The ageless Alfa was pressed into service once more and won the Seaman Memorial Historic Trophy at Silverstone and a Libre race at Boreham. He took a win and 3rd at Ibsley, 7th in the Festival of Britain Trophy at Goodwood, as well as 8th in an F2 race at Boreham with

Denis Poore (Alfa Romeo) at Silverstone in July 1952.

Photo: Ferret Fotographics.

a Connaught. On the hills he won at Rest and be Thankful, took 2nd at Bouley Bay and Prescott, 2nd and 3rd at Shelsley Walsh and 2nd in the Snetterton Speed Trials.

1952 His first entry on the Grand Prix stage came with a Connaught at the British Grand Prix, qualifying 8th and finishing 4th. His only other Grand Prix start came in the Italian, where he qualified 19th and finished 12th. The Connaught was also taken to Charterhall where he finished 2nd in the Newcastle Journal Trophy, and Goodwood, where he was 2nd in the Madgwick Cup and 4th in the Daily Graphic Trophy. Further outings in his Alfa brought a 2nd victory in the Seaman Memorial Trophy at Oulton Park and a Libre win at Boreham. He took 3rd in the Sussex International Trophy and 4th in the Chichester Cup at Goodwood, as well as a win at Prescott Hillclimb, 2nd at Bo'ness and 3rd at Bouley Bay and Rest and be Thankful. He was also in action for Aston Martin with victory at Ibsley in a DB3S and 3rd in Goodwood's Easter Handicap in a DB2.

1953 He won his 3rd consecutive Seaman Memorial Trophy at Oulton Park in the old Alfa, but spent most of his year with Aston Martin. There were two class wins and a 3rd at Prescott, he partnered Eric Thompson at Le Mans and crashed out of the TT in a DB3S.

1954 A class win at the Prescott Silver Jubilee and 13th in the TT with Graham Whitehead were the highlights of his season with an Aston Martin DB3S. He also shared a Lagonda at Le Mans until Thompson crashed out.

1955 Further success with Aston Martin brought a victory in the BARC 9 hours with Peter Walker, the same pairing collecting 4th in the TT. At Le Mans he was back in a Lagonda, this time sharing with Reg Parnell.

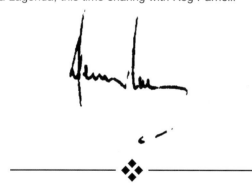

❖

JOHN RISELEY-PRICHARD
Born January 17th 1924

A national and club sports car racer from the early fifties who suddenly came to the fore with Rob Walker's Connaught in 1954. A number of top finishes in Libre races earned him a drive in the British Grand Prix the same year, his one and only Grand Prix appearance which ended in retirement. After joining the Aston Martin team a year later, he partnered Tony Brooks at Le Mans but disappeared from the racing scene for good at the end of the 1955 season.

GRAND PRIX RECORD	
Starts	1
Wins	0
Poles	0
Fastest laps	0
WC points	0
Best finish	DNF

1951 Raced a Jaguar XK120 in smaller national meetings.

1952 Finished 2nd in the sports car race and 3rd in a handicap at Silverstone in a Riley.

1953 Won a Goodwood handicap race in his Riley.

1954 His one and only Grand Prix appearance came at the British with Rob Walker's Connaught A-Type, qualifying 21st and retiring after spinning off when a steering arm broke. He took the car to a double victory at Davidstow and won the F1 class at a Prescott Hillclimb as well as an F1 race at Crystal Palace. He also took 3rd in a Davidstow Libre race and the Joe Fry Memorial at Castle Combe, 4th in the London Trophy at Crystal Palace, Snetterton Libre and the Madgwick Cup and F2 at Goodwood, 7th in the Goodwood Trophy and 8th in Libre. For sports car events he had a Cooper Connaught, taking a 2nd, two 3rds and three 4ths at Brands Hatch, 2nd at Davidstow, 6th in the British Grand Prix and 25th in the International Trophy support races.

1955 As part of the Aston Martin sports car team, he shared a DB3S with Tony Brooks, including at Le Mans. He also used his own Connaught to win a Libre race at Castle Combe, take 2nd at Ibsley, 3rd at Snetterton, 4th in the London Trophy at Crystal Palace and 6th in the Silverstone International Trophy. On occasions the car was also entered for Brooks to drive.

TONY ROLT
Born October 16th 1918

Having made his name as a teenager winning races before the war, he then won the Empire Trophy at Donington Park in 1939. His war years included an escape from the infamous Colditz Castle. Returning to the circuits when peace was restored, his regular single-seater outings were more than eclipsed by his sports car successes for Jaguar which were crowned by his victory at Le Mans in 1953 with Duncan Hamilton. He eventually retired from driving at the end of 1955, to head the development of the Ferguson four wheel drive system.

Tony Rolt (Jaguar C Type) in the 1953 Goodwood nine hours.

1935 Trialed a three-wheeler Morgan and represented Eton.

1936 Started racing with a Triumph Southern Cross and took 4th in class and a new 2-litre lap record in the Belgian 24 hours at Spa.

1937 Raced a Triumph Dolomite, mainly at Donington Park.

1938 Began a long association with an ERA, winning three scratch and two handicap races at the Donington Coronation Trophy, as well as taking 2nd in the feature race. He also won the Brooklands October Handicap and finished 2nd in the Crystal Palace Cup and at Phoenix Park. He finished 4th in the Imperial and Sydenham Trophies at Crystal Palace, 5th in the JCC International and Nuffield Trophies at Donington, 6th in the Leinster Trophy, 7th in the JCC200 at Brooklands and 9th in the Prix de Berne.

GRAND PRIX RECORD

Starts	3
Wins	0
Poles	0
Fastest laps	0
WC points	0
Best finish	DNF

1939 Won the British Empire Trophy aged 19, finished 2nd at Phoenix Park and continued racing at Donington and Crystal Palace until war intervened.

1947 Finished 3rd and 7th at Shelsley Walsh hillclimbs, 8th in the Chimay Grand Prix and contested the Empire and Gransden Trophies with an Alfa Romeo.

1948 Took 2nd place at Zandvoort with his Alfa Romeo, but retired from the British Grand Prix and Empire Trophy. He also shared an Aston Martin with Andre Pilette in the Spa 24 hours.

1949 A further year with the Alfa Romeo brought 6th in the Empire Trophy, 10th in the Silverstone International Trophy, but retirement in the British Grand Prix. However, there was a victory in a Goodwood handicap, 3rd in class at Luton Hoo and Weston Speed Trials and 3rd with an Alfa Sports in the Dolomite Grand Prix. Other outings included retiring a Delahaye at Le Mans with Jason-Henry and finishing 4th in the International Trophy Production race in a Healey.

1950 Retired from the inaugural World Championship British Grand Prix, when the ERA he was sharing with Peter Walker had gearbox failure. The ageing Alfa was taken to 3rd in the Brighton Speed Trials and he shared a Healey with Duncan Hamilton to finish 4th at Le Mans. Other finishes were recorded with 7th in the Empire Trophy and with Jaguar in the International Trophy Production Race, after retiring Rob Walker's ERA Delage from the feature race and the Jersey Road Race.

1951 He continued to race the ERA Delage in national events. He took a win and 2nd at Boreham, 3rd in the Daily Graphic Trophy and Woodcote Cup at Goodwood,

6th in the Festival of Britian Trophy and 7th on the Isle of Man. Sharing a Jaguar with Leslie Johnson he took 4th in the Mille Miglia and the TT, as well as 6th at Le Mans with Hamilton in a Healey.

1952 The ERA Delage was taken to victory again in two Snetterton races, along with 2nd place in the Chichester Cup. Victory came in the Goodwood International Sports with a C-Type Jaguar, but he retired at Le Mans. An outing in a HWM secured 2nd place in the Silverstone International Trophy.

1953 After qualifying Rob Walker's Connaught in 10th for the British Grand Prix, a broken halfshaft ended his only Grand Prix outing of the year. Throughout the year the Connaught otherwise proved very reliable, winning the Coronation and Crystal Trophies at Crystal Palace, two Snetterton F2 races, the USAF Trophy at Snetterton, F2 and Libre at Thruxton and the feature F2 race at the opening meeting at Oulton Park. There was also 2nd in the London Trophy and the Charterhall International, 3rd in the Silverstone International Trophy, Lavant Cup at Goodwood and at Snetterton, 4th at Castle Combe and 5th in Godwood's Richmond Trophy. The ERA Delage secured a 2nd at Crystal Palace, but all this was overshadowed by victory at Le Mans with Hamilton in the works C-Type Jaguar. He retired his C-Type Jaguar on the Mille Miglia.

1954 The Connaught was raced again on the home front, with victory at Crystal Palace in the Glade Trophy and 3rd in the August Trophy. He added a further win in a Goodwood handicap, along with 7th place in the Silverstone International Trophy. Concentrating on sports and saloon races, 2nd place at Le Mans and in the Reims 12 hours were taken with Hamilton in the Jaguar D-Type. He claimed two 2nd places with a C-Type at Goodwood, along with 10th in the British Grand Prix sports car race and 2nd in the International Trophy Production Touring race with a Jaguar MKVII.

1955 Made his farewell to the Grand Prix scene at Aintree when a broken throttle put his Rob Walker Connaught, shared with Peter Walker, out of the race. He finished 2nd in Silverstone Libre and 4th in the Chichester Cup with the same car, and took his Jaguar to 3rd in the International Trophy sports car race and 4th at Goodwood.

❖

ROY SALVADORI
Born May 12th 1922

An all-rounder who was equally at home in single-seaters, sports cars or saloons. He started racing as soon as the sport emerged after the war and was fortunate to survive a serious accident at Silverstone in 1951. But he was fit enough to make his Grand Prix debut there a year later but it was not until 1958 that he collected his best finish when he took a works Cooper to second in Germany.

While a Grand Prix victory eluded him, success in the other formulae more than made up for it, with victory for Aston Martin at Le Mans in 1959 with Carroll Shelby the icing on the cake. In a 20-year career, sports car racing remained his most successful arena although he contested 47 Grands Prix. After retiring in 1965 he became Cooper team manager for a couple of seasons and has taken part in numerous historic races to this day.

GRAND PRIX RECORD	
Starts	47
Wins	0
Poles	0
Fastest laps	0
WC points	19
Best finish	2nd

1946 Finished 2nd at Gransden Lodge with an MG R-Type on his race debut, and secured fastest time of the day at Finchampstead's West Court Speed Trials in a Riley.

1947 Graduating to an Alfa Romeo Monoposto, he journeyed to the Grand Prix des Frontieres at Chimay and took 5th, plus 3rd in the Gransden Trophy and Southsea Speed Trials and 2nd in class at Shelsley Walsh.

1948 After a few speed trial outings in the Alfa, he changed to a Maserati 4CL. Results included 7th at Goodwood, 8th in the British Grand Prix at Silverstone, 8th at Zandvoort and the Jersey Road Race, 4th in class at Brighton Speed Trials and 7th overall with 3rd in class at Luton Hoo.

1949 His Maserati retired from both the British Grand Prix and the International Trophy, but finished 8th in the Paris GP at Montlhery. During the Wakefield Trophy at the Curragh, the car was hit by Gordon Watson's Alta and burned out.

1950 His one and only race of the year netted 5th in the Wakefield Trophy with a Healey Silverstone.

1951 On his debut with a new Frazer Nash LM Replica at Silverstone, he was critically injured after a crash at

Roy Salvadori at Aintree in 1954.

Photo: Ferret Fotographics.

Stowe. His return in the rebuilt car at Castle Combe secured 3rd place, while outings in a Jaguar XK120 secured a brace of 2nd places at Boreham.

1952 His Grand Prix debut came in a privately-entered Ferrari 500 at the British, finishing in 8th place. Further outings with the car brought an F2 win at Castle Combe and 6th in the Daily Graphic Trophy and Woodcote Cup at Goodwood. The Frazer Nash had three victories in a day at Thruxton as well as wins at Snetterton and Goodwood, 2nd at Ibsley, Boreham and Snetterton, 2nd and 3rd at Castle Combe and 4th in the Empire Trophy. He shared Bobby Baird's Ferrari Tipo 225 to 3rd in the Goodwood 9 hours, won at Charterhall and took 4th at Boreham. He also had a number of 2nd places in a Jaguar XK120 and raced a Bristol Saloon.

1953 From five Grand Prix starts in a works Connaught A-Type, he had five mechanical retirements. He did however win with the car at the Goodwood Madgwick Cup and Snetterton Libre, took 2nd in the Crystal Palace and Silverstone International Trophies, 2nd at Charterhall and in the Lavant Cup, 3rd at Charterhall, 4th in the Glover Trophy at Goodwood and 5th in the Libre race. He took 2nd in the Nurburgring 1000km with Ian Stewart for Jaguar, finished 2nd at Silverstone and 4th in the Casablanca 12 hours with Mike Sparken for Aston Martin. He added two victories at Snetterton and numerous other placings with his Frazer Nash. He also raced an ERA Delage, Maserati A6GCS Sports and Ferrari 500, securing at least one 2nd place with each.

1954 Two Grand Prix outings in the Gilby Engineering Maserati 250F ended in retirement, but the car was taken to victory in the Curtis Trophy at Snetterton, plus two

other wins at the same circuit. He was also 2nd in the Chichester and Lavant Cups at Goodwood, 2nd at Crystal Palace, 3rd at Rouen and Goodwood, 3rd in the Goodwood Whitsun Trophy, 5th in the Woodcote Cup at Goodwood and 5th in the Aintree Daily Telegraph Trophy. He took the Maserati A6GCS to 2nd in the Empire Trophy, two wins at Castle Combe, victory at Goodwood and Brands Hatch, along with two wins and two 2nds at Crystal Palace. He also claimned four 2nds and two 3rds at Snetterton, 3rd at Ibsley, 4th at Goodwood and Crystal Palace, and a class win at Aintree. Further outings in a Jaguar C-Type brought 2nd in the Pedralbes Barcelona Cup and Penya Rhin Grand Prix, two wins and a 3rd at Snetterton and wins at Goodwood and Charterhall. At the wheel of an Aston Martin he took 2nd at the British Grand Prix sports race, won at Ibsley and Snetterton and recorded numerous other top five finishes.

1955 A solitary Grand Prix outing with the Gilby 250F ended in retirement again at the British. However the car proved reliable otherwise and won the Daily Telegraph Trophy at Aintree, the Glover Trophy at Goodwood, the Curtis Trophy and two Libre races and the Eastern Counties Trophy at Snetterton as well as the Ibsley Libre race. He took 2nd in the Silverstone International Trophy, Aintree and Snetterton Libre, Chichester Cup and Goodwood Easter Handicap, 3rd in the Crystal Palace International Trophy and Rochester Cup at Brands Hatch, 4th in the Empire News Libre and Avon Trophy at Castle Combe and Oulton Park Gold Cup. He won the Lavant Cup at Goodwood and Charterhall Libre in a Connaught, drove an Aston Martin DB3S to wins at Ibsley, Snetterton, Goodwood, Aintree and Crystal Palace, plus 2nd at Silverstone and in the Norbury Trophy, 7th in the TT and in the Swedish Grand Prix. He also had occasional races in the Maserati sports, had a 3rd place at Castle Combe in a Lister Bristol and picked up victories at Aintree and Snetterton in Cooper Maserati and Climax sports.

1956 Three more Grands Prix in the Gilby 250F brought relatively little success, but he once again proved victorious on home soil, winning the Vanwall and HW Sear Trophies at Snetterton. He also claimed 2nd in the Richmond Trophy, 3rd in the Caen Grand Prix and 3rd at Brands Hatch. He drove a Cooper T41 to victory in the Oulton Park Gold Cup, Woodcote Cup, Sussex Trophy, Brands Hatch and Silverstone F2. He raced a Cooper T39 sports car to victory in the Lavant Cup at Goodwood, at Silverstone and in the Oporto City Cup, as well as 2nd at Aintree and 3rd in the Rhine Cup and Empire Trophy sports car race. Further wins were taken with the Aston Martin DB3S, twice at Aintree and once at Silverstone, with 4th in the Sebring 12 hours, 2nd in the Goodwood Trophy and at Silverstone, 4th in the Daily Herald Trophy at Oulton Park and 5th at Rouen. He also took a sports car victory at Snetterton with a Lotus Climax.

1957 Having failed to qualify a works BRM for the Monaco Grand Prix, he retired a Vanwall from the French, before three further starts in a works Cooper. 5th place in the British brought his first World Championship point, followed by retirement in Germany and Pescara. He won the Woodcote Cup, took 2nd at Caen, the London Trophy and Brands Hatch F2, 4th at Reims and 8th overall with an F2 win at the Silverstone International Trophy. His Aston Martin outings netted 2nd in the Empire Trophy, the Sussex Trophy, the Spa National race and at Aintree. He took a victory at Silverstone, 4th in the Spa GP and 6th in the Nurburgring 1000km A further race in the Vanwall brought 5th at Reims, and there were occasional outings on the national scene in Cooper and Lotus Climax sports.

1958 A full Grand Prix season with a works Cooper resulted in four points finishes, 2nd in Germany, 3rd in the

British, 4th in the Dutch and 5th in the Italian, with only one failure from nine starts. He also took 2nd at the International Trophy, 3rd in the Aintree 200, Glover Trophy and Goodwood 100. He took his Lotus 19 to victory in the Oulton Park Gold Cup, with 2nd at the British Grand sports and 3rd in the Chichester Cup. He collected 2nd in the TT, 2nd at Aintree, and 4th at the International Trophy sports in Aston Martins.

1959 Seven Grand Prix starts were spread between Tommy Atkins' Cooper and a works Aston Martin, with 6th place in the British and Portuguese being the only finishes, both in the Aston Martin. The Cooper was also used to win the London Trophy and take 2nd in the Goodwood 100, Lavant Cup and John Davy Trophy at Brands Hatch, while the DBR4 Aston Martin finished 2nd in the International Trophy. He shared an Aston Martin with Carroll Shelby to victory at Le Mans, and was class winner in the British Saloon Car Championship after numerous podium finishes in his 3.4 Jaguar. He finished 4th in the Oulton Park Gold Cup with an F1 Cooper Maserati and was a regular winner on the national scene with his Cooper Monaco sports, including the Norbury Trophy at Crystal Palace.

1960 Another year divided between Aston Martin and the Atkins' Cooper, resulted in an 8th place at the United States GP, from four starts. Cooper-mounted, he took 4th at the Snetterton Lombank Trophy with an F1 car and had two wins at Oulton Park. He finished 3rd in the Lavant Cup and Oulton Park Trophy in an F2 car, and took victory in the Sussex Trophy, wins at Oulton Park, Aintree, Silverstone International Trophy sports, Raffles Club Trophy at Brands Hatch, finished 3rd at Watkins Glen and 6th at Riverside in the Monaco sports. His Aston Martin outings brought 2nd in the TT, 3rd at Le Mans and 6th in the Paris 1000km. In the Jaguar 3.8 saloon he claimed wins at Silverstone and Brands Hatch, and two 2nd places at Goodwood.

Roy Salvadori at Brands Hatch.

Photo: BRDC Archive.

1961 The Grand Prix season was spent partnering John Surtees in the Yeoman Credit Cooper team, with 6th place in both the British and Italian Grand Prix, 8th in France and 10th in Germany. He won the London Trophy again, took 3rd in the Glover Trophy, Goodwood 100, International Trophy and Copenhagen Grand Prix, 4th in the Silver City Trophy and Cannon race at Karlskoga, 5th in the Brands Hatch Guards & Snetterton Lombank Trophies. He jointly debuted the E-Type Jaguar with 3rd place at Oulton Park, followed by victory in the Norbury Trophy, 2nd at Snetterton and 2nd and 3rd at Brands Hatch. His Jaguar saloon won at Crystal Palace, Oulton Park and Aintree, the Cooper Monaco collected the Green Helmet Trophy at Crystal Palace and the Aston Martin DB4GT finished 4th in the TT. A trip to New Zealand with a Lotus 18 also brought success, with victories at Teretonga and Longford.

1962 Stayed with Surtees as they both moved to Bowmaker Lola, where he failed to record a solitary finish from 10 starts, and made his final Grand Prix appearance in South Africa. The car did manage to take 2nd in the Crystal Palace Trophy, Lavant Cup and at Karlskoga, plus 4th in the Goodwood 100 and 6th in the Reims GP. Sharing a Jaguar E-Type with Cunningham he finished 4th at Le Mans, and 4th in the TT. Regular podium finishes continued with Jaguar saloons and the Aston Martin DB4GT, as well as the occasional race in a Ferrari GTO.

1963 A successful year with the Cooper Monaco sports brought wins at Oulton Park, the Lavant Cup at Goodwood, the International Trophy sports car race, at Silverstone and Aintree. He finished 2nd in the Brands Hatch Guards Trophy and the Snetterton Molyslip Trophy and 7th at Riverside. He won the Motor 6 hours with Hulme and Jaguar at Brands Hatch, followed by further wins at Snetterton and a handful of 2nd places. The Aston Martin DB4GT claimed the Coppa Europa at Monza and his Jaguar E-Type outings brought 2nd at the International Trophy and 3rd in the TT and Mallory Park Grovewood Trophy.

1964 In his last full year of racing, he collected the Scott-Brown Memorial Trophy at Snetterton and 2nd in the Coppa Europa in a Ferrari 250LM. His Cooper Maserati drives resulted in a win at Goodwood, 2nd at Silverstone and 3rd at Brands Hatch and he finished 3rd in the Ilford Films Trophy at Brands Hatch in a Cobra Ford.

1965 His role as development driver for the King Cobra ended when the project was abandoned after one race at Silverstone, and he finished 2nd in his final race with Ronnie Hoare's Ford GT40 at Goodwood.

❖

ARCHIE SCOTT-BROWN
Born May 13th 1927
Killed May 19th 1958

A fairly short but eventful career for this brave Scot, who had to battle against officialdom to gain an International racing licence, due to having only a partly formed right arm. His one and only Grand Prix ended with retirement in a works Connaught at the 1956 British, but his name became almost inseparable with that of Lister sports cars. His bravery and talent won many admirers as he scored many wins in sports cars and single-seaters despite the physical handicap he suffered. Sadly, it was at the wheel of a Lister Jaguar that he was to lose his life, after crashing out on a damp track during a sports car race at Spa in May 1958.

GRAND PRIX RECORD	
Starts	1
Wins	0
Poles	0
Fastest laps	0
WC points	0
Best finish	DNF

1951 Began sprinting an MG TD, winning his class at Bottisham Speed Trial, a scratch race at Snetterton and 4th place in a handicap race at Silverstone for novice drivers.

1952 Another year with his MG brought two class wins and a 2nd at Bottisham, a class win at Cambridge Speed Trial, victory at Great Chishill Hillclimb, a win and two 2nds racing at Snetterton and 2nd place on the WECC Rally.

1953 A fairly mixed year marked his first acquaintance with Lister, bringing 5th overall and a class win in the British Grand Prix sports car race. He carried on campaigning his MG and also used a JAP-engined Tojeiro, taking two wins, a 2nd and a 3rd at Snetterton, 3rd overall and a class win at Thruxton, a class win at Silverstone and on the London Rally. The Tojeiro was also a class winner at a Prescott Hillclimb, while the MG clinched 3rd in class at Bottisham. Another 3rd in class at the Bedwell Hay sprint was achieved driving a Bugatti.

1954 Starting the year with an MG-powered Lister, he won at Fairwood, Silverstone and four times at Snetterton. He claimed 2nd in the Anerley Trophy at Crystal Palace, at Snetterton, Fairwood twice, three times at Oulton Park and Brands Hatch. He added 5th and 7th in the British Grand Prix support races and a 3rd in class at a Wethersfield sprint. He also drove a Lister Bristol to a win at Snetterton, victory and 2nd at Fairwood, 2nd at

Archie Scott-Brown (Connaught) at Goodwood, Easter 1957.

Photo: Ferret Fotographics.

Brands Hatch and Aintree and twice at Castle Combe. He was 5th in the Norbury Trophy at Crystal Palace and took 2nd in class at Brighton Speed Trials. He still had time to win the Cambridge driving test and his class on the Little Rally with his Ford Zephyr, take 3rd in the Gransden Sprint and win the ECMC Autocross in his MG.

1955 The Lister Bristol was taken to victory in the Empire Trophy at Oulton Park and also won the Norbury Trophy at Crystal Palace, Goodwood Easter sports, three sports car races at Snetterton and at Charterhall. He also won at Ibsley, the Wrotham Cup and Kingsdown Trophy at Brands Hatch, and took 2nd in the John Brown Trophy at Charterhall. Other results included 2nd in the Hundred Trophy, Curtis Trophy and 100 miler at Snetterton, at Crystal Palace and 3rd at both Snetterton and Charterhall. He shared a Connaught with Leston to 6th overall and a class win in the Goodwood 9 hours and won the Brands Hatch Air India Trophy in an F1 Connaught. A few races with a Jaguar C-Type collected a win and 2nd at Brands Hatch and a win and two 3rds at Snetterton. Elsewhere, a Peugeot 203 was taken to 2nd in class at Templesford Speed Trial.

1956 His one and only Grand Prix opportunity came with a works Connaught B-Type at the British, qualifying 10th and running well inside the top ten until the rear hub collapsed. He also drove the Connaught to 2nd in the Silverstone International Trophy and won a Formula 1 and three Libre races at Brands Hatch. With a Maserati-powered Lister he collected a win and 2nd at Brands Hatch, 4th overall and a class win at Aintree, 5th and a

class win in the Daily Herald Trophy. He also claimed 9th and a class win at the International Trophy and 13th with 2nd in class at the Empire Trophy. With an Elva sports he won at Brands Hatch and Silverstone, with a Lotus XI sports he was 2nd at Brands Hatch and Snetterton and 3rd at Aintree, and he took a Connaught sports to victory at Brands Hatch. In saloons he drove a DKW to two wins at Silverstone and a class win at the Cambridge Sprint. He was 4th in the Redex Trophy at Snetterton in an Aston Jaguar, had FTD and two class wins at a Snetterton Sprint with a Jaguar D-Type and XK140, and finished 76th in the Monte Carlo Rally with Jack Sears.

1957 A planned British Grand Prix drive failed to materialise when BRM withdrew the car. His Lister Jaguar again proved to be the car to beat, winning the Empire Trophy for a second time, along with the Goodwood Trophy. He also won at Crystal Palace, Aintree, Goodwood, took three victories at Snetterton, including the Vanwall Trophy, won the Kingsdown Trophy at Brands Hatch, and took 2nd places at Goodwood and Silverstone. The Elva was used again to take 2nd in the Norbury Trophy, plus four wins at Brands Hatch and a 3rd at Mallory Park. Other results included a Snetterton Libre victory in a Tojeiro, 8th in the Swedish Grand Prix with John Lawrence in a Jaguar D-Type and 3rd at Brands Hatch in a Lotus XI. Showing his versatility, he took 2nd in a 6 hour relay race at Silverstone in an Austin A35, a Snetterton sprint victory in the Lister Jaguar and victory again in the Cambridge University Auotmobile Club's driving test with his Zephyr.

1958 Starting the year in New Zealand he won the Lady Wigram Trophy and at Teretonga, was 2nd in Libre at Levin and 6th in Libre at Teretonga, all with his Lister Jaguar. On his return home he secured Libre and sports car wins at Snetterton, sports car wins at Mallory Park and Aintree, 2nd in the International Trophy sports car race and 3rd at the Empire Trophy. He shared a Lister Jaguar with Cunningham at the Sebring 12 hours, and took an F1 Connaught to 4th in the Aintree 200 and 6th in the Goodwood Glover Trophy. Tragically, only a few days after his 31st birthday, he crashed fatally at Spa in the Lister Jaguar.

A Pre-War winner at Donington Park who became better known Post War for his national successes in his ERA. Having been born in Dublin, his family moved to England when his father was shot dead in a Sinn Fein ambush in 1920. Having served with the royal artillery, he resumed racing after the war with the same ERA. He also drove works Aston Martins and the highlight of his career was being part of the fifth-placed team at Le Mans in 1951. However, he was seriously injured in an accident at Goodwood in 1951, rolling his ERA end over end. He broke his neck and was on the critical list for some time, but later made a full recovery although he never raced again.

BRIAN SHAWE-TAYLOR
Born January 29th 1915
Died May 1st 1999

GRAND PRIX RECORD	
Starts	2
Wins	0
Poles	0
Fastest laps	0
WC points	0
Best finish	8th

Brian Shawe-Taylor at Reims in 1951.

Photo: Ferret Fotographics.

1939 Won the Nuffield Trophy at Donington Park.

1948 Shared an ERA with Geoffrey Ansell at the British Grand Prix, the car retiring when Ansell rolled spectacularly.

1949 Took 5th in the Daily Graphic Trophy and 7th in the Chichester Cup at Goodwood, with his ERA, and retired a Maserati 4CL from the Silverstone International Trophy.

1950 With his entry for the British Grand Prix rejected, on the grounds that his ERA was too old, he took over Joe Fry's Maserati 4CL but failed to be classified. The ERA did however win and take a 2nd place at Castle Combe at the circuit's opening meeting. He added 3rd in the Richmond Trophy, 4th in the Empire Trophy and 5th in the Jersey Road Race, Silverstone International Trophy and Daily Graphic Trophy at Goodwood.

1951 He failed to get a start in the Thinwall Special at the French Grand Prix, when Parnell took over the car after qualifying. He did however make the start of the British Grand Prix, and after qualifying 12th, he brought his ERA home in 8th. The ERA also secured victory in the Daily Mail Trophy at Boreham, 2nd in the Richmond Trophy and Chichester Cup at Goodwood, 3rd in the Ulster Trophy, 4th in Goodwood Festival of Britain Trophy and 5th in the Prescott International Hillclimb. As part of the Aston Martin team he finished 5th at Le Mans with Abecassis and 7th in the TT. A one-off race with a new Connaught netted 2nd place in a Goodwood handicap. His final race was the Daily Graphic Trophy at Goodwood, where a serious accident ended his career.

❖

ALAN STACEY
Born August 29th 1933
Killed June 19th 1960

A Lotus driver for almost his entire career, Stacey earned a place in the Grand Prix team after a string of victories in the Lotus XI sports car. Reliability robbed him of finishes in all but one of his seven Grands Prix, but he continued to show his pace in sports car, despite having an artificial lower right leg. **His fairly short career came to a tragic end at the 1960 Belgian Grand Prix, when he was hit in the face by a bird, knocking him unconscious before his Lotus 18 crashed with fatal consequences.**

GRAND PRIX RECORD	
Starts	7
Wins	0
Poles	0
Fastest laps	0
WC points	0
Best finish	8th

1955 Began racing with a Lotus Mk6, taking two wins at Silverstone, plus 2nd in a handicap race, 2nd and a class win at Snetterton and 6th at Brands Hatch.

1956 Changing to a new Lotus XI he had three wins each at Silverstone and Goodwood as well as in the Snetterton Speed Trial. He also had a 2nd in a Brands Hatch handicap and at Snetterton, 4th in the Madgwick Cup at Goodwood, 4th and 6th at Brands Hatch, 4th at Crystal Palace and 5th in the August Trophy at the same circuit.

1957 Became part of the works Lotus XI team with Ashdown and Hall, winning the Madgwick Cup and a further race at Goodwood. He was 2nd at Snetterton and in his class at Aintree, 3rd in class at the International Trophy support race, along with Roskilde, Brands Hatch and twice at Crystal Palace, plus 3rd and 5th places at the Whit Goodwood meeting.

Alan Stacey.

Photo: BRDC Archive.

1958 His Grand Prix debut came at the British, qualifying his Lotus 16 in penultimate place and retiring with low oil pressure. Back in sports cars he won the Farningham and Rochester Trophies at Brands Hatch, the Crystal Palace Trophy, Oulton Park International and national events at Snetterton, Crystal Palace and three times at Brands Hatch. He had a 2nd in class at the International Trophy, 3rd at Rouen, and in the Chequered Flag Sports at Brands Hatch, 4th in class at the British Grand Prix, 17th in the TT and 20th at Le Mans. 3rd place in a Tojeiro was also achieved in the National Benzole Trophy race at Snetterton and he claimed 2nd in a Brands Hatch Libre race in the F2 Smith Climax.

1959 Two further Grand Prix outings in the Lotus 16 brought 8th place at British and retirement in the US. Driving the new XIV in sports cars, he had a win at Oulton Park, with 2nd in class and 13th overall at Rouen, 2nd overall and a class win at the British Grand Prix meeting, 3rd at Crystal Palace and the Farningham Trophy at Brands Hatch.

1960 Following Graham Hill's departure from Lotus, he became works number two driver behind Innes Ireland. He took 4th in the International Trophy and despite changing from the Lotus 16 to the new 18 Grand Prix car, was plagued with unreliability. After retiring in Argentina, Monaco and at the Dutch, he crashed fatally during the Belgian Grand Prix. Earlier in the year he had shared a Lotus Elite with John Wagstaff to take a class win in the Nurburgring 1000km.

Ian Stewart (Connaught).

IAN STEWART
Born July 15th 1929

As a founder member of Ecurie Ecosse it comes as no surprise that most of his successes came at the wheel of a Jaguar. 2nd place at the Nurburgring and 4th at Le Mans are probably the highlights of what he recalls as a very short career, which included one Grand Prix at the British in 1953 and victory in the last ever Jersey Road Race. After an accident at the 1954 Buenos Aires 1000km and his father's sudden death, he had to retire and concentrate on the family business in Scotland.

1949 Contested sprints and hillclimbs mainly in Scotland, with an MG TC and Jaguar SS100.

1950 After another year of speed events, his race debut came at Winfield in October, where his Healey Silverstone took 3rd in the sports car race and 4th in the Libre race.

GRAND PRIX RECORD	
Starts	1
Wins	0
Poles	0
Fastest laps	0
WC points	0
Best finish	DNF

50 years of British Grand Prix drivers

1951 A year of racing a Jaguar XK120 in Scotland, brought victories at Crimond, Turnberry and two at Winfield. He also took 4th in a Libre race at Crimond and 3rd in an F1 Invitation race at Winfield, but a single foray to Silverstone resulted in retirement.

1952 His Ecurie Ecosse Jaguar XK120 and C-Type proved successful further afield, with a victory in the last ever Jersey Road Race, and both the Frank O'Boyle and Wakefield Trophies at the Curragh. He also had two wins at Turnberry, four at Charterhall, two at Crimond and two at Castle Combe. He added 2nd at Castle Combe (twice), 3rd at Turnberry and Crimond, and 9th in the sports car race supporting the Silverstone International Trophy. He retired from both Le Mans and the Goodwood 9 hours in his C-Type and retired an HWM from a Libre race at Charterhall.

1953 A one and only Grand Prix opportunity came at the British, qualifying the Ecurie Ecosse Connaught A-Type in 20th, but retiring with engine failure. Three other outings with the car brought a win at Ibsley on his single-seater debut, 3rd in a Thruxton Libre race and retirement at Charterhall. Most of the year was spent concentrating on the Jaguar C-Type, sharing with Peter Whitehead to 3rd in the Goodwood 9 hours and 4th at Le Mans, and with Roy Salvadori to 2nd in the Nurburgring 1000km. He had wins at Ibsley, Charterhall and three at Snetterton, along with 2nd and 4th at Charterhall, 5th in the Leinster Trophy and British Grand Prix support race, and 9th at Silverstone. However, he retired from his last race of the year, the TT at Dundrod.

1954 His only race of the year was the Buenos Aires 1000km in January, when after crashing his C-Type he retired to concentrate on the family business.

❖

50 years of British Grand Prix drivers

Part One
1950s

CHAPTER 6

JIMMY STEWART
Born March 6th 1931

Jimmy, the elder brother of Jackie Stewart, made his mark in Scottish hillclimbs, before joining Ecurie Ecosse with whom he spent the rest of his fairly short career. He only graced the Grand Prix stage on one occasion and was running in 5th place at the 1953 British at Silverstone, until his Cooper Bristol spun off after hitting a deep puddle. He tasted sports car success with Ecosse Jaguars and Aston Martins, but after breaking his arm for a second time in 1955 at the Nurburgring, he retired from racing.

1950 Contested the hillclimbs at Bo'ness and Rest & be Thankful in his MG TC.

GRAND PRIX RECORD	
Starts	1
Wins	0
Poles	0
Fastest laps	0
WC points	0
Best finish	DNF

1951 Won his class at Bo'ness and finished 3rd at Rest & be Thankful, with a Healey Silverstone, while completing his National Service.

Jimmy Stewart (Jaguar C Type) at Goodwood in May 1954.

Photo: Ferret Fotographics.

1952 A class win at Bo'ness and 2nd in class at Rest & be Thankful were claimed in his Healey Silverstone.

1953 As part of the Ecurie Ecosse he had his first opportunity in Grand Prix racing, qualifying a Cooper Bristol in 15th and retiring from 6th place after spinning off at Copse. Further outings in the Cooper Bristol brought a win in the Goodwood Easter Handicap and 3rd at Charterhall. He also drove an F2 Connaught, tying for victory at Snetterton with Nuckey's Cooper Bristol. But it was with the C-Type Jaguar that the majority of his success was achieved, including wins at Thruxton and Oulton Park. He also took 2nd in class in the Mille Miglia, 3rd at Charterhall, Ibsley and Thruxton, 4th in the Goodwood 9 hours and Lyons Trophy at Snetterton, and 6th in the Empire Trophy, Nurburgring 1000km and British Grand Prix support race.

1954 Success continued with the Ecosse C-Type, with two wins each at Goodwood and Silverstone and one at Ibsley. He also took 2nd at Aintree, Goodwood, Ibsley and Castle Combe, 3rd at Aintree (twice), 4th at Silverstone and 6th in the Empire Trophy. He scored a 2nd in a Castle Combe Libre race with the F2 Connaught, but the season was cut short after he was thrown from an Aston Martin DB3S at Le Mans and broke his arm.

1955 After taking a MKVII Jaguar to 2nd in the Touring Car race at the Silverstone Intenational Trophy meeting, he crashed an Ecosse D-Type Jaguar at the Nurburgring and broke his arm again, but this time more seriously. He never raced again.

HENRY TAYLOR
Born December 16th 1932

An equally competent race or rally driver, Taylor served a successful apprenticeship in 500cc F3 before making his Grand Prix debut in the F2 class at the 1959 British. His Grand Prix career spanned two seasons, while during the first in 1960, he also raced in Formula Junior for Ken Tyrrell taking wins at Monaco and Albi. As his rally commitments began to outweigh the racing, he debuted the Cortina for Ford and later became its Competition Manager after retiring from the competitive side of the sport in 1965. He also drove the bobsleigh for the British Olympic team.

GRAND PRIX RECORD	
Starts	8
Wins	0
Poles	0
Fastest laps	0
WC points	3
Best finish	4th

1953 Took part in the London Rally driving a Morris Minor.

1954 Built an Austin 7 Special with Bob Anderson and won the Guy Fawkes Trial. Started racing at the end of the year with a Cooper Vincent and Cooper JAP, taking 2nd at Crystal Palace and 5th at Silverstone.

1955 Won both the JAP and Clubmans F3 Championships, with wins at Charterhall, Silverstone, Brands Hatch and Snetterton. Also took three 2nds and a 3rd at Brands Hatch, 2nd at Silverstone, 3rd at Oulton Park, a class win at Bushmead Speed Trials, 2nd in class at Prescott and Westbrook Hay Hillclimbs and 3rd in class at Stapleford Hillclimb.

1956 Won the JAP and Clubmans F3 Championships again, with 15 wins in total, including four each at Brands Hatch and Silverstone. He also had two 2nds and a 6th at Silverstone, 5th and 6th at Brands and 6th at Aintree. He added BTD at the CUAC Speed Trial, a class win at Prescott, a class win, 2nd and 3rd at Shelsley Walsh, 2nd overall and 2nd in class at Great Auclum, 2nd in class at Westbrook Hay and a class win at Brighton Speed Trials. He also drove a D-Type Jaguar to victory in a Silverstone handicap, with 2nd at Snetterton, a further 2nd, 3rd and 5th at Silverstone and 8th in the Daily Herald Trophy at Oulton Park.

1957 Continuing in F3 he had a win and 2nd at Mallory Park, with 4th at Brands Hatch, 5th at Goodwood and 2nd in class at Shelsley Walsh. He finished 3rd in the Belgian Sports GP and 3rd at Goodwood in his Jaguar D-Type and was 2nd in class with a Lotus in the International Trophy sports car race.

1958 Racing mainly in F2 with a Cooper T43, he won the Grand Prix de Paris and a Mallory Park Libre race, with 2nd in both the Vanwall Trophy and Libre at Snetterton, 5th in the French F2 Grand Prix and 6th in the Brands Hatch Kentish 100. Driving a Lotus Sports he took 7th at the International Trophy and 11th in the TT, and drove a Cooper Sports to 4th at Aintree.

1959 His Grand Prix debut came at the British, bringing a Parnell Cooper T51 home in 11th place, 2nd in the F2 class. He also won the feature race at the only meeting to be held at Whitchurch near Bristol, and finished in the Auvergne Trophy at Clermont Ferrand, took 6th at Pau and Reims, and 11th at Rouen. On home soil he tended to race an older T45, taking 2nd and 3rd in Mallory Park F2 races and 3rd and 4th in Libre. He finished 3rd in the

Henry Taylor (Lotus 18) at Silverstone in 1960.

London Trophy, 3rd in Snetterton F2 and 2nd in Libre, 6th in the John Davy Trophy at Brands Hatch and in the F2 section of the Aintree 200.

1960 Five Grand Prix appearances with a Yeoman Credit Cooper T51 brought 4th in the French, 7th in the Dutch, 8th in the British, 14th in the US and a non-start in Portugal after an accident in practice. At home he took the Cooper to 5th in the Brands Hatch Silver City Trophy and 7th in the Oulton Park Gold Cup. He also raced a Ferrari 250GT with Graham Whitehead, taking 5th in the Paris 1000km and retiring at Le Mans. He also won the British Empire Trophy in Formula Junior Lotus 18. There was also time to drive for Ken Tyrrell's works Cooper Austin Formula Junior team, collecting prestigious victories at Monaco and Albi, with 2nd at Oulton Park and Aintree, 4th at Goodwood and 4th in a Brands Hatch Libre race.

1961 He joined the UDT Laystall team for the Grand Prix season, but after failing to qualify his Lotus 18 in Monaco, he was unable to practice at the Belgian after Allison crashed their shared car. At the French he finished 10th and, after crashing in the rain at the British, he took 11th in Italy. He finished 2nd in the London and Lombank Trophies, 4th at the International Trophy, 6th in the Goodwood 100 and 8th in both the Silver City Trophy at Brands Hatch and the Oulton Park Gold Cup. He also raced the UDT Lotus 19 to sports car success with a win and three 3rds at Oulton Park, a class win at the International Trophy, a win and 2nd at Goodwood, two

2nds at Aintree and a win at Snetterton. On the Monte Carlo Rally he finished 26th overall for Ford.

1962 Rallied a Ford Anglia, finishing 6th on the RAC, 10th overall and 2nd in class on the Acropolis and 29th on the Monte Carlo.

1963 He gave the Ford Cortina its first rally in Monte Carlo, finishing 36th overall. He went on to finish 3rd overall on the Alpine, 4th on the Acropolis, 4th on the Marathon de la Route and 6th on the RAC. He also raced a Cortina to 2nd in the Marlboro 12 hours in the USA and 10th in the Brands Hatch 6 hours, sharing on both occasions with Jimmy Blumer.

1964 Won the team prize with Lotus Cortinas on the RAC rally. Finished 5th on the Tulip Rally and 77th on the Monte Carlo, followed by a win at a post Monte event at Prescott. He also raced a Lotus Cortina in the European Touring Car Championship, with 2nd at Karlskoga and in the Brands Hatch 6 hours, with 2nd in class at Zolder.

1965 Took 2nd with a class win on the Shell Rally of Canada, 3rd on the Alpine, 9th on the Monte Carlo and a class win on the Scottish for Ford.

MIKE TAYLOR
Born April 24th 1934

Mike Taylor.

A prolific sports car racer from the late fifties who graduated to F2 during the 1959 season. He made his Grand Prix debut in an Alan Brown-entered Cooper at the British and was due to have driven in the US until being struck down with jaundice. For the following year he bought a Lotus 18, but was seriously injured when the steering column broke during practice for the Belgian Grand Prix at Spa. He later successfully sued Lotus for damages over the loss of his career, as he never raced again. He did, however, return to the sport to contest the London-Sydney marathons of 1988 and 1974.

GRAND PRIX RECORD	
Starts	1
Wins	0
Poles	0
Fastest laps	0
WC points	0
Best finish	DNF

1958 Raced his own Lotus XI and won the Brooklands Trophy after four wins, a 2nd and a 3rd at Goodwood. He added two wins and two 2nds at Brands Hatch, two wins and a 3rd at Mallory Park, victory in the Benzole Trophy at Snetterton, 5th at Aintree and 10th in the TT. With his car's preparation in the hands of works Lotus driver Innes Ireland, he joined the works team at Le Mans.

1959 He made his Grand Prix debut in the F2 class of the British, retiring with broken transmission. Jaundice stopped him racing in the USGP, but he finished 4th in the German F2 race at Avus. He won the Grand Prix des Frontieres at Chimay in his Lotus XI and the F2 class of the Aintree 200 in a Tyrrell-entered Cooper. As a works Lola sports car driver he won the Danish Grand Prix at Roskilde, the Governors Trophy at Nassau, the Coupe de Paris at Montlhery, along with seven national victories and 3rd in the Chichester Cup and at Aintree. He also had a win at Snetterton with a Lotus XV.

1960 Debuted his new Lotus 18 with 17th at the International Trophy, before taking it to Spa for the Belgian Grand Prix. During practice his steering column broke, leaving him seriously injured in a meeting that later claimed the lives of Bristow and Stacey. He had also raced an Aston Martin DB4GT earlier in the season and took his Lotus XI to a victory at Snetterton, 2nd at Oulton Park and Aintree.

1968 Contested the London-Sydney Marathon with Innes Ireland and Andrew Hedges, winning the first to Bombay private entrants award. He also partnered Stirling Moss on the London Sahara, when their car broke down in the middle of the desert.

1974 Finished 3rd overall and won the team prize with Paddy Hopkirk on the London-Sydney Marathon.

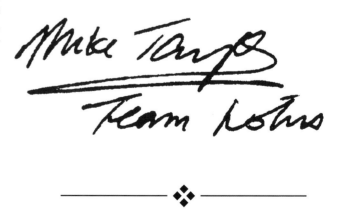

ERIC THOMPSON
Born November 4th 1919

A successful sports car racer who made relatively few appearances in single-seaters. One of them was a one-off Grand Prix outing with a works Connaught A-Type, which brought a remarkable 5th place at the British in 1952 after qualifying 9th. Although his job as a stockbroker rather restricted his racing career, he won the Goodwood nine hours, had a 2nd in the Tourist Trophy and 3rd at Le Mans as part of the Aston Martin team. He virtually retired from racing at the end of 1955.

GRAND PRIX RECORD	
Starts	1
Wins	0
Poles	0
Fastest laps	0
WC points	2
Best finish	5th

Eric Thompson.

1948 Made his race debut in the Paris 12 hours at Montlhery sharing Robin Richard's HRG, and finished 4th in class and 17th overall.

1949 Continuing to race an HRG he took a class win and 8th overall at Le Mans and a further class win at the Spa 24 hours, sharing on both occasions with Jack Fairman. He also won two Goodwood handicaps, had 11th overall and a class win at the Silverstone International Trophy sports car race and a 6th in class at a Prescott Hillclimb.

1950 He joined the Aston Martin sports car team and finished 4th in class and 14th overall at Silverstone in a one-hour production race, but retired a DB2 at Le Mans. Further races with an HRG resulted in 7th overall and a class win at Blandford, 3rd in a Goodwood handicap, and a class win and 3rd overall in the Cambridge University Sprint at Bedwell Hey. A rare outing in an F3 Cooper Vincent ended in retirement at Castle Combe.

1951 Sharing his Aston Martin DB2 with Lance Macklin, he collected a class win and 3rd overall at Le Mans and 3rd in class and 8th overall in the TT. As well as driving Rob Walker's ERA/Delage and Delahaye in Libre events, he took his Cooper Vincent to 5th in the Lavant Cup at Goodwood and drove a Bugatti T51 to 5th in a Libre race at Boreham.

1952 His one and only Grand Prix outing saw him take a works Connaught to an astonishing 5th place. He used the same car to take 6th at Charterhall, but crashed out of the Madgwick Cup at Goodwood. He shared his works Aston Martin with Reg Parnell, the pair retiring at Le Mans and ending the Goodwood 9 hours with a burnt out car. Driving Rob Walker's Aston Martin DB2 in national events, he was a winner in two Goodwood handicaps and at Snetterton, added a 7th and 8th at Snetterton and 3rd in class at the CUAC Bottisham Sprint. He took the ERA/Delage to two 2nds, 7th and 10th at Snetterton, and 3rd at Boreham and Castle Combe, drove the Delahaye to 5th in a Goodwood handicap and was 10th in the British Grand Prix Libre race in an ERA.

1953 As Parnell's partner at Aston Martin he won the Goodwood 9 hours and took 2nd in the TT, but retired at Le Mans again sharing with Dennis Poore in the DB3S. Further Connaught outings brought an F2 win and 2nd in Libre at Snetterton. He finished 2nd in a Thruxton sports car race and 6th in a Libre race with a DB3 and 5th in the Goodwood Easter Handicap in a DB2. He also retired a Riley from the 6 hour relay at Silverstone and had an outing in Stirling Moss's Cooper Alta at Snetterton.

1954 Apart from crashing out of Le Mans in a Lagonda, the season was mostly spent racing a DB2 Aston Martin on the national scene.

1955 He shared McAlpine's Connaught at Le Mans where they retired and managed 16th at the Goodwood 9 hours despite pushing the car to the finish. He went into virtual retirement at the end of the year.

1956 Finished 2nd in class at the CUAC Speed Trials with a 498cc Jason.

❖

LESLIE THORNE
Born June 23rd 1916
Died July 13th 1993

An occasional hillclimber who started competing before the war. After the war, it was not until 1953 that he returned to competition. He had only brief circuit racing experience when he joined Ecurie Ecosse to race an F2 Connaught A-Type. After barely a handful of outings he made his solitary Grand Prix appearance at the 1954 British Grand Prix, finishing 14th on the road but unclassified. He disappeared from the racing scene after a couple of races in 1955.

GRAND PRIX RECORD	
Starts	1
Wins	0
Poles	0
Fastest laps	0
WC points	0
Best finish	NC (14th)

1936-38 Made occasional appearances in hillclimbs and speed trials. Finished 2nd overall and took a class win at Bo'ness Hillclimb in his Alexandra Special.

1953 Raced an F3 Cooper, and finished 3rd in his heat at the inaugural Oulton Park meeting, followed by another 3rd place at the same circuit later in the year. He also took the car to a 2nd and 3rd in class at Bo'ness Hillclimb and a class win at Rest & be Thankful.

1954 He qualified the Ecurie Ecosse Connaught in 23rd place for his only Grand Prix outing in the British, but failed to be classified as a finisher as he was 12 laps behind. He also raced a Cooper Bristol, retiring from the International Trophy, taking 6th at the Chichester Cup at Goodwood. Back in the Connaught he was 6th at Goodwood, 7th at Aintree, 7th and 9th at Oulton Park.

1955 Apart from the occasional non-productive outing in the Connaught, his career virtually ended.

DESMOND TITTERINGTON
Born May 1st 1928

A truly talented all-rounder who was also a school friend of Archie Scott-Brown. His single-seater experience was fairly limited, but apart from debuting the Vanwall with 3rd place at the 1955 Oulton Park Gold Cup, he took 3rd at the 1956 International Trophy at Silverstone. That result was achieved driving the Connaught that gave him his only taste of Grand Prix racing during the British of the same year. He raced works Mercedes sports cars and Jaguars but turned down the chance to race for Ferrari. Although he retired at the end of 1956 to concentrate on his business, he made occasional appearances in rallies and trials into the early sixties.

1950 Started trialling and hillclimbing in a J2 MG.

1951 He raced a Fiat Balilla to 2nd at Phoenix Park and 3rd in the Champion Trophy at Dundrod, a Sunbeam MG to 3rd at Newtonards, an Allard to 6th in the Wakefield Trophy, and shared an MG TD to 3rd in class on the Alpine Rally with Ernie McMillen.

1952 A full year with the Allard brought home the Leinster Trophy at Wicklow, 5th place at Phoenix Park and 15th in the Champion Trophy at Dundrod, along with record breaking performances on both Bo'ness and Rest & be Thankful hills.

1953 Started the year with the Allard again, he won the Phoenix Park Handicap. He finished 2nd at Kirkistown, 5th in the Wakefield Trophy, 6th in the O'Boyle Trophy, 9th in the Champion Trophy and 18th in the Empire Trophy. He won his class twice at Craigantlet Hillclimb, as well as Bo'ness and Rest & be Thankful, and took FTD at Knockagh. After sharing Bobby Dickson's Aston Martin DB3 to 6th in the TT, David Murray issued an invitation to join Ecurie Ecosse, resulting in 4th on his debut at Snetterton. He also drove a Frazer Nash to 2nd and 4th at Charterhall and won the Connacht Winter Trial in a Dellow.

1954 6th place on the Monte Carlo Rally with Ronnie Adams and Jaguar got the year off to a good start. With his own Triumph TR2 he won the Goodwood Sports Whitsun Handicap and the Baird Trophy at Kirkistown, was 8th at Phoenix Park, took a class win at Carncastle Hillclimb and finished 2nd overall on the Circuit of Ireland. His successful outings in a Jaguar C-Type netted a win, 3rd and 4th at Snetterton, victory at Oulton Park, 4th at Goodwood and 6th in the British Grand Prix support race. After sharing Joe Kelly's Ferrari in the TT, he was invited to be part of the works Jaguar team for the following year. He was a regular sprinter and trialist, winning both the Knock and UAC final trials.

1955 Jaguar drives for both the works team and as deputy for Jimmy Stewart at Ecurie Ecosse, brought wins in the Newcastle Journal Trophy at Charterhall, the Ulster Trophy at Dundrod and at Snetterton. He finished 2nd in the BARC 9 hours with Ninian Sanderson, in the John Brown Trophy at Charterhall and atAintree, 3rd in a Snetterton Libre race and 9th with a class win at the Leinster Trophy. He led the TT with Hawthorn until retiring, which prompted Mercedes to offer a drive on the Targa Florio. Having turned down a similar offer from Ferrari, he shared his Mercedes with John Fitch to a remarkable 4th place. His other drives included giving the Vanwall its debut with a 3rd place at the Oulton Park Cup on his own single-seater debut. He also took 3rd in the saloon car race at the International Trophy in a Jaguar MKVII, 2nd again on the Circuit of Ireland sharing his TR2 with wife Paddy, and became Victor Ferguson Memorial UAC Trials Champion.

1956 Further single-seater outings with a works Connaught included his one and only Grand Prix start at the British, qualifying 11th but retiring when a cam rod broke and destroyed the engine. He was also 3rd in the International Trophy, but retired at Syracuse. With Jaguar he secured a win at Goodwood, two 2nds at Aintree, 3rd in the British Grand Prix support race and at Reims where

GRAND PRIX RECORD

Starts	1
Wins	0
Poles	0
Fastest laps	0
WC points	0
Best finish	DNF

Peter Walker (left) with Raymond Mays.
Photo: BRDC Archive.

he shared with Fairman, plus 7th at Rouen. He shared an XK140 with Hawthorn and Cunningham at Sebring until it ran out of brakes, took 2nd on the Circuit of Ireland once more and 2nd on the UAC Night Trial in a McCandless. He decided to retire at the peak of his form to concentrate on business commitments.

1958 Finished 3rd in class with a TR3 on the Alpine Rally, and shared a Ford Zephyr with Adams and McMillen to 43rd on the Monte Carlo Rally.

1963 Won the Armagh Sporting Trial in an Alexis.

1964 Won the Irish Experts and Carlig Lead Mines Trials, plus 2nd at Slieve Croob in his Alexis.

1966 Finished 5th in the Armagh Christmas Trial with his Alexis.

--- ❖ ---

PETER WALKER
Born December 7th 1912
Died March 1st 1984

Already well established in the thirties thanks to success at Brooklands and Donington Park, he soon returned to his winning ways when racing recommenced after the war years. Although a successful single-seater racer, his reputation in sports car racing overshadowed his four Grand Prix starts. He won Le Mans for Jaguar in 1951 with Peter Whitehead and also scored two wins in the Goodwood 9 hours. He retired from racing after an accident at Le Mans in 1956.

1935 Started racing with Peter Whitehead's Alta.

1936 Took 3rd place in the Donington Park Grand Prix, sharing Whitehead's ERA and scored two victories on the Brooklands Mountain Circuit. He also took a 2nd in the Brooklands Mountain Handicap and Donington scratch race in the ERA, plus a 2nd in class at a Shelsley Walsh Hillclimb in an Alta.

1937 Concentrated on racing the ERA and finished 2nd in the Siam Challenge Trophy at Brooklands, 3rd in the Empire Trophy, the Donington Coronation Handicap and Campbell Handicap at Brooklands and 5th in the RAC International Race on the Isle of Man.

1947 Began racing again with the ERA.

1948 Failed to finish the British Grand Prix and Empire Trophy in his ERA, but took 2nd in the Supercharged Race at the inaugural Goodwood meeting and 8th in the Goodwood Trophy. Also claimed FTD at Prescott Hillclimb and a class win at Shelsley Walsh.

1949 Continued to race Whitehead's ERA and the newer E-Type, retired from the British Grand Prix, took second places at Goodwood (twice) as well as in the Woodcote Cup and Daily Graphic Trophy at the same circuit. There was also a 3rd in a Goodwood handicap, 5th in the Empire Trophy, and hillclimb success with 2nd overall and two class wins at Prescott, 2nd in class at Shelsley Walsh, 3rd at Rest and be Thankful and 2nd overall at Craigantlet. A class win was taken at the Luton Hoo Speed Trials and on the debut of the Jaguar XK120, he secured 2nd place at Silverstone.

1950 Retired from the British Grand Prix after sharing an ERA with Tony Rolt, and retired his works BRM V16 from the International Trophy and Penya Rhin Grand Prix. There was however success with Jaguar, with victory and 3rd at Silverstone and 2nd in class at Shelsley Walsh in the XK120.

1951 His one Grand Prix outing in the BRM V16 resulted in 7th at the British, but the season was

GRAND PRIX RECORD

Starts	4
Wins	0
Poles	0
Fastest laps	0
WC points	0
Best finish	7th

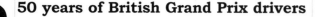

highlighted by victory for Jaguar at Le Mans with Peter Whitehead in the C-Type. Other results included 2nd in the TT and 15th in the International Trophy Production Race, along with 8th in the Ulster Trophy with Rob Walker's ERA Delage.

1952 Once again he was part of the works Jaguar team, taking 5th in the Goodwood 9 hours with Moss in a C-Type, 7th in the International Trophy sports car race, plus class wins and records at Prescott and Shelsley Walsh Hillclimbs. He also raced a Cooper ERA to 2nd in a Castle Combe Libre race and at the Brighton Speed Trials, took 4th at Charterhall and drove a Ferrari to 4th in the Monza Grand Prix.

1953 Continuing success came with Jaguar including victory in the Goodwood 9 hours, 2nd at Le Mans and 4th in the TT with Moss, 5th in the International Trophy Sports and two class wins at Prescott Hillclimbs. The Cooper ERA was taken to 2nd place in a Thruxton Libre race and there was a 2nd in class at Prescott and 3rd at the Brighton Speed Trials with a Connaught.

1954 Finished 3rd in the International Trophy Sports and 4th at Aintree in his Jaguar, but only managed 18th in the TT and retired from Le Mans sharing his D-Type with Moss. The Cooper ERA was taken to 3rd in class at Brighton and an ERA to 4th in class at Prescott.

1955 After retiring Moss's Maserati 250F in the Dutch Grand Prix, he made his final Grand Prix start at the British, retiring a Rob Walker-entered Connaught after sharing with Rolt. The Connaught did win a Libre race at Snetterton, but it was Aston Martin which was now bringing sporting success. Took victory in the Goodwood 9 hours and 4th in the TT with Dennis Poore, 5th at the British Grand Prix meeting and 7th in the International Trophy sports car race with a DB3S, but retired from Le Mans.

1956 After retiring his Aston Martin from the Nurburgring 1000km, an accident at Le Mans gave him concussion and prompted retirement from the sport.

1957 A one-off comeback at Syracuse ended in retirement with Rob Walker's Connaught.

KEN WHARTON
Born March 21st 1916
Killed January 12th 1957

A four times British Hillclimb champion, multiple RAC Trials champion, rally winner and race winner in single-seaters, sports and saloon cars. Never a Grand Prix winner, but unquestionably one of the greatest all-rounders in the history of the sport. Wharton topped his Grand Prix career by taking a Frazer Nash to fourth in the 1952 Swiss. He continued to excel in all forms of motorsport until losing his life early in 1957, when he crashed his Ferrari during a sports car race at Ardmore in New Zealand.

1935 Finished 3rd in an up to 850cc race at Donington Park in an Austin.

GRAND PRIX RECORD	
Starts	15
Wins	0
Poles	0
Fastest laps	0
WC points	3
Best finish	4th

1936 Won his class at the Madresfield Speed Trial and took a 3rd and 4th at Donington Park in his Austin Seven.

1947 Trials wins came in the Gloucester, Clee, Full Moon, Roy Fedden, Colmore and Lawrence Cup, as well as an award on the West of England Spring Trial. He won the Blackpool Rally and took 1st and 3rd in class in the Southsea Speed Trial and 2nd in class at Brighton and Shelsley Walsh.

1948 Became the RAC Trials champion with victories on the Hagley, High Peak, MCC, SUNBAC Whittington Cup and Gloucester Trials. He took a Ford Anglia to 2nd place in the Lisbon Rally and with his Wharton Special and MG he took 8th overall and 2nd in class at Shelsley Walsh hillclimb, 12th overall, a class win and 3rd at Prescott, and victory in the Burghfield Common Speed Trials. He also had time to race in F3.

1949 He retained his RAC Trials title, with wins on the Coventry, Plymouth and Hagley Winter Trials and 2nd on the Roy Fedden and Colmore. With his V8 Ford Pilot he won the Tulip Rally, took 2nd in Lisbon and 5th in Monte Carlo. He also took the Pilot to 2nd in class at Lydstep Hillclimb and took a 3rd in class at Shelsley Walsh in the Wharton Special.

1950 RAC Trials champion for the third successive year winning the Clee and Hagley Trials, and he also won the Lisbon and Tulip Rallies in his Pilot. His F3 outings brought success with 3rd at Zandvoort and the Ostend Coupe du Monde, 5th at Goodwood, 6th at the Silverstone International Trophy and a victory at Castle Combe. He won hillclimbs at Bo'ness, Bouley Bay and Lydstep in his Cooper JAP, and was 2nd at Rest and be Thankful, 3rd at Shelsley Walsh and 4th at Prescott 4th in a Cooper sports and 5th in a Kieft at Lydstep and 3rd at Shelsley Walsh in an ERA. He also raced an Austin A90 in production races.

1951 Won his first British Hillclimb Championship, driving a Cooper JAP, ERA and Kieft. He won at Bouley Bay, three times at Shelsley Walsh, twice at Bo'ness, Prescott and Lydstep, plus 2nd at Bo'ness, 2nd, 4th and 9th at Shelsley Walsh, 2nd and 3rd at Rest and be Thankful and numerous class wins. He won the Snetterton Speed Trials in his ERA and journeyed overseas to win the Freiburg Hillclimb in his ERA, the Vue

Ken Wharton (ERA) at Shelsley Walsh, June 1954.

Photo: BRDC Archive.

des Alpes and take 3rd at Susa-Mont Cenis. He finished 6th on both the Lisbon and Monte Carlo Rallies for Ford. On the race circuits he won at Castle Combe, took 2nd in the British Grand Prix F3 race and 3rd in Genoa with his Cooper and took his ERA to victory at Castle Combe, with 2nd at Winfield and 6th in the Daily Graphic Trophy at Goodwood.

1952 His Grand Prix debut came in the Swiss, where he qualified his Frazer Nash in 13th place and finished 4th. After retiring the Frazer Nash in the Belgian and Dutch, he changed to a Cooper Bristol for the Italian and finished 9th. There were a number of outings in the BRM V16 throughout the season which brought 2nd at Charterhall and 3rd in the Daily Graphic Trophy at Goodwood. The Cooper Bristol was taken to 2nd at Castle Combe in F2 and 3rd in Libre and the Frazer Nash collected 2nd in the Jersey Road Race, 3rd in the Eifelrennen and Goodwood International sports car race and 7th in the Silverstone International Trophy meeting. He also retained his British Hillclimb title with the ERA and Cooper JAP, winning at Bouley Bay, Bo'ness, Craigantlet, Prescott, Rest and be Thankful and Shelsley Walsh, with either 2nd, 3rd or class wins at most events. He also found time to win the Tulip Rally again in his Ford Consul.

1953 Five Grand Prix outings with his Cooper, resulted in 7th at the Swiss and 8th at the British. But he took the car to victory in the Daily Record Trophy, Newcastle

Journal Trophy and F2 at Charterhall, the Richmond Trophy at Goodwood and a Snetterton Libre race. He added 2nd in the Coronation Trophy at Crystal Palace and Ulster Trophy at Dundrod, 3rd in a Goodwood handicap and at Castle Combe, 4th in the Madgwick Cup, 5th in the Silverstone International Trophy and 6th at Cadours. Regular outings in the V16 BRM were rewarded with victories in the Glover Trophy at Goodwood, the Hastings Trophy and Libre race at Castle Combe, the Snetterton Invitation and USAF Trophy and Charterhall Libre. He was also 2nd in the Chichester Cup and Goodwood Trophy, 3rd in the British Grand Prix Libre race, Woodcote Cup, Bordeaux Grand Prix and Charterhall Libre. At Le Mans he collected a class win and 13th overall in his Frazer Nash. He also took 2nd in the Empire Trophy, 3rd in the TT, 2nd in the Isle of Man and Goodwood sports car race. For the third successive year he won the British Hillclimb title, winning at Bouley Bay, Craigantlet, Prescott and twice at Shelsley Walsh, took 2nd and 3rd at Bo'ness and 2nd at Prescott and Shelsley Walsh. The ERA was taken to the Vue des Alpes and finished 3rd and he helped England win a TV Hillclimb match race at Bo'ness. He also raced a Kieft Bristol sports car to 4th at Castle Combe.

1954 The Owen Organisation Maserati 250F was used for his five Grand Prix appearances, with a best result of 6th in the Swiss from three classified finishes. He continued to shine with the V16 BRM in Libre events and won the Chichester Cup and Glover Trophy, with 2nd in

Ken Wharton (BRM) at Goodwood, September 1953.

Photo: BRDC Archive.

the Woodcote Cup, 3rd at Lady Wigram Trophy and New Zealand GP and 4th in the Goodwood Whitsun Trophy. In long distance sports car races he shared a Jaguar with Peter Whitehead to take victory in the Reims 12 hours and 5th in the TT, he raced a Lister in the Empire Trophy and took his Frazer Nash to 3rd in a sports car race at Aintree. For the fourth successive year he was British Hillclimb Champion with three wins at Shelsley Walsh, plus Bouley Bay, Craigantlet, and Bo'ness, and 2nd at Craigantlet, Bo'ness and twice at Shelsley Walsh. He won the Brighton Speed Trials in his ERA and ventured overseas once more to win the Col Bayard Hillclimb and take a class win on the Rheineck-Walzenhausen-Lachen.

1955 As a member of the Vanwall team he crashed and burnt his arms and neck at the Silverstone International Trophy but made his Grand Prix debut for the team at the British. The car was taken over by Harry Schell and finished many laps adrift. He also ventured to the Italian Grand Prix in what was to be his last World Championship outing, which ended in retirement. He did however race the car to 2nd place at Snetterton. His sports car outings resulted in 2nd place at the Goodwood 9 hours with Sanderson in a Jaguar and 11th in the Empire Trophy with an Aston Martin. On the hills he had a win, two 2nds and a 3rd at Shelsley Walsh, a win and 4th at Bouley Bay, victory at Craigantlet and the Brighton Speed Trials in his ERA. He rallied a Daimler to 22nd place in Monte Carlo and 2nd in class in Sestriere and

took a Ford Zephyr to 4th overall and a class win in a Silverstone saloons race and an Austin Westminster to 2nd in the Sporting Life Trophy at Oulton Park.

1956 A very mixed year in which he finished 3rd in the Australian TT with a Ferrari Monza, 6th at Aintree in a Maserati sports, 7th at the Bari sports GP in his Ferrari and 10th in the Empire Trophy in an Alfa Romeo. He finished 56th overall and 4th in class on the Monte Carlo Rally with his Austin and was 5th with a Cooper in the Oulton Park Gold Cup, winning the supporting saloon car race with his Zephyr. 2nd overall and a class win were claimed in Silverstone saloon races in an Austin A95 and for the second successive year he won the Brighton Speed Trial but on this occasion in his Cooper. Further victories came from the hills, at Shelsley Walsh, Prescott and for the seventh consecutive year Bouley Bay. He had a 2nd and 3rd at Shelsley Walsh, two 3rds and a 4th at Prescott, 3rd at Rest and be Thankful and won the Staverton Speed Trial in his ERA.

1957 Only weeks into the new year he crashed his Ferrari Monza fatally during a New Zealand sports car race at Ardmore.

GRAHAM WHITEHEAD
Born April 15th 1922
Died January 15th 1981

A successful sports car racer in Jaguars, Aston Martins and Ferrari, Whitehead often sharing in many of the classic long distance races with his half-brother Peter. Basically a national single-seater racer, he made his only Grand Prix appearance in the 1952 British driving Peter's Alta. His most creditable result came at Le Mans in 1958, when he shared an Aston Martin DB3S to 2nd place with Peter. Later the same year they were contesting the Tour de France, when they crashed off the road and Peter was killed. He returned to racing in 1959 and enjoyed more success before retiring at the end of 1961.

1949 Drove an ERA and retired from the International Trophy at Silverstone.

1950 Continued racing the ERA and finished 2nd at Castle Combe, 4th in the Richmond Trophy, 6th in the Daily Graphic Trophy and 10th in the Chichester Cup at Goodwood.

1951 Although he had outings in an Alta, his results were mainly claimed in the ERA. They included 2nd in the Daily Mirror Trophy at Boreham, 3rd in the Winfield Libre, Kenning Trophy at Gamston, and International Trophy at Silverstone, and 10th in the Chichester Cup at Goodwood.

1952 His only Grand Prix outing netted 12th place after qualifying 12th at the British, in Peter's Alta. Continued success with the ERA resulted in two 2nd places at

GRAND PRIX RECORD	
Starts	1
Wins	0
Poles	0
Fastest laps	0
WC points	0
Best finish	12th

Boreham, 2nd at Ibsley, 3rd in the Scottish Daily Express Trophy Turnberry, Goodwood September Handicap, 4th in the Sussex International Trophy and 8th in the Libre race at the British Grand Prix. He also raced a Ferrari 500 to 3rd at Charterhall, 4th at Castle Combe and 5th and 6th at Goodwood; and a Ferrari sports in which he finished 2nd in the Goodwood 9 hours.

1953 The ERA was raced on the domestic scene with wins at Crystal Palace and Goodwood, 2nd in the Seaman Trophy, 4th at the Goodwood Trophy and Snetterton Libre and 6th in the British Grand Prix Libre race. He had his first taste of sports car racing with an Aston Martin DB3 in which he was 5th at Caen, Roubaix and in the TT, 3rd at Castle Combe, 5th at Goodwood, in the Casablanca 12 hours and 7th in the British Grand Prix sports car race. He drove a Cooper Bristol to 6th in the Coronation Trophy at Crystal Palace, took 6th in the International Trophy sports at Silverstone in a Jaguar and was lying 3rd in the Goodwood 9 hours until his HWM retired. The ERA was also taken to the Bordeaux GP and finished 6th.

Graham Whitehead (Aston Martin) at Silverstone, May 1958.
Photo: BRDC Archive.

1954 Further outings with his Aston Martin brought 5th in the Supercorte-maggiore, 6th in the Penya Rhin GP, 12th in the International Trophy sports at Silverstone and 13th in the TT. He also finished 95th in the Monte Carlo Rally with Peter Collins. He shared an HWM to 7th at Reims with Tony Gaze, and had two wins at Castle Combe and 4th at Ibsley in his ERA.

1955 Concentrating on the Aston Martin once more, he finished 10th in the Lisbon GP, 12th in the Empire Trophy and 5th in the Kingsland Trophy at Brands. He also finished 95th again in the Monte Carlo Rally. He raced a Lister sports car at home and abroad, winning the Whitsun

Trophy at Goodwood and took 2nd in class at Castle Combe racing an F2 Connaught.

1956 Victory at Goodwood, 2nd at Brands Hatch, 3rd at Chimay, 7th in the Daily Herald Trophy at Oulton Park and a class win in a Brands Hatch sprint were taken in his Aston Martin. Racing a Jaguar D-Type with Peter they claimed 4th in the Swedish GP and 5th at Dakar.

1957 Racing almost exclusively in his Aston Martin DB3S, he had a win, 2nd and 3rd at Silverstone. He added 2nd at Crystal Palace, 3rd in the Kingsdown Trophy at Brands Hatch, 4th in the Empire Trophy and Forez 6 hours at St.Etienne, 6th at Goodwood, 6th and 9th at Spa and 9th in the Nurburgring 1000km.

1958 Another year with the DB3S saw a further improvement in results, with 2nd at Le Mans, 2nd in class at the International Trophy, victory and 3rd at Silverstone, 3rd at Crystal Palace, 4th in the Sussex Trophy, 5th at Kristianstad and 6th in the Nurburgring 1000km. Tragedy struck however on the Tour de France, claiming the life of brother and co-driver Peter. The occasional outing in a Lister Jaguar resulted in a victory at the Goodwood Whit meeting.

1959 Still bearing allegiance to Aston Martin, he raced a DBR1 to 3rd in the Goodwood 100 and 5th at Aintree and the Silverstone International Trophy sports car race.

1960 Changing to a Ferrari 250GT he won the Taca Cida de Luanda, took 3rd in the Angola GP, 5th in the Paris 1000km and TT, and drove a Lola sports to a class win at Rouen.

1961 Continuing with his Ferrari he had a 2nd at Snetterton, 3rd in the Norbury Trophy at Crystal Palace, 3rd at Spa, 4th in the Fordwater GT at Goodwood, the Coupe de Mare Deboutteville and at Silverstone, before retiring at the end of the year.

PETER WHITEHEAD
Born November 12th 1914
Killed September 21st 1958

Whitehead was one of the first British drivers to travel the world in pursuit of his motor racing passion. His Pre War wins included the Australian Grand Prix at Bathurst, and during the early fifties there was victory at Le Mans in 1951 in a C Type Jaguar and a double victory in the Reims 12 hours. His Grand Prix career was highlighted by third place on his debut in the 1950 French race but it was in sports car racing that this successful businessman really excelled.

He regularly entered cars for other drivers, notably Peter Walker and his own half-brother Graham, and it was with Graham that he met his death, when their Jaguar crashed down a ravine during the 1958 Tour de France. A couple of months earlier they had finished second at Le Mans in an Aston Martin DB3S.

1934 Started racing in a Riley Nine.

1935 Graduated to an Alta and won the Dancers End Hillclimb, took 3rd in the Limerick Street Race, 2nd at a Shelsley Walsh Hillclimb and a class win at Prescott.

GRAND PRIX RECORD	
Starts	10
Wins	0
Poles	0
Fastest laps	0
WC points	4
Best finish	3rd

1936 After sharing his ERA with Peter Walker to 3rd in the Donington Park Grand Prix, he secured 3rd in the Nuffield Trophy and Donington Handicap, 7th in the Limerick Grand Prix and 3rd in class at Shelsley Walsh. He also took a class win at Syston Park Speed Trials in an MG.

1937 Continued to gain success with his ERA, 3rd in the JCC200 at Donington, 3rd in the Brooklands 200 and Easter Mountain Handicap, 5th in the RAC International on the Isle of Man and 8th on the Circuit of Milan. He retired from the Donington Grand Prix.

1938 A trip to Bathurst with his ERA was rewarded with victory in the Australian Grand Prix.

1939 Finished 3rd in the Nuffield Trophy in his ERA.

1946 Raced his ERA at Gransden Lodge, GP de Nations in Geneva and retired the E-Type version in Turin. He did, however, record a victory at the Prescott Hillclimb.

1947 2nd place in the Empire Trophy and 6th in the Supercharged Race at the inaugural Goodwood meeting highlighted another year with his ERAs.

1948 Forced to take a year out after an air crash at Croydon Aerodrome on his way to Italy, to buy a Ferrari.

1949 Now at the wheel of his Ferrari 125, he tasted victory in the Czech Grand Prix and 3rd in the French Grand Prix after being robbed of victory by gearbox maladies. He finished 7th in the Jersey Road Race, 8th in the British Grand Prix sharing with Dudley Folland, 9th in the Swiss Grand Prix and 10th in Lausanne. He continued to race his ERAs, with 2nd in the Richmond Trophy, 5th in the Chichester Cup, 9th in the Goodwood Easter Handicap and 10th overall with 5th in class at Prescott.

1950 Having missed the Monaco Grand Prix after three engine failures during practice, his World Championship debut came in the French Grand Prix, where his Ferrari 125 finished 3rd. One further outing brought 9th place in the Italian, but nearer to home there were victories in the Jersey Road Race and Ulster Trophy, as well as 3rd in the Silverstone International Trophy. Other results included 3rd with the ERA in a Godwood handicap, plus 2nd in the TT and 15th at Le Mans in a Jaguar XK120.

1951 Although there were four Grand Prix starts, there was only one finish. His works Ferrari 125 crashed out of

Peter Whitehead (Ferrari) in the Silverstone International Trophy, August 1950.
Photo: BRDC Archive.

the Swiss, while his own car had headgasket failure in the French and engine failure in the Italian. But driving the Vandervell Thinwall Ferrari he came home 9th in the British. The Ferrari was taken around the world and won at Erlen, took 2nd at the Colombian Grand Prix, 2nd in Genoa, 3rd at Rouen and Bordeaux, 5th at Bari and Pescara and 6th at Monza. The ERA continued to make occasional outings and took a 2nd and two 3rds at Castle Combe. The highlight of the year however was his Le Mans victory with Walker in the Jaguar C-Type.

1952 Clutch failure on his Alta caused retirement in the French Grand Prix, but a return to his Ferrari brought 10th in the British. The car was also taken to the Italian, where he failed to qualify. He took 2nd place at an Oulton Park F2 race with a Cooper Alta, and 4th at Comminges. The Ferrari proved more successful, with 4th in Turin, 5th at Syracuse, Albi and in the Silverstone International Trophy and 6th at Boreham.

1953 His only Grand Pix of the year resulted in 9th place in the British with a Cooper Alta, in a season that brought victories in the Reims and Hyeres 12 hours in a Jaguar C-Type. The Jaguar also finished 3rd in the Goodwood 9 hours, 4th at Le Mans and 6th in the Portuguese Grand Prix. Further outings in the Cooper Alta resulted in 2nd place in the Goodwood Easter Handicap, Snetterton and Oulton Park F2, 3rd in the Coronation Trophy at Crystal Palace and Snetterton Libre, 4th in the Ulster Trophy, 5th at Albi, Syracuse and in the Crystal Palace Trophy. Debuting a Cooper Jaguar sports car he secured 9th at the International Trophy, before winning at Snetterton, and he took 7th in the British Grand Prix sports car race with an Aston Martin,

which he later shared with Graham to take 5th in the Casablanca 12 hours.

1954 His final Grand Prix ended with engine failure in his Cooper Alta at the British, but it finished 5th in the Glover Trophy. The Cooper Jaguar was used to take victory at Snetterton and in the Wakefield Trophy, along with 3rd in the Oporto Grand Prix, 4th in the O'Boyle Trophy and 9th in the International Trophy sports car race. Sharing with Ken Wharton he won the Reims 12 hours again and took 5th in the TT for Jaguar. He took 3rd in the Coupe Du Salon at Montlhery in an HWM Jaguar and 4th in an Oulton Park Libre race with his Ferrari, which also won the Lady Wigram Trophy in New Zealand.

1955 The Ferrari gained further success in New Zealand, with 2nd place in the Grand Prix, but most of the year was spent racing the Cooper Jaguar. He took 4th in the Portuguese Grand Prix, 5th at Aintree and 14th in the Oulton Park Daily Herald Trophy, as well as taking the fastest sports car time at Brighton Speed Trials. The car was also shared with Graham in the TT until the chassis broke.

1956 Further trips to Australia and New Zealand proved successful, with another victory in the Lady Wigram Trophy driving the Ferrari. He took 3rd in the Australian and New Zealand Grand Prix, 4th in Dunedin and victory in the Bryson Industrial Cup at Melbourne with a Ferrari Super Squalo. There was also 6th place in the Australian TT and 2nd with the Cooper Jaguar at Ardmore, as well as a trip to Africa where he won the Central African International Trophy in Rhodesia. He added wins at Limpopo and Kafue in his Ferrari. Nearer to home he shared a Jaguar with Graham to 4th in the Swedish Grand Prix and took his Aston Martin to 3rd at Chimay. He drove a Maserati to 3rd in the Double 12 Trophy at Snetterton, a class win in the Leinster Trophy and 11th in the International Trophy Sports.

1957 Continued with his Super Squalo winning his third Lady Wigram Trophy, won at Invercargill, and took 2nd in the New Zealand Grand Prix and 3rd in Dunedin. His Aston Martin DB3S also brought success with 2nd and 3rd at Snetterton, 7th and 8th at Spa, 8th in the Forez 6 hours and 9th in the Nurburgring 1000km. He also took a class victory with a Lister in the Leinster Trophy and retired his Jaguar XK150 in the Tour de France, sharing with Graham.

1958 Victory at Goodwood, a class win in the Leinster Trophy and 9th at Spa were taken with the Lister. But the season had already been highlighted when Peter and Graham shared their Aston Martin DB3S to 2nd at Le Mans and 6th at the Nurburgring. Then, tragedy struck when Peter was killed during a crash in the Tour de France.

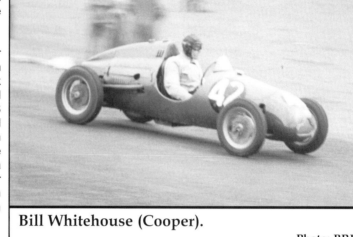

Bill Whitehouse (Cooper).

Photo: BRDC Archive.

P. N. Whitehead

❖

BILL WHITEHOUSE
Born April 1st 1909
Killed July 14th 1957

Whitehouse was another motorcycle racer who found a successful home in 500cc F3 car racing at the start of the 1950s. After graduating to a Connaught in which he mainly contested national libre events, he not only made his solitary Grand Prix appearance in the 1954 British but was forced into semi-retirement after a serious accident. A further comeback in 1957 coincided with the purchase of a Cooper for his son. During a meeting at Reims his own Cooper was put out of action, and so the works loaned him its spare. A burst tyre caused the car to crash, somersault and catch fire, killing him instantly.

1949 Finished 3rd in the Madgwick Cup at Goodwood and at Silverstone in his F3 Cooper.

1950 A successful year in F3 with his Cooper Norton included a win at Rouen, and two at the inaugural Brands Hatch meeting. He also took two 2nds, two 3rds and a 4th at Brands Hatch and was 17th in the British Grand Prix F3 race.

1951 Continuing in F3 he won the Daily Telegraph Trophy at Brands Hatch, had two 2nds at Castle Combe as well as 2nd places at Rouen, Genoa and in the Columbus Centenary GP. He had 3rd places at the Nurburgring and Brands Hatch and had a couple of outings in Gordon Watson's Alta, which brought a 2nd in class at Castle Combe. An outing with Aston Martin in the International Trophy production race was rewarded with 16th overall.

1952 After taking 4th in F3 at both the British Grand Prix and International Trophy meetings, his season was cut short by a crash in the Dutch F3 Grand Prix. Armed with a Connaught A-Type he qualified in 19th place for his only Grand Prix, but retired with engine failure. He did however win the Rochester Cup and a Libre race at Brands Hatch along with two 2nds and a 3rd at Snetterton. He added 4th in the Crystal Palace Trophy and Oulton Park Libre, 6th in the Oulton Park Gold Cup and 7th in the Joe Fry Memorial Trophy at Castle Combe, before another accident shortened his season.

1953 Having recovered from injuries that forced his temporary retirement, he returned to racing initially with his Connaught. After taking 2nd at Syracuse he bought a Cooper for his son to race, but took it to a couple wins and 2nd places himself. After problems during qualifying for a race at Reims, he was loaned a car by the works team, crashing fatally after a tyre burst.

GRAND PRIX RECORD	
Starts	1
Wins	0
Poles	0
Fastest laps	0
WC points	0
Best finish	DNF

50 years of British Grand Prix drivers

Part Two
1960s

CHAPTER 7

BOB ANDERSON
Born May 19th 1931
Killed August 14th 1967

After a successful motor cycle racing career, Anderson made the change to cars at the relatively late at the age of 29. After two years in Formula Junior he graduated to F1 and made his Grand Prix debut at the 1963 British. He was probably the last true privateer and performed miracles with his under-financed and outdated machinery. A particular highlight was his 3rd place in the 1964 Austrian GP. Sadly, he lost his life in a testing accident at Silverstone in 1967.

GRAND PRIX RECORD	
Starts	25
Wins	0
Poles	0
Fastest laps	0
WC points	8
Best finish	3rd

Bob Anderson.

Photo: BRDC Archive.

1961 Raced a Lotus in Formula Junior and finished 4th in the Chichester Cup at Goodwood and 12th at Silverstone.

1962 Drove a works Lotus in Formula Junior as team mate to Arundell and Rees. He finished 2nd at Monthlery, 3rd at Goodwood, Zandvoort and Rouen and 6th at Clermont Ferrand in the Coupe de Vitesse.

1963 After buying an ex-Bowmaker Lola Climax he contested most of Europe's non-championship F1 races. Results included 3rd at Imola and 4th at Syracuse before his victory in the Rome GP. He made his Grand Prix debut at the British qualifying 16th and finishing 12th, and followed that by a further outing at the Italian again finishing 12th. His other F1 appearances brought 8th at Solitude and Karlskoga and retirement in the Mediterranean Grand Prix.

1964 Changing to a Brabham BT11, he started his Grand Prix season with 7th at Monaco and 6th in the Dutch, but failed to start the Belgian after ignition problems. His career best result came with 3rd in Austria, and he took 7th at the British, 11th at the Italian, 12th at the French but retired from the German. Away from his World Championship campaign he took 3rd in the Rand Grand Prix and at Solitude, and drove a Brabham BT8 sports car to 2nd in the Silverstone Martini Trophy and 4th in class at the International Trophy.

1965 A further year with the Brabham brought 9th at Monaco and in the French from five starts, his season ending when the car was wrecked in a qualifying accident at the German GP. He was also 6th at Syracuse and 14th in the International Trophy.

1966 With his Brabham rebuilt, the change to the 3-litre Grand Prix formula meant an outdated Coventry Climax 2.7 litre unit was sourced for the season. Apart from 7th in the French Grand Prix, the season brought little reward until he clinched a well deserved point with 6th in the Italian. As well as taking the Brabham to 7th in the International Trophy, he drove the Aurora BMC to 3rd in a Goodwood sports car race and an F2 Cooper to 11th at Montlhery.

1967 The season started with his ageing Brabham collecting 5th at the South African Grand Prix, before failing to qualify in Monaco. He had already taken 2nd at Killarney in South Africa, 7th in the Oulton Park Spring Cup and 8th in the International Trophy, when he went on to collect 9th from the Dutch GP and 8th from the Belgian. He retired from the French and British but returned to Silverstone about a month later, where he crashed fatally during a test session.

❖

PETER ARUNDELL
Born November 8th 1933

A double Formula Junior Champion who stayed loyal to Lotus for most of his career. After years of waiting patiently for his break into the Grand Prix team, he was finally promoted in 1964. Third place in his first two races at Monaco and Zandvoort were to be the best results of his career for a serious accident during an F2 race at Reims that year brought a premature end to his season and kept him out for the whole of 1965. Although he returned to the team for 1966 he was never able to regain his form and apart from a couple of saloon car outings in 1968, he was racing career was over.

1954 Made his motorsport debut with an MG TC Midget in a club rally.

1955 Rallied and hillclimbed his MG.

1956 Spent another year in rallies and hillclimbs with his MG.

1957 His race debut came at Goodwood, taking his MG to 2nd place behind Alan Foster's MGA. His first win was at Oulton Park, just ahead of Tim Parnell, and he also had 3rd places at Mallory Park and Brands Hatch. Other

GRAND PRIX RECORD	
Starts	11
Wins	0
Poles	0
Fastest laps	0
WC points	12
Best finish	3rd

results included a class win and 2nd overall at the Stapleford Hillclimb and class wins at Oulton Park and Silverstone (twice).

1958 He won his first two races in a Lotus XI, but had eight crashes from 25 starts. He also finished 2nd at Snetterton, 3rd at Goodwood (twice) and 15th in the TT.

Peter Arundell.

Photo: BRDC Archive.

1959 Moving to a newer Lotus XI he won at Goodwood, Mallory Park and Snetterton, with 2nd at Goodwood, 3rd at Mallory Park, 4th in the International Trophy and in the Crystal Palace August Trophy, and 5th at Aintree. Later in the season he began his Formula Junior career, taking an Elva DKW to victory in the John Davy Trophy at Brands Hatch.

1960 Racing with Lotus in Formula Junior he finished 2nd in the Empire Trophy behind Henry Taylor and won at Brands Hatch, Snetterton and Mallory Park (three times). Other results included 2nd at Silverstone and

Brands Hatch, 3rd at Aintree, Brands Hatch and Oulton Park, 4th at Monaco, Solitude and Oulton Park. He also had a win at Snetterton in the Formula Junior Elva and finished 2nd in a Mallory Park Libre race with his Lotus. In sports cars he won the Scott-Brown Memorial Trophy at Snetterton and was 8th in the Empire Trophy meeting in a Gilby Climax. He also drove a Lotus to 2nd in class in the British Grand Prix support race.

1961 As a regular Formula Junior frontrunner for Lotus, he won at Monaco, the Eastern Counties Trophy at Snetterton, at Mallory Park, Silverstone (twice) and Brands Hatch and shared the Chichester Cup after a tie with Tony Maggs' Cooper at Goodwood. He had 2nd places at Solitude and Goodwood, and a 4th at Snetterton. Occasional sports car outings for Team Elite brought a best result of 2nd at Snetterton.

1962 He dominated the Formula Junior scene with 18 wins from 25 starts to crown him champion for Lotus. His victories included the Chichester Cup at Goodwood, the Vanwall Trophy at Snetterton, Oulton Park, Albi, Snetterton, Goodwood, Aintree, Silverstone, Monaco, Monza, Rouen, Zandvoort and Montlhery, with 2nds at Brands Hatch and Mallory Park. At the Reims GP he had his first taste of F1 power, until Clark took over the Lotus BRM for the race.

1963 Still waiting for his F1 break, he was forced to spend another year in Formula Junior, taking the Express and Star British Championship. He won the Anglo European Trophy at Brands Hatch, at Albi, Oulton Park, Mallory Park, Silverstone, Zolder, Goodwood and Solitude. With a Lotus 23 he tasted sports car success with class wins at Oulton Park and Aintree and 3rd in class in the Lavant Cup at Goodwood, and in saloons he took a Lotus Cortina to 5th overall in the British Saloon Car Championship. He did manage to get a couple of Formula 1 outings, taking 2nd at Solitude and sharing the 2nd place car at the Mediterranean Grand Prix with Spence. He also practiced for the French Grand Prix.

1964 Finally got a place in the Lotus Grand Prix team, taking 3rd on his debut at Monaco after qualifying 6th. He matched that performance again at the Dutch, and took 9th in Belgium and 4th in the French after qualifying 4th for both races. He had also taken 2nd in the News of the World Trophy at Goodwood, 3rd in the International Trophy, the Aintree 200 and at Syracuse. In F2 he was 2nd at Mallory Park, 3rd at Pau and 4th at Crystal Palace, but had a huge accident at Reims, when he was thrown from the car after spinning and being hit by Richie Ginther. He sustained a broken arm, collarbone and thigh, and serious head injuries. Despite missing half of the Grand Prix season, he was still 8th in the World Championship. In saloons he had continued to race a Cortina, taking 3rd in the St.Mary's Trophy at Goodwood, 2nd in class at Crystal Palace and 4th in class at Aintree. In GTs he drove an Elan to a class win in the Sussex Trophy at Goodwood and 2nd in class at Mallory Park.

1965 The whole year was spent convalescing.

1966 Beginning the year with 3rd in the non-championship South African Grand Prix, he reclaimed his

seat for the World Championship. In Belgium engine failure kept him off the grid and that was followed by retirements in the French, British and Dutch races. In the German he finished 12th behind four F2 cars, and was 8th in Italy, 6th in the US and 7th in Mexico. He finished 10th overall in the F2 Championship after 5th at Keimola, 6th at Karlskoga, 7th at Brands Hatch and 9th at Pau. In saloons his Lotus Cortina took 2nd places at Goodwood, Snetterton and Brands Hatch, with 3rd in the Lombank Trophy at Brands Hatch. At the end of the year he was released by Lotus.

1968 After a year out he had a couple of outings in an Alan Mann Ford Escort, taking 4th at Mallory Park and 26th at Silverstone before retiring from the sport.

GERRY ASHMORE
Born July 25th 1936

Gerry Ashmore.

The son of former Grand Prix driver Joe, Gerry was a rather reluctant starter in motorsport, making his racing debut at Silverstone in an ex-Duncan Hamilton Jaguar D-Type. After combining single-seaters with sports cars in 1960, his Grand Prix debut came at the British in 1961, during a year in which he contested most of Europe's non-championship F1 races. His Grand Prix career was brief and when plans to buy a BRM were abandoned, he concentrated on sports car racing from 1962 onwards. Through the mid-sixties his appearances became more intermittent, before finally hanging up his helmet at the end of 1972, after some success in national racing with a Lotus Elan.

1957 A race debut at Silverstone in his D-Type Jaguar was intended to be a one-off. "It went straight on at all the corners and understeered everywhere," was how he described the car, but he survived and returned home with the car undamaged.

1958 His second race appearance again at Silverstone, was under the watchful eye of his uncle Fred, himself a former Grand Prix driver. From eight races in the D-Type, he had a win and a couple of 2nds and was always just behind Jon Bekaert's Lister.

1959 Another year with the D-Type brought a 2nd at Brands Hatch and 3rd places at Snetterton (four times), Brands Hatch (twice) and Aintree.

1960 Moving into single-seaters he collected the Leinster Trophy at Dunboyne and took 2nd in the Aintree F2 Trophy, 3rd overall with a lap record at Innsbruck in a Cooper T45 Climax and 3rd and 4th places at Kirkistown. He also took 14th in the Empire Trophy in a Formula Junior Alexis. He now drove the ex-Bekaert Lister in sports cars, but was no match for the Cooper Monacos and Lotus 19s. He did however take a win at Oulton Park, 2nd at Aintree, 3rd at Snetterton and 5th in the British Grand Prix support race.

1961 Having bought a Lotus 18 he made his Grand Prix debut at the British, qualifying 26th but retiring with a chronic misfire. After finishing 16th in the German, his Italian Grand Prix outing was over on the first lap. "The rear suspension broke into Parabolica, sending the car over a 9ft earth bank and clearing telegraph wires, before hitting a tree about 18ft up and settling in a bomb crater. With a front wishbone piercing the cockpit I had a broken ankle and split tank leaking fuel onto my legs, with the battery inches away," he recalls. In the non-championship Naples Grand Prix he took pole and finished 2nd, despite breaking the gear lever at half distance. He had wins at Phoenix Park and Dunboyne, with 2nd on handicap in the Leinster Trophy, 3rd at Mallory Park and spun out of contention in the Vienna GP after shadowing Moss for the lead.

1962 With his Lotus 18 rebodied to look like a 24, thanks to a £1200 kit from Ken Gregory, he contested mainly domestic F1 races. The car was, however, taken to the Italian Grand Prix where it failed to qualify when a cam follower broke. With the Lotus sold to Kurt Kuhnke,

GRAND PRIX RECORD	
Starts	3
Wins	0
Poles	0
Fastest laps	0
WC points	0
Best finish	16th

the plan was to buy a BRM until the order was cancelled due to the lack of competitiveness of the car.

1963 Raced Bill Rigg's Jaguar D-Type and Peter Mould's Lister in national sports car races, taking the D-Type to 5th in the Oulton Park 5 hour race.

1964 Had occasional outings in the ex-David Prophet Lotus 30, making his debut at Croft sitting on a briefcase, as he couldn't get into the car with a proper seat.

1965 The Lotus 30 was converted to a GT car, with the addition of gullwing doors. He also raced a Lotus 40, with a win, 2nd and 3rd at Silverstone, 2nd at Castle Combe and 7th in the Guards International at Brands Hatch.

1966 A further year was spent racing Allan Eccles' Lotus 40, but with less success.

1967 Continued to persevere with the Lotus 40, but with little or no reward.

1968 Two 3rd places and class wins at Silverstone with the Lotus 40 preceded a spectacular crash at Croft, when brake failure sent it careering through an ambulance gate. The car was repaired and raced once more, taking 8th in a wet Guards Trophy at Brands Hatch.

1969 Shared a lightweight bodied Lotus Elan 2+2 with Max Payne. The car was built from used parts and used an engine loaned by the works.

1970 Another year with the Elan was cut short after Payne crashed the car at Silverstone.

1971 Finished 5th overall in the Chevron Oils Modsports Championship, winning twice at Silverstone, with 2nd at Mallory Park and 3rd at Croft in the Elan. His final race was at Thruxton, after which he retired to concentrate on fatherhood.

RICHARD ATTWOOD
Born April 4th 1940

After a success period in Formula Junior, he tended to spend most of his Grand Prix career covering as a deputy. Despite always putting in a competitive performance, it failed to secure him a regular berth with any of the teams. He scored his best result in Formula 1 when he joined the BRM team after Mike Spence was killed at Indianapolis in 1968. In his debut race for the team he finished a remarkable second at Monaco, but he left the team later that year with his Grand Prix career virtually over.

What he missed in Grand Prix racing, however, he more than made up for in F2 and sports cars, including taking victory at Le Mans with Hans Herrmann and Porsche 1970. With the awesome Porsche 917, he was a front-runner in all the major sports car races of the era. After a break in the early seventies he came back to race some of the classic sports cars in which he had previously been so successful, and to this day he still races regularly in classic and historic events.

1959 Had a few races in a Standard 8.

1960 Began racing more seriously with a Triumph TR3A, winning at Mallory Park, finishing 3rd at Rufforth and taking a class win at Oulton Park.

1961 Moved into Formula Junior with an MRP-entered Cooper and won at Goodwood, took 2nd at Mallory Park, 3rd at Snetterton and Charterhall and 6th at Silverstone.

1962 Another year with his Cooper brought Formula Junior victories at Oulton Park (twice), Silverstone (twice), Aintree and Snetterton, with 2nd in the Coupe de Vitesse, 2nd and 7th at Silverstone, 2nd at Goodwood, 4th at Mallory Park and 5th at Brands Hatch. He also drove the car in Libre races, taking two wins at Silverstone and a 3rd place at Snetterton.

1963 Changing to an MRP Lola, he won the Monaco Formula Junior race, as well as at Kirkistown. He also finished 2nd at Rouen, at Mallory Park, in the British Grand Prix support race and at Goodwood, 3rd in the Chichester Cup at Goodwood and Reims, 4th at Oulton Park and 5th at Solitude, at Silverstone and in the Circuit D'Auvergne. He raced a Lola GT at Le Mans and became the first ever Grovewood Award winner, but had his season shortened after breaking his leg at Albi. He returned to take 2nd in Mallory Park's Christmas Libre race with his Lola.

1964 His first taste of F1 power came with BRM, when after taking 4th in the News of the World Trophy at Goodwood, he was entered for the British Grand Prix. After practicing the four-wheel drive P67, it was withdrawn before the race. He concentrated on F2 with an MRP Lola, with a win in Vienna, 2nd at Pau, Albi and the Eifelrennen, 6th at Reims, 7th at Brands Hatch, 8th in the Aintree 200 and at Crystal Palace, and 9th in the

Richard Attwood receives the winners' laurels.

Photo: BRDC Archive.

GRAND PRIX RECORD	
Starts	17
Wins	0
Poles	0
Fastest laps	1
WC points	11
Best finish	2nd

Oulton Park Gold Cup. As part of the Ford works sports prototype team he raced a Ford GT40 at Le Mans, and shared an AC Cobra with Schlesser to 23rd place in the Nurburgring 1000km.

1965 Moving to the Parnell team to race a Lotus BRM in F1, he qualified 6th at Monaco on his Grand Prix debut, only to retire from the race after losing a wheel. From 14th in Belgium, he improved to 13th in the British, 12th in the Dutch, and after retiring in Germany he collected his first World Championship point with 6th in Italy. He matched his performance with a second point in Mexico, after finishing 10th in the US. In the non-championship races he took 6th in the Sunday Mirror Trophy at Goodwood and 8th in the International Trophy. He continued to race in F2 with a Lola, and won the Rome Grand Prix, with 2nd at Pau, 3rd at Crystal Palace, 4th at Snetterton, 5th at Karlskoga and 6th at Reims and Brands Hatch. Sharing David Piper's Ferraris he won the Rand 9 hours and was 4th at the Reims 12 hours, while other results included 2nd at Mallory Park with a Ford GT40 and 2nd place in an historic race at Silverstone with a Maserati 250F.

1966 There was no Grand Prix racing this year, but he did contest the Tasman Series for BRM, winning the Gold Leaf Trophy at Levin, followed by 2nd in the Lady Wigram Trophy. Continuing to race in F2 he took 5th at Reims and Le Mans, 6th at Albi, 8th at Rouen and 10th at Brands Hatch. But in sports cars he won the Rand 9 hours again with Piper's Ferrari, took 2nd in the Circuit D'Auvergne with Guichet in a Ferrari and was 3rd in the Scott-Brown Memorial Trophy at Snetterton in a Ford GT40.

1967 A further visit to the Tasman Series with BRM netted 2nd in the Lady Wigram Trophy and at Teretonga, 3rd in the New Zealand Grand Prix and at Levin. He finished 5th in the championship. He made a brief return to the Grand Prix scene with a Cooper Maserati in Canada, qualifying 14th and finishing 10th and had a few F2 outings in an MRP Lola. His main successes were again in sports cars. He drove a variety of Ferraris and won the Wills Trophy and Grand Prix support race at Silverstone, took 3rd at Brands Hatch, at Oulton Park and in the Spa 1000km with Bianchi. He finished 5th in the Rand 9 hours with Piper, 6th in the Paris 1000km with Redman, 7th in the Brands Hatch BOAC 500 with Piper, but retired at Le Mans, Daytona and Sebring. He also shared a Porsche with Bill Bradley to 2nd in the Austrian GP.

1968 Following Mike Spence's death, he joined the BRM Grand Prix team. On his debut for the team at Monaco, he qualified 6th and finished 2nd with the fastest lap of the race. After retiring in the Belgian, he was 7th in both the Dutch and French, retired from the British and took 14th in the German, after which he was released from his contract. He had been to the Tasman races again at the start of the year, finishing 10th in the championship with 4th at Longford and 6th in the Australian Grand Prix for BRM. In F2 he raced a Tecno to 3rd at Zandvoort, 9th at Hockenheim and 13th at Albi and had a Lotus Cortina for the occasional saloon car race, collecting 2nd in class at Zolder and a victory at Mallory Park. Most of his sports car outings were again with Piper's Ferraris, taking 2nd in the TT and 3rd in the Cape International 3 hours at Killarney. They finished 7th at Le Mans and 14th in the Kyalami 9 hours, while with Porsche he took 6th in the Watkins Glen 6 hours with Ikuzawa and also raced the new Ford 3-litre Prototype.

1969 A brief return to Grand Prix racing as Rindt's deputy at Monaco, brought a remarkable 4th in the Lotus 49B. He also contested the F2 section of the German Grand Prix in Frank Williams' F2 Brabham, securing 2nd in class and 6th overall. However, most of his sporting success came with Porsches with 2nd in the BOAC 500 at Brands Hatch and in the Watkins Glen 6 hours with Elford. He finished 3rd in the Austrian 1000km with Redman, 4th in the Nurburgring 1000km with Lins, and led at Le Mans with Elford until the 917's gearbox failed. He also raced a Lola T70 taking 4th at the Norisring, 5th at Anderstorp, and 10th with Parkes at the Paris 1000km. His partnership with Piper brought victory at the Kyalami 9 hours in a Porsche 917 and 3rd in the Lourenco Marques 3 hours with a Mirage.

1970 Driving works Porsches he won at Le Mans, with 2nd at Nurburgring, 3rd in the BOAC 500 and 6th in the Spa 1000km with Herrmann. He finished 5th in the Targa Florio with Waldegaard, 4th in the Austrian 1000km with Elford, 6th in the Watkins Glen 6 hours with Ahrens and 3rd in a Watkins Glen CanAm race. He shared the Springbok Championship title with Redman in a Chevron B19 and won the Capetown 6 hours with Redman in a B16. He had a win at Dijon and 5th in a Hockenheim Interserie race with a Lola T70 and finished 2nd in the Phoenix Park Libre race with an F2 Brabham BT30.

1971 Sports car success continued with a variety of machinery. He won the Austrian 1000km with Rodriguez in a Gulf Porsche, was 2nd at Le Mans with Muller and 3rd at the Watkins Glen 6 hours with Bell in 917s. He finished 3rd in the Targa Florio with Bonnier in a Lola T212, won the Goldfields 3 hours and took 8th at Paul Ricard with Redman in a Chevron B19 and finished 13th at Watkins Glen with a 917K Porsche in a CanAm race. He was 7th overall in the Sports Prototype Drivers' Championship. At the end of the season he stopped racing.

1977 Made his racing comeback with 2nd in class at Oulton Park in a Chevron B8.

1981 Finished 3rd in the Marlboro Cup Supersports at the Dubai Grand Prix with a Ferrari 330P.

1982 Raced in Supersports, taking victory at Montlhery and 2nd at Phoenix Park in a Porsche 917K and 7th at

Zandvoort in a Ferrari 275LM. He also took 2nd place at Silverstone in an historic race with a BRM P25.

1983 He was a Supersports regular, winning at Hockenheim and Zolder, with 2nd at Montlhery and 4th at Donington Park, with a Porsche 917K and 908/2.

1984 Raced an Aston Martin Nimrod, but retired from both the Silverstone 1000km and Le Mans, with Sheldon and Salmon respectively. He was 15th at Daytona with Elford and Meister in a Porsche 928S and took three Supersports wins at the Nassau Speed week in his Porsche 917K as well as 3rd at the UK/US Challenge at Dallas.

1985 Finished 7th in the Willhire 24 hours at Snetterton in a Mercedes 190, had a 2nd place in the Brands Hatch Historic Grand Prix in a Maserati 250F, and took Supersports wins at Spa and Pau.

1986 Won at Silverstone in a Supersports race in a Porsche 917.

1988 Finished 5th in the Pirelli Porsche race at Birmingham in a 944 Turbo and 3rd at Donington Park.

1989-1999 Continued to race in International Supersports and numerous other classic and historic races, which included Groveair Endurance victories at Snetterton in 1995 and Donington Park 1996, sharing a Lister Jaguar with Gary Pearson.

Derek Bell.

Photo: BRDC Archive.

DEREK BELL
Born October 31st 1941

With five Le Mans wins and numerous other classic successes, Bell is one of the legends of sports car racing. He started racing in a Lotus 7, he soon switched to single-seaters and worked his up through F3 and F2. He joined Ferrari in 1968, making both his F1 and Grand Prix with the team later in the year. His nine Grand Prix starts produced a single championship point when he finished sixth in the 1970 US Grand Prix for Surtees.

Although his Grand Prix career never really took off, he more than made up for it in sports cars, continuing to be a frontrunner well into the nineties with a career spanning more than 30 years. By then, he was able to partner his son Justin who had followed his father into World class sports car racing.

1964 Began racing with a Lotus 7 and came 2nd in a works backed championship, with two wins at Silverstone, a class win at Brands Hatch and a handicap win at Goodwood. He also drove an F3 Lotus to 3rd place in the Christmas Libre race at Mallory Park.

1965 His Lotus 31 F3 car was used in both F3 and Libre, taking a win and 2nd at Goodwood, a class win at Castle Combe, 2nd in class at Brands Hatch and 2nd overall at the Bodiam Sprint. He also raced a Marcos GT and took a class win at Brands Hatch.

1966 He started the year with a Lotus 41 before changing to a Brabham BT21 for F3 and Libre. Wins came at Goodwood and Brands Hatch, with a 2nd and 3rd at Goodwood, 3rd at Silverstone and Oulton Park (twice), 4th and 5th at Crystal Palace, 4th at Enna and 6th at Albi.

1967 Teamed up with Peter Westbury in a pair of F3 Brabham BT21s, winning the Les Leston £1000 race at Oulton Park. He also won at Zolder, Brands Hatch, Snetterton, Silverstone, Castle Combe and Oulton Park, with 2nd at Barcelona, Albi, Snetterton, Crystal Palace, Nogaro and Brands Hatch. Other results included 3rd at Monaco, Chimay and Clermont Ferrand, 4th and 6th at Silverstone, 5th at Pau and Crystal Palace and a class win at the Ollon-Villars Hillclimb. Earned 2nd place in the end of season Grovewood Awards.

1968 Finished 4th in the F2 Championship, starting the year in a Brabham before joining the works Ferrari team.

He was 3rd at Thruxton, in the Eifelrennen and at Hockenheim, 5th at Enna and 6th at Valellunga, but had a huge crash at Monza on his Ferrari debut. After a successful F1 debut in the Oulton Park Gold Cup, he made his Grand Prix debut in Italy, qualified 8th but retired from the race. A further outing in the US GP also ended in retirement.

1969 The year started with 4th place in the Tasman Series for Ferrari, with 2nd places in the Australian Grand Prix and twice at Warwick Farm, with 4th in the New Zealand GP and 5th in the Lady Wigram Trophy, at Invercargill, Sandown and Christchurch. He was 9th in the International Trophy and took the F2 Ferrari to 5th at Monza and 8th at Jarama before he was out of a drive. A one-off drive for McLaren ended in retirement in the British Grand Prix, but he took 5th in the F2 Championship after his Brabham finished 4th at Vallelunga and 5th at Nurburgring.

1970 With Tom Wheatcroft's support he went to the Tasman Series with a Brabham and finished 2nd in the New Zealand Grand Prix. He was runner-up in the F2 Championship after winning at Barcelona, and taking 2nd at the Nurburgring and Zolder, 3rd at Thruxton and Imola, 3rd and 6th at Hockenheim, 4th at Tulln Langenlebarn and Pau, and 6th at Nurburgring and Crystal Palace. In the Belgian Grand Prix he retired his Wheatcroft Brabham, but gained his only World Championship point after taking a works Surtees TS7 to 6th in the US GP. His other results included 8th in the Spa 1000km and 6th in the Kyalami 9 hours with a Ferrari 512S.

1971 A further drive with Surtees in the British Grand Prix ended in retirement, with further F1 outings in a March 701 resulting in 5th in the non-championship Argentine GP and 15th in the Questor GP. With a March 712M in F2 he was 2nd at Monza, 3rd at Thruxton and 3rd in the Colombian Grand Prix. He finished 5th in the World Sports Car Championship with the John Wyer-managed Porsche 917 team, after winning the Buenos Aires and Paris 1000kms. He also finished 2nd at Barcelona, Monza and Spa, 3rd in the BOAC and at Watkins Glen and 5th at Sebring.

1972 He joined the Martini Tecno Grand Prix team, but from five attempts he only made the start in the German and US Grands Prix, retiring from both. In sports cars he was 3rd at Watkins Glen and 4th at Spa and the Nurburgring with a Mirage. He won at Jarama, with 3rd at Nogaro and 7th at Imola in an Osella Abarth, and finished 8th at Le Mans in a Ferrari 365GTB. He also raced a McLaren M18 in F5000 at Elkhart Lake and finished 3rd.

1973 Further races with the Mirage brought victories at Spa and Imola, with 2nd in the Kyalami 9 hours, 4th at Watkins Glen and 5th at the Osterreichring. He won the TT with a BMW CSL, took 4th in a Mid-Ohio CanAm race in a McLaren M8F, 2nd in a Michigan F5000 race with a Lola T330 and with an F2 Surtees he was 3rd at Hockenheim and 4th at Monza and the Nurburgring.

1974 His final attempt at Grand Prix racing resulted in one start from five races, with 11th in the German in a works Surtees. In F5000 at Thruxton he finished 4th in a

GRAND PRIX RECORD	
Starts	9
Wins	0
Poles	0
Fastest laps	0
WC points	1
Best finish	6th

Lola, but continued to find success with the Mirage in sports cars. Results included 2nd at Spa, 3rd at Paul Ricard, in the BOAC 1000 and in the Kyalami 6 hours and 4th at Le Mans, Monza, the Osterreichring and Nurburgring.

1975 Won his first Le Mans with Ickx in a Mirage, but shared further success with Pescarolo in an Alfa Romeo 33TT12. They won at Spa, Watkins Glen and the Osterreichring, with 2nd at Enna and 4th at Mugello and Dijon. He was also 3rd in the Wynns 1000 at Kyalami in a BMW CSL with Redman.

1976 Spent the year persevering with the Jaguar XJ12C. His other varied results included 3rd at Elkhart Lake in a F5000 race with a Lola and 2nd and 4th at Brands Hatch in British F5000 with a Penske PC3. He finished 3rd at the Nurburgring in a Porsche 934T, 4th in the Austrian 1000km with a 935, 5th at Le Mans in a Mirage and 2nd overall with a class win in the British Grand Prix Saloon Car race in a Triumph Dolomite.

1977 Continued with the XJ12C and finished 2nd at the Nurburgring and 4th at Silverstone. At Avus he was 2nd with an Alfa Romeo TT33/12 in an Interserie race, and drove the Hexagon Penske PC3 to victory in the Oulton Park Gold Cup, along with 4th at Brands Hatch and 5th at Donington Park.

1978 Started the year in South African Formula Atlantic, taking a Kauhsen March 77B to 5th at Welkom. With BMW he finished 3rd in the Mugello 6 hours and 6th in the Spa 600, and finished 8th at Brands Hatch in the British Saloon Car Championship in a Hermitite-sponsored Triumph Dolomite.

1979 He won the IMSA Elkhart 500 mile race in a BMW with Hobbs, and was 3rd in the championship round at Riverside in a Porsche 935. A regular in the BMW County Championship, he won at Thruxton and finished 2nd at Brands Hatch and Castle Combe as well as 4th at Silverstone and Brands Hatch. He also finished 2nd in class with an Alfetta GTV at Bathurst.

1980 Racing a variety of sports cars his only top finish was 2nd at Vallelunga with Brunn in a Porsche 908/3. Another year in the BMW County Championship brought 5th at Oulton Park and 6th at Castle Combe and at the wheel of Roy Lane's March 79SF1 he just missed the run-offs at the Loton Park Hillclimb.

1981 In a wide selection of Porsches he won his 2nd Le Mans with Ickx in a 936, won at Silverstone in a 917, Mid-Ohio and the Lumbermans 500 in a 935, with 2nd at Daytona in a 935 and 3rd at Kyalami in a 908/3. He took a BMW M1 to 2nd and a class win in the Silverstone 6 hours and 3rd at the Brands Hatch 1000km and finished 3rd at Bathurst in a Mazda RX7. He finished 7th overall in the World Drivers Endurance Championship.

1982 Won his 3rd Le Mans with Ickx in a Porsche 956, followed by victory in the Shell 1000 Brands Hatch. He finished 2nd in the Silverstone 6 hours, the Spa 1000km and the Kyalami 9 hours to finish 3rd in the drivers' championship. In IMSA races he had a 935, taking 2nd and 3rd at Daytona, 4th at Riverside and Mosport and 7th at Road Atlanta to take 6th in the championship. He also took an Alfa Romeo Giulia to a win and 3rd at a Donington Park historic meeting.

1983 Finished as runner-up in both the World and European Endurance Championships with victories in the Silverstone and Fuji 1000kms and at Kyalami. He finished 2nd at Le Mans and Spa, 3rd at Brands Hatch and Mugello, 4th at Imola and 7th at Monza in a 956. He won the LA Times Grand Prix at Riverside in a 935, finished 8th at Miami with Mass, won a Brands Hatch Thundersports race in Brunn's 908/3 and shared an Alfa GTV6 to 5th in the Kyalami 2 hours.

1984 Took 4th place in the World Endurance Championship, winning at Spa, Sandown and Nurburgring, with 4th at Mosport and 10th at Silverstone in a 956. Finished 3rd in the IMSA Series with a 935 and a 962, winning at Mid-Ohio, Watkins Glen, Elkhart Lake, Pocono and the Eastern Airlines 3 hours at Daytona. He also took 2nd in the LA Times GP at Riverside and the Daytona 24 hours and 3rd at Sebring at Portland. He also contested the last ever F2 race, taking a March 842 to 9th at Brands Hatch.

1985 Won the World Sports drivers title with Stuck in a Rothmans Porsche, winning at Hockenheim and Brands Hatch. He also finished 2nd at Silverstone, Monza and Spa, 3rd at Le Mans and 4th at Mugello. Runner-up in the IMSA Series, he won at Miami, Charlotte, in the Lumbermans 500 at Mid-Ohio, at Watkins Glen and Pocono, with 2nd at Daytona and Sebring in Holbert's 962.

1986 Became World Sports Car Champion again with Stuck and Rothmans Porsche, winning his 4th Le Mans. He won at Monza and finished 2nd at Silverstone and Brands Hatch, 3rd at Spa and 4th at Hockenheim. In IMSA he won the Daytona 24 hours, at Mid-Ohio and at Watkins Glen, with 2nd at Sears Point and Watkins Glen. He also took 3rd at Sebring and Road Atlanta, 4th at Lime Rock and Palm Beach and 6th at Miami and in the Daytona 3 hours with Holbert's 962 to take 3rd in the championship.

1987 Won his 5th Le Mans with the Rothmans Porsche. Other results included 2nd at Jarama, Nurburgring and Monza, 3rd at Jerez and Silverstone, 4th at Brands Hatch, 5th at Spa, 6th at Fuji and he came 5th overall in the World Sportscar Championship. In IMSA he won the Daytona 24 hours and at San Antonio, with 2nd at Palm Beach, 4th at Miami, Columbus and Road America to finish 6th in the championship.

1988 Finished 2nd at Le Mans and 4th at Jerez in the World Sports Car Championship with 962s. In IMSA he was 2nd at Watkins Glen and Road America, 3rd at Road Atlanta, 4th at Miami, 6th at Mid-Ohio and Sears Point, and 7th at Daytona in Porsche 962Cs.

1989 Shared a Porsche 962 in World Sports, taking 4th at Mexico City and 5th at Dijon. Won at Daytona again in IMSA, with 4th at Sebring and finished 5th on the Tour of Britain.

1990 Racing in IMSA he shared Moretti's Porsche to 4th at Road Atlanta, 6th at Watkins Glen and 7th at Tampa. He was 4th at Le Mans with Jelinski and Stuck in a Porsche 962, 8th at Fuji, and had a 5th and 8th in the Japanese series sharing with Needell.

1991 Took 5th at Road Atlanta, 6th at Portland and West Palm Beach, and 7th in Miami with Moretti's Porsche 962C. In the World Series he was 5th at Mexico City and 7th at Le Mans.

1992 Finished 12th at Le Mans sharing a Porsche 962 with Needell and son Justin.

1993 Finished 4th in the IMSA GTP Championship for Nissan, including 2nd at Sebring, 4th at Miami, Portland and Laguna Seca and 6th at Daytona. At Le Mans he shared a Courage to 10th place.

1994 Took 5th at Le Mans in a Kremer K8 Porsche and raced an IMSA Spice to 2nd at Sebring and retirement at Daytona.

1995 Finished 2nd at Sebring and retired at Daytona in a Spice, 3rd at Le Mans sharing a McLaren F1 GTR with son Justin and won a Prototype race at Silverstone in a Porsche 917K.

1996 Shared a McLaren with Wallace and Grouillard to 6th at Le Mans.

1998 Raced with son Justin again in a Porsche 911GT2 at Vallelunga, leading the class until retiring. He also finished 2nd in the Richmond Trophy with a Cooper Maserati at Goodwood's re-opening.

❖

JOHN CAMPBELL-JONES
Born January 21st 1930

After some success in small capacity sports cars in the late fifties, he worked his way through F2 to make his Grand Prix debut in 1962. Despite travelling throughout Europe contesting non-championship F1 races, he found little success and apart from a one-off return in 1966, his career virtually ended in 1963.

GRAND PRIX RECORD	
Starts	2
Wins	0
Poles	0
Fastest laps	0
WC points	0
Best finish	11th

1958 Raced a Lotus XI and won the Chichester Cup at Goodwood, with 3rd in class in the International Trophy Sports Car race and 4th overall with a class win at Vila Real.

1959 Won his class in the Nurburgring 1000km in his Lotus XI and had a 3rd at Snetterton. He also raced a Cooper F2 in selected races.

1960 Concentrating solely on his Cooper, he was 2nd in the Silver City Libre Trophy, the Leinster Trophy and a Snetterton single-seater race. He finished 7th in the Brussels GP, 8th at Pau, 16th in the International Trophy at Silverstone and retired from the Crystal Palace Trophy.

1961 A further season with the Cooper brought 7th in the Lewis-Evans Trophy at Brands Hatch, 9th in the Brussels GP and 12th in the Silver City Trophy, before a crash at Modena ended his season prematurely. He had also raced a Lotus Elite to a class win in the Auvergne Trophy.

1962 Joined Emeryson to race in F1, but borrowed a Lotus 18 for his Grand Prix debut in Belgium after his Emeryson broke its gearbox during qualifying. He finished a distant 11th after further gearbox problems. His only other results of note came with 5th in the Brussels GP and 6th in the Aintree 200.

1963 Contested national F1 races and the British Grand Prix in a Parnell Lola Climax, where he finished 13th. There were no other finishes of note.

1966 Returned to contest the Oulton Park Gold Cup in ageing BRP Climax, and retired from both the race and finally from the sport.

JIM CLARK
Born March 4th 1936
Killed April 7th 1968

Jim Clark.

Photo: BRDC Archive.

One of the true greats of the sport, a double World Champion and Indianapolis 500 winner, Tasman and British Saloon Car Champion, who spent most of his successful career as a works Lotus driver. His relationship with Lotus boss Colin Chapman was as close as any team boss/driver partnership before or since in the sport.

The Scot remains one of the most highly-rated of all drivers for his consummate skills were complemented by an unassuming personality. He took the world title in 1963 and 1965 and was surely destined to add at least another title with the advent of the Cosworth DFV engine in 1967. His statistic of 25 wins and 33 poles from 72 Grand Prix starts is evidence of his position as the best driver of the era.

In 1965 he won the Indianapolis 500 at his second attempt and he was equally at home in single seaters, sports, Saloons or rally cars. He had begun another successful season in 1968, when his F2 Lotus crashed fatally during a race at Hockenheim. No cause for this accident was ever confirmed, but driver error seems unimaginable for such a peerless talent. His death robbed the sport of an all-time great and British fans of a true hero.

1956 Drove his own MK3 Sunbeam to a victory at Stobs Camp, took a double class win at Winfield Sprints and 6th in the Burton Beadnell Speed Trials. He also competed in Ian Scott-Watson's DKW, taking a 6th at Beadnell, 8th at Crimond and two further class wins at Winfield.

1957 After taking 4th at Charterhall in the DKW, he also drove Scott-Watson's Porsche 1600S to victory in the BMRC Trophy, 2nd in production touring and 3rd in production sports in one day at Charterhall. He also had a modified saloon win at a Winfield Sprint, along with 2nd in the sports car class.

1958 Driving the Porsche again he collected two wins in the saloon car class and a win and 2nd in sports cars at a Winfield Sprint. He won a sports car race at Stobs Camp and the class at the Rest & be Thankful Hillclimb. He won in saloons, sports and GT at Full Sutton and claimed more top finishes at Crimond and Charterhall. He also took the Porsche to Spa and finished 5th in his first overseas event and raced a Border Reivers run Jaguar D-Type, taking two double wins at Full Sutton in racing and sports car classes. He won in Libre and sports cars at Charterhall, and won at Crimond and Mallory Park. A couple of outings in a Triumph TR3 also brought 2nd in class at Stobs Sprint with 2nd and 3rd in class at the Rest & be Thankful hillclimb, while with a Lotus Elite he had a 2nd at the Boxing Day Brands Hatch.

1959 Further success with his Elite brought victory in the Autosport 3 hours at Snetterton, wins at Mallory Park (twice), Oulton Park, Charterhall (twice), Brands Hatch and class wins at the Bo'ness Hillclimb and Winfield Sprint. He also finished 10th overall with 2nd in class at Le Mans. Further outings with the Porsche brought a class win and FTD at a Stobs Sprint. With a Lister Jaguar he won at Mallory Park (three times), at Charterhall (twice), at Rufforth and at Brands Hatch. He also took the car to FTDs at both Bo'ness and Winfield. At the TT he retired a Tojeiro and made his single-seater debut at the Boxing Day Brands Hatch meeting, retiring a Formula Junior Gemini.

1960 After his planned Grand Prix drive for Aston Martin failed to materialise, he joined Lotus, retiring on his debut at the Dutch in a Lotus 18. He went on to take 3rd in Portugal, 5th in Belgium and France and 16th in both the British and US. Those results took him to 8th in the World Championship. He also took the car to 2nd in the Lombank Trophy at Snetterton and won the Kentish Trophy at Brands Hatch, with 8th at Solitude in F2. Racing in Formula Junior he became joint champion, winning the Chichester Cup at Goodwood, with further victories at Solitude, Oulton Park (three times), Goodwood and Brands Hatch (twice each), and Snetterton and 7th at Monaco. From six outings with Aston Martin he came 3rd at Le Mans with Salvadori and 3rd at Oulton Park.

Jim Clark.

Photo: BRDC Archive.

Jim Clark.

1962 Six pole positions from the nine-race Grand Prix season confirmed the pace of the Lotus 25, winning the Belgian, British and USGPs, with 4th in Germany and 9th in the Dutch, to finish as runner-up to Graham Hill in the World Championship. He won the Oulton Park Gold Cup, the Aintree 200, the Lombank Trophy, the Mexican Grand Prix (sharing with Trevor Taylor) and the Rand Grand Prix. During his trip to South Africa he was also 2nd at Westmead and in the Cape GP. He finished 6th at Sandown in Australia and 2nd in the Silverstone International Trophy. His other results included a 3rd in class at the Ollon-Villars Hillclimb in a Lotus 21, 4th in class at the Daytona 24 hours in a Lotus Elite, 3rd at Silverstone in an Aston DBR1 and victory at the Snetterton 3 hours in a Lotus 23.

1963 After a disappointing 8th in the Mexican Grand Prix, he proved almost unbeatable on his way to his first World title. His tally was seven pole positions, victories in the Belgian, Dutch, French, British, Italian, Mexican and South African, with 2nd in the German and 3rd in the US. In non-

1961 A first full year of Grand Prix racing in the Lotus 21 produced 3rd in the Dutch and French, 4th in the German, 7th in the US, 10th in Monaco and 12th in the Belgian, for 7th overall in the World Championship. His first F1 win came in the Pau Grand Prix and was followed by wins at the Rand GP, Westmead and East London on an end of season tour of South Africa. There was also 2nd place in the Silver City and Guards Trophies at Brands Hatch, 4th at Modena and in Austria, 6th at Syracuse, 7th at Solitude, 8th in the Aintree 200 and International Trophy. Earlier in the season he had taken 2nd at Levin and 7th in the New Zealand GP, while further outings for Aston Martin brought 4th in the TT and 6th in the Paris 1000km.

GRAND PRIX RECORD	
Starts	72
Wins	25
Poles	33
Fastest laps	28
WC points	274
Won his 17th Grand Prix	

championship races he won at Pau, Imola, in the International Trophy, at Karlskoga and in the Oulton Park Gold Cup, with 2nd in the Lombank Trophy, 3rd in the Aintree 200 and 8th at Solitude. He won his first Indycar race at the Milwaukee 200 and came 2nd at the Indianapolis 500 in a Lotus 29. He also drove a Lotus 23B to sports car success winning at Oulton Park (twice), winning the Crystal Palace Trophy, the Snetterton 3 hours, at Riverside and finishing 3rd in class at Mosport. In saloons he won at Brands Hatch in a Ford Galaxie and at Snetterton in a Lotus Cortina.

1964 Victories came in the Dutch, Belgian and British Grand Prix, along with five more pole positions, 4th in Monaco and 5th in Mexico resulted in 3rd in the World Championship. He won the News of the World Trophy at Goodwood, the Solitude GP and took 2nd in the Oulton Park Gold Cup and Mediterranean GP. In F2 he won the British Eagle Trophy at Brands Hatch, the Grovewood Trophy at Mallory Park, at Pau and in the Eifelrennen, with 2nd at Karlskoga and 4th at Reims. He became the British Saloon Car Champion with a Lotus Cortina, with class wins at Oulton Park (twice), Crystal Palace, Brands Hatch, Goodwood, Aintree, Snetterton and Silverstone, plus a class win and 2nd on a trip to Sebring. His other results included victory in the Oulton Park Trophy with a Lotus 19 sports car, a GT win at Oulton Park and 2nd in class at Silverstone in an Elan. With the un-loved Lotus 30 sports car, he took a victory at Mallory Park, 2nd at Aintree, 3rd in the LA Times GP at Riverside and 12th in the TT.

1965 After winning the Grand Prix season opener in South Africa, he missed Monaco as he was away winning the Indianapolis 500. He returned with successive wins in the Belgian, French, British, Dutch and German, followed by 10th in Italy and retirements in US and Mexico, by which time his second World Championship title was sealed. Victories at Levin, in the Lady Wigram Trophy, the Teretonga Trophy, at Warwick Farm and Lakeside, with 2nd at Sandown secured the Tasman title. He won the non-championship races at Syracuse and the Goodwood Glover Trophy, with 2nd in the Mediterranean GP. In F2 he won the British Eagle Trophy at Brands Hatch, the London Trophy at Crystal Palace, at Albi, Pau, Rouen, with 3rd at Reims and Snetterton and 6th at Oulton Park, becoming the Autocar British F2 Champion. With the Lotus 30 he won the Lavant Cup at Goodwood and the Guards Trophy at Silverstone, while in the Lotus 40 he was 2nd at Riverside. With a Lotus Cortina he won the Sebring 3 hours and at Goodwood, with 2nd at Oulton Park and Snetterton.

1966 By his own standards it was a poor year for Grand Prix results, but victory in the US, 3rd in the Dutch and 4th in the British were still enough to clinch 6th in the World Championship. He was runner-up in the Tasman Championship, with a win at Warwick Farm, 2nd at Sandown and Levin, 3rd in the Australian GP and 7th at Longford. He finished 3rd in the Oulton Park Gold Cup, and in F2 was 2nd at Montlhery, and 3rd at Keimola, Karlskoga and Brands Hatch. With the Lotus Cortina he had wins at Oulton Park, Snetterton, Goodwood and Brands Hatch and retired a similar version from the RAC

Rally. Back at the Indy 500 his Lotus managed 2nd place behind Hill's Lola.

1967 His Grand Prix form was restored with victories in the Dutch, British, US and Mexican, which when added to 3rd in Italy and 6th in Belgium secured 3rd in the Championship for his Lotus 49. He was Tasman Champion again, winning the Lady Wigram Trophy, Lakeside, Levin, the Teretonga Trophy and Sandown, with 2nd at Longford and the New Zealand and Australian GPs. In F2 he won in Madrid, Barcelona and Keimola, with 2nd at Zolder, 3rd at Albi, Karlskoga, Hameenlina and Albi and 4th at Pau. He retired from the Indy 500, retired a Vollstedt Ford from the Rex Mays 300 at Riverside and a Ford Fairlane from Rockingham.

1968 Started the year in winning form at the South African Grand Prix, and had taken Tasman wins in the Australian Grand Prix, the Lady Wigram Trophy, at Surfers Paradise and Warwick Farm. His first F2 outing ended in retirement in Barcelona, but his second ended fatally at Hockenheim when his Lotus left the track and hit a tree on that black day in April.

PIERS COURAGE
Born May 27th 1942
Killed June 21st 1970

The son of the chairman of Courage Brewery, Piers had no desire to join the family business, preferring instead to go racing. But he had to make his own way in the sport and was not allowed any family money to fund his career. He had three fairly successful years in Formula 3, before making the jump to F2 and then his Grand Prix debut in 1966. After just over a year with Parnell's team, he joined his former F3 team mate Frank Williams to race a Brabham and then a De Tomaso. After shedding a reputation for crashing, he was beginning to make his mark on the Grand Prix scene, notably with a fine second at Monaco in the Brabham in 1969. The following season he raced the less competitive De Tomaso but crashed during the 1970 Dutch Grand Prix. Sadly, with his potential still to be fully realised, he perished in the flames that engulfed the car.

Piers Courage.

Photo: BRDC Archive.

1962 Began racing with a Lotus 7 at Brands Hatch and contested 25 races with little success, apart from 3rd in his heat for the Jack Fairman Trophy at Castle Combe.

1963 Continuing with sports cars but with a Merlyn MK4, he collected 3rd in class at both Snetterton and Oulton Park.

1964 He teamed up with Jonathan Williams and they toured Europe with their F3 cars. After starting with a Lotus 22, he changed to a Brabham, collecting 2nd at Zandvoort, 3rd at Reims and 4th in the Eifelrennen.

1965 Joined the Charles Lucas F3 team to partner Frank Williams in a pair of Brabhams, winning at Silverstone (three times), Brands Hatch (twice), Goodwood, Caserta, Rome, Rouen, Oulton Park and Mallory Park. He also took 2nd at Reims and in Goodwood's Chichester Cup, 3rd at Monza, 4th at Oulton Park and 10th at Zandvoort. He also came 2nd in a Brands Hatch sports car race with a Lotus 23 and was the Premier Grovewood Award winner.

1966 With his F3 Lotus 41 he was a member of the English World Cup winning team. He also collected victories at Pau, Rouen, Brands Hatch (twice) and Albi, with 2nd at Karlskoga, Crystal Palace and Brands Hatch. His Grand Prix debut followed in a Ron Harris-entered F2 Lotus 44, but he crashed out of the race. At Le Mans he shared a Ferrari 365GTB with Roy Pike to 8th and

finished 3rd in a GT race at Crystal Palace in a Lotus Elan.

1967 He joined the Parnells to partner Chris Irwin in the semi-works BRM Grand Prix team, but after retiring in South Africa and Monaco and failing to get a start at the British, he left the team to concentrate on F2 with John Coombs. After starting with a McLaren he changed to a Brabham, collecting 2nd at Zandvoort, 3rd and 5th at Hockenheim, 5th at Crystal Palace, 7th at Brands Hatch, 8th at Jarama, 9th at Tulln Langenlebarn and 10th at Albi, to secure 4th in the Championship. Crashes at Pau, Brands Hatch and Enna however still cast doubts over his future. He drove at Le Mans again sharing a Ferrari 412P with Attwood, but retired.

1968 After acquiring the McLaren from John Coombs, he tackled the Tasman Series, taking 2nd at Levin, 3rd in the New Zealand Grand Prix, at Surfers Paradise and Warwick Farm. He added 4th in the Lady Wigram Trophy, 5th at the Australian Grand Prix and victory in the finale at Longford, beating Clark and Hill in a wet race to clinch third in the championship. With new found confidence he rejoined Parnells for the Grand Prix season, but started with four consecutive retirements in Spain, Monaco, Belgium and the Dutch. His first championship point followed with 6th in the French Grand Prix, and that was followed by 8th in the British and German, 4th in the Italian, 7th at the US and further retirements in Canada and Mexico. He took his BRM to 5th in the International

GRAND PRIX RECORD	
Starts	28
Wins	0
Poles	0
Fastest laps	0
WC points	20
Best finish	2nd

Trophy, while in F2 he raced a Brabham BT20 for Frank Williams. Results included 2nd at Enna, 3rd at Reims, Hockenheim and Albi, 4th at Barcelona, 7th at Hockenheim, 10th at Zandvoort and 14th at Tulln Langenlebarn, to finish 6th in the F2 Championship. At the end of the year he also contested the Temporada F2 Series, finishing 1st and 3rd at Buenos Aires and 6th at Cordoba, to take 3rd in the championship.

1969 The year began again with 3rd place in the Tasman Series, winning at Invercargill and Longford, with 2nd at Levin, 3rd in the New Zealand Grand Prix and 4th in the Lady Wigram Trophy. His Grand Prix year was spent with Frank Williams in a Brabham BT26A, retiring from the Spanish but after qualifying 8th in Monaco he finished an astonishing 2nd. Although he retired in the Dutch, French, German and Canadian races, he was 2nd again in the US, 5th in the British and Italian and 10th at the Mexican, securing 8th in the World Championship. He had also driven the Brabham to 5th in the International Trophy, and raced in F2 again with a victory at Enna, 3rd at Hockenheim, Pau, Zolder, Reims and Madrid, and 7th at Thruxton and Albi. At Le Mans he shared a Matra to 4th place with Jean-Pierre Beltoise.

1970 Staying with Williams but racing the De Tomaso chassis, he was 3rd in the International Trophy, but retired from the opening Grand Prix in South Africa. He failed to start the Spanish after a crash in practice, was unclassified at Monaco and retired in the Belgian. Tragically, he lost his life at Zandvoort in June when he crashed during the Dutch Grand Prix and his car rolled and caught fire. Earlier in the year he raced for Alfa Romeo, sharing a T33-3 with De Adamich to victories in the Buenos Aires 200 and Temporada race, with 6th in the Buenos Aires 1000km and 8th at Sebring.

❖

VIC ELFORD
Born June 10th 1935

Vic Elford.

Photo: BRDC Archive.

One of the last genuine all-rounders, Elford had a European Rally Championship title under his belt before settling down to a circuit racing career. Having started rallying in 1960, he enjoyed a great deal of success but by the mid 1960s he was starting to split his time between rallying and racing.

He was a winner in saloon cars and sports cars winning many of the world's classic races. In Grands Prix he raced a works Cooper in 1968 and took a career best fourth place on his debut in France. Amazingly, he had only made his single-seater debut earlier that season in a Formula 2 car at the Nurburgring. He continued in Formula 1 the following year with Colin Crabbe's McLaren. At the end of 1972 he retired from full-time racing, but made occasional returns as recently as the early eighties. From 1977 to 1980 he was involved in team management with ATS, Inaltera and Audi.

1960 Navigated David Siegle-Morris' Triumph TR3A to numerous rallying successes.

1961 Continued navigating, and started racing his ex-Whitmore Mini, taking 2nd at Brands Hatch and Oulton Park and 3rd at Mallory Park.

1962 Started his year rallying with a loaned DKW, winning the Maidstone & Mid-Kent Hopper National Rally and taking 2nd on the Birmingham Post Rally. After joining Standard Triumph he took 6th in class on the Tulip and lay in the top 10 of the RAC Rally until his gearbox broke.

GRAND PRIX RECORD

Starts	13
Wins	0
Poles	0
Fastest laps	0
WC points	8
Best finish	4th

1963 Continuing with Triumph he took 4th in class on the Tulip Rally and was 4th on the Alpine until his TR3 left the road. He was 24th on the Monte Carlo and drove a prototype Vitesse on the Liege-Rome-Liege until it was burnt out after a carburettor fire.

1964 Rallying with Ford he won the Touring Car category on the Alpine, finished 10th overall and 3rd in class on the Safari, 3rd in class on the RAC and 4th in class in the Tour de France with a Cortina.

1965 Another year with Ford brought 2nd on the Circuit of Ireland, 3rd on the RAC Rally and the lead on the Alpine until the distributor broke just before the end. He also raced an Anglia to 3rd in class at the Snetterton 500 and 4th in the Birkett 6 hours at Silverstone, and a Lotus Cortina to 2nd in class at Castle Combe.

1966 With Ford he was disqualified from victory in the Rally of the Flowers, but took 2nd on the Tulip and 10th with a class win on the Swedish Rally, before changing to Porsche and claiming 3rd on the Tour de Corse.

1967 Won the Group 3 Rally title with Porsche, after winning the Tulip, Geneva, German and Lyon-Charbonnieres events. He also took 3rd on the Monte Carlo and Tour de Corse, 4th on the Marathon de la Route, and 5th on the Rally of the Flowers with a Lancia Fulvia. He won the 2000cc class in the British Saloon Car Championship in a Porsche 911, with 2nd in the International Trophy support race, a win and 3rd at Croft, 3rd at Brands Hatch, 5th at Oulton Park, 3rd in the Lombank Trophy at Brands Hatch and 5th at Silverstone (twice). He also had a rallycross win at Lydden. In sports car racing he took 3rd on the Targa Florio, at Mugello and in the Nurburgring 1000km, 6th at Reims and 7th at Le Mans with Porsche.

1968 Made his Grand Prix debut with Cooper in the French and finished 4th. After retiring in the British, German and Italian races, he took 5th in Canada, retired again the US and finished 8th in Mexico before the team withdrew at the end of the year. In rallying he won the Monte Carlo, in sports cars he won at Daytona, Nurburgring and on the Targa Florio for Porsche. He added 2nd at Paris and Sebring, 3rd in the BOAC 500, 8th in Austria, 9th at Monza and 10th at Solitude. He started the year in saloons again, with class wins at Brands Hatch and Silverstone and 4th at Thruxton. Finally, in F2 he drove a Winkelman Brabham and Harris Costin Protos, taking 7th at the Nurburgring in his first single-seater race.

1969 After starting the Grand Prix season with 7th at Monaco in Colin Crabbe's Cooper, he changed to a McLaren and took 10th in the Dutch, 5th in the French, 6th in the British and crashed in the German, breaking his arm and collarbone. He had earlier finished 12th in the International Trophy in the Cooper, but concentrated on sports cars with Porsche. He led at Le Mans until his 917's gearbox failed, finished 2nd at the Norisring and Watkins Glen and 3rd at the Nurburgring and Spa. He won an Interserie race at Hockenheim in a McLaren M6B, won at the Nurburgring in a Chevron B16, retired from the Monte Carlo Rally and raced in the NASCAR Daytona 500.

1970 With a Porsche 917 he won at the Nurburgring, with 2nd in the BOAC 500, 3rd at Spa, 4th at Watkins Glen and in the Austrian 1000km. In CanAm he was 3rd at Watkins Glen in a 917 and 6th at Road Atlanta in a Chaparral. He had an Interserie win at Hockenheim in a McLaren M6B/12, won the Nurburgring 500km in a Chevron B16 and had a TransAm win at Watkins Glen in a Chevrolet Camaro.

1971 A one-off Grand Prix drive with BRM ended with 11th in the German. He was 8th in the World Sports Car Championship with Porsche, winning at the Nurburgring. In CanAm he finished 9th in a McLaren M8E, with 3rd at Road America, 4th at Minnesota and 8th at Watkins Glen. He was runner-up in the European Sports 2-litre Series in a Lola T212, winning at the Nurburgring, with 2nd at Paul Ricard and Hockenheim, 3rd at Vallelunga and 4th at the Salzburgring. His other outings included 3rd in a Hockenheim Interserie race with a Lola T222, 4th in the Tour de France with a Ferrari and another run at the NASCAR Daytona 500.

1972 Changing from Porsche to Alfa Romeo, he took 3rd in the Daytona 6 hours, 4th in the Buenos Aires and BOAC 1000kms and 11th at the Nurburgring. He also had a 2nd at Enna in a Lola T290 sports and F2 outings with 4th at Crystal Palace and 10th at the Nurburgring in a Chevron B20, before announcing his retirement at the end of the year.

1973 Came out of retirement to take 6th at Le Mans in a Ferrari 365 GTB and another Interserie win.

1982 Contested the Paris-Dakar rally in a Subaru.

1983 Was due to race a BMW M1 in the Nurburgring 1000km but the car expired during qualifying. He also raced at Le Mans, retiring a Rondeau with a blown engine.

1984 Finished 15th in the Daytona 24 hours in a Porsche 928S.

KEITH GREENE
Born January 5th 1938

The son of Gilby Engineering boss Syd Greene came into the sport at a very early age, competing in minor events before the age of 18. Much of his career was linked with Gilby cars, including his three Grand Prix starts. Although his single-seater outings came to an end in 1962, he continued to race successfully in sports and saloons. Since his retirement from driving, he has managed teams in virtually every category of racing from the Brabham Grand Prix, through Group C sports to the Spice Capris and works Renaults in Touring Cars.

1955 Took a class win at the Stapleford Hillclimb in a Cooper Climax sports car.

1956 Continued to race his Cooper, winning both Brands Hatch and Goodwood Handicaps, with 2nd at Goodwood, 2nd and 5th at the inaugural Mallory Park meeting, 4th at Silverstone and 6th at Brands Hatch.

1957 Another year with the Cooper brought 2nd and at 3rd at Snetterton, a Handicap victory, plus two 2nds, 3rd, 4th and 7th at Goodwood, and a class win at the Stapleford Hillclimb. He drove a Lotus XI sports to 2nd at Goodwood and drove the Gilby Maserati to 4th place at Snetterton.

1958 Further success came with the Lotus XI, notably at Goodwood with three wins and six 2nds. He added three wins at Brands Hatch, a 3rd at Snetterton, 5th in class at the Nurburgring 1000km, 7th in the British Grand Prix sports car race, 10th in the TT and 2nd overall at the Stapleford Hillclimb.

1959 Moving up to a Gilby F2 Cooper T45, brought a win at Snetterton and 2nd place in the F2 section of the Aintree 200. He also claimed 2nd at Whitchurch, 3rd in a Snetterton Libre race, 4th in a Goodwood Libre race, 8th at Pau and 2nd in class at the Stapleford Hillclimb, but failed to qualify for the British Grand Prix. He won at Snetterton on his debut with a Lotus 17, taking two further sports car wins at the same circuit, along with 3rd at Whitchurch and 2nd in class at Stapleford.

1960 His Grand Prix debut came in the British, where his Gilby Cooper T45 Maserati retired due to overheating. Further outings with the car brought F1 and Libre wins at Snetterton, 12th in the Silver City Trophy at Brands Hatch and 13th in the International Trophy. With the Gilby Climax sports car he had a win and 3rd at Brands Hatch, victory at Snetterton, 2nd at Mallory Park, 3rd at Aintree and Silverstone, a class win at the Stapleford Hillclimb, but rolled the car during the Empire Trophy. He also shared a Lotus XI with Douglas Graham to 3rd in class at the Nurburgring 1000km.

1961 He finished 15th in the British Grand Prix in the F1 Gilby Climax and won a Snetterton Libre race with the

Keith Greene (Gilby Climax) at Aintree in 1960.

Photo: Ferret Fotographics.

GRAND PRIX RECORD	
Starts	3
Wins	0
Poles	0
Fastest laps	0
WC points	0
Best finish	15th

same car. He also took 2nd in the National Benzole Trophy at Snetterton and 4th in the Lewis-Evans Trophy at Brands Hatch. Continuing to race the sports version he took 2nd at Snetterton and shared a Porsche to 17th place in the TT.

1962 Although he practiced John Dalton's 18/21 Lotus at the British Grand Prix, the car was raced by Tony Shelly. He did however race a BRM-powered Gilby in Germany until the front suspension broke, but failed to qualify for the Italian. He also finished 3rd in Naples, 4th at Goodwood, at Snetterton and in the Brussels GP, 7th in the London Trophy at Crystal Palace and 15th in the International Trophy.

1963 Having forsaken single-seaters, he had a successful year on the national scene with a Lotus 23, in both sports and Libre races. He had two wins at Snetterton, a win at Brands Hatch, 2nd in the British Grand Prix sports car race and in the Lavant Cup. He added 3rd at Aintree, Crystal Palace and in the Guards Trophy, and two 4ths at Oulton Park. Partnering Andrew Hedges in an MG Midget, he was 3rd in class at the Nurburgring and 15th overall in the TT. Finally, he drove a Cortina to 3rd in class in an Aintree saloon car race.

1964 Shared an MG Midget with Hedges to 24th overall at the Nurburgring 1000km and with Alan Foster to 6th in the 500km.

1965 Raced Alan Foster's BMW in the British Saloon Car Championship, finishing 10th at the British Grand Prix. Shared an MG Midget with Hedges again at the Nurburgring 1000km, and finished 27th.

1966 Finished 8th at Silverstone with Foster's BMW in the British Saloon Car Championship and 5th in the Ilford Films 500 at Brands Hatch with Robert Ellice in a Lotus Elan.

1967 Shared a Lotus 47 at the BOAC Brands Hatch International.

1971 Took a Ford Escort to 6th overall and 2nd in class in a one-off return to the British Saloon Car Championship at Snetterton.

MIKE HAILWOOD
Born April 2nd 1940
Killed March 23rd 1981

Probably the greatest motorcycle racer ever, with nine World titles in 250cc, 350cc and 500cc, and a Tourist Trophy winner on no less than 12 occasions. However, he then tried to emulate John Surtees by bidding to win the World Championship on both two and four wheels during a career in which he traded back and forth between two and four wheels. Ironically, his best F1 result came with Surtees' team when he took second in the 1972 Italian GP.

Both his car racing and Grand Prix debut came in the same year, but after retiring at Monaco in 1965, he returned to full time motorcycle racing. Apart from a few sports car races his car racing career began to take off once more with Formula 5000, before taking the European F2 title with Surtees. After two successful years back in Grands Prix, he crashed heavily during the 1975 German Grand Prix and sustained serious leg injuries. Although his car racing career was all but over, he returned to further success on bikes and took another TT win in 1979. Sadly, he was killed along with his two children in a road accident near his home in 1981.

1963 Already famous for his motorcycle success, his car racing debut came in Formula Junior at Brands Hatch, finishing 5th in a Brabham. Following victories at Oulton Park, Mallory Park and a 3rd at Aintree, he found himself at the wheel of a Parnell Lotus 24 Climax in the British Grand Prix. He qualified 17th and finished 8th, while further outings with a Lola brought 10th in the Italian Grand Prix and 7th in the Oulton Park Gold Cup.

1964 A full Grand Prix campaign with Parnell's Lotus 25 BRM, brought a first World Championship point with 6th at the Monaco Grand Prix. He also took 8th in the French, Austrian and US races, but retired on his other four outings. In the non-championship races he collected 6th in the International Trophy, 7th at Syracuse and 9th at Solitude, along with 3rd in a Mallory Park Libre race with a Brabham.

1965 His only Grand Prix start of the year ended in retirement at Monaco, when the gearbox broke in his Lotus. He had already taken the car to 9th in the International Trophy, but frustrated by the lack of results, returned to bikes for the rest of the year.

1966 Concentrating on bikes, he made an end of year appearance at the Dickie Dale 3 hours race in South Africa, sharing a Bernard White-entered Ford GT40 to victory with David Hobbs.

1967 Another end of year break from bikes brought 3rd place in the Rand 9 hours at Kyalami, sharing Eddie Nelson's Ford GT40.

1968 Won the Lourenco Marques 3 hours, with 2nd in both the Cape International 3 hours at Killarney and the Roy Hesketh 3 hours, sharing a Mirage with Guthrie.

1969 Returned to cars and finished 3rd in the inaugural European Formula 5000 Championship with a Lola T142. He won at Brands Hatch, took 2nd at Snetterton, Hockenheim and Mondello Park, 3rd at Zandvoort, 5th in the Oulton Park Gold Cup, 8th at Oulton Park and 10th at Koksijde. At Magny Cours he won the Bourgogne Trophy with a Ferrari P4, finished 3rd at Le Mans and 5th at the Brands Hatch BOAC 500 sharing a Ford GT40 with Hobbs, and also claimed 7th in the Spa 1000km and 12th at the Norisring in a Mirage.

1970 Another year in F5000 brought victories for his Lola T190 in Silverstone's GKN Vanwall Trophy and at the Salzburgring. He collected 2nd places at Brands Hatch, Snetterton and Mallory Park, 3rd at Zolder and Brands Hatch, 4th at Anderstorp and Thruxton, 5th at Oulton Park, 7th overall and a class win in the International Trophy and 11th at Oulton Park. In South Africa he shared an Alfa Romeo T33/2 with Paddy Driver to 6th in the Capetown 3 hours and a Lola T210 with Hobbs to take 15th in the Kyalami 9 hours. He also had a one-off saloon car race at Brands Hatch in a Ford Escort.

1971 A late season return to Grands Prix with a works Surtees TS5 resulted in 4th place in the Italian and 15th in the US, despite spinning off on oil towards the end. He had continued to race in F5000 with a Surtees TS8 and finished as runner-up in the championship. He won the GKN Vanwall Trophy at Silverstone, the Yellow Pages Trophy at Mallory Park, the Uniflo Trophy at Silverstone as well as taking a further win at Mallory Park. Other results included 2nd places at Mallory Park, Thruxton and Oulton Park, along with 3rd at Mondello, 5th overall and a class win in the International Trophy, 8th at Brands Hatch and 11th overall with 6th in class at the Oulton Park Gold Cup. With a victory in the Bulawayo 3 hours with Driver and 2nd with Redman at the Capetown 3 hours in a Chevron B19, his 2nd place with Charlton in a Lola T210 at the final round of the Springbok Series was enough to secure 3rd overall in the championship.

1972 A full season of Grand Prix racing with Surtees brought plenty of promise, but both good fortune and wins

GRAND PRIX RECORD

Starts	50
Wins	0
Poles	0
Fastest laps	1
WC points	29
Best finish	2nd

Mike Hailwood in the McLaren in Yardley colours.

Photo: BRDC Archive.

eluded him. In South Africa he retired from 2nd place, he retired from the Spanish and Monaco before collecting 4th at the Belgian and Austrian, 6th at the French and a career best 2nd in the Italian to finish 8th in the World Championship. He comfortably won the European F2 title for Surtees, with wins at Mantorp Park and the Salzburgring, plus 2nd places at Crystal Palace, Rouen, the Osterreichring and Hockenheim, 5th at Mallory Park and Pau, 12th at Imola and 14th at Albi. In Brazil he contested the mini-F2 series and tasted success in the Tasman F5000 Series. 2nd in the New Zealand Grand Prix and the Lady Wigram Trophy, 3rd at Levin, 4th in the Australian Grand Prix, 5th at Warwick Farm and 6th at Surfers Paradise led to 2nd overall in the championship. With his F1 car he was 2nd in the Race of Champions, returning to Brands Hatch later in the year to take 9th in the John Player Challenge.

1973 A further year with Surtees brought little success, his TS14A retiring on 10 of its 15 starts. 7th in the Italian Grand Prix, 8th in Monaco, 9th in Canada, 10th in Austria and 14th in Germany were his only classified finishes. In F2 he finished 18th at Enna, but shared a Gulf Mirage with Bell and Schuppan to victory in the Spa 1000km, followed by 5th at Dijon, 4th at the Osterreichring and 5th at Watkins Glen with Watson. He was also awarded the George Medal for rescuing Clay Regazzoni from his blazing car at the South African Grand Prix.

1974 Moved to McLaren and became a regular top 10 finisher in the M23. He was 3rd in South Africa, 4th in the Argentinean and Dutch, 5th in the Brazilian, 7th in the Belgian and French, 9th in the Spanish, and retired at Monaco, the Swedish and British. But in Germany he crashed and broke his leg badly, effectively bringing an end to his single-seater career. He had already taken 4th in the Race of Champions and shared a Mirage with Bell to finish 2nd at Spa and 4th at Monza, Le Mans and the Osterreichring.

1976 Finished 20th at Pukekohe in the Benson & Hedges 1000km, sharing a Holden GTS with Phil Kerr.

1977 Raced a Lotus 18 in Historics at Amaroo Park.

1978 Having returned to bikes yet again, he took time out to race at Pukekohe, where he led the race with Hulme in an Escort RS2000 until the headgasket blew. He also retired from the Kyalami 1000km, sharing a BMW with Driver.

❖

Brian Hart.

Photo: BRDC Archive.

BRIAN HART
Born September 7th 1936

A successful driver in Formula Junior and Formula 2, whose own driving career began to take a back seat to his engineering expertise from the seventies onwards. His only Grand Prix appearance came in the F2 class of the 1967 German, but after making a name for himself building engines for F2 and sports cars, his first Grand Prix engine saw the light of day with Toleman. He continued to provide the power units for numerous categories, from hillclimb and rally cars to current Grand Prix cars.

1958 Had a win at Snetterton in his 1172 Lotus.

1959 Won the 1172 Championship with a Terrier, taking 19 wins from 21 races, including five wins at Silverstone, three at Snetterton, and two at Oulton Park. He also had a 2nd at Brands Hatch and drove a Lola sports to 3rd at Silverstone.

1960 With his Terrier Sports he collected a win at Snetterton, but concentrated on the Formula Junior version. He had a 2nd at Brands Hatch, 3rd at Snetterton and Mallory Park and 12th in the British Grand Prix support race.

1961 A further year with the Formula Junior Terrier brought a win at Mallory Park, 2nd at Goodwood and 5th in the Chichester Cup.

1970 Had a few races again in an F2 Brabham, finishing 2nd in the Rhine Cup.

1971 A final year of racing again in the F2 Brabham, brought 3rd at Mallory Park, 6th and 7th at Hockenheim and Monza, before his ever-growing competition engine business took over.

GRAND PRIX RECORD

Starts	1
Wins	0
Poles	0
Fastest laps	0
WC points	0
Best finish	12th

1962 Still in Formula Junior but with a Lotus 20, he won at Brands Hatch and Silverstone, with 2nd in the National Benzole Trophy at Snetterton, 3rd at Oulton Park and 4th in the Yorke Trophy at Silverstone. He had three Libre victories at Mallory Park, plus one each at Snetterton and Cadwell, had a 2nd in class at Snetterton and took 5th in the London Trophy against some F1 machinery.

1963 Moving up to a Lotus 22 his Formula Junior success continued, winning the Scott-Brown Memorial at Snetterton, with a further win at Crystal Palace, 2nd in the London Trophy and 5th at Goodwood. He used the same car in Libre races to win the Leicester Trophy at Mallory Park, he also won at Brands Hatch, with a further 2nd at Mallory Park and a class win at Silverstone. The Terrier sports collected a class win and 2nd at Mallory Park, with 3rd in class at Brands Hatch and he also drove the Godiva Climax to 3rd in a Mallory Park GT race. He was also 3rd in the end of season Grovewood Awards.

1964 A step up to F2 with Ron Harris and Lotus brought a win at Enna, 4th at Montlhery and Zolder, 12th with a class win at the Aintree 200 and 13th in Berlin.

1965 Continuing in F2 with a Lotus he was 7th in the Oulton Park Gold Cup, 8th at Brands Hatch and 11th at Albi. He also shared a Jaguar E-Type with Robert Ellice to 3rd in class at the Brands Hatch Guards 100.

1966 Stepped back down to F3 and finished 3rd at Monthlery and 5th at Brands Hatch in the Euro Challenge.

1967 Raced the wooden Harris Costin Protos in F2 and finished 12th overall and 4th in class at the German Grand Prix, his only World Championship appearance. He also took 2nd and 10th places at Hockenheim, 6th at Zandvoort, 8th at Enna and 10th at Crystal Palace.

1968 Another season in F2 started with a Gerard-run Merlyn and ended in a Church Farm Brabham. He had a 5th at Reims, 6th at Hockenheim, 7th at Jarama and Enna, 11th at Zandvoort and 13th at Tulln Langenlebarn.

1969 Due to the pressure from his growing business, race outings were rare. He won the Rhine Cup at Hockenheim in a Gerard F2 Brabham, with 11th at Enna, 12th at Tulln Langenlebarn. He also had the occasional Libre races with the same car, taking a win at Mallory Park and 2nd at Silverstone.

50 years of British Grand Prix drivers

Part Two
1960s

CHAPTER 8

DAVID HOBBS
Born June 9th 1939

David Hobbs.

Having served his apprenticeship in Sports Cars, Hobbs progressed through Formula Junior and F2, but made only occasional Grand Prix appearances. One-off races for both BRM and Honda failed to lead to permanent positions with the teams, and he only started seven races in all over a seven year period.

His single-seater career peaked when he won the US Formula 5000 title in 1971, before settling into CanAm, IMSA and the World Sports Series. The latter part of his career was spent almost entirely in the US, where after finally retiring from driving in the early nineties, he took up race commentary.

GRAND PRIX RECORD	
Starts	7
Wins	0
Poles	0
Fastest laps	0
WC points	0
Best finish	7th

1959 Made his race debut in a Morris Oxford automatic, taking 3rd in a Silverstone handicap.

1960 Moved on to a Jaguar XK140, taking a win and three 2nds at Silverstone and wins at Goodwood and Snetterton before rolling the car at Oulton Park.

1961 Driving a Lotus Elite automatic, he secured 14 wins from 22 starts, including three wins at Oulton Park, four at Silverstone, plus Brands Hatch, Aintree, Mallory Park and Snetterton. Other results included a 2nd and two 3rds at Silverstone, a 2nd and two 3rds at Mallory Park, 2nd at Snetterton and a class win sharing with Bill Pinckney in the Nurburgring 1000km.

1962 A varied year which saw further outings in a Lotus Elite, taking two wins at Snetterton, a win at Silverstone and 8th with a class win at Le Mans sharing with Frank Gardner. He also raced a Jaguar E-Type to 3rd in class in the Sussex Trophy, 4th at Mallory Park and 5th at Oulton Park. He drove a Jaguar Saloon to 3rd at Aintree and 4th at Mallory Park and collected his first single-seater win with an MRP Cooper at Oulton Park.

1963 Finished 4th in the Formula Junior Championship with an MRP Lola, with 2nd in the International Trophy support race and at Oulton Park. He too 3rd at Mallory Park and in the British Grand Prix support race, 4th at Goodwood and in the Anerley and Crystal Palace Trophies, and 6th at Reims. He won at Brands Hatch and had a two 2nds in class with a Lotus Elite at Silverstone.

1964 Moving into F2 with a works Merlyn and a Lola, he had a best result of 5th at Zolder. At Roskilde he had a win with a Lotus Cortina and also raced a Lotus 23 and Porsche 904. He finished 21st at Le Mans with Slotemaker in a Triumph Spitfire.

1965 Another varied year which saw him take 7th at Pau and 12th at Snetterton in an F2 Lotus. He raced a Willment F3 Lotus and a Triumph Spitfire at Le Mans, but most of his success came with a Lola T70. He won the Daily Mirror Trophy at Croft, the Guards Trophy at Mallory Park and a GT race at Snetterton, with 2nd in the TT and 3rd at the Lavant Cup at Goodwood.

1966 Had his first F1 race taking Bernard White's BRM to 3rd at Syracuse. His other single-seater outings included 4th at Barcelona in an F2 Lola and 6th in the Leston International Trophy at Brands Hatch in an F3 Lotus. In GTs he won the Dickie Dale 3 hours at Roy Hesketh with Hailwood in a Ford GT40 and took 3rd in the Silverstone Martini Trophy at Silverstone with a Lola T70. He finished 4th at the Ilford Films 500 at Brands Hatch and British Eagle Trophy with Salmon in a Ferrari 250LM. He also raced a Mini to 2nd place in a Snetterton saloon car race.

1967 His Grand Prix debut came with Bernard White's BRM in the British, qualifying 14th and finishing 8th. He also drove the second works car in Canada, finishing 9th. In F2 he drove a Surtees Lola, taking 10th overall and 3rd in class at the German Grand Prix, and also raced an Alexis. He raced Malcolm Gartlan's Ford GT40 in the Autosport GT Series.

1968 A one-off Grand Prix drive with Honda at the Italian ended in engine failure. In the International Trophy and Oulton Park Gold Cup he was 6th in a BRM and drove a Ferrari P261 to 9th in the Race of Champions. F2 outings in a David Bridges Lola T100 and a Harris Tecno brought a best of 5th at Hockenheim, while a year in saloons with a Gartlan Ford Falcon resulted in a wins at Silverstone and Brands Hatch. He also took 2nd at Thruxton, Croft and in the Motor 200 at Brands Hatch, 3rd at Oulton Park and Mallory Park and 4th at Brands Hatch. With the Gulf Mirage he won the Monza 1000km with Hawkins and the Rand 9 hours with Ickx, plus 2nd in the Cape 3 hours, and 2nd at Watkins Glen, 4th at Spa and 6th at Nurburgring in a Ford GT40. He was also 2nd in the Oulton Park Spring Trophy in Piper's Ferrari 330 P3/4.

1969 Raced for Surtees in both the European and US Formula 5000 Championships. He missed out on the US title by one point, after winning at Sebring and taking 2nd at Lime Rock. In Europe he was eighth in the championship, winning at Mondello Park, with 2nd at Oulton Park and Mallory Park. With a Ford GT40 he came 3rd at Le Mans and 5th in the BOAC 500 at Brands Hatch, plus 7th at Spa in a Mirage with Hailwood.

1970 Continued in the US Formula 5000 Championship, with victories at Donnybrooke and Lime Rock and 3rd at Mosport to secure 3rd overall in the championship. His best result in the European series was 5th at Zandvoort in the Surtees TS5A. His other results included 8th at Riverside in a Pontiac TransAm.

1971 Changing to a Hogan Lola T300 he won the US F5000 title, winning at Laguna Seca, Seattle, Road America, Edmonton and Lime Rock, with 2nd at Mid-Ohio and 7th at Donnybrooke. At the Indy 500 he finished 20th in a Lola and deputised for Donohue at the US Grand Prix in a Penske McLaren, finishing 10th. In sports cars he was 3rd at Daytona, 6th at Sebring and 5th in the BOAC 500 with Ferrari 512Ms. He also raced a CanAm McLaren M8D and took 4th in the STP Trophy in Bermuda with a McLaren M10B.

1972 In US F5000 he won for Hogan and Lola in Edmonton with 6th at Donnybrooke. He was 7th in the CanAm Championship in a Lola T310, after 4th at Watkins Glen, 5th at Edmonton and Riverside and 6th at Mid-Ohio. He too 5th in the Tasman Series with a McLaren M18/22, following a win at Adelaide, 3rd in the New Zealand and Australian Grands Prix, and 4th at Surfers Paradise.

1973 Another year with Hogan's F5000 Lola brought 3rd at Laguna Seca, 4th at Riverside and Elkhart Lake, 6th at Mid-Ohio and Watkins Glen and 7th at Pocono. In the Indy 500 he finished 11th in an Eagle Offenhauser, while his CanAm McLaren M20 finished 2nd at Watkins Glen and 4th at Road Atlanta and Edmonton. Back in the European F5000 Championship he won the GKN Vanwall Trophy at Silverstone and took 5th at Brands Hatch in his Lola.

1974 Two final Grand Prix outings in a works McLaren, deputising for Hailwood, brought 7th in Austria and 9th in Italy, but the highlight of his year was 5th place in the Indy 500 with a McLaren Offenhauser. He finished 5th in the US F5000, with a win at Mosport, 3rd at Ontario and 4th at Mid-Ohio and Elkhart Lake. He was 6th in the Rothmans European F5000 Championship, winning at Mallory Park and Mugello, with 2nd at Oulton Park, 3rd at Silverstone and 5th at Monza. Sharing a Gulf Ford with Bell he also secured 3rd in the BOAC 1000 and Kyalami 6 hours, plus 8th at Watkins Glen sharing a Porsche Carrera with Posey.

1975 Apart from occasional USAC and CanAm outings, he raced exclusively in US F5000, finishing 6th in the championship. He was 3rd at Mid-Ohio, 4th at Mosport, 5th at Long Beach and Road Atlanta and 6th at Laguna Seca.

1976 Started the year sharing a BMW CSL with Parsons to 10th at Daytona, before concentrating on the unreliable Jaguar XJ12C Saloon.

1977 Returned to the US to race a McLaren BMW 320i in IMSA, winning at Sears Point, Ontario and Monterrey, with 4th at Atlanta.

1978 Finished 6th in the IMSA Championship with a win at Hallett and shared a BMW 535 with Keizan to 5th in the Wynns 1000 at Kyalami.

1979 Took his IMSA BMW to 5th in the championship, winning at Hallett and Elkhart Lake, with 2nd at Monterrey, Lime Rock and Brainerd, 3rd and 4th at

Gamesville, 5th at Lexington and 6th at Daytona. His other results included 2nd at Oulton Park and Silverstone and 3rd at Brands Hatch in the BMW County Championship.

1980 Won the Lumbermans 500 at Mid-Ohio with Redman in a Lola T333CS.

1981 Racing a BMW M1 he collected 4th in the Silverstone 6 hours, 6th in the LA Times 6 hours and 16th at Daytona. In IMSA he took 4th at Portland, 5th at Mid-Ohio and 6th at Laguna Seca. He also shared a BMW 635 CSI with Grice to 7th at Bathurst.

1982 Sharing a Porsche 935 with Fitzpatrick he was 4th at Le Mans and 3rd in the Shell 1000 at Brands Hatch. He won the IMSA races at Mid Ohio and Elkhart Lake with 5th at Laguna Seca in Fitzpatrick's 935. He shared a BMW 635 CSI with Richards to 6th at Bathurst and also raced a Lola T610, Triumph Dolomite and Nissan Skyline.

1983 Won the TransAm title in a Chevrolet Camaro, winning at Summit Point, Sears Point, Elkhart Lake and Riverside, with 2nd at Moroso Park, Mid-Ohio and Brainerd and 4th at Portland and Las Vegas. Sharing Fitzpatrick's Porsche 935 he was 3rd at Spa, 5th at Monza, 6th at the Nurburgring and 8th at Silverstone, plus 4th in the Miami IMSA race. He also finished 2nd at Imola and 4th at Mugello in a 956.

1984 Finished 8th in the World Sports Endurance Championship, with 2nd at Mosport and Nurburgring, 3rd at Le Mans and 6th at Brands Hatch in a 956. He collected 3rd at the Daytona 24 hours with Tullius and Bundy in a Jaguar XJR-5 and took 2nd at Elkhart Lake and 4th at Daytona with Leven's 962. His Corvette was 6th in the TransAm Series, with 2nd at Summit Point, 3rd at Road Atlanta, Watkins Glen and Las Vegas and 4th at Seattle.

1985 At Le Mans he was 4th with Gartner and Edwards in a Porsche 956. He finished 5th at Hockenheim, 2nd in the Miami IMSA race with a March 85G, 3rd at Atlanta and 2nd in the Lumbermans 500 in a 962 and 10th in the Detroit TransAm race with a Pontiac.

1986 Concentrating on an IMSA BMW his best result was 4th at Portland.

1987 Drove for Nissan in IMSA, taking 5th at Laguna Seca and also drove a Joest Porsche 962 at Le Mans.

1988 Shared Porsche 962s to 5th at Le Mans with Theys and Konrad, 4th at Silverstone with Wollek and Streiff, and 7th at the Nurburgring with Donnelly. He also shared a Corvette in IMSA with Forbes-Robinson, taking 4th at Columbus.

1989 Retired at Le Mans when sharing a Porsche 962 with Hill.

1990 Finished 21st at Fuji in a Spice and 8th at Dijon sharing a Porsche 962 with Palmer.

1993 Took 2nd at Indianapolis in the Fast Masters Jaguar XJ220 Challenge.

❖

CHRIS IRWIN
Born June 27th 1942

Chris Irwin.

Irwin was a star in the making after rising successfully through F3 and F2, with numerous victories under his belt. His Formula 1 break came with Brabham in 1966, before a season at Parnell's team in 1967. Despite not having the best of machinery, he collected his only points-scoring Grand Prix finish with fifth in the French GP at Le Mans.

But after stepping back to F2 for the following year, he earned a drive in Alan Mann's Ford F3L Sports Prototype. At the Nurburgring he crashed and sustained serious head injuries and although he eventually recovered, his racing career was over.

GRAND PRIX RECORD	
Starts	10
Wins	0
Poles	0
Fastest laps	0
WC points	2
Best finish	5th

1961 Made his racing debut with a Jim Russell-entered Lotus 18.

1962 Had one further race in the Lotus 18 and finished 2nd at Oulton Park in an Austin Healey Sprite.

1963 With a Merlyn MK4 he had a sports car win at Snetterton, with 2nd at Silverstone, a class win at Goodwood, 2nd in class at Brands Hatch and Snetterton, and two 3rds at Brands Hatch.

1964 Moved into single-seaters with a Chequered Flag F3 Merlyn, taking wins at Goodwood, (twice) Aintree, Mallory Park and Crystal Palace, 2nd at Silverstone, Oulton Park and Brands Hatch (twice), with 3rd at the Auvergne Trophy and in an Oulton Park Libre race. He collected 3rd place in the end of year Grovewood Awards.

1965 Still with Merlyn he graduated to F2 and led the Eifelrennen until retiring. He finished 8th at Oulton Park, 13th at Snetterton and 16th at Reims. He also took over the F3 car again from the injured Roger Mac taking 2nd at Monaco and in the Auvergne Trophy, and 3rd at Roskilde. Further F3 races with a Brabham secured victories at Brands Hatch (twice), at Karlskoga and Crystal Palace, with 3rd at Copenhagen and Zandvoort.

1966 Another year in F3 brought 17 wins from 30 starts. His Brabham won the European Challenge at Brands Hatch and was part of the victorious World Cup winning team. He won the Chichester Cup at Goodwood, at Roskilde, Karlskoga and Crystal Palace (twice), with 2nd in the International Trophy, Leinster Trophy, at Brands Hatch, Monaco and Silverstone, 3rd at Monza, 3rd and 4th at Reims and 5th at Brands Hatch. In the Temporada F3 Series he finished 2nd after winning in Buenos Aires, taking 2nd at Mendoza and 4th at Mar del Plata. His reward was a Grand Prix debut with a works Brabham BT11 at the British, qualifying 12th and finishing a very promising 7th. He also had an F2 run in a works Brabham Honda, finishing 3rd at Albi.

1967 Entered the Grand Prix arena with Parnells and started the year with 8th place in the Tasman Series, after taking 3rd at Longford and 4th at Sandown in his BRM. Back in Britain he collected 6th in the Race of Champions and 7th in the International Trophy, but made his first Grand Prix appearance of the year with an ageing Lotus BRM at the Dutch, still finishing 7th. After retiring from the Belgian, he took a career best 5th in the French, 7th in the

British and 9th in the German, ending the year with four consecutive retirements in Canada, Italy, US and Mexico. He had also taken the Lotus BRM to 4th at Syracuse, while in F2 he raced a Lola to 3rd at Jarama, 5th at Albi and 7th in the Eifelrennen and Tulln Langenlebarn and shared a Lola Aston Martin with Peter de Klerk at Le Mans.

1968 He finished 6th in the F2 Championship driving a Surtees-entered Lola T100, winning the Eifelrennen and taking 3rd at Zolder and the Nurburgring. With a year out from Grand Prix, he raced Alan Mann's Ford F3L Sports Car and was seriously injured after crashing during a race at the Nurburgring. He never raced again.

❖

CHRIS LAWRENCE
Born July 27th 1933

A name synonymous with the Morgan sports car marque, that took him to a championship title and a class win at Le Mans and numerous national successes. He also raced the Deep Sanderson sports and Formula Junior cars of his own design and had a brief foray with Formula One in the mid-sixties. His two Grands Prix were in 1966 at the wheel of a Ferrari V12 engined Cooper T73.

Through his tuning expertise and team management of the Morgan GT team, he is still actively involved in the sport, and continues to make occasional appearances in the driving seat.

1959 Became the Marque Sports Car champion in his Lawrencetune Morgan, Amongst his numerous class wins came one in the Silverstone International Trophy sports car race and at Goodwood, as well as being part of the Morgan team that won the 750MC relay.

1960 Continued to race his Morgan, with wins at Brands Hatch and Goodwood (twice) and 24th in the TT. Sharing a Lola he finished 2nd in class at the Nurburgring 1000km and 3rd at Goodwood, while in Formula Junior he took his Deep Sanderson to victory at Oulton Park and to 18th in the Silverstone International Trophy meeting.

1961 Further success at the wheel of his Morgan, included 2nd in class at Brands Hatch and in the British Grand Prix support race, 4th in class at Silverstone and in the Scott-Brown Memorial at Snetterton and 11th overall in the TT.

Chris Lawrence racing the Cooper Ferrari in the 1966 British Grand Prix.

Photo: Ferret Fotographics.

1962 Taking his Morgan to Le Mans he collected 13th overall and a class win with Richard Shepherd-Baron. At home he had a class win at Brands Hatch, 2nd in class at the Wiscombe Hillclimb, 3rd in the Autosport 3 hours at Snetterton, 5th at Crystal Palace and 8th in the TT.

1963 In a fairly mixed year he had a 2nd in class at Oulton Park and 4th at Goodwood in his Morgan but retired his Deep Sanderson at Le Mans. He finished 19th in the Brands Hatch 6 hours sharing a Vauxhall VX4/90 with Bill Blydenstein, and took 5th at the Boxing Day Brands Hatch in a Jaguar 3.8 saloon.

1964 Further outings in the Deep Sanderson brought little success and included another retirement from a return trip to Le Mans.

1965 With his more familiar Morgan he collected 2nd places at Brands Hatch, Silverstone and Aintree, and drove a TVR Griffith to class wins at both the Harewood and St. Ursanne Les Rangers hillclimbs. He also raced an AC Cobra, collecting 2nd place at Silverstone.

1966 Moving to Formula 1 to drive Jack Pearce's Ferrari V12-engined Cooper T73, brought a Grand Prix start at the British and an 11th place finish. He also contested the German but retired with broken suspension, and collected 5th at the Oulton Park Gold Cup. He still raced his Morgan and amongst his successes were two wins and a 2nd in class at Goodwood.

1967 After taking 8th at the Race of Champions in a Pearce-Ferrari, the project had to abandoned when all the cars were destroyed in a transporter fire.

1968 Finished 20th overall with John Wingfield in a Deep Sanderson at the Spa 1000km.

1973 Returned to Thoroughbred Sports Car racing with a Morgan +4, taking a win at Brands Hatch, 3rd at Thruxton and 2nd with a class win at Silverstone.

GRAND PRIX RECORD	
Starts	2
Wins	0
Poles	0
Fastest laps	0
WC points	0
Best finish	11th

JACK LEWIS
Born November 1st 1936

Jack Lewis.

Lewis made a rapid rise through F3 and F2 and won the British F2 title in 1960. From there he progressed rapidly and made a Grand Prix debut at the 1961 Belgian in his own Cooper Climax. Finishing fourth in the Italian GP that same year was a fine result for this rising star, but it was a success that would not be repeated.

A year later he left the racing scene after returning his new **BRM** to the factory, totally disillusioned with its performance. At only 26 years of age, his full talent was never truly realised.

1958 Began his career with lessons at the Brands Hatch Cooper Racing Drivers' School, before buying an ex-Bueb Cooper 500. He was 2nd on his F3 debut at Brands Hatch, won his second race at Full Sutton and

then won again at Oulton Park. At Goodwood he was 6th in the Lavant Cup and his tally for the year was three wins from 13 races, with three 2nds and a 3rd.

1959 Racing his own F2 Cooper, he won at Montlhery, finished 3rd in the Aintree 200, took pole and 7th at Pau and 10th at Reims, but had to fight all year to get his entries accepted.

1960 Won the Autocar F2 Championship in his Cooper, with wins at the Grand Prix des Frontieres at Chimay, the Coupe du Salon at Montlhery and the Lombank Trophy at Snetterton. He added 2nd in the Vanwall Trophy at Snetterton, 2nd at Brands Hatch F2, 7th in the Kentish 100, 8th in the Grand Prix of Brussels and 12th at Pau.

1961 He qualified 13th on his Grand Prix debut in the Belgian, finishing 9th in his own Cooper T53 Climax. After retiring from both the French and German races, he collected 9th in Germany before a career best 4th in Italy. Also contesting non-championship F1 races he was 5th at Pau, 6th in the Aintree 200 and succeeded in obtaining an A grading for the 1962 season.

1962 After finishing 8th in the Dutch Grand Prix with his Cooper, he took delivery of a new BRM P48/57. After failing to qualify the car in Monaco he took it to 3rd at Pau, but was dissatisfied with its competitiveness and returned it to the factory. Returning to his trusty Cooper, he retired from the French Grand Prix when he hit Graham Hill after his brakes had failed, finished 10th in the British and retired from his final GP in Germany. He also took 8th in the International Trophy and 10th in the Reims GP, but after retiring from the Oulton Park Gold Cup when he lost a wheel, he retired from the sport.

GRAND PRIX RECORD	
Starts	9
Wins	0
Poles	0
Fastest laps	0
WC points	3
Best finish	4th

❖

JOHN MILES
Born June 14th 1943

Miles was a works Lotus driver for the majority of his career, winning GT Championships and being a Formula 3 frontrunner. After working on the development of the 4 wheel drive Grand Prix Lotus, he became Rindt's number two in 1970, but after the World Champion's death in qualifying at Monza that September, he never raced in another Grand Prix. He continued for one further year in sports cars, before pursuing a career in journalism.

GRAND PRIX RECORD

Starts	12
Wins	0
Poles	0
Fastest laps	0
WC points	2
Best finish	5th

1962 Drove an Austin Nippy in trials, autotests and rallies.

1963 Raced an Austin 7 Ulster and shared a Marcos to 5th in the Nurburgring 500.

1964 Started a successful career with a Diva GT, taking class wins at Goodwood, Mallory Park and Brands Hatch, with 3rd at Snetterton and 37th overall in the Nurburgring 1000km.

1965 Won the Redex GT Championship in his Diva, with two class wins and two 2nds at Brands Hatch, four class wins at Mallory Park, 2nd at Monthlery and 3rd at Snetterton. He also raced on occasions for Willment and came 3rd in the end of season Grovewood Awards.

1966 An exceptionally successful season with a Willment Lotus Elan, starting the season with nine straight wins to secure the Autosport Championship. He had two wins at Brands Hatch, three wins and a 2nd at Mallory Park, two wins and a 2nd at Goodwood, victory at Oulton Park and in the British Eagle Trophy at Snetterton. At the Christmas Brands Hatch meeting he also won the GT race with a Lotus 47 and came 3rd in the saloon car race with a Hillman Imp.

1967 Joining Lotus as a works driver he contested F3 in a 41 and GT in a 47. He won at the Ingliston Lombank Trophy, Brands Hatch, Mallory Park, Oulton Park and Snetterton to finish as runner-up in the Les Leston F3 Championship. In GT he won at Crystal Palace, and twice each at Mallory Park and Brands Hatch. He also took 9th overall at the BOAC Brands Hatch race sharing with Oliver. A couple of outings in the British Saloon Car Championship also netted 6th places with a Lotus Cortina.

1968 Continuing in F3 he gave the Lotus 41X a debut win at Silverstone. That was followed by a double victory

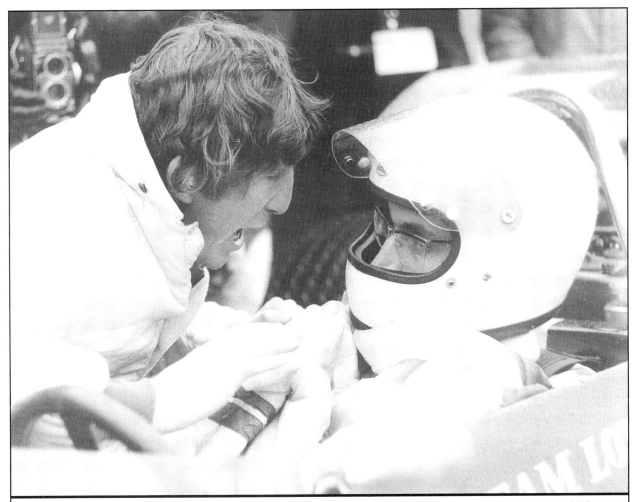

John Miles (right) in discussion with Jochen Rindt at the Nurburgring, May 1970.
Photo: Ferret Fotographics.

at Croft, in the Lombank Trophy at Ingliston, the Clearways Trophy at Brands Hatch and at Zandvoort. He shared a 47 to a class win in the BOAC 500 with Oliver and won the Special GT Championship after victories at Crystal Palace (twice), Thruxton, Brands Hatch and Ingliston. He also finished 2nd at Snetterton, 3rd at Oulton Park, 5th at Vila Real, 6th at Silverstone, 8th in the Martini 300 at Silverstone, 9th at Croft, 10th at Oulton Park and in the TT and was also 2nd in a Libre race at Snetterton in his Europa.

1969 His season started in F2 with Lotus, but he dropped out after three races, in which he took 3rd at Vallelunga with 5th at Hockenheim. After doing the initial testing of the Lotus 63 Grand Prix car, he gave the four-wheel drive machine its debut at the French. Although he retired from four of his five Grands Prix, he reached the finish of the British in 10th place. He raced the 62 GT car regularly, taking wins at Ingliston and Brands Hatch, with 3rd in the TT, 4th in the Trophy of the Dunes at Zandvoort and 13th in the BOAC 500.

1970 Became Rindt's number two in the Lotus Grand Prix team and started the year with 5th in South Africa. After failing to qualify for both the Spanish and Monaco races, he retired in Belgium, took 7th in the Dutch, 8th in the French, followed by further retirements in the British, German and Austrian. His car was withdrawn from the Italian after Rindt's death during qualifying. He had also made an F2 appearance at the Nurburgring, finishing 8th.

1971 Two further F1 outings in a BRM brought 7th at the Race of Champions and retirement from the Rindt Memorial at Hockenheim. He continued to race successfully in sports cars with a Chevron B19, winning both the RAC and Scottish Sports Car Championships. He won the John Leith Trophy at Croft, the King Hussein and SMT Trophies at Ingliston and at Silverstone and Brands Hatch. He added 2nd at Thruxton (twice) and at Oulton Park, 7th in the BOAC 1000, 8th in the Nurburgring 1000km and 9th in the Martini Trophy at Silverstone. At Paul Ricard he managed to come both 3rd and 6th in a European 2-litre round, sharing a Lola T212 with Hezemans and a Chevron B19 with Birrell.

1972 Won a European Saloon Car race at Paul Ricard and came 2nd at Zandvoort with Brian Muir in a Ford Capri.

1981 Finished 27th on the Paris-Dakar with a Janspeed prepared Range Rover.

JACKIE OLIVER
Born August 14th 1942

Jackie Oliver.

Photo: BRDC Archive.

After an early grounding in sports cars and one season in F3, Oliver's career began to take off in 1967 with some impressive performances in his semi-works F2 Lotus and a Ford Mustang. He earned a place in the Lotus Grand Prix team the following year after the death of Jim Clark. He also raced in Formula 1 for BRM, McLaren and Shadow.

He won the CanAm title for Shadow, raced successfully in US F5000 and won at Le Mans and Sebring for the Gulf Ford Team during a varied and successful racing career that spanned 17 seasons. From his 50 Grand prix starts, he took a best result of third in a wet Canadian race in 1973. Indeed, so confused was the race that some observers considered him to have been the winner. His last season in 1977 included racing for the Shadow team where he became increasingly involved in team management. The following year he split from Shadow to be instrumental in the formation of the Arrows Grand Prix team.

1960 Began racing with a Mini.

1961 Continued with his Mini, before purchasing a Marcos.

1962 Had a win, two 2nds and a 3rd at Brands Hatch and two 2nds at both Cadwell Park and Silverstone, before wrecking his Marcos in an accident at Snetterton.

GRAND PRIX RECORD

Starts	50
Wins	0
Poles	0
Fastest laps	1
WC points	13
Best finish	3rd

1963 With his rebuilt Marcos run under the Ecurie Freeze banner, he had a 4th overall and class win in the Martini Trophy at Silverstone, with further class wins at Snetterton and Mallory Park (twice), with two 2nds and a 3rd at Snetterton.

1964 Starting the year with a Diva, he took a 2nd in class at Brands Hatch, before changing to a Lotus Elan. He was 3rd in class in the British Grand Prix support race with his new car, followed by class wins at Brands Hatch and Crystal Palace, 3rd at Brands Hatch and 4th in the Scott-Brown Memorial at Snetterton.

1965 Continuing with the Elan he won at Brands Hatch, Crystal Palace and Monthlery, with 2nd at Croft, Snetterton, Crystal Palace (twice), Rufforth and Brands Hatch. Driving a Ford Mustang he was 3rd at Brands Hatch and sharing a Jaguar E-Type with Craft he was 3rd in the Guards 100 at Brands Hatch.

1966 Finished 3rd in the Les Leston F3 Championship, after changing from a Brabham to a works Lotus mid-season. He won at Brands Hatch, Mallory Park and Snetterton, with 2nd at Crystal Palace and Silverstone. With a Mustang he took 2nd in his class in the British Saloon Car Championship, after winning at Brands Hatch, Silverstone, Snetterton (twice). He also won the Edward Lewis Trophy, and took 2nd at the British Grand Prix meeting, in the Lombank Trophy and at Oulton Park. He also raced a Mini, led the Ilford Films 500 at Brands Hatch in a Jaguar E-Type and came 2nd in the end of season Grovewood Awards.

1967 Moved into F2 with a Lotus Components run Lotus, winning his class from 5th overall in the German Grand Prix. He also had a class win in the Oulton Park Gold Cup, won at the Nurburgring, took 4th in the Oulton Park Spring Cup, 5th at Barcelona, 6th at Crystal Palace and Brands Hatch, and 7th at Pau and Reims. Racing a Mustang again in saloon car events, he won at Silverstone, Brands Hatch and Snetterton. He shared a Lotus 47 with Miles to 9th in the BOAC 500 at Brands Hatch.

1968 Following Clark's death he became Graham Hill's partner in the Gold Leaf Team Lotus Grand Prix team. After crashing out on his debut at Monaco, he finished 5th in Belgium, followed by a non-classified finish in the Dutch. He failed to start the French and US races after practice accidents, retired from the British after leading in the early stage and also retired in Italy and Canada. He finished 11th in the German and 3rd in the end of year Mexican. He also took 3rd in the Oulton Park Gold Cup in his F1 car. Continuing in F2 he finished 5th in the championship with a best result of 2nd at Hockenheim. In the Temporada Series he finished 6th, with a 3rd and 4th in Buenos Aires, 5th in San Juan and 10th in Cordoba. With a Lotus Europa he took a class win in the BOAC 500 with Miles, plus two wins at Thruxton, 3rd at Brands Hatch, 6th overall and a class win in the Guards International Trophy at Brands Hatch, 6th at Croft and 9th with a class win at Oulton Park. He had a 2nd in saloons at Brands Hatch in an Alan Mann Escort and 3rd in the Wills Trophy at Croft with a Ford Falcon.

1969 Moving to the BRM Grand Prix team he secured only two classified finishes from 10 starts, with 7th in the South African opener and 6th in the Mexican finale. His BRM did survive to take 5th in the Race of Champions. However the highlight of his season came with victories at Sebring and Le Mans with Ickx in a Gulf Ford GT40. His other outings included 13th in CanAm at Monterrey in an Autocoast Ti22 and 6th in the Nordic Cup at Anderstorp in a Lola T70.

1970 Another dismal year with BRM, with only 5th in the Austrian Grand Prix, 7th in Mexico and 3rd in the Oulton Park Gold Cup to show for his efforts. In the CanAm Series he finished 5th with the Autocoast and Norris Chevrolets, taking 2nd at Mosport, Laguna Seca and Riverside. He shared a Porsche 917 to victory at Daytona, Monza and Spa and with a Lola T70 he recorded 4th in the Buenos Aires 200 and 11th in the 1000km with Reutemann.

1971 From four outings with McLaren he retired from the British Grand Prix after a startline shunt, took 7th in Italy, 9th in Austria and retired from the Brands Hatch Victory race. In CanAm he had a 3rd at Edmonton with Shadow and finished 3rd in a Riverside TransAm race for Penske. He was 3rd in the World Sports Car Championship, after sharing victories in a Porsche 917 with Rodriguez at Daytona, Spa and Monza, with 2nd at Buenos Aires and 4th at Sebring.

1972 The year was spent developing the Shadow CanAm car, finishing 8th in the series after 2nd at Mid-Ohio, 3rd at Donnybrooke and 4th at Riverside. Had a one-off Grand Prix return with BRM at the British, ending in retirement.

1973 Had a full season back in Grands Prix with Don Nicholls' UOP Shadow Team. After retiring from the South African, Spanish and Belgian races, his first finish came with 10th at Monaco. From a further nine outings he secured 15th in the US, 11th in the Italian, 8th in the German and 3rd in a very wet Canadian, even though some observers considered him the winner. He also finished 2nd at Laguna Seca and 3rd at Edmonton with the CanAm Shadow.

1974 Won the CanAm Championship with Shadow, winning at Mosport, Road Atlanta, Watkins Glen and Mid-Ohio.

1975 Finished 4th in the US Formula 5000 Championship in a Shadow DN6, following 2nd at Elkhart Lake, 3rd at Pocono, 4th at Mid-Ohio and Road Atlanta and 5th at Laguna Seca.

1976 Another year in US F5000 brought 3rd in the championship with his Shadow, winning at Elkhart Lake and taking 2nd at Mid-Ohio, Mosport and Riverside. He also won a sports car race at Mosport in a Shadow DN4 Chevrolet.

1977 A brief return to F1 with Shadow brought 5th at the Race of Champions and 9th in the Swedish Grand Prix, before retiring to a managerial role with the team.

❖

ARTHUR OWEN
Born March 23rd 1915

continued to take part in speed events until 1964. He was also responsible for writing the 'Racing Coopers' books.

1954 Finished 7th overall in a Cooper and 2nd in class with a Skinner Special in the Bouley Bay Hillclimb.

1955 Had class wins in the Bouley Bay Hillclimb and Brighton Speed Trials in his Cooper, took three 500 F3 victories at Brands Hatch in a Cooper JAP and broke seven class K and five class G World Speed records at Montlhery.

1956 Finished 2nd in class at both Bouley Bay and Westbrook Hay Hillclimbs in a Cooper Sports, and also won all three parts of a race at Roskilde. He came 4th in the Rome Grand Prix and collected a further seven class E World Speed records at Monza.

1957 Returned to Roskilde to take 3rd in his heat, only to retire from the final. He was 5th in class at the Empire Trophy and returned to Monza to set two class G and five class K World Speed Records.

1958 Another record breaking year in Coopers, with the standing quarter mile in class E and two records in classes J and K at Bedford, along with six further records

Arthur Owen (Cooper).

Owen was an expert in both Coopers and hillclimbs, which combined to make him the British Hillclimb Champion in 1962. As well as his numerous successes on the hills, he was a world speed record holder in numerous classes during a competition career spanning 10 years.

He made his one and only Grand Prix appearance in the 1960 Italian driving his own Cooper Climax. Although his racing experience was fairly limited, he

in class K at Montlhery. He also took 2nd in class at the Bouley Bay Hillclimb in a Cadillac Allard.

1959 On the hills his Coopers collected two class wins at Stapleford, 2nd in class at Shelsley Walsh and 3rd overall with a class win at Bouley Bay. He also raced in the Oulton Park Gold Cup and collected five more class E World Speed records at Monza.

GRAND PRIX RECORD

Starts	1
Wins	0
Poles	0
Fastest laps	0
WC points	0
Best finish	DNF

MIKE PARKES
Born September 24th 1931
Killed August 28th 1977

Mike Parkes at Silverstone in 1961.
Photo: BRDC Archive.

1960 His one and only Grand Prix was in the Italian, where his own Cooper Climax qualified 11th, but retired when the suspension broke after a brake lock-up. He finished 2nd overall in the British Hillclimb Championship with FTD at Wiscombe, two class wins at Prescott in the F1 car and 3rd in a Formula Junior. He took class wins at Bouley Bay and Stapleford, 2nd with a class win at Craigantlet, 3rd with a class win at Rest & be Thankful and 2nd in class at Great Auclum. By the end of the year he held 41 International speed class records, spread over four classes, a record itself at the time.

1961 Finished 2nd in the British Hillclimb Championship again, with FTD at Wiscombe, overall victories at Bo'ness, Stapleford and twice at Firle. He took 3rd with a class win at Westbrook Hay, further class wins at Bouley Bay, Shelsley Walsh and Rest & be Thankful and 2nd overall in the Coventry & Warwickshire Sprint. He also revisited Roskilde and won again.

1962 RAC British Hillclimb Champion in a Cooper T53 Climax with FTD at Westbrook Hay, Staverton and at Firle (twice). He took 2nd with a class win at Great Auclum, and 2nd at Bo'ness and Prescott each on two occasions. At Bouley Bay he was 2nd with two class wins, 2nd at Brunton, had three 3rds at Wiscombe, 3rd at Craigantlet, 3rd with a class win at Rest & be Thankful, 3rd with 2nd in class at Prescott and 4th at both Prescott and Shelsley Walsh. He also contested the Brighton Speed Trials and took a class win. He travelled to Hong Kong where he won an unlimited capacity race and to Helsinki where he collected a 2nd place in the 2-litre class.

1963 Finished 2nd in class and 6th overall in the Great Auclum hillclimb in a Lotus 23B, and took 3rd in the Japanese Grand Prix, followed by victory in a sports car race at Suzuka.

1964 Took 8th overall and a class win at Great Auclum in the Lotus 23B.

Born into the automobile business as the son of the Alvis MD and chairman, Parkes was a development engineer for the Rootes Group before moving into motorsport on a more permanent basis. An outstanding sports car racer who won many of the classic races during his time with Ferrari, but a combination of his height and development duties for Ferrari restricted his single-seater outings. He did, however, win the 1967 International Trophy at Silverstone having taken second in both the French and Italian races for Ferrari the previous year. Indeed, two seconds from six Grand Prix starts was a fine record.

He retired from racing at the end of 1972, to work on various projects for Fiat and Lancia, including the Stratos rally car. Five years later he was killed in a road accident in Turin.

1952 Made his racing debut at the SUNBAC Silverstone meeting in a 1933 PB MG.

1953 Graduated to racing an MG TD, which had been a 21st birthday present.

1954 Continued to race his MG with moderate success.

1955 Changed to a chain-driven Frazer Nash for club racing.

GRAND PRIX RECORD

Starts	6
Wins	0
Poles	1
Fastest laps	0
WC points	14
Best finish	2nd

1956 A further year spent racing the Frazer Nash.

1957 Spent the year racing his own Lotus XI and went to Le Mans as reserve driver for the works Lotus team.

1958 Raced a Fry F2 car originally destined for Lewis-Evans, collecting occasional 2nd and 3rd places.

1959 Continued to race the Fry mainly in Libre races, failing to qualify the Climax-powered car for the British Grand Prix.

1960 Raced Sir Gawaine Baillie's Lotus Elite, taking two class wins at Brands Hatch, 3rd at Silverstone and 13th overall in the TT. Racing a Sunbeam he finished 2nd in a Silverstone saloon car race, and in the Chequered Flag Formula Junior Gemini he recorded a 3rd at Brands Hatch.

1961 An outstanding year in sports, saloons and Formula Junior. At Le Mans he shared a works Ferrari Testa Rossa to 2nd place with Mairesse, won at Snetterton (twice), Brands Hatch and Goodwood and took 2nd in the TT in a Berlinetta. He drove an Equipe Endeavour Jaguar E-Type to victory in the Scott-Brown Memorial Trophy and scored further wins at Snetterton and Brands Hatch as well as 2nd at Spa. In total he had 14 GT wins and eight 2nds, winning every International and National GT race in the UK bar three, including six wins in one weekend at Brands Hatch and Snetterton. In saloons his Jaguar won at Brands Hatch, Snetterton, Silverstone and in the St. Mary's Trophy at Goodwood. He added 2nds at Silverstone and Snetterton and 4th at Aintree to secure the 3000cc class in the British Saloon Car Championship. His Formula Junior Gemini took him to two wins each at Snetterton and Brands Hatch, with two 2nds at Brands Hatch, 2nd places at Crystal Palace and Snetterton, and 9th at Silverstone. He also took part in the Monte Carlo Rally, sharing his Talbot with Autosport Editor Gregor Grant to finish 108th.

1962 He won the Autosport Sports Car Championship, winning at Oulton Park, the Autosport 3 hours at Snetterton, plus at Brands Hatch, Silverstone (twice), Mallory Park and Goodwood, and took 3rd in the TT with his Ferrari 250 GTO. He won the Guards Trophy at Brands with a 246SP and shared works GTOs with Surtees and Mairesse to 2nd in Paris 1000km and victory at Nurburgring respectively. With his Jaguar Saloon he won at Brands Hatch, Snetterton and in the Motor 6 hours at Brands Hatch sharing with Jimmy Blumer, with 2nd at the British Grand Prix and 3rd at Oulton Park. He also

made his F1 debut with a Cooper taking 4th place in the Mallory Park 2000 Guineas.

1963 Having joined Ferrari as a reserve works driver, he won the Martini Trophy at Silverstone in a GTO. He won the Sussex Trophy at Goodwood, took 2nd places in the TT and Snetterton 3 hours and shared a 250P to 3rd at Le Mans with Maglioli.

1964 He won the Sebring 12 hours with Maglioli in a 275P and the Spa 500km with Scarfiotti in a GTO. Further success came with 2nd at the Nurburgring 1000km (with Guichet) and 3rd in the Reims 12 hours (with Scarfiotti).

1965 His Ferrari successes continued and with Guichet he won the Monza 1000km and took 2nd at Nurburgring in a 275P2. He won the Paris 1000km with Piper, shared 2nd in the Reims 12 hours with Surtees, took 2nd in the Austrian Grand Prix and 6th in the Guards Trophy at Brands Hatch.

1966 From the French Grand Prix onwards he replaced Surtees in the Ferrari Grand Prix team, qualifying and finishing 2nd on his Grand Prix debut. After retiring from both the Dutch and German, he was 2nd again in the Italian after starting from pole position. From only four starts he was 8th in the World Championship. In sports cars he won the Monza, Spa and Paris 1000km races, sharing with Surtees, Scarfiotti and Piper. He also took 6th in the British Grand Prix support race and 6th at Brands Hatch.

1967 Starting the year in F1 again, he won the International Trophy at Silverstone and dead-heated at Syracuse with Scarfiotti. After taking 5th at the Dutch Grand Prix he crashed at the Belgian and broke both legs. His earlier sports car outings had brought a win at the Daytona 24 hours, 2nd at Le Mans and Monza, 5th at Spa with Scarfiotti in a 330P4 and 2nd at Crystal Palace with a 250LM.

1968 The whole year was spent recovering from the injuries sustained in the Belgian Grand Prix.

1969 He returned to racing sharing Piper's Lola T70 with Attwood to finish 10th at the Paris 1000km.

1970 Racing for NART and Scuderia Fillipinetti, he was 4th at Daytona with Posey in a Ferrari 312P and 6th at Sebring with Parsons in a 312P. In Europe, he finished 4th in the Austrian 1000km, 6th in the Targa Florio, 7th at Monza and 13th in the BOAC 1000 at Brands Hatch with Muller in a 512S.

1971 Having been retained for a second season by both teams, he was 5th at the Targa Florio sharing a Lola T212 with Westbury, 7th in the Buenos Aires 1000km sharing a Ferrari 512M with Bonnier and had a class win at Vallelunga.

1972 Finished 7th at Le Mans with Lafosse in a Ferrari 365 GTB.

TIM PARNELL
Born June 25th 1932

Son of former Grand Prix driver Reg, Tim had reasonable success during the late fifties with Coopers mainly in national F2 and Libre races. After failing to qualify for the British Grand Prix 1959, he made his Grand Prix debut two years later with a Lotus 18. Having made his debut in the 1961 British Grand Prix, he went on to record his only Grand Prix finish in the Italian race that year.

He continued racing all over Europe until his driving career was brought to an abrupt end by his father's sudden death. Not only did he take over the reigns of Parnell Racing, he became BRM team manager from 1968 to 1975, had a spell as Motor Circuit Development Regional Director for Mallory Park and Oulton Park, managed Donington Park and is currently a director of the British Racing Drivers' Club.

1958 Moving up to a Cooper T45 Climax, he won the USAF Trophy at Snetterton and was 2nd in F2 at Silverstone. He came 8th and 11th in Brands Hatch F2 races, while at Crystal Palace he took 9th in the Anerley Trophy. However, he crashed and cleared a 10ft earth bank before landing unhurt on the infield during the Crystal Palace Trophy.

1959 Continuing with his Cooper, he failed to qualify for the British Grand Prix and at Rouen, but had wins at Mallory Park (four times), Silverstone (twice) and at Brands Hatch. He also took 3rd places at Rufforth and Whitchurch, 10th in the Trophee D'Auvergne at Clermont Ferrand and 13th in both the International Trophy at Silverstone and the Silver City Trophy at Brands Hatch.

1960 Another year in F2 with the Cooper brought a win at Mallory Park, 4th in the Grand Prix des Frontieres, retirements at Zeltweg and Innsbruck and non-qualification at Modena. Success however came in Formula Junior, when after taking 2nd at Mallory Park in a Cooper, he changed to a Lotus 18. 8th overall and a class win at the Aintree Trophy was followed by a 2nd and two 3rds at Mallory Park, 2nd in the Coupe de Vitesse at Reims, 3rd at Roskilde and 8th at both Monaco and in the Brands Hatch John Davy Trophy.

1961 Graduating to an F1 Lotus 18, he made his Grand Prix debut at the British but retired when the clutch failed. He also went to Monza and took 10th in the Italian GP. Elsewhere, he had two Libre wins and a 2nd at Mallory Park, 3rd in the Lewis-Evans Trophy at Brands Hatch and at Phoenix Park. He finished 5th in the Lombank Trophy at Snetterton, 7th in the Silver City Trophy at Brands Hatch, 7th at Zeltweg Flugplatzrennen, 8th in the Naples GP and 10th in the Danish GP.

Tim Parnell (Lotus 18) at Silverstone.

Photo: BRDC Archive.

1957 Made his racing debut in a Frazer Nash LM Replica, but also raced a Cooper Bobtail taking a 2nd place at Mallory Park.

1962 From only a handful of races in the Lotus 18, he collected 7th in the Naples GP and 9th in the Aintree 200, retiring from both the Lombank and International Trophies.

1963 He failed to qualify his updated Lotus for the German Grand Prix, but had a Libre win at Silverstone, 6th in Austria and 9th in Rome, but retired from the International Trophy, Aintree 200 and Solitude GP. The sudden death of his father in January 1964 brought his racing career to an abrupt halt.

GRAND PRIX RECORD	
Starts	2
Wins	0
Poles	0
Fastest laps	0
WC points	0
Best finish	10th

DAVID PROPHET
Born October 9th 1937
Killed March 29th 1981

Although never a major star, Prophet had a competent career through the sixties and early seventies. He raced in most of the single-seater categories and made both of his Grand Prix appearances in South Africa in 1963 and 1965. Some of his best performances were saved for sports car racing, where he raced a mouth-watering collection of cars. After three years in Formula 5000, he retired at the end of 1972, but came back to racing with a Surtees for a couple of British Formula 1 races during 1977. He was killed when his helicopter crashed in poor weather conditions as it was leaving the 1981 International Trophy at Silverstone.

1961 Finished 2nd at Aintree and twice at Mallory Park with a Kieft Formula Junior.

1962 Continued in Formula Junior with an Alexis, winning twice at Rufforth, with 3rds at Mallory Park (twice) and at Oulton Park, 4th at Silverstone and a Libre victory at Rufforth.

1963 Raced in Formula Junior with a Brabham BT6 and won at Snetterton and Goodwood. He added 2nd places at Mallory Park and Aintree, 3rd at Silverstone and Crystal Palace, 7th at Zolder and Reims, 8th at the British Grand Prix support race, 9th in the Anglo-European

GRAND PRIX RECORD	
Starts	2
Wins	0
Poles	0
Fastest laps	0
WC points	0
Best finish	14th

Trophy, 11th at Karlskoga and 2nd in class in an Aintree Libre race. He took the car to the South African Grand Prix and qualified 14th but retired with falling oil pressure. At the Rhodesian GP he finished 2nd and was 6th in the Rand GP. In sports cars he raced a Lotus 23 to class wins at Aintree and Oulton Park, plus 3rd in class at Silverstone.

1964 Raced mainly in Formula 2 with a Brabham and a Lotus, finishing 4th in the Leinster Trophy, 6th at Avus and the Oulton Park Gold Cup, 7th at Zolder and 14th at Reims. In sports car he raced an Elva and won his class in the Lavant Cup at Goodwood and at Aintree. He also finished 2nd at Aintree and Oulton Park, 3rd in class in the International Trophy meeting and 13th overall in the Guards Trophy at Brands Hatch.

1965 A second Grand Prix appearance in South Africa brought 14th place with his Brabham BT10, but once

David Prophet at Brands Hatch.

Photo: BRDC Archive.

again he concentrated on Formula 2. Results included 6th at Karlskoga, 11th in the Rome GP and the Oulton Park Gold Cup, 12th at Brands Hatch and 17th at Reims. He also continued to race a Lotus 30 in sports cars, with 4th at the British Grand Prix meeting, 3rd and 5th at Silverstone and 9th in the TT. Other results included a win at Oulton Park and 7th in the Spring Cup with a McLaren Elva sports, plus 3rd and 5th in Mallory Park Libre races with his F2 Brabham.

1966 Another year in F2 brought 7th in the Eifelrennen, 8th at Reims and 10th at Karlskoga with his Brabham. He continued to race his McLaren Elva, with victory in sports cars and 2nd in Libre at Silverstone, 7th at the British Grand Prix meeting, 9th in Silverstone's Martini Trophy and 20th in the TT. At Phoenix Park he collected a class win with his F2 Brabham and was 3rd at Mallory Park in a Libre race.

1967 With the emphasis on sports cars, success was on the increase. With a Ferrari 275LM he was 2nd and 6th at Oulton Park, 5th in the Auvergne Trophy and 18th at Brands Hatch. But with his Ford GT40 he won a Libre race at Phoenix Park, came 2nd in the Lourenco Marques 3 hours, 3rd in the Rhodesian GP and 9th in the Killarney 3 hours, sharing with Peter de Klerk.

1968 His Ford GT40 finished 4th in the Oulton Park Gold Cup, 7th at Anderstorp, 8th at Spa, 9th in the TT and 10th at the Solituderennen and Martini 300 at Silverstone. He also raced a Lola T70 to victory at Silverstone, with 2nd place in the supporting Libre race.

1969 With the Lola T70 he shared 8th in the Spa 1000km with Paul Hawkins, finished 9th in the Mantorp Park Nordic Cup race and 11th in the Kodak Super 8 Trophy at Thruxton. He also raced a pair of McLarens, taking an M8GT to victory at Crystal Palace and an M6B to 11th at Hockenheim.

1970 Driving a McLaren M10B in the new Formula 5000 series, he finished 4th at Hockenheim, 5th at Oulton Park (twice) and Snetterton, 6th at Mondello Park and Thruxton, 7th at the Salzburgring and Zandvoort and 10th at Silverstone, also taking a Libre victory at the same circuit. His McLaren M12 finished 2nd at Diepholz, 4th at Croft, 8th at Thruxton and 10th at Hockenheim in Interserie races as well as a 2nd at Magny Cours. There were also outings in a Chevrolet Camaro in the British Saloon Car Championship, with 6th at the British Grand Prix meeting, two 3rds in class at Silverstone and 4th in class at Croft.

1971 Another year with McLaren in F5000 brought the bonus of 4th place in the non-championship Argentine Grand Prix. Although he had two wins and a 2nd in Silverstone Libre races, his F5000 campaign brought only 10th overall in the championship. Results included 2nd in class in the Oulton Park Gold Cup, 4th at Mallory Park and Oulton Park, 5th at Snetterton, 6th at Mondello and Snetterton and 7th at Thruxton.

1972 A third year in F5000 saw the McLaren in 4th at Brands Hatch, 5th at Mallory Park, 6th at Oulton Park, 7th

in class and 14th overall at the International Trophy. He added 8th at Oulton Park and in the British Grand Prix support race, 9th in the Rothmans 50,000 race at Brands Hatch, 9th at Mallory Park and Silverstone, 10th at Oulton Park and took two wins and a 2nd in Silverstone Libre races. At the end of the season he stopped racing.

1977 Made a comeback in a couple of Shellsport Group 8 races, with a best result of 9th at Mallory Park in his Surtees TS16.

IAN RABY
Born September 22nd 1931
Killed November 7th 1967

A fairly long career through Formula 3 in the fifties led to a Grand Prix debut in 1963. Raby gained a reasonable amount of success in national racing, but relatively little from his International exploits. His three Grand Prix starts were all in the British, but resulted in only one finish.

After three years of dabbling in Grand Prix and non-championship Formula 1 races he stepped back into Formula 2. It was in this category at Zandvoort that he had a serious accident in the autumn of 1967, sustaining injuries from which he died a few weeks later.

1953 After a couple of years in minor events, he began to race in F3 with an IER Special. His racing was mainly confined to Brands Hatch where he had a 3rd and 4th as well as a 3rd place in a sprint.

1954 Continued to race the IER with no notable success.

1955 Moving to a Cooper but still racing in F3, he won the Petit Prix at Crystal Palace, took 2nd in a Cadwell Park handicap, 4th at Snetterton, 4th and 5th at Brands Hatch and a class win in the Brighton Speed Trials.

1956 A further season with his Cooper brought wins at Brands Hatch and Silverstone, with 2nd and 5th at Brands Hatch, 3rd at Snetterton, 4th at Mallory Park and Crystal Palace, 6th at Silverstone, 8th in the British Grand Prix support race and 3rd in class at Brighton.

1957 For his F3 racing he piloted a Flash Special (collecting 3rd at Crystal Palace and Brands Hatch) and his Cooper which secured two 2nd places at Brands Hatch. A couple of outings in an F2 Cooper brought 2nd at Brands Hatch and 3rd at Roskilde, while in sports cars he raced an Elva and a Cooper. He took BTD and 3 class wins in a Brands Hatch sprint, 2nd in the Crystal Palace August Trophy, 3rd at Roskilde, four 2nd places at Brands Hatch, 2nd at Oulton Park and 15th at Le Mans.

1958 He continued to race the Elva and Cooper in sports car races, taking 2nd at Mallory Park, 4th at Crystal Palace and 2nd in class at Brighton. With the Flash Special he collected 2nd and 3rd in Crystal Palace F3 races.

Ian Raby.

Photo: BRDC Archive.

1962 After starting the year in Formula Junior again, with a Lotus 20 and later a Merlyn, he had a 2nd in Helsinki, 4th and 6th at Brands Hatch, 5th at Silverstone and a 3rd at the Bodiam hillclimb. He also raced a Turner in GT events and had a win at Oulton Park.

1963 Having bought the Gilby BRM Formula 1 car, he made his Grand Prix debut in the British, qualifying 19th but retiring when the gearbox broke. Further trips were made to the German and Italian races where he failed to qualify on both occasions. He did finish 3rd in the Rome Grand Prix, 8th at the International Trophy, 9th at Karlskoga and 2nd in a Silverstone Libre race, but retired from the Aintree 200 and at Solitude. Earlier in the year he raced his Formula Junior Lotus 22, finishing 2nd at Goodwood, and had occasional outings in a Merlyn sports car.

1959 In sports cars he raced his Cooper and a Hume Climax, winning at Oulton Park, with 2nd and 3rd at Snetterton, 3rd at Mallory Park and 3rd in the Brands Hatch Easter Trophy. He was a fairly regular Libre racer, winning at Silverstone in an F2 Cooper and the same car was used in the Oulton Park Gold Cup, where it retired. In F3 he continued to race occasionally, taking a class win at Brands Hatch in a Moorland.

1960 With the end of F3, he moved into Formula Junior with a Cooper BMC, finishing 3rd in the Coupe de Vitesse at Reims. At Monaco he raced a Formula Junior Envoy without success, and drove the single-seater Hume to 8th at Syracuse. In Libre he had a win at Mallory Park in his F2 Cooper, and in sports cars he took a Ferrari-engined Cooper to 2nd at Mallory Park.

1961 Another year concentrating on Formula Junior brought little success of note.

1964 Moving up to a Brabham BT3 BRM, he was back in action at the British Grand Prix. But after qualifying 16th he crashed out of the race after a hub failure. Another trip to the Italian Grand Prix proved fruitless, as he again failed to qualify. In the non-championship races he collected 8th at Syracuse and 15th in the Aintree 200, and with a Lotus 23 he finished 4th in a Snetterton sports car race.

1965 A further year with the F1 Brabham brought him 11th place at the British Grand Prix but he failed to qualify for the German. He finished 2nd with the same car in a Brands Hatch single-seater race, and was 8th at Syracuse and 12th in the International Trophy. In F2 he had a Merlyn and finished 8th in the Oulton Park Gold Cup, 12th at Solitude and 15th at Snetterton. He also raced an F2 Brabham in Libre, taking 2nd at Crystal Palace and 3rd at Brands Hatch.

1966 The decision was made to drop out of F1 and concentrate on racing his F2 Brabham. He took 4th in the Eifelrennen and finished 4th overall in the Bob Gerard Mallory Park Libre Championship. His season finished prematurely though after a crash at Brands Hatch.

GRAND PRIX RECORD	
Starts	3
Wins	0
Poles	0
Fastest laps	0
WC points	0
Best finish	11th

1967 Continuing in F2 with his Brabham, he was 5th and 9th at Hockenheim, 6th at Mallory Park, 8th at Brands Hatch, 9th at Zolder, 11th at Silverstone, 13th at Tulln Langenlebarn and 16th in the Eifelrennen. He also took 2nd in a Brands Hatch Libre race. Sadly, his last race was at Zandvoort, when his Brabham crashed during an F2 race, six weeks later he died from his injuries.

BRIAN REDMAN
Born March 9th 1937

A triple champion in US Formula 5000 and a massively successful sports car racer who never quite managed to get established on the Grand Prix scene. His best finish was third with Cooper in the 1968 Spanish and his last Grand Prix starts were in 1974 with the Shadow team.

His 12 Grands Prix were spread across seven different teams, but his sports car successes were mainly with Porsche and Ferrari, winning most of the classic races in a long and extremely successful career. Having settled in the US he won the IMSA title and had success in CanAm, and still races regularly in Classic and Historic events around the world, as well as setting up his own team in Formula 3000.

1959 Started racing in a Morris Mini Traveller.

1960 Finished 2nd in class at Rufforth, 2nd at Oulton Park in both a race and a sprint, and 3rd in class at Linton-on-Ouse, with his Mini.

1961 Racing mainly with a Jaguar XK120, his best result was 3rd in class at Ouston.

1962 Moved to a Morgan +4 and won the Chorley Speed Trials.

1963 Had a class win at Castle Howard and 2nd in class at Southport Speed Trials with a Mini.

1964 Took two class wins at Woodvale sprints, and one each at Southport and Loton Park, plus 3rd in class racing at Mallory Park with his Mini.

1965 Concentrated on racing Charles Bridges' Jaguar E-Type, with six wins at Oulton Park, plus Ouston, Rufforth (twice), Goodwood, Croft and Aintree. His Mini won at Oulton Park and Cadwell Park and had two class win at Woodvale sprints and a 3rd at Ouston. He also had BTD at Woodvale in a Jaguar XK120.

Brian Redman.
Photo: BRDC Archive.

1966 Graduating to Bridges' new Lola T70, he took two wins at Rufforth and Oulton Park, and 13th in the TT. He was 2nd twice at Oulton Park in the Jaguar E-Type and won at Croft and Snetterton in a Brabham BMW. He raced a Brabham BT14 to a Libre victory at Rufforth, with 2nd at Croft and Oulton Park. Sharing a Ford GT40 with Peter Sutcliffe he finished 4th at Spa, followed by 3rd at Crystal Palace and earned 3rd place in the end of season Grovewood

1967 Moved into Formula 2 with David Bridges in a Brabham and Lola, finishing 2nd at Crystal Palace, 4th at Vallelunga, 6th at Jarama and Albi, 8th at Barcelona and Brands Hatch. He won the Daily Mirror Trophy at Oulton Park in a Chevron GT, followed by two further Oulton Park victories, plus a win and 3rd at Crystal Palace. Among his other sports car results were victory with Ickx in a Mirage at the Rand 9 hours, 6th with Sutcliffe in a Ford P40 at Spa and 6th with Attwood in a Ferrari 275LM in the Paris 1000km.

1968 A sudden leap into Grand Prix racing saw him join the Cooper team for the early part of the year. He retired in South Africa, took a magnificent 3rd in Spain, but crashed in the Belgian sustaining a broken arm. He had earlier finished 5th in the Race of Champions for Cooper, taken 4th in the Eifelrennen F2 race on his debut for Ferrari and taken the Lola F2 to 2nd at Crystal Palace and 5th at Zolder. In sports cars he won the BOAC 500 and Spa 1000km with Ickx and took 6th with Hobbs in the Nurburgring 1000km in a Ford GT40. He won the Oulton Park Gold and Spring Cups in a Lola T70, and took 3rd in the Lourenco Marques 3 hours, 4th in the Kyalami 9

GRAND PRIX RECORD	
Starts	12
Wins	0
Poles	0
Fastest laps	0
WC points	8
Best finish	3rd

hours, 3rd and 4th in the Rhodesian GP and 14th in the Cape International with a Chevron B8.

1969 Driving works Porsches he won the Watkins Glen 6 hours, BOAC 500, Monza, Nurburgring and Spa 1000kms with Siffert in 908s. He also had success with Sid Taylor's Lola T70, winning the Embassy Trophy at Thruxton, plus at Karlskoga, Keimola, Norisring and Snetterton with 2nd at Anderstorp and at Silverstone (twice). Continuing with Chevron, he won the Nurburgring 500 in a B16.

1970 His Grand Prix attempts with Frank Williams' De Tomaso ended with a non-start at the British after hub failure in qualifying and non-qualification at the German. But with Porsche he won the Targa Florio, the Imola 500 and the Austrian and Spa 1000kms. He took 2nd at Watkins Glen and Daytona, sharing mainly with Siffert, and finished 7th in a CanAm race at Watkins Glen. He won the European and Springbok Sports Car Championships for Chevron, winning the Nurburgring 500, at Capetown, Pietermaritzburg, Lourenco Marques and the Bulawayo 3 hours and at Paul Ricard and Spa. He finished 2nd at Anderstorp, Thruxton and Hockenheim, 3rd at Enna, 4th at Silverstone and 5th at Kyalami in B16s and 19s. He also took the Lola T70 to Monthlery and finished 2nd.

1971 A couple of drives with Surtees brought 7th in the South African Grand Prix and retirement in the International Trophy at Silverstone. He raced a McLaren M18 to 5th in the Rothmans Formula 5000 Championship, with two wins at Brands Hatch, 2nd and 3rd at Mallory Park and 2nd at Snetterton. He took 4th in Interserie, after wins at Imola and Hockenheim in a BRM. For the second successive year he was the Springbok Sports Car Champion, with six straight wins in a Chevron B19. He also won the Kyalami 9 hours with Regazzoni in a Ferrari 312P and took 4th at Laguna Seca in a CanAm BRM.

1972 Three Grand Prix outings for McLaren resulted in 5th places at Monaco and the German and 9th in the French, while a late season run with BRM in the USGP ended in retirement. He also took a McLaren to 7th in the John Player Challenge and 2nd in the Rothmans 50,000 at Brands Hatch, but retired from the Race of Champions. In the Rothmans European F5000 he finished as runner-up with a Chevron B24 and McLaren M10B, winning at Oulton Park, in the Dublin Grand Prix at Mondello Park

and Brands Hatch (twice). He also won the F5000 class in the Oulton Park Gold Cup. In US F5000 he was joint 3rd, winning at Riverside, with 2nd at Road Atlanta and Lime Rock and 4th at Watkins Glen in his Chevron B24. Racing for Ferrari in sports cars he won the Spa 1000km and took 2nd at Nurburgring with Merzario. He won the Austrian 1000km with Ickx and took 2nd in the Buenos Aires 1000km, 4th in the Daytona 6 hours and 5th in the BOAC with Regazzoni, all in 312Ps.

1973 His only Grand Prix appearance ended in disqualification from the USGP, after his Shadow received a push-start. He was runner-up in the US F5000 Championship with a Haas-Hall Lola, after winning at Riverside, Elkhart Lake, Road Atlanta, Pocono and Seattle, with 2nd at Mid-Ohio. Sharing a works Ferrari 312P with Ickx he won at Monza and Nurburgring, with 2nd at Dijon and Watkins Glen and 3rd at the Osterreichring and Vallelunga.

1974 Three final Grand Prix outings with Shadow brought 7th in Spain, retirement in Belgium and a multiple accident in Monaco. He had earlier finished 8th in the International Trophy at Silverstone with an Ensign. He won the US F5000 title with his Haas-Hall Lola, with victories at Mid-Ohio, Ontario and Laguna Seca, with 2nd at Watkins Glen, Elkhart Lake and Riverside. In the European F5000 Championship he won the Vanwall Trophy at Silverstone and at Oulton Park, with 2nd and 3rd places at Brands Hatch. His other results included 4th in the BOAC 1000 at Brands Hatch with Gethin in a Chevron B26 and 2nd at Mid-Ohio in CanAm with a Porsche 917K.

1975 Retained the US F5000 title for Haas, winning at Long Beach, Mid-Ohio, Pocono and Watkins Glen, with 2nd at Mosport and Road Atlanta, 3rd at Laguna Seca and Riverside, and 8th at Elkhart Lake. He drove for BMW in IMSA, winning the Sebring 12 hours and taking 6th at the Watkins Glen 6 hours. He also shared a BMW to 3rd in the Wynns 1000 at Kyalami.

1976 His third successive US F5000 title was clinched with a Haas Lola, winning at Pocono, Mid-Ohio and Elkhart Lake, with 3rd at Riverside and 6th in both championship and non-championship races at Watkins Glen. He contested the New Zealand Formula Atlantic Series with a Chevron, taking 2nd at Manfield and 4th in the New Zealand Grand Prix. He won the Daytona 24 hours with Gregg and took 6th in the Watkins Glen 6 hours for BMW.

1977 Was seriously injured during qualifying for the opening CanAm round at St.Jovite, after his car rolled.

1978 Returned to racing and became IMSA Champion after winning his comeback race at Sebring in a Porsche 935. He was also 5th at Le Mans and 8th in the Watkins Glen 6 hours in a 935 and gave the Mercedes 450 SLC Automatic its debut in the TT at Silverstone.

1979 Further races in a Porsche 935 brought 2nd at Sebring and Watkins Glen, 3rd in the Nurburgring 1000km and at Daytona and 6th at Riverside. He also won a 500 mile race at Mid-Ohio in Tony Cicale's CanAm Ralt.

1980 Finished 3rd in the World Endurance Championship for drivers, winning at Mosport, with 3rd at Watkins Glen and Silverstone and 5th at Le Mans and Elkhart Lake IMSA in a Porsche 935. He also shared the winning Lola T333 with Hobbs in the Lumbermans 500 at Mid-Ohio.

1981 Won the IMSA title in a Lola T600, with victories at Laguna Seca, Lime Rock, Mid-Ohio, Portland and Road Atlanta, with 2nd at Daytona, Elkhart Lake and Sears Point. He also finished 2nd in the Mosport 6 hours with the Lola and shared a Porsche 935 to victory in the Daytona 24 hours and 3rd in the LA Times 6 hours at Riverside.

1982 Retired a Lola T620 from Le Mans, sharing with Kent-Cooke and Adams.

1983 Had occasional outings in an IMSA Lola.

1984 Finished 6th in the IMSA Championship with a Jaguar XJR-5. He won at Miami, with 2nd in the Eastern Airlines 3 hours at Daytona, 3rd at Road Atlanta, Charlotte, Watkins Glen and Sears Point, and 5th at Elkhart Lake.

1985 Continued with the XJR-5 in IMSA and finished 7th overall, winning at Atlanta. He also finished 2nd at Charlotte, Lime Rock and in the Eastern Airlines Daytona 3 hours, 3rd at Watkins Glen and Laguna Seca, 4th at Portland and 8th at Elkhart Lake.

1986 Sharing Haywood's IMSA Jaguar XJR-7 he took 3rd at Palm Beach, Columbus and Sears Point, 4th at Miami, 5th at Mid-Ohio and Watkins Glen, and 9th at Portland.

1987 Raced in IMSA sharing a Porsche 962 with Kneifel, finishing 3rd at Sebring, 5th at Road Atlanta, 8th at Miami, and retiring at Daytona.

1988 Shared a Porsche 962C with Wollek and Baldi to 2nd at the Daytona 24 hours and 10th at Le Mans with Elgh and Jarier.

1989 Drove an Aston Martin AMR1 with Leslie, Dickens and Sears, taking 4th at Brands Hatch, 7th at Donington Park and Spa, and 8th at the Nurburgring and Mexico City. He also took 9th at Daytona in a Mazda RX7.

1990-99 Continued to race in various Supersports, historic and classic events throughout the world, mostly at the wheel of a variety of Chevrons. But he made brief returns to modern machinery, with 12th at Sebring in 1991 in a Mazda RX7 and shared a Porsche 911 RSR to 52nd at Daytona with Chambers and Koenig in 1998.

50 years of British Grand Prix drivers

Part Two
1960s

CHAPTER 9

ALAN REES
Born January 12th 1938

A successful Formula Junior driver, Rees became a stalwart of the Formula 2 scene in the mid-sixties, despite being overshadowed by team mate Jochen Rindt in their Roy Winkelman-entered Brabhams. Apart from his appearances in the F2 class of the German Grand Prix, his only other World Championship outing came with a third works Cooper Maserati at the 1967 British Grand Prix. After hanging up his helmet at the end of 1968, he went into team management, and was a founder member of the March, Shadow and Arrows Grand Prix teams.

GRAND PRIX RECORD	
Starts	3
Wins	0
Poles	0
Fastest laps	0
WC points	0
Best finish	7th

1959 Racing a Lola in sports cars, he had wins at Brands Hatch, Goodwood, Snetterton and Silverstone, finished 2nd at Mallory Park, Oulton Park and Silverstone, and took 3rd places at Aintree and Brands Hatch.

Alan Rees (Lola Mk1) at Silverstone in 1960.

Photo: Ferret Fotographics.

1960 A further year with the Lola sports car brought wins at Snetterton, Aintree, Oulton Park and Mallory Park (twice), Brands Hatch and Silverstone, with 2nd at Brands Hatch and Mallory Park. He also had a 4th in a Formula Junior race at Goodwood.

1961 Concentrating on Formula Junior with a Lotus 20, he won the Anerley Trophy at Crystal Palace, also won at Goodwood, took 2nd at Snetterton and Aintree, and 3rd at Silverstone.

1962 Becoming a works Lotus driver in Formula Junior, he won the Anerley Trophy again. Further wins came at Crystal Palace and at Mallory Park (twice), plus 2nd places at Rouen, in the Trophee D'Auvergne, the London Trophy and at Monza. He took 4th at Clermont Ferrand and in the International Trophy meeting, and 16th at Monaco. His season ended prematurely after he was injured crashing a Lotus 23 during the Nurburgring 1000km sports car race.

1963 Joining the Winkelman team he continued to race in Formula Junior with a Lola. He finished 2nd at Crystal Palace and Snetterton, 3rd in the Anerley Trophy, 7th in the Anglo-European Trophy and Trophee d'Auvergne, 8th at Goodwood and 10th at Reims. He also raced a Lotus 23B, winning the Lavant Cup at Goodwood, with a further win at Crystal Palace and 2nd at Goodwood, and took his Lola to Oulton Park to win his class in a Libre race.

1964 Moving into F2 with a Winkelman Brabham, he won at Reims. He also finished 3rd at Albi and Crystal Palace, 4th at Mallory Park and Zolder, 5th at Karlskoga, 6th at Clermont Ferrand, 8th at Brands Hatch and 13th at Aintree.

1965 Continuing in F2 he won at Enna, took 2nd at Solitude, 3rd at Oulton Park, 4th at Reims and 5th at Snetterton, Albi and Crystal Palace in his Brabham. He also raced an F2 Lola at Brands Hatch, winning a single-seater race and the British Eagle Libre Trophy.

1966 It was a case of more of the same with the Winkelman Brabham, winning at Le Mans. He took 2nd at Reims and Rouen and 4th at Goodwood, Barcelona and the London Trophy, 5th at Pau and Zolder to secure 4th overall in the championship. At the German Grand Prix he made his World Championship debut, retiring from the F2 section. He also shared a Ferrari 250LM to 11th place in the TT.

1967 Became Autocar British F2 Champion and was 5th in the European Series. His Grand Prix outing resulted in 7th overall at the German with 2nd place in the F2 class. He also took 2nd at Silverstone, 3rd at Pau and Brands Hatch, 4th at Keimola, 5th at Rouen and Zandvoort, 6th at Hockenheim, Zandvoort, Enna, Hameenlinna and in the Oulton Park Gold Cup, 7th at Vallelunga and Karlskoga, 9th at the Eifelrennen and 11th at Jarama and Tulln Langenlebarn. He had the use of the third works Cooper Maserati at the British Grand Prix, qualifying 15th and finishing 9th.

1968 His final year of racing was again in F2 with a Brabham. Results included 2nd at Monza, 6th at Barcelona, 7th at Reims, 8th at Zolder, 10th at Enna and 14th at Hockenheim. He also went to the Temporada Series, finishing 10th in Buenos Aires.

JOHN RHODES
Born August 18th 1927

Such was Rhodes' success and spectacular style at the wheel of the works Mini Coopers, that his single-seater exploits are often overshadowed. A fairly successful Formula Junior career in the early sixties failed to provide the appropriate launch up the racing ladder. He had regular outings in Formula Libre with Bob Gerard's Coopers and it was with a rather outdated T60 that he made his one and only Grand Prix appearance at the 1965 British.

1958 Had occasional speed event outings in John Handley's Turner, including a class win at the Lydstep Hillclimb.

1959 Began racing in Formula Junior.

1960 Graduated to a Cooper BMC in Formula Junior, taking wins at Linton-on-Ouse and Mallory Park, with a further 2nd and 3rd at Mallory Park and 3rd at Snetterton.

1961 With his Cooper entered by MRP, he won Irish Formula Junior Championship, with wins at Phoenix Park, Kirkistown and Dunboyne. He also won at Snetterton, Mallory Park (twice) and Silverstone, with 2nd at Mallory Park and 6th at Brands Hatch. In Libre races he had a win and 3rd at Mallory Park, with two 2nds at Snetterton and a 3rd at Silverstone.

GRAND PRIX RECORD	
Starts	1
Wins	0
Poles	0
Fastest laps	0
WC points	0
Best finish	DNF

John Rhodes in a Formula Junior Ausper at Silverstone, May 1962.
Photo: BRDC Archive.

1962 Continuing in Formula Junior he raced an Alexis and an Ausper, winning at Brands Hatch, with 3rd at Silverstone, 6th at Goodwood and Zandvoort and 14th at Silverstone. He made his F1 debut with a Gerard Cooper at the International Trophy at Silverstone, and had two Libre victories with the same car at Mallory Park.

1963 As a works Cooper driver he raced in Formula Junior for Ken Tyrrell and had a Mini for the British Saloon Car Championship. He best Formula Junior results came with 6th at Oulton Park and in the Chichester Cup at Goodwood, along with 9th at the British Grand Prix meeting. In saloons he was 8th at Brands Hatch with Rob Slotemaker, and at Crystal Palace he finished 3rd in class, with 4th at both Aintree and in the Small Car Trophy at Crystal Palace.

1964 He finished 9th overall in the British Saloon Car Championship with his Mini, winning the Motor 3 hours at Mallory Park with Warwick Banks. Other results included took 3rd at Brands Hatch, 6th at Oulton Park, 15th in the Coppa Europa at Monza and 16th at Brands Hatch with Slotemaker, along with numerous class wins. He also continued to race a Cooper BMC in F3, with a best result of 4th at Zandvoort.

1965 His one-off Grand Prix appearance came at the British, where he retired Bob Gerard's Cooper after ignition problems. In further outings for Gerard he collected 8th in the Sunday Mirror Trophy at Goodwood and a 4th in a Libre race at Mallory Park. He won the 1300cc class in the British Saloon Car Championship and was 3rd overall, with wins at Mallory Park in the Ilford Films Trophy and at Crystal Palace. Overall he was also 3rd at Silverstone, 4th at Oulton Park, 5th at Brands Hatch, 6th and 7th at Oulton Park and was a class winner on the majority of occasions. At Brands Hatch he also won the Guards 100 with Banks in an MGB and finished 12th at Le Mans sharing a Sprite with Paul Hawkins.

1966 A class winner again in the British Saloon Car Championship, as his giant-killing Mini collected an overall win at Crystal Palace. He also claimed 2nd places at Oulton Park, Brands Hatch and Goodwood, 3rd and 6th at Brands Hatch, 5th and 6th at Silverstone, and 9th at the British Grand Prix meeting, with a plethora of class wins along the way.

1967 For the third successive year he was 1300cc class champion in the British Saloon Car Championship with his Mini. He won at Oulton Park, Mallory Park and Brands Hatch, with 3rd at Silverstone, 4th and 6th at Brands Hatch and 9th at the British Grand Prix meeting. At Sebring he shared an MGB with Timo Makinen and finished 12th.

1968 Now almost unbeatable in his class, he collected his fourth successive 1300cc title. He won his class at Brands Hatch (twice) and Silverstone, with 2nd at Thruxton and Mallory Park, 3rd at Crystal Palace, Brands Hatch and Silverstone. He also won his class in the European Championship, with class wins at Zolder, Zandvoort, Snetterton and Jarama and 4th at Brands Hatch. Finally, he rounded off the year by winning the World of Sport Rallycross at Croft, in a Mini of course.

1969 He spent a final year racing Minis, but without the works backing. He was 4th in the Anerley Trophy at Crystal Palace and at Mallory Park, 2nd in class at Silverstone and 4th in class at Brands Hatch, Oulton Park and in the British Grand Prix support race. He finished 7th overall and 2nd in class with Hopkirk in the Guards 6 hours at Brands Hatch, while in rallycross he won at Cadwell Park and took the runner-up spot in the Croft World of Sport Championship.

1970 He continued to rallycross a Mini, but spent the racing season campaigning a quick but unreliable Steinmetz Opel Commodore.

1972 He raced a works Group 1 Opel Ascona with little success.

1973 Had occasional outings deputising for John Handley in a Production Sports Triumph TR6.

---------- ❖ ----------

MIKE SPENCE
Born December 30th 1936
Killed May 7th 1968

After overcoming polio as a child, Spence began racing in the late fifties with his father's backing. Although his Formula 1 debut came in 1961, a step back into Formula Junior earned him a works Lotus drive, with a Grand Prix debut at the 1963 Italian. After two full seasons with Lotus, Peter Arundell was sufficiently recovered from injury to reclaim his seat with the team, forcing Spence to move to Parnell's team.

Notable victories away from Grand Prix racing came at Brands Hatch, where he won the non-championship Race of Champions and the BOAC 500 sports car race. During his second year with BRM in 1968, he was invited to race for Lotus at Indianapolis following Jim Clark's death. But a test drive in his team mate's car ended fatally when he crashed into the retaining wall and a detached wheel struck his head. The accident came exactly one month after Clark's death during one of the blackest periods in the history of the sport.

1957 Made his motorsport debut rallying his father's Turner.

1958 He bought an AC Bristol to race and came 4th in a five lap handicap at Goodwood on his debut. His only other race during the year ended with 2nd at Silverstone.

1959 Another year with the AC brought a couple victories.

1960 Moved into Formula Junior with a Cooper BMC, taking part in 15 races throughout the year including a few Libre outings. His first win was at Snetterton, with a heat win at Monza and further victories at La Chatre, Snetterton and Silverstone. He was 2nd at Oulton Park and Snetterton, 5th in the Empire Trophy and in the British Grand Prix support race, 6th at Oulton Park and 2nd in a Silverstone Libre race. A couple of late season F2 races in a Cooper Climax brought 10th at Goodwood and retirement at Goodwood after running in 6th place.

1961 His F1 debut came with Emeryson at the Solitude Grand Prix, retiring from 7th place when the gearbox broke. At Brands Hatch he was 2nd in the Lewis-Evans Memorial Trophy and took 6th in a Libre race at Silverstone. With the Formula Junior Emeryson he won the Commander Yorke Trophy at Silverstone and was 6th at Goodwood. He also helped his team to 6th at the Silverstone 6 hour relay with the AC Bristol.

1962 A change to a Lotus 22 in Formula Junior brought a change of fortune. He won at Reims and took 2nds at Albi, Monaco, Snetterton and Crystal Palace (twice). He finished 3rd in Goodwood's Chichester Cup, at Rouen and Brands Hatch, 5th at Clermont Ferrand and 6th in the International Trophy

Mike Spence in the Lotus Climax.

Photo: BRDC Archive.

Mike Spence.

support race. After taking 2nd in his heat in the Monza Lotteria, he crashed out of the final after tangling with a backmarker. He also raced a works Lotus 23 sports car for Ian Walker, taking 2nd in class at the Brands Hatch Guards Trophy.

1963 With a full works Formula Junior drive for Lotus he collected 2nd in the Circuit D'Auvergne, at Nurburgring and Innsbruck. He also claimed 4th at Reims, Rouen and Silverstone, 5th and 6th at Aintree and 7th at Silverstone. With Trevor Taylor injured, his Grand Prix debut came in Italy, qualifying 9th and finishing 14th despite falling oil pressure. He also shared an F1 car with Arundell to 2nd place at the Mediterranean Grand Prix, and raced a Lotus Elan for Chequered Flag.

1964 His Grand Prix year started with the British as deputy for Arundell in the Lotus team, finishing 9th. From five further outings he collected his first championship points with 6th in Italy and 4th in Mexico, along with 7th in the US and 8th in the German. He retired from the

Austrian and in non-championship races he shared 3rd at Syracuse with Arundell and took 5th in the Mediterranean Grand Prix. In F2 he won his class in the Aintree 200, with 3rd at Reims and in the Eifelrennen, 4th in the Oulton Park Gold Cup, 6th at Enna, 11th at Brands Hatch and clinched the Autocar British F2 title. In saloons he raced a Lotus Cortina, taking a 2nd at Roskilde, while in GT racing he continued with an Elan, taking 2nd at Brands Hatch.

1965 Became a fully-fledged member of the Lotus Grand Prix team, partnering Clark. Her scored a 3rd in Mexico, 4th in the South African and British, 7th in the Belgian and French, 8th in the Dutch and 11th in the Italian. He posted retirements in the US and German races to finish 8th in the World Championship. He had earlier won the Race of Champions at Brands Hatch and taken 3rd at Silverstone's International Trophy. In F2 he was 3rd in the Eifelrennen, 4th at Karlskoga, 6th at Albi, 7th at Brands Hatch and 10th at Reims. With his Lotus Cortina he took 7th in class in the British Saloon Car Championship, taking 4th overall at the International Trophy meeting. He was 6th in the Rand 9 hours sharing a Ferrari 250LM with John Love.

1966 He started the year by winning the non-championship South African Grand Prix for Lotus, but joined Parnell's team to race to its Lotus BRM in Grands Prix after Arundell reclaimed his Lotus seat. From eight starts he finished 5th in both the Dutch and Italian Grands Prix, but retired from the rest. With the Parnell BRM sports car he won the Lavant Cup at Goodwood, took a further win at Crystal Palace and 2nd at Silverstone. He also had occasional F2 outings, which brought him 4th at Reims.

GRAND PRIX RECORD	
Starts	36
Wins	0
Poles	0
Fastest laps	0
WC points	27
Best finish	3rd

1967 Joined the works BRM Grand Prix team with the troublesome H16. He collected points from 5th in Belgium, Canada, Italy and Mexico and 6th in Monaco. At the International Trophy he finished 6th, with 7th at the Race of Champions. In F2 he continued to race for Parnell, with 9th at the Wills Trophy at Silverstone. He raced a Chaparral to victory at the BOAC 500 at Brands Hatch with Phil Hill, but retired at Sebring and Spa. There were also CanAm outings in a McLaren, taking 3rd at Mosport and Las Vegas.

1968 Having re-signed for BRM, he retired from the seasons opener in South Africa. Following Clark's death, Lotus invited him to race for them at the Indy 500. But during qualifying he tested his team mate's car and crashed fatally.

❖

JACKIE STEWART
Born June 11th 1939

A triple World Champion and pioneer of driver safety, who won a staggering 27 of his 99 Grand Prix and barring retirement, only failed to finish a Grand Prix in the points on five occasions. Stewart had earlier won the British F3 Championship and been a race winner in F2 and sports cars. Prior to starting racing in 1960, he had been an Olympic standard shot, but it was at the wheel of Ken Tyrrell's Formula 3 cars that Stewart started to make his name in motor racing.

One of the greatest drivers of all, Stewart was not always popular for his crusade on safety at a time when it was not seen as a major issue by many people. But his work set the scene for the high safety standards that are now accepted as normal. Three world titles in five seasons with Tyrrell was an astonishing achievement, but his career ended in tragic circumstances when team mate Francois Cevert was killed in qualifying for what was scheduled to be Stewart's final Grand Prix. Unlike so many, once Jackie retired he stayed retired.

After retiring at the end of 1973 he came back into the sport with son Paul, building a successful team that graduated from Formula Vauxhall, through F3, F3000 to the Stewart Grand Prix team in 1997. A canny businessman, a great ambassador for the sport and, above all, a truly gifted racer.

Jackie Stewart on the grid with Stirling Moss (left).

Photo: BRDC Archive.

GRAND PRIX RECORD

Starts	99
Wins	27
Poles	17
Fastest laps	15
WC points	360
Won his 8th Grand Prix	

1962 Racing a variety of sports cars which included an Austin Healey Sprite, Jaguar E-Type, Aston Martin DB4GT and Marcos, he became the Master of Charterhall.

1963 Following in his brother Jimmy's footsteps he joined Ecurie Ecosse, and took its Jaguar E-Type to victories at Rufforth, Charterhall and Ouston. He also raced a Tojeiro with a victory at Charterhall, and had occasional races in a Cooper Monaco.

1964 Became a member of Ken Tyrrell's works Cooper F3 team and won 11 out of 13 races to become the Express & Star British F3 Champion. His victories included two at Oulton Park, at Silverstone and in the Chichester Cup at Goodwood. An F2 debut quickly followed, taking Ron Harris' works Lotus to victory in the Vanwall Trophy at Snetterton, with 2nd at the Circuit D'Auvergne and Monthlery, and 3rd in the Oulton Park Gold Cup. Before the end of the year he made his F1 debut, winning a heat of the Rand Grand Prix for BRM. His other results included victory in the European Grand Prix GT race in a Jaguar E-Type, victory at Oulton Park and 2nd in class at Silverstone in the Tojeiro Sports, a win in the Marlboro 12 hours with a Lotus Cortina and 3rd at Silverstone with a Lotus Elan.

1965 As a member of the BRM Grand Prix team he finished 6th on his debut in South Africa, which started a run of six consecutive points finishes. 3rd at Monaco, 2nd at the Belgian and French, 5th at the British and 2nd at the Dutch followed until the sequence was broken with retirement in Germany. He came back to take his maiden victory in Italy and clinched 3rd place in the World Championship behind Clark and Hill. He had also won the International Trophy, taken 2nd in the Race of Champions, and finished 10th at Le Mans with Hill in the experimental Rover BRM Turbine. In F2 he had a Cooper BRM and came 2nd at Oulton Park and 5th at Pau and Reims.

1966 Continuing with BRM, he opened the Grand Prix season with a win at Monaco, but crashed during practice for the Belgian and was trapped in the car. He missed the French due to his injuries and retired from the British. After further points finishes with 4th at the Dutch and 5th in the German, he ended the season with retirements in Italy, US and Mexico. Earlier in the year his BRM won the Tasman Championship, with wins in the Lady Wigram Trophy, at Teretonga and Sandown, plus 2nd in the New Zealand Grand Prix. Victory seemed probable at the Indy 500, until his engine failed in sight of the finish. His other results included 2nd in F2 at Barcelona with a Matra, a victory at Mount Fuji in a Lola and at the Surfers Paradise 12 hours in a Ferrari 275LM.

1967 The year started with success in the Tasman Series once more, winning both the New Zealand and Australian Grands Prix to finish second in the championship. On the Grand Prix scene it was a disastrous year with the troublesome H16 BRM, securing only two classified finishes from the entire season, 2nd in Belgium and 3rd in France. Continuing in F2 with a Tyrrell Matra, he won at Enna, Albi and Karlskoga, plus his class at the Oulton Park Gold Cup. He also finished 2nd in the BOAC 500 at Brands Hatch sharing a Ferrari P4 with Amon, and retired his Lola again in the Indy 500.

1968 Having worked with Ken Tyrrell in F3 and F2, he became the number one driver in the new Tyrrell Matra Grand Prix team. After retiring in South Africa, the points began to flow. After 4th in the Belgian he collected the team's first win in the Dutch, followed by further victories in the German and US, with 3rd in the French, 6th in the British and Canadian and 7th in the Mexican, securing 2nd in the World Championship.

1969 The Matra became the dominant force from the start of the year, never qualifying lower than 4th, taking wins in the South African, Spanish, Dutch, French, British and Italian Grand Prix, with 2nd in the German and 4th in the Mexican to crown him World Champion. He was the Vat '69 British F1 Champion after winning the Race of Champions and taking 3rd in the International Trophy, and raced in F2 again with victory in the Eifelrennen and Madrid Grand Prix, 2nd at Tulln Langenlebarn and Thruxton, and 4th at Reims.

1970 With Matra running its own team, Tyrrell turned to a March 701. Apart from a victory in Spain, points were claimed from 2nd in the Dutch and Italian Grands Prix and 3rd in the South African. But the season ended with the great promise of Tyrrell's own F1 car, that had secured pole on its Grand Prix debut in Canada. He ended the relatively disappointing season 5th in the World Championship. He won the Race of Champions again and was 2nd in the International Trophy, won at Crystal Palace and took 2nd at Thruxton in John Coombs F2 Brabham BT30. He also debuted the new Chapparal CanAm car at Watkins Glen.

1971 Seven poles and seven victories clinched a second World title, as the Tyrrell more than fulfilled its promise. He won in the Spanish, Monaco, French, British, German and Canadian races, and was 2nd in South Africa. In non-championship races he took 2nd in the Race of Champions and the Questor Grand Prix in Ontario, with 3rd in the Brands Hatch Victory race and Oulton Park International Trophy. In the CanAm Championship he finished 3rd with a Lola T260, with wins at Mont-Tremblant and Mid-Ohio, 2nd at Edmonton and Laguna Seca, 6th at Minnesota and 11th at Road Atlanta.

1972 Another successful start to the year for Tyrrell came with a victory in the Argentinean Grand Prix. Despite further wins in the French, Canadian and US, 2nd in the British, 4th at Monaco and 7th at the Austrian, he was pipped to the title by Fittipaldi's Lotus.

1973 Any disappointment at losing the '72 title was quickly overcome, with eight podium finishes to clinch his third World title. Victories came in South Africa, Belgium, Monaco, the Dutch and German, with 2nd in Brazil and Austria, 3rd in Argentina, 4th in France and Italy and 5th in Canada and Sweden. The season ended on a tragic note, however, when Tyrrell team mate Francois Cevert was killed during practice for the USGP at Watkins Glen. With his third title won, retirement from racing came with immediate effect. Earlier in the year he had won the International Trophy again, and shared a Ford Capri on a couple of occasions with Jochen Mass, finishing 5th at Paul Ricard.

❖

JOHN SURTEES
Born February 11th 1934

The only man ever to have taken World titles on both two and four wheels, Surtees won the World Championship in 1964 with Ferrari. On two wheels, he won seven World Championships between 1956 and 1960. He then proved his all-round ability by finishing second in his maiden Formula Junior race at Goodwood.

Within a few weeks of his car racing debut he joined the Lotus Grand Prix team, taking an amazing 2nd place at the 1960 British Grand Prix in only his second race. He drove for seven different Grand Prix teams, before racing for his own Surtees marque in 1970. He was a successful sports car racer but retired from racing in 1972, as the after-effects of a major CanAm accident in 1965 still dogged him. However, he continued to run his team until the end of 1978. He now regularly demonstrates both classic cars and motorbikes, including those of Mercedes and Honda.

1960 Although racing both cars and motorcycles, he finished 2nd on his car debut with Ken Tyrrell's Formula Junior Cooper at Goodwood. He then bought his own Cooper and within a few weeks made his F1 debut with Lotus in the International Trophy. His Grand Prix debut

soon followed, qualifying his works Lotus 18 in 15th place for the Monaco race before retiring with broken transmission. After taking 2nd at the British, he had two further outings, retiring in Portugal after taking pole position, followed by another non-finish in the USGP. He also took the Lotus 18 to 6th in the Silver City Trophy at Brands Hatch, while the F2 version collected 4th at Snetterton. His own F2 Cooper finished 2nd at Oulton Park and 4th in the Aintree 200, while Tyrrell's Cooper collected a further 2nd at Silverstone and 4th in the John Davy Trophy at Brands Hatch.

1961 After retiring from two early season Tasman races, he turned down a Lotus Grand Prix contract and signed for Yeoman Credit to drive its Cooper T53 Climax. After retiring in Monaco, he finished 7th in the Dutch and 5th in the Belgian and German, but posted four further retirements. In non-championship races he won the Glover Trophy at Goodwood, and was 3rd in the Snetterton Lombank Trophy, and at Karlskoga, 4th in the Aintree 200 and 10th in the Austrian Flugplatzrennen. He also drove a Cooper to 3rd in the Empire Trophy, the rear-engined Vanwall to 5th at Silverstone and took 2nd with a Jaguar in a Snetterton saloon car race.

1962 Moving to the Bowmaker Lola team he started the year with pole for the Dutch Grand Prix, but retired with broken suspension. He had 2nd places in the British and German Grand Prix, 4th in Monaco and 5th in the French and Belgian, to finish 4th overall in the World Championship. At Mallory Park he won the F1 2000 Guineas race, took 3rd at the International Trophy and finished the year with 3rd in the Rand Grand Prix. Earlier in the Tasman series he had won the South Pacific

John Surtees.

Photo: BRDC Archive.

John Surtees in the Cooper Maserati during the 1966 Mexican Grand Prix.

Trophy, with 2nd in the New Zealand Grand Prix, 3rd in the Vic Hudson Memorial Trophy at Levin and the Lady Wigram Trophy with a Cooper. He shared a Ferrari 250 GTO with Mike Parkes to 2nd in the Paris 1000km and took a 3rd at Mallory Park and in the Archie Scott-Brown Memorial Trophy at Snetterton.

1963 Joined Ferrari and finished 4th in Monaco on his Grand Prix debut for the team. After taking 3rd in the Dutch and 2nd in the British Grand Prix, he collected his first victory in the German. Despite five retirements and a disqualification in Mexico after a push start, he was 4th overall in the World Championship. He retired from the International Trophy on his Ferrari F1 debut, but won both the Mediterranean and Rand Grand Prix. In sports cars he won the Sebring 12 hours and Nurburgring 1000km for

Ferrari, sharing with Scarfiotti and Mairesse respectively, and finished 4th in the Times GP at Riverside. At the beginning of the year he had taken the Lola to the Tasman races, winning the New Zealand Grand Prix and the Lakeside International, with 2nd in the Australian GP.

1964 His season only netted six finishes from 10 starts but all were on the podium. He won the German and Italian Grands Prix, finished 2nd in the Dutch, US and Mexican and 3rd in the British to be crowned World Champion. His title was clinched in an unfamiliar blue and white Ferrari, as the works cars ran under the NART banner due to a licence suspension. He also won at Syracuse and took 2nd at Solitude, while in sports cars he was 2nd at Reims in a 275LM and 3rd at both Sebring and Le Mans sharing a 330P with Lorenzo Bandini. He crashed a 250GTO out of the TT suffering concussion.

1965 A second year with Ferrari in Grands Prix opened with 2nd place in South Africa, followed by 3rd in the French and British and 7th in the Dutch to take 5th in the World Championship. He also took 2nd at Syracuse in the F1 Ferrari, while in sports cars he won the Nurburgring 1000km and was 2nd in the Monza 1000km with Scarfiotti in a 330P2. He shared a 365P2 with Parkes to 2nd in the Reims 12 hours. In F2 he won the Oulton Park Gold Cup in a Lola T60 and had a couple of unsuccessful outings in a Cooper. Entering his own Lola T70, he won the Guards Trophy at Brands Hatch, and took 2nd and 7th with a class win at Silverstone. The car was also taken to

GRAND PRIX RECORD	
Starts	111
Wins	6
Poles	8
Fastest laps	11
WC points	180
Won his 27th Grand Prix	

Canada where it won the Players 200 at Mosport and the Quebec St. Jovite race. However, it failed to start a second race at Mosport after he crashed and sustained serious back injuries, causing him to miss the final two Grands Prix of the year.

1966 Having started the year with Ferrari he retired at Monaco and won the Belgian Grand Prix and the non-championship Syracuse, along with 2nd at the International Trophy. He then joined Cooper to race their Maserati V12-powered car from the French Grand Prix onwards. After a run of three retirements, he took 2nd in the German, 3rd in the US and won the Mexican to take the runner-up spot in the World Championship. He had won the Monza 1000km with Parkes in a 330P3 before his Ferrari departure and took a Matra F2 car to 7th at Rouen. His Lola T70 won the Guards Trophy at Brands Hatch, the Wills Trophy at Croft and took the CanAm title with victories at St. Jovite, Riverside and Las Vegas.

1967 Having left Cooper he headed the fledgling Honda Grand Prix team, finishing 3rd in South Africa on his debut with the raucous V12. He went on to take 6th in the British, 4th in the German and Mexican and a debut win in the Italian with a new Lola-developed chassis to share 4th in the World Championship with Amon's Ferrari. He also finished 3rd in the Spring Cup at Oulton Park in the F1 Honda, while in F2 he won at Zolder and Mallory Park, with 3rd at Reims and Silverstone, and 7th at Crystal Palace in a Lola. Continuing to race his Lola T70 he took 3rd in the CanAm series, winning at Las Vegas with 3rd at Elkhart Lake and 4th at Bridgehampton. At the Riverside Indy car race he retired a Lola T90 Offy in the Rex Mays 300 and ran the Aston Martin-powered Lola, retiring at Le Mans and the Nurburgring 1000km.

1968 Continuing with Honda he always qualified well and showed plenty of speed, but lacked reliability. From his 12 starts he secured pole for the Italian Grand Prix, but only made the finish in four races. 2nd in the French, 3rd in the US, 5th in the British and 8th at the South African was still enough for 7th in the World Championship. Returning to the CanAm series he found little success, retiring a Lola T160 at Bridgehampton and Riverside.

1969 Joined BRM for his Grand Prix campaign, taking 3rd in the USGP, 5th in the Spanish, 9th in the Dutch and 11th in the Italian. He drove a McLaren M12 in CanAm taking 3rd at Mosport and 12th at Watkins Glen, before changing to a Chaparral with 4th at Edmonton on his debut with the car and 5th at Lexington.

1970 His own Team Surtees Grand Prix team made its debut with a McLaren M7C, retiring from three of the first four starts, before taking 6th at the Dutch. The new Surtees TS7 also retired on its debut at the British Grand Prix, but went on to collect 9th in Germany, 8th in Mexico and 5th in Canada. He did however win the Oulton Park Gold Cup with the TS7, while his GT exploits in a Ferrari 512S resulted in 2nd at the Spa 1000km with Ickx, 3rd at the Nurburgring 1000km with Schetty and 3rd in Nurburgring 1000km with Vaccarella.

1971 The TS9 Surtees with Brooke Bond Oxo backing proved fairly reliable, with only three non-finishes from the Grand Prix season. He was 5th in the Dutch, 6th in the British, 7th in Monaco and the German, 11th in Spanish and Canadian and 17th in the USGP. For the second successive year he won the Oulton Park Gold Cup in the TS9, and took 3rd at the Race of Champions and Rindt Memorial at Hockenheim. He added 6th in the Brands Hatch Victory race and 11th in the International Trophy. As well as contesting an early season F5000 race in a Surtees TS8, he shared a Capri with Graham Hill at the Paul Ricard 12 hours, finishing 11th.

1972 After taking the new TS14 to 3rd in the International Trophy, he only made one Grand Prix appearance, ending in retirement at the Italian. He failed to start the USGP due to a shortage of engines, but rounded off his career with F2 victories at the Japanese Grand Prix and Imola in a TS10.

1980 Finished 3rd at Silverstone in the Lloyds & Scottish Historic Championship, with a JCB Ferrari 246 Dino.

1981 Won his fourth Oulton Park Gold Cup again with a JCB Maserati 250F.

JOHN TAYLOR
Born March 23rd 1933
Killed September 8th 1966

Having spent most of his career racing in Formula Junior and Libre for his mentor Bob Gerard, his talents had just reached the Grand Prix stage when he crashed with fatal consequences during the 1966 German Grand Prix. He will best be remembered for his domination of club single-seaters races, particularly at his home circuit of Mallory Park.

GRAND PRIX RECORD

Starts	5
Wins	0
Poles	0
Fastest laps	0
WC points	1
Best finish	6th

1962 Found instant success with his Gerard Cooper Ford in Formula Junior, with wins at Cadwell Park, Castle Combe and Mallory Park (twice). He also had a 2nd and 4th at Mallory Park, 3rd at Cadwell Park and Silverstone, and 12th in the International Trophy support race. In Libre he had a win and 2nd at Mallory Park, with 2nd at Cadwell Park, while at the Prescott hillclimb he took 3rd in the F1 class and 5th in Formula Junior.

1963 Racing Coopers in Libre and Formula Junior again for Gerard, he took 4th in the Von Trips Memorial at Nurburgring. He had three wins and two 2nds in Mallory Park Libre races, a win and 3rd in Silverstone Libre races, 9th in the Aintree 200 and retired from the International Trophy. His Formula Junior outings brought two wins at Mallory Park and 6th at the British Grand Prix meeting, and he also tried a Lola Climax in Libre, and finished 2nd at Mallory Park.

1964 At the British Grand Prix he made his World Championship debut, finishing 14th with his ageing Cooper T73 Ford after gearbox problems. With the same car he was 5th in the Aintree 200 and 10th in the International Trophy, but had a newer Climax-engined car at the Mediterranean Grand Prix, where he took 7th. With his F2 Cooper he secured 7th in the Oulton Park Gold Cup and he had an F3 win at Mallory Park. But in Libre races he was the man to beat, securing the Bob Gerard Mallory Park Championship, with three wins, plus one at Oulton Park.

1965 Raced the Cooper Climax in non-championship F1 races, taking 7th in the Sunday Mirror Trophy at Goodwood, 11th in the International Trophy and victory in a Mallory Park single-seater race.

1966 After taking 6th for Gerard in the International Trophy, he joined David Bridges to race his Brabham BRM in Grands Prix. Having started well with 6th at the French, he followed up with 8th in the British and Dutch. But in Germany he spun on the opening lap and was hit by Ickx, the car burst into flames and although he fought for recovery for a couple weeks, he finally succumbed to his serious burns. He had also raced a Ford GT40 to 6th in the Nurburgring 1000km with Peter Sutcliffe and an F3 Lola to 2nd in an Oulton Park Libre race.

John Taylor in a Gerard Racing Cooper at Mallory Park, September 1963.
Photo: Ferret Fotographics.

TREVOR TAYLOR
Born December 26th 1936

Trevor Taylor.

Photo: BRDC Archive.

Taylor was a champion in both 500 F3 and Formula Junior before making his Grand Prix debut with Lotus in 1961. After a couple more fairly successful seasons partnering Jim Clark, he was released by Lotus and joined BRP for his last full Grand Prix year. Second in the 1962 Dutch GP was the best result from his 27 Grand Prix starts.

After his GP career stalled in the mid sixties, the era of big V8 sports cars and Formula 5000 relaunched him and he continued with F5000 until his retirement at the end of 1972. However his career was littered with a number of huge accidents, some of which he was lucky to walk away from. "I was good at escaping, but not as good as Masten Gregory, because he would be standing on the seat before the impact," recalls Taylor.

1953 Built his own Ford 8 with brother Mike, and took part in minor events.

1954 Hillclimbed and sprinted the Ford.

1955 Began racing with a Triumph TR2, finishing 7th on his debut at Aintree despite a first lap spin. He rallied the car and also took part in minor speed events.

1956 Started the year with an Erskine Staride in 500 F3, before moving on to a Cooper Norton. Apart from 2nd in his first race, success was rather scarce.

1957 Racing in F3 with his Cooper Norton again, brought a maiden victory at Mallory Park, followed by a win Silverstone and another two at Mallory Park. He ended the year with eight wins, plus 2nd and 3rd at both Silverstone and Snetterton, 4th at Oulton Park and in the Redex Trophy at Crystal Palace.

1958 Became the British F3 Champion in a Cooper tuned with a Beart Norton engine. After taking 2nd to Lewis-Evans first time out with the car at Goodwood, he took 10 straight wins, including Mallory Park, Crystal Palace, Brands Hatch (twice) and the Commander Yorke Trophy at Silverstone for the second successive year. He had 2nd places at Snetterton, Goodwood and in the World Sports Trophy at Brands Hatch, but his accidents included crashing into a public address pylon at Crystal Palace and somersaulting into the Oulton Park lake.

1959 Moved into F2 with his own Cooper and had two wins at Rufforth, 2nd in a Silverstone Libre race and 6th in the London Trophy. He failed to qualify his Cooper for the British Grand Prix and broke his ribs at Mallory Park after colliding with Henry Taylor.

1960 At the behest of Colin Chapman, he stepped back to Formula Junior and with a semi-works Lotus 18 he shared the title with Jim Clark. He won at Aintree, Goodwood, Oulton Park and twice each at Brands Hatch and Crystal Palace. He added 2nd at Oulton Park, 2nd and 3rd at Goodwood and scored a heat win at Aix les Bains on his continental debut, followed by 3rd at both Monaco and Solitude. At Crystal Palace he also had a race in an F2 Lotus and won.

1961 His Grand Prix debut came at the Dutch, finishing 13th in a works Lotus 18. He won the Formula Junior Championship outright with his works Lotus, winning at Snetterton, Oulton Park, Aintree, Reims, Solitude, Goodwood and Crystal Palace, with 2nd at Silverstone and 3rd at Brands Hatch. His F1 debut resulted in 9th at Pau, and was followed by 9th in the Silver City Trophy at Brands Hatch, and at Solitude. He spent the winter in South Africa where he won the Cape GP and finished 2nd in the Rand GP. At Le Mans he shared a Lotus Elite with Bill Allen, finishing 12th overall with a class win.

1962 Now a fully-fledged member of the Lotus Grand Prix team, he qualified 10th and finished 2nd in the Dutch GP on his debut in a Lotus 24. He retired in Monaco before crashing and wrecking his car at the Belgian, then returned with a new Lotus 25 to take 8th in both the French and British GP. However his finish at the French proved rather dramatic when he hit Trintignant's stalled car on the line. He then crashed through a hedge in the German, before rounding off the year with 12th in the US and retirements in Italy and South Africa. He ended the year 10th in the World Championship. In the non-championship races he was 3rd at Solitude, 5th in the

GRAND PRIX RECORD

Starts	27
Wins	0
Poles	0
Fastest laps	0
WC points	8
Best finish	2nd

Aintree 200 and 6th in the Danish GP. He shared victory in the Mexican GP with Clark, was 10th in Brussels and won the end of season Natal GP and at Killarney, with 2nd in the Rand GP. With an Elite he took a class win and 5th overall in the International Trophy GT race, a class win and 10th at Oulton Park and 9th in the TT with Gil Baird.

1963 Continuing with Lotus he took 6th at Monaco in the opening Grand Prix, but failed to improve on it throughout the season. He was 8th in Germany and South Africa, 10th in the Dutch and 13th in the French, but retired from the Belgian, British, US and Mexican. Earlier in the year he was 2nd at Pau and Karlskoga, 3rd at the International Trophy and shared a car with Clark to 3rd in the Aintree 200. In South Africa he took 10th at the Rand GP, but had another huge accident in the Mediterranean GP when his car rolled to destruction after throwing him out at 100mph. He was fortunate to escape with severe bruising. He won at Oulton Park with the Team Elite Lotus Elite, as well as taking a class win in the International Trophy meeting, 3rd at Brands Hatch and 9th with a class win in the Nurburgring 1000km. Driving a Lotus Cortina he collected 3rd with a class win at Snetterton and 4th with a class win at Oulton Park.

1964 Following his release by Lotus, he joined BRP for the Grand Prix season. After retiring in Monaco he was 7th in the Belgian, but apart from 6th in the US, he failed to qualify in Italy and the rest ended in retirement. In the non-championship races he was 3rd in the News of the World Trophy at Goodwood and 6th at Solitude. He also shared an Aurora-backed Mini with his sister Anita, taking a class win at Silverstone and 21st in the Brands Hatch 6 hours.

1965 Without a Grand Prix drive he concentrated on racing an F2 Brabham, taking 2nd in the Senior Service Trophy at Silverstone, 3rd in an Oulton Park Libre race, 4th in the Oulton Park Gold Cup, 8th at Reims, 12th at Albi and 13th at Oulton Park. His other results included 4th at Silverstone in the Senior Service 200 with an Aurora BMC, 7th in the Guards Trophy at Brands Hatch with Anita in an MGB, as well as outings in a JCB-backed Lotus 30.

1966 One further Grand Prix ended in retirement at the British, when the fuel tank split on Aiden Jones' Shannon Climax. Further races with the Brabham F2 brought 4th at

Karlskoga and 9th at Montlhery, and he was 2nd at Mallory Park with a Lotus Elan and won at Roskilde in a Ford Anglia.

1967 A few F2 races in a Gerard Cooper were supplemented by outings in a Lotus 47, bringing a win at Ingliston and 3rd at Mallory Park.

1968 His Lotus 47 won both GT and Libre races at Brands Hatch and a GT race at Oulton Park. He also took 2nd in a European race and 20th in the Martini International, both at Silverstone. He shared a Ford Escort to 10th at the Nurburgring with John Fitzpatrick and was 21st in a Ford Anglia at Silverstone.

1969 Finished runner-up in the inaugural European Formula 5000 Championship, only losing the title after a collision with champion Peter Gethin at the final round. He collected four successive wins in his Surtees TS5, the North Sea Trophy at Koksijde, at Zandvoort, Snetterton and Hockenheim, along with 4th at the Oulton Park Gold Cup and 12th at Brands Hatch. Success also came at the wheel of a Lola T70, winning the TT at Oulton Park, taking 2nd at Croft, 6th at Keimola and 19th in the BOAC 500 at Brands Hatch sharing with Hugh Dibley. At the Brands Hatch Guards 6 hours saloon car race his Broadspeed Ford Escort, shared with John Fitzpatrick, led until the last 30 minutes but had to settle for 2nd.

1970 Another year in F5000 with Surtees brought a win in the Dublin Grand Prix at Mondello, before changing to a Lola. At the Oulton Park Gold Cup he took 5th overall and 2nd in class, with 3rd at Mallory Park, 4th at Zolder, Snetterton, Oulton Park and Brands Hatch, 5th at Silverstone and 12th overall at the International Trophy. But he had another big crash at the Salzburgring when a tyre punctured at maximum speed on the banking and the car rolled. Once again he escaped slightly dazed, but otherwise unhurt.

1971 Changing to a Leda chassis he finished 9th in the F5000 Championship, taking 2nd at Monza, 3rd at Hockenheim, 4th at Thruxton, 5th at Mallory Park, 6th at Brands Hatch, 7th at Castle Combe, 8th at Mallory Park and 9th at Brands Hatch. He also went to Ingliston and collected 3rd overall and a class win with a Ford Escort and to the Buenos Aires 1000km, where he shared a McLaren M8C to finish 9th with Chris Craft.

1972 Further appearances with the Leda in F5000 preceded his decision to retire at the end of the year.

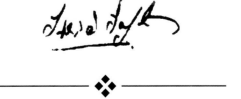

❖

PETER WESTBURY
Born May 26th 1938

Peter Westbury in his Formula 2 Brabham.

A British Hillclimb Champion who moved on to the race circuits with Formula 3 in 1967. After two fairly successful years in F3 he took the next step to F2, which also gave him a Grand Prix debut in the F2 class at the 1969 German Grand Prix. During his three years in F2 he also had a one-off Grand Prix chance with BRM at the 1970 US, but failed to qualify. Mixing sports car racing with his F2 outings, he continued racing until announcing his retirement mid way through 1973.

1960 Secured BTD in the Cambridge University sprint at Snetterton with an F2 Cooper.

1962 Became a regular competitor in the British Hillclimb Championship with a Cooper Daimler, finishing 6th overall. He scored BTDs at Dyrham Park and Brunton, with 2nd at Craigantlet and Shelsley Walsh, 4th at Bouley Bay, 6th at Great Auclum, 7th at Prescott, a class win at Wiscombe, plus an overall victory in the Snetterton Speed Trial.

1963 Won the Hillclimb Championship in a Felday Daimler, taking BTD and wins at Dyrham Park, Craigantlet, Rest & be Thankful and Bouley Bay. He took a BTD and a 2nd at both Prescott and Great Auclum, 2nd at Barbon, Wiscombe and Shelsley Walsh, 3rd at Loton Park, 5th at Prescott, 6th at Bo'ness, a BTD and further class win at Brunton and two BTDs at Wiscombe.

1964 Took the Ferguson 4 wheel-drive onto the hills and retained the British Championship, taking BTD and victories at Loton Park, Prescott, Barbon, Bouley Bay, Craigantlet, Dyrham Park and Harewood. He took a BTD and 2nd at Wiscombe, with a further 2nd at Great Auclum

and a class win at Prescott. He also drove a Bugatti at Wiscombe and took BTD at Castle Howard in a Lotus 7 BRM.

1965 Made occasional hillclimb appearances, recording BTD at Wiscombe and 2nd in class at Ollon-Villars with his BRM. He also took a Formula Libre victory at Mallory Park in an early race outing.

1966 Took BTD with his Felday Sports at Harewood and a class win at Wiscombe. He also contested the Gerard Libre Championship at Mallory Park and finished 6th.

1967 Teamed up with Derek Bell in a two-car Brabham F3 team. He won the International Trophy support race at Silverstone, at Chimay, Clermont Ferrand, Djurslandring and Castle Combe. He finished 3rd at Silverstone and Reims, 4th in the British Grand Prix support race, 5th at Barcelona and Zolder, 7th at Pau, 8th at Monaco and 2nd in a Snetterton Libre race. He also shared Mike D'Udy's Lola T70 in the BOAC race at Brands Hatch.

1968 Stayed in F3 and won the French Craven A Championship, with wins at Chimay and Reims, 3rd at Albi, 4th at Pau and 5th at Monaco in his Brabham. Nearer to home he finished 3rd at Brands Hatch and 4th at Silverstone (twice). He had a couple of races in the Church Farm Racing F2 Brabham, after Bell had joined Ferrari.

1969 Finished 5th in the European F2 Championship with a Brabham BT30, winning the Flugplatzrennen. He also took 2nd at Monza and Vallelunga, 3rd at

GRAND PRIX RECORD	
Starts	1
Wins	0
Poles	0
Fastest laps	0
WC points	0
Best finish	9th

Hockenheim and 5th in class at the German Grand Prix, 7th at Jarama, 8th at Albi, 9th at Tulln Langenlebarn and 10th at Enna and the Nurburgring. He took his F2 car to 2nd in a Formula 5000 race at Zandvoort, won a Libre race at Brands Hatch, and finished 10th overall and 4th in class in a Silverstone saloon car race with a Ford Escort.

1970 Had a one-off drive with BRM at the USGP, but failed to qualify after the engine blew during qualifying. Continuing in F2 with a Brabham, he was 3rd at Hockenheim, 4th at Enna and Paul Ricard, 5th at Nurburgring, 6th at Mantorp Park, 9th at Barcelona and 10th at Rouen. He also finished 3rd in the Flugplatzrennen Libre race.

1971 A further year in F2 brought 3rd at Monza, 4th at the Nurburgring, Brands Hatch and Mallory Park, with 8th at Albi, Hockenheim and Tulln Langenlebarn. He took his car to the Torneio Brazil and collected 4th at Cordoba and 5th at Porto Allegre, taking in further South American races to finish 2nd in the Colombian Grand Prix, with a 3rd and 4th at Bogota. His Brabham also collected 2nd in the Leinster Trophy at Mondello Park. In sports cars he finished 5th in the Targa Florio with Parkes and 8th in the BOAC 500 with Bonnier in a Lola T212, plus 7th in a Hockenheim Interserie race with a Lola T222.

1972 Began the year in F2 again, but had little success. He shared a Ferrari 365 GTB with Hine and Koenig at Le Mans, but retired just before midnight with a holed piston.

1973 Started the year yet again in F2, but retired from racing before the season was completed, with little to show for his efforts.

ROBIN WIDDOWS
Born May 27th 1942

After quickly graduating through national sports cars and Formula 3, most of Widdows' career was spent in Formula 2. His one and only Grand Prix chance came with a works Cooper in the 1968 British, after which he continued in F2 with the occasional foray into International sports cars events. He retired from racing midway through 1970 and had also represented Britain at the 1964 and 1968 Winter Olympics, driving the bobsleigh.

1964 Had 10 races with a MG Midget in his debut year, including a win in a Silverstone handicap.

1965 Won the Autosport Championship in a BRM powered Lotus 23, with two class wins at Silverstone,

Robin Widdows (Formula 2 McLaren M4A) at Thruxton in 1968.

Photo: Ferret Fotographics.

GRAND PRIX RECORD	
Starts	1
Wins	0
Poles	0
Fastest laps	0
WC points	0
Best finish	DNF

JONATHAN WILLIAMS
Born October 26th 1942

Jonathan Williams.

victory and two 2nds at Snetterton, 2nd at Oulton Park, and 3rd in the Lavant Cup at Goodwood and Brands Hatch.

1966 Moving into F3 with a Brabham BT18, he secured pole on his debut at Goodwood, but spun out of the lead. He won at Silverstone (twice), with 2nd at Brands Hatch, Snetterton, Goodwood and Castle Combe, 6th at Snetterton and 2nd in a Libre race at Castle Combe.

1967 With the help of a group of friends, the Witley Racing Syndicate was formed to run an F2 Brabham BT23. He won the Rhine Cup at Hockenheim, took 7th at Zandvoort, 8th at Silverstone, Reims and Karlskoga, 9th at Jarama, 10th at Zolder and 11th at Vallelunga. He also drove a DAF F3 to 7th in the Coupe de Vitesse and shared Nelson's Ford GT40 in the Spa 1000km, from which they retired.

1968 His one and only Grand Prix with Cooper at the British ended in retirement after ignition failure. He also drove a Chequered Flag entered McLaren in F2, taking 2nd at Pau, 3rd at Monza, 6th at Zolder and Zandvoort, 9th at Albi and 11th at Jarama. He also deputised for Redman in the Bridges F2 Lola and was injured himself testing a Mirage at the Nurburgring. He returned at the end the year to share Norinder's Lola T70 at the Paris 1000km.

1969 Another year in F2 driving a Merlyn and Brabham for Gerards, brought a win at Monza, 2nd at Reims, 5th at Enna, 6th at Albi and 8th at Pau, plus a Libre victory at Mallory Park. His other results included 7th at Le Mans sharing a Matra with Galli. He finished 2nd in the Lourenco Marques 3 hours and 13th in the Kyalami 9 hours sharing Alistair Walker's Ferrari P3, 21st in the BOAC 500 with Norinder's Lola T70 and 5th in a Mallory Park F5000 race with Sid Taylor's Lola T142.

1970 Finished 6th in the F2 Championship with Alistair Walker's Brabham, taking 2nd at Hockenheim, 4th at Thruxton and Barcelona, 6th at the Eifelrennen and 8th at Zolder. However he retired from racing before the end of the season.

After a Formula Junior and F3 career during which he spent more time on the continent than in the UK, Williams' performances earned him a works Ferrari drive. However, apart from one Grand Prix, a few sports car races and an F2 race, his time at Maranello is best forgotten. His only World Championship outing was in the Mexican GP of 1968 when he finished eighth. But it was not enough to secure his place with the Italian team and the following season he returned to Formula 2. He continued to race F2 for a number of teams, before drawing his career to a close in sports cars in 1971.

1960-61 Contested minor speed events in a Mini.

1962 Became a front-runner in the Brands Hatch Molyslip Saloons with his Austin A40. With 12 wins he finished 2nd in the Championship.

GRAND PRIX RECORD	
Starts	1
Wins	0
Poles	0
Fastest laps	0
WC points	0
Best finish	8th

1963 Joined the Merlyn Formula Junior team with Pike, but the season was cut short after he was injured in a crash at Monaco. He returned with a Brabham and took 3rd in a Formula Junior race in Dresden.

1964 Toured Europe with Piers Courage and their F3 cars, taking 2nd at Innsbruck, 3rd at Crystal Palace, 3rd and 4th at the Nurburgring, 4th at Brands Hatch and 6th at Zolder with a Lotus.

1965 Continued to race throughout Europe in F3, winning the Monza Lotteria and at Zolder in his Lucas-entered Brabham. He also took 2nd at Brands Hatch and Chimay, 3rd in the Chichester Cup and at Monza and Silverstone, 4th at Monza and 5th at Brands Hatch. He also drove an F3 De Sanctis in the F2 race at Syracuse.

1966 Spent the year racing F3 in Italy with De Sanctis. He won at Enna, tied with Beckwith at Monza, had two further wins and a 2nd at Monza, won at Mugello and Garda, took 2nd at Vila Real, 4th at Buenos Aires and Monaco, 6th at Imola and 10th at Reims.

1967 Joined Ferrari and had his one and only Grand Prix drive to finish 8th in Mexico. He shared a Ferrari with Venturi to 4th in the Targa Florio and with Hawkins to 6th in the BOAC 500 at Brands Hatch. His other limited outings included 6th at Laguna Seca in a CanAm Ferrari, retiring from Riverside and Las Vegas. He took another Monza Lotteria victory with De Sanctis.

1968 After being dropped by Ferrari, most of the year was spent in F2, driving for Frank Williams, Church Farm, Gerards and Harris Tecno. He won at Hockenheim and in the F2 Monza Lotteria, with 8th at Zandvoort and 10th at Reims, before going to the Temporada races to take 11th in Cordoba and 14th in San Juan. A trip to Le Mans with Muller ended in retirement with a Ferrari 275LM and he was 2nd in the Enna City Cup with a Serenissima GT.

1969 Finished 7th with fastest lap in the Enna City Cup with a Serenissima, 14th at Brands Hatch in a Lola T142 F5000 and gave the De Tomaso F2 car its debut at Monza, finishing 9th. A further outing with the De Tomaso ended with 13th at Tulln Langenlebarn and he also drove the Serenissima at the Norisring.

1970 Took 7th in the Targa Florio with an Alfa Romeo T32/2 and 4th at the Salzburgring in an Abarth.

1971 Contested the Targa Florio again, finishing 7th with Nicodemi in a Lola T212.

VIC WILSON
Born April 14th 1931

Although British born, Vic made his motorsport debut in Rhodesia in the late fifties before hitting the British national scene in 1960. Moderate success followed, but after a couple of seasons out of racing, he took a Lotus 30 and Ferrari 250LM to numerous victories. After one Grand Prix back in 1960, he was lined up to partner Bob Bondurant in a privately-entered team of BRMs for 1966, but the drive failed to materialise.

GRAND PRIX RECORD	
Starts	1
Wins	0
Poles	0
Fastest laps	0
WC points	0
Best finish	DNF

1959 Raced a Lotus XI in Rhodesia.

1960 Deputised for the injured Dick Gibson in his Cooper T43 at the Italian Grand Prix, but retired when the engine blew. He also finished 2nd with the same car in the USAF Trophy race at Snetterton.

1964 Secured FTD at an Olivers Mount hillclimb in a Lotus 18.

1965 Raced a Lotus 30 in sports car and Libre races, with a double victory at Rufforth, a win and two 2nds at Croft, a win at Oulton Park, 3rd at Kirkistown, 4th at Mallory Park but retired in the TT. He also campaigned a Ferrari 250LM, winning at Croft, Silverstone, Aintree and Montlhery, with 4th in the Angola Grand Prix and he finished 3rd at Crystal Palace in an F2 Lola.

1966 After taking 4th at Syracuse and 9th in the Silverstone International Trophy in a Team Chamaco Collect BRM P261, he practised the car at the Belgian Grand Prix. But from thereon the team decided against running a second car and he was out of a drive.

Part Three
1970s

CHAPTER 10

IAN ASHLEY
Born October 26th 1947

Ian Ashley in March 1975.
Photo: BRDC Archive.

GRAND PRIX RECORD	
Starts	5
Wins	0
Poles	0
Fastest laps	0
WC points	0
Best finish	14th

One of the main stays of Formula 5000 racing in its heyday, Ashley started in Formula 3 and moved down to Formula Ford before climbing the ladder again. His Grand Prix debut came in the 1974 German with the unfashionable Token, but he enjoyed more success that year in F5000 by finishing 3rd in the championship. He dabbled in various single-seater categories over the next few years and sampled Williams, BRM and Hesketh in his quest to stay on the Grand Prix grid. However, an accident during qualifying for the 1977 Canadian race ended his Grand Prix career after he broke both ankles. He has since raced Indy Cars, Superbikes, Sidecars and even played polo, before returning to racing in 1999 in the UK-based TVR Tuscan Challenge.

1964 Raced karts.

1965 Drove a Jim Russell Lotus 31 and won his first race.

1966 Raced an Austin Healey Sprite in club racing.

1967 Moved into F3 with an Ashlowe Racing Lola and Merlyn, finishing 2nd at Albi in a consolation race, 3rd at Avus, 4th at Hameenlinna, 10th in the Coupe de Vitesse and 12th at Zolder.

1968 Raced for the Chequered Flag team in F3 with a Merlyn, taking 7th at Pau and Zandvoort and 12th at Montlhery and Karlskoga.

1969 He started the year in Formula Ford with an Alexis, taking two wins, a 2nd and two 3rds at Brands Hatch, a win and 2nd at Croft, 2nd at Oulton Park and 3rd at Silverstone until the team withdrew the car. Changing to a Lotus 61 he had a 3rd and 5th at Brands Hatch, and 4th at Snetterton on his way to finishing 6th overall in the Les Leston Championship. He also had a Libre win at Brands Hatch in a Lotus 59B and drove a K3 in F5000, taking 5th and 6th at Brands Hatch and 11th at Hockenheim.

1970 Started the year by taking 2nd in the Brazilian Formula Ford Championship behind Emerson Fittipaldi. Results included a win and 2nd at Curtiba, 2nd and 3rd at Sao Paulo, 3rd and 4th at Fontalenza, 4th and 5th at Rio and 4th and 6th at Jacarepagua in his Lotus 61. On his UK return he went back into F3, taking 2nd at the International Trophy support race in a Chevron and winning a Snetterton Libre race in a March.

1971 Another varied year, with 8th at Hockenheim and Brands Hatch in a Lola T190 F5000, 3rd at Brands Hatch in an F3 Lotus 59 and 22nd at Brands Hatch in an F3 EMC.

1972 With a Lola T190 and T191 he concentrated on F5000, taking 3rd in class at the Brands Hatch John Player Trophy, 4th at Silverstone, 2nd, 5th and 6th at Brands Hatch, 7th at Mallory and 8th in the Oulton Park Gold Cup, to finish 10th in the championship. He also raced a Royale RP11 in F3, finishing 3rd at Brands Hatch and 12th in the British Grand Prix support race.

1973 Another year in F5000 brought his first victory at the Jyllandsring. His Lola T330 also took 5th in the Oulton Park Gold Cup, 7th in the Vanwall Trophy at Silverstone, 8th at Brands Hatch, 9th in the Dublin GP at Mondello and 10th in the Race of Champions Brands Hatch. He spun out of the race at Mugello after starting from pole.

1974 Made his Grand Prix debut at the German with the Token, qualifying 26th and finishing 14th. He finished but was unclassified with the same car in Austria and then attempted to qualify the Chequered Flag Brabham BT42 unsuccessfully in the Canadian and USGPs. In F5000 he finished 3rd in the championship with his Lola T330, winning the Oulton Park Gold Cup and at Thruxton, with 2nd and 3rd at Mallory, 2nd, 3rd, 4th and 6th at Brands Hatch, 3rd at Oulton Park and 4th at Silverstone.

1975 His one Grand Prix appearance for Williams in Germany got no further than practice, after crashing and breaking his legs. He still managed to finish 4th in the Rothmans Formula 5000 Championship, only losing the title due to a series of engine failures. He won at Brands Hatch and then Thruxton, where he actually took the flag with a blown engine. He also took 2nd at Zolder, 4th at Thruxton, 5th in the Oulton Park Gold Cup, at Silverstone, Brands Hatch and Snetterton and 7th at Brands Hatch.

1976 Apart from racing a BRM in the Brazilian Grand Prix and failing to start the Thruxton F2 race in a Leda, it was a very quiet year.

1977 Joined the Hesketh Grand Prix from the Austrian race, but failed to qualify there and for the Dutch and Italian Grands Prix. He qualified in the US and finished 17th, but had another qualifying accident in Canada and broke both his ankles. He had also contested six rounds of the British F3 Championship in a Lola T570, finishing 7th at Cadwell Park, 10th at Brands Hatch, 13th at Donington Park but failed to qualify at Monaco.

1985 Made a comeback racing in Indy Cars, retiring a Lola at Miami after qualifying 16th.

1986 Had a couple of Indy Car outings with a Dick Simon-entered Lola T86, finishing 9th at Mid-Ohio and 23rd at Elkhart Lake.

1987 Raced at Miami in CART and retired the Lola T86, from his only outing of the year.

1988 Raced Superbikes in the USA.

1989 Continued in Superbikes and had a couple of outings in the Barber-Saab single-seater series, taking 5th at both Elkhart Lake and Lime Rock.

1990 Moved into Sidecars in the USA.

1991 Had two unsuccessful races with a Sotul Kitcar at Mallory Park and Spa.

1993 Contested the British Touring Car Championship with a Vauxhall Cavalier, taking 7th in the Donington Park end of season TOCA Shoot-Out. He finished 9th and 17th at Oulton Park, 9th, 12th and 15th at Donington Park, 12th at Snetterton, 13th at Pembrey, 13th, 17th and 21st at Brands Hatch, and 17th and 19th at Silverstone. In the TOCA Challenge for privateers he finished 3rd, after leading early in the year.

1996 Returned to race in the USA with 750 Superbikes.

1997 Played polo in the USA.

1998 Raced in the World Sidecar Championship.

1999 Returned to the UK to contest the TVR Tuscan Challenge.

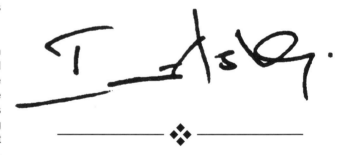

MIKE BEUTTLER
Born August 13th 1940
Died December 29th 1988

After a reasonable career in Formula 3 Beuttler was suddenly launched onto the Grand Prix scene, with only a handful of not particularly impressive F2 drives behind him. From 28 Grand Prix starts, he only managed to qualify in the top half of the grid on two occasions and was never more than a midfield runner. As in his Formula 3 days, he was privately entered and most of his Grands Prix were at the wheel of customer Marches. He gave up on F1 at the end of 1973 and made one sports car appearance in 1974 before hanging up his helmet.

Mike Beuttler.

Photo: BRDC Archive.

GRAND PRIX RECORD	
Starts	28
Wins	0
Poles	0
Fastest laps	0
WC points	0
Best finish	7th

1960 Had an occasional outing in a Chequered Flag Formula Junior Gemini, including a class win at the WECC Speed Trial.

1965 Raced an F3 Brabham mainly in Formula Libre events.

1967 Began racing more regularly in an F3 Brabham BT21, scoring a best finish of 4th in a Brands Hatch Libre race.

1968 Continued with his BT21 in F3 and finished 9th in the Lombank Championship, after a win at Snetterton and 3rds at Oulton Park (twice), Brands Hatch and Mallory Park. In Libre he won at Castle Combe, with two 2nds and two 3rds at Mallory Park, two 2nds and a 3rd at Brands Hatch and a 3rd at Snetterton. He also shared a Porsche 911S with Spero to 10th in the Barcelona 6 hours.

1969 A further year in F3 brought a mixture of success and accidents. He was 3rd at Pau and Mallory Park, 4th at Barcelona, 5th and 6th at Brands Hatch, 6th at Crystal Palace and Magny Cours, 7th at Snetterton and 10th at Cadwell Park. He also continued to race in Libre, taking 2nd at Brands Hatch and 4th at Silverstone.

1970 He started the year with a series of accidents, but ended up 3rd in the Shell F3 Championship and 10th in

the Forward Trust Championship. He won at Silverstone, Brands Hatch in the Grand Prix support, Thruxton and Montlhery. He also took 2nd at Crystal Palace, 3rd at Croft and Rouen, 4th at Thruxton and Pau, 5th at Snetterton, 6th at Paul Ricard, Zolder and Cadwell Park and 9th at Oulton Park. He shared a Porsche 910 with Nick Gold to 11th in the BOAC 1000. He was awarded second place in the end of season Grovewood Awards.

1971 The season began in F2 with a March 712 finishing 10th at Mallory Park and 18th at the Nurburgring, and ended with 4th and a victory at Vallelunga to secure 7th in the championship. He had also made his F1 debut in the Race of Champions at Brands Hatch, but retired his March 701. That was followed by 10th in the International Trophy at Silverstone and 13th in the Rindt Memorial at Hockenheim. His Grand Prix debut came at the British in a March 711 and ended in retirement. From four further Grand Prix outings he failed to record a finish. At the end of the year he took his F2 car to Brazil, and finished 4th at Interlagos and 19th at Porto Allegre.

1972 Another attempt at Grand Prix racing was undertaken in a March 721 F2 car modified for F1. Having failed to qualify for the Spanish Grand Prix, he finished 13th in Monaco, a result equalled in both the British and US races. His best results came with 8th in the German and 10th in the Italian, while in the non-championship races he took 4th at Vallelunga and 15th in the John Player Trophy at Brands Hatch. From his occasional F2 forays he secured 2nd in the Clark Memorial and 4th in the Rindt Memorial, both at Hockenheim, along with 7th at Mantorp Park.

1973 A final year on the Grand Prix scene with his March 721G brought a small improvement overall. Although he failed to record a finish on seven occasions, he did secure 7th in Spain, 8th in Sweden, 10th in Argentina and US, 11th in Belgium and 16th in Germany. He continued to race occasionally in F2 with success, finishing 3rd at Thruxton and 4th at Pau and Nivelles with his March.

1974 After a brief appearance in the 1000km sports car race at Brands Hatch, he retired from racing.

TONY BRISE
Born March 28th 1952
Killed November 29th 1975

Tony Brise in July 1975.

Photo: BRDC Archive.

GRAND PRIX RECORD	
Starts	10
Wins	0
Poles	0
Fastest laps	0
WC points	1
Best finish	6th

each at Croft, Lydden and Thruxton. He had two Libre wins and 3rd in F3 at Brands Hatch with a Brabham, plus BTD at a Brands Hatch sprint and received a Grovewood Commendation for his efforts.

1972 Started the year racing Formula Ford in South Africa with his Merlyn, he won at Lourenco Marques and Bloemfontein and took 2nd at Kyalami. Back in England he had wins at Brands Hatch and Mallory Park, before moving to F3 with a Brabham and later a GRD. He won at Thruxton, Mallory Park, Brands Hatch and Oulton Park. Other results included 2nd and 3rd at Silverstone, 2nd and 3rd at Snetterton, 2nd, 3rd and 4th at Thruxton, 2nd and 3rd at Brands Hatch, 2nd at La Chatre and Cadwell Park, 4th at Chimay and Oulton Park and a win in the Brands Hatch Yuletide Trophy. He was runner-up in the Lombard North Central Championship and 4th in the Forward Trust Championship.

1973 Won the John Player F3 Championship, shared the Lombard North Central title with Richard Robarts and finished as runner-up in the Forward Trust Championship, starting with his GRD before changing to a new March 733. Victories came at Brands Hatch (five times) at Silverstone, Mallory Park, Oulton Park and at Snetterton. He finished 2nd in the Grovewood Awards at the end of the season.

1974 Finished 2nd in the Monaco F3 race but spent the year racing a March 73B and a Modus in Formula Atlantic. He won at Silverstone, Brands Hatch and Mondello Park, with 3rd at Phoenix Park, 4th at Oulton Park (twice) and 5th at the British Grand Prix meeting to take 3rd in the John Player Championship.

1975 His first F1 chance came with Williams at the Spanish Grand Prix, qualifying 18th and finishing 7th. Although that proved to be a one-off, he joined Embassy Hill for the rest of the year but retired in Belgium. He followed that up with 6th in the Swedish, 7th in the Dutch and French, 15th in the British and Austrian and retirements in the German, Italian and US races. He won the John Player Formula Atlantic Championship and finished 3rd in the Southern Organs Series for Modus, with wins at Brands Hatch (three times), Silverstone (three times), Snetterton (twice) and at Oulton Park. In the Monaco F3 race he was battling for the lead in his Modus until a clash with Ribeiro at the Mirabeau put him out. He also led F5000 races at Brands Hatch and Long Beach before finishing 4th in both. Further outings netted

A rising star who won championships in every category he attempted. His rise through karting and the junior single-seater categories was meteoric and was indication of a very fine talent. Not surprisingly Brise was quickly snapped up for Grand Prix racing, and although he made his debut for Williams in the 1975 Spanish, he completed the year with Graham Hill's Embassy Lola team. Plans were already well advanced for 1976 when the team went testing in France, but their plane crashed on the return flight killing everyone on board. It was a cruel blow and Brise's full potential was destined never to be seen. Many experts consider he had the talent to be a Grand Prix winner and perhaps even a British World Champion. He was just 23 when he died.

1969 Joint British Karting Champion, having started racing at the age of 8.

1970 Began the year in karts before moving into Formula Ford with an Elden.

1971 Won the Brands Hatch Formula Ford Championship and finished runner-up in the BOC Championship driving an Elden and a Merlyn. He had eight wins at Brands Hatch, four at Oulton Park, plus one

a 2nd at Brands Hatch, 4th at Laguna Seca and 6th Riverside, taking 10th overall in the US Championship. Sadly this was to be his last year, after he was killed in the aircrash with Graham Hill when returning from testing in France.

CHRIS CRAFT
Born November 17th 1939

A top class saloon and sports car driver who only tended to have brief flirtations with single-seater racing. He won the European Sports Car Championship in 1973 and partnered Alain de Cadenet at Le Mans on numerous occasions. A solitary Grand Prix appearance came at the 1971 US in a privately-entered Brabham, but the car failed to finish. That was followed by a couple of years in Formula 5000 and he continued with a very heavy race schedule in sports cars and saloon cars until retiring in 1984. One of his best results was finishing third at Le Mans in 1976 while many successes in saloons and sports cars made him one of Britain's top drivers of the era.

1961 His debut race at Mallory Park ended in an accident with his Ford Anglia, but he returned to clinch a 2nd in class at Silverstone.

1962 Continued to race his orange Anglia, with two class wins at Brands Hatch and one each at Castle Combe and Silverstone, with 2nd at Mallory Park and Silverstone, and 3rd at Crystal Palace.

1963 Another year with the Anglia brought two class wins and two 2nds at Snetterton, a win, 2nd and 3rd at Brands Hatch, two wins at Mallory and a win and 2nd at Silverstone.

1964 Having started the year with a Lotus Cortina, he had a 6th at Crystal Palace before rolling the car to destruction at Brands Hatch. After wheeling out the Anglia again, he had a win and 2nd at Brands Hatch, with 4th at Crystal Palace.

1965 The season started again with a Lotus Cortina until his cash ran out and he moved on to a Superspeed Anglia. He was 3rd at Crystal Palace, 9th at Oulton Park and 12th at the British Grand Prix meeting. He also drove a Ford Mustang to an overall and class win at Brands Hatch and 2nd at Snetterton, and a McLaren Elva to 2nd

in the Rand Sports Car race and 4th at the Roy Hesketh circuit. At the Brands Hatch Guards 100 he shared a Jaguar E-Type with Oliver to 3rd, and shared a Lotus Cortina with Hobbs at Road America to finish 3rd.

1966 Continued with the Superspeed Anglia in the British Saloon Car Championship, winning his class at Snetterton, Oulton Park and Goodwood, with 3rd at Brands Hatch to finish 3rd in class in the championship. He also drove a Shelby Mustang at Brands Hatch, collecting 2nd and 3rd and had occasional races in a Techspeed-entered Chevron B8.

1967 Went to Italy to race a BWA in Formula 3, but also drove a Merlyn to take 3rd in the Lakeside Trophy at Mallory Park. When time permitted he also raced the Superspeed Anglia.

1968 Began the year with an Anglia, taking class wins at Thruxton, Silverstone and Oulton Park. After changing to a Broadspeed Escort he had wins at Brands Hatch (twice) and Oulton Park, 2nd at Silverstone and 9th overall at the Nurburgring with Roger Clark. In F3 he raced his own Tecno to 2nd at Crystal Palace, 3rd at Silverstone and added 3rd and 5th at Brands Hatch. At Phoenix Park he broke the lap record in Sid Taylor's F5000 Lola and also raced a Chevron B8 to 2nd at Brands Hatch and Croft, and 5th at Oulton Park. He finished 3rd in the end of season Grovewood Awards.

1969 Finished 2nd overall with class titles in both the British Sports and Saloon Car Championships. With his

Chris Craft.

Photo: BRDC Archive.

GRAND PRIX RECORD

Starts	1
Wins	0
Poles	0
Fastest laps	0
WC points	0
Best finish	DNF

Broadspeed Escort he won his class at Snetterton (twice), Brands Hatch, Oulton Park, Silverstone and at he British Grand Prix meeting, with 2nd at Brands Hatch. In sports cars he won at Vila Real with Piper, took 2nd at Mantorp Park and Barcelona and 3rd at Montlhery in a Porsche 908, and won at Croft, with 4th at the International Trophy and 8th in the BOAC 500 driving a Lola T70.

1970 Began racing in F5000 firstly with a Leda and then a McLaren M10B. In the British Saloon Car Championship he finished 5th overall and won his class with the Broadspeed Escort, taking class wins at Brands Hatch (twice), Snetterton, Crystal Palace, Silverstone and Croft, with 2nd at Oulton Park and Silverstone and 26th overall in the TT sharing with Stewart. His other results included victories at Karlskoga in a McLaren M8C and in the Guards Trophy at Brands Hatch in a Lola T210. He took 2nd at Thruxton in an Interserie race with the Lola and 3rd at the Nurburgring in the McLaren.

1971 His Ecurie Evergreen Brabham BT33 was taken to the Canadian Grand Prix, but failed to start after engine problems. He did make the grid for the US GP, but retired on what was to be his only Grand Prix start. He earlier raced the same car to 5th in the Oulton Park Gold Cup. Once again he was a class champion in the British Saloon Car Championship and came 5th in Interserie with a McLaren M8E, after winning at the Norisring and taking 2nd in the Coppa Shell at Imola and 12th at Zolder. He also went to Le Mans and finished 4th with David Weir in a Ferrari 512M, shared a McLaren M8C with Trevor Taylor to 9th in the Buenos Aires 1000km and drove a Chevron B19 to victory at Oulton Park, 2nd at the Nurburgring and 3rd at Silverstone.

1972 Concentrated almost entirely on sports cars, with 3rd at Keimola and 6th at Hockenheim in Interserie with a Porsche 917K. He took 7th in the Buenos Aires 1000km in a Lola T280 and 12th at Le Mans with De Cadenet in the Duckhams Special Ford.

1973 Won the European Sports Car Championship in a Lola T292, winning the Coppa Giunti at Misano, the Coppa Shell at Imola, with 2nd at Barcelona and Clermont Ferrand. He retired the Duckhams Ford at Le Mans, but won at Misano in a Lola T212. He returned to F5000 to partner Pilette in the VDS team, taking 5th at Zandvoort, 7th at Mallory Park and 9th at Brands Hatch in his Chevron B24.

1974 Another year in F5000 brought 3rd at Zolder and Mondello Park, 4th at Zandvoort and Thruxton, 5th at Brands Hatch and 8th at Mallory Park in his Chevron, along with 7th at Brands Hatch in a Brabham BT43. With his Porsche 917K he was a regular top ten Interserie finisher and drove an Osella Abarth in European 2-litre Sports Car races, finishing 4th at Enna. He also had occasional saloon car appearances, finishing 6th at Snetterton in a Ford Capri and 4th in class at Brands Hatch with a Triumph Dolomite Sprint.

1975 Racing a Ford Capri in the British Saloon Car Championship, he finished 4th and 5th at Oulton Park and 7th at Brands Hatch, along with 3rd in class at Thruxton in a Dolomite. He shared a Lola T380 with De Cadenet at Le Mans, finishing 15th with the fastest lap.

1976 Contested the British Saloon Car Championship in a Hammonds Sauce-backed Ford Capri, taking 2nd at Brands Hatch and Mallory Park, 3rd at Thruxton (twice) and 4th at the British Grand Prix and Snetterton. He also shared a Dolomite with Bell to 14th overall in the TT at Silverstone and came 3rd overall at Le Mans sharing De Cadenet's Lola.

1977 Contested the British Saloon Car Championship in the Capri again, finishing 2nd in class with a win at Thruxton, 2nd at Silverstone, Donington Park and Brands Hatch, 3rd at Oulton Park and Thruxton, 4th at Silverstone and 6th at Thruxton. He shared his Capri with Edwards to 4th in the Spa 1000km, finished 5th at Le Mans with De Cadenet's Lola and took 4th in class at Estoril on the World Sports Car debut of the Lola T296.

1978 Joined the Spice Capri team and won the Spa 24 hours. He also won at Donington Park, with 2nd at Silverstone and Thruxton, 3rd at Oulton Park, 4th at Mallory Park, Brands Hatch and Donington Park and 5th at Brands Hatch to take 9th overall and 3rd in class in the British Saloon Car Championship. He also contested the Porsche 924 Championship, taking 2nd at Donington Park and 5th at Silverstone, and went to Le Mans again to share De Cadenet's 15th-placed Lola.

1979 Continuing with a Spice Capri he had two 2nds and a 5th at Silverstone, two 3rds at Donington Park, 2nd at Brands Hatch, 3rd at Oulton Park and 4th at Thruxton to finish 3rd in class. At the Spa 24 hours his Capri was 4th when shared with Jeff Allam, while sharing a Dome with Spice he took 12th in the Silverstone 6 hours but retired at Le Mans.

1980 Finished 7th in the Silverstone 6 hours with O'Rourke and Norman in a Ferrari 512 and 25th at Le Mans with Evans in a Dome.

1981 Won his class and took 3rd overall in the Brands Hatch 1000km sharing a BMW M1 with Bell, and retired his Dome at Le Mans, after sharing with Evans.

1982 Retired his Dome at both Silverstone and Le Mans, sharing with Boesel and Salazar.

1983 Retired the Dome at Le Mans again when sharing with Nick Mason, but the same partnership secured 7th in a Brands Hatch Thundersports race with a Lola T298.

1984 Retired from Le Mans again, after partnering De Cadenet and Grice in a Porsche 956.

❖

JIM CRAWFORD
Born February 13th 1948

Jim Crawford in April 1981.
Photo: BRDC Archive.

After a couple of years rallying and preparing Steve Choularton's racing cars, Crawford's break came courtesy of Choularton with the chance to race. He quickly proved his talent by becoming Formula Atlantic Champion in 1974, in what was his first full season of racing. Remarkably, his Grand Prix chance came the following season.

However, a couple of outings in an out-dated works Lotus gave him little opportunity to prove his worth on the Grand Prix scene. His first GP was the infamous 1975 British at Silverstone that ended in a cloud-burst. However, it did not lead to a permanent Grand Prix opportunity and he stepped back into national racing. After a successful spell in F2 and domestic championship, he went to the USA to finish as runner-up in the CanAm and race occasionally in Indycars. His racing ambitions were curtailed by a serious crash at the 1987 Indianapolis 500 during qualifying, when he broke both ankles. He did however return to the brickyard to contest the Indy 500 from 1988 to 1992 and topped those attempts with an excellent sixth place in '88.

1967 Began rallying in a Mini.

1968 Continued in rallying and contested the Gulf International in his Mini.

1969 His rallying exploits came to an end when his Mini hit a tree on the Express & Star Rally.

1970 Spent the year out of competition as a mechanic in America.

1971 Had an outing in Choularton's Alexis Formula Ford, and finished 2nd at Oulton Park.

1972 Another one-off in Choularton's Lotus 69, brought him 2nd place in a Formula Libre race at Croft.

1973 He smashed the outright circuit record at Croft in Choularton's March 73B, and was rewarded with further outings in a Chevron B25. He had Libre wins at Aintree and Snetterton, while in Formula Atlantic he took 2nd at Oulton Park and 5th at Brands Hatch.

1974 His first full year in racing brought him the Southern Organs Atlantic title and 2nd place in the John Player Championship, after starting with a March 73B before changing to a Chevron. He had two wins and 2nd at Oulton Park, a win and two 2nds at Mallory Park, 3rd and 6th at Snetterton, 2nd at Phoenix Park, 3rd at the British Grand Prix meeting, a win, 3rd and 7th at Brands Hatch and 4th, 5th and 6th places at Silverstone. He also had a Libre win at Snetterton, finished 5th in a non-championship F2 race at Nogaro, and earned himself a Grovewood Commendation.

1975 A testing contract with Lotus led to his F1 debut in the International Trophy at Silverstone, where he crashed

GRAND PRIX RECORD	
Starts	2
Wins	0
Poles	0
Fastest laps	0
WC points	0
Best finish	13th

out of the race. His Grand Prix debut followed at the rain-lashed British, spinning out after qualifying 25th and was followed by a further opportunity at the Italian, where he finished 13th. Continuing to race in Formula Atlantic he finished runner-up with a Chevron B29, after two wins and a 2nd at Mallory Park, 2nd at Brands Hatch, 2nd at Snetterton and 2nd, 4th and 6th at Silverstone.

1976 After plans to race in F2 fell apart, he had relatively few opportunities. At Mallory Park he won a Renault 5TS race, followed by a couple of races in the Shellsport Series with his Chevron B29, taking 3rd at Oulton Park and 8th at Brands Hatch.

1977 A one-off British F3 outing netted 8th at Mallory Park.

1978 In F3 again with a Chevron, he took 3rd and 4th at Oulton Park, 5th at Mallory Park, 7th at Thruxton and 8th and 10th at Brands Hatch.

1979 Returned to Formula Atlantic again and finished runner-up in the Hitachi Championship, with a Plygrange-backed Chevron B45. He won at Mallory Park, had a win and two 2nds at Brands Hatch, two wins at Oulton Park, won at Ingliston, had a 2nd, 3rd and 5th at Silverstone, 2nd at Donington Park and Snetterton, 3rd at Phoenix Park and won the Triple Crown. He also raced in the BMW County Championship, finishing 5th at Mallory Park.

1980 Won the F2 class and finished 4th overall in the Aurora AFX Championship with his Chevron B45, after 3rd and 4th places at Mallory Park, a win and 4th at Oulton Park, 6th and 8th at Silverstone, 6th at Brands Hatch and 13th at Thruxton. He won a Libre race at Aintree, had two F2 outings, retiring at Silverstone and taking 10th at Zolder, and shared Barrie Williams' Colt in the Brands Hatch European Touring Car round.

1981 A full year in F2 with a Toleman TG280B brought 4th at Silverstone, 6th at Spa, 7th at Hockenheim and Misano, 9th at Vallelunga and Donington Park, 10th at Pau and 11th at Mugello. He also took Libre wins at Croft and Aintree and shared a Sunbeam in the Willhire 24 hours at Snetterton and a 3 hour Brands Hatch production car race.

1982 Became British F1 Champion in an AMCO Ensign N180B, with wins at Thruxton, Donington Park and Brands Hatch. The car was then converted to CanAm specifications and finished 2nd at Trois Rivieres, 3rd at Laguna Seca, 4th at Las Vegas and 5th at Mosport, to finish 5th in the championship. His other results included 10th overall and 2nd in class sharing a Lancia Beta Monte Carlo with Castellano at the Silverstone 6 hours, and 6th with Leslie in a March 81S in an Oulton Park Sports 2000 enduro.

1983 Finished 2nd in the CanAm Championship in his RK Carbon Fibres-backed Ford, winning at Lime Rock and Mosport and taking 2nd at Sears Point, Trois Rivieres and Mosport. He won the Madras Grand Prix in a Chevron B42, raced an F1 Ensign in the British Open, and a Ford C100 and Chevron B16 in Thundersports.

1984 He made his Indycar debut at Long Beach with 4th in the Theodore DFX 83. He then changed to a March 82C, failed to qualify for the Indy 500 and retired at Meadowlands and Laguna Seca. For the second successive year he was runner-up in the CanAm Championship with an RK March 847, winning at Road Atlanta, Trois Rivieres and Green Valley, with 2nd at Mosport (twice), Dallas, Lime Rock, Sears Point and Riverside.

1985 Raced a Lola T900 Indycar, finishing 4th at Long Beach, 5th at Phoenix, 9th at Meadowlands, 13th at Cleveland and 16th Miami, but retired from the Indy 500 after qualifying 27th. He also won the Madras Grand Prix again in a Chevron B42.

1986 Retired from the top ten in the Indy 500 when the Buick engine blew in his March 86C. He also shared a March Buick with Whitney Ganz in IMSA, without success.

1987 Raced in IMSA with a Buick Hawke, and retired from Miami after sharing with Michael Andretti. During qualifying for the Indy 500 he crashed heavily in his Patrick March Buick, breaking both ankles.

1988 Returned to contest the Indy 500 again, qualifying his Lola T87 Buick 18th, before finishing a remarkable 6th.

1989 Finished 19th in the Indy 500 after his Lola developed engine problems, having qualified in 4th.

1990 Retired his Lola T89 Buick at Phoenix, but finished 15th in the Indianapolis 500.

1991 Qualified 8th at Indianapolis but retired with engine failure in his Lola T91 Buick.

1992 His final appearance at the Indy 500 ended with his Lola T92 Buick crashing into the Penskes of Fittipaldi and Mears. Crawford sustained a fractured left foot in what proved to be his final race.

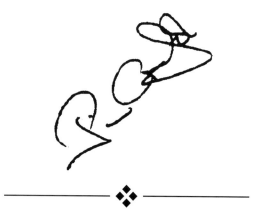

GUY EDWARDS
Born December 30th 1942

Guy Edwards.

Photo: BRDC Archive.

One of the acclaimed masters at gaining sponsorship for his racing, Edwards scored major successes worldwide in sports cars and Formula 5000. His Grand Prix career spanned two seasons, with Embassy Hill and Hesketh, starting in Argentina in 1974. Seventh place in the Swedish GP of that season was his best finish. During his GP career, he was awarded the Queens Gallantry medal for his part in rescuing Niki Lauda from his burning Ferrari during the German Grand Prix at the Nurburgring in 1976. After a successful spell in British F1, he turned back to long distance sports car racing, before a final period racing in touring cars in the late eighties.

1965 Made his racing debut at Snetterton in a Ford Anglia, before changing to a Mini and taking 5th on his debut in that car.

1966 Finished 3rd in class sharing a Mini Marcos at Mugello.

1967 Raced a Mini and had a win and 2nd at Oulton Park, plus 3rd at Brands Hatch. He also shared a Mini Marcos to 2nd in class at the Nurburgring.

1968 His Mini took a 2nd and 3rd overall with first in class at Brands Hatch, and 7th at Karlskoga. He also drove an MG Midget to 7th at Oulton Park and took over the Lola T62 F3 car briefly at the end of the year.

1969 Racing mainly in a Chevron B8, he finished 3rd and 5th at Croft, 4th in the Barcelona 12 hours, 9th in the TT and 15th in the Spa 1000km with Franey. He claimed 2nd in the Danish Grand Prix, 9th in the Trophy of the Dunes at Zandvoort and at Keimola, 10th in the Brands Hatch Lombank Trophy and 12th in the Nordic Cup at Anderstorp. He also drove the F3 Lola at Silverstone and finished 19th.

1970 Continued to race in GT but with an Astra, winning the Zandvoort Benelux Cup, with 2nd at the Flugplatzrennen, 3rd at Brands Hatch, 7th at the Danish Grand Prix and the Nurburgring and 8th at Karlskoga.

1971 A change to a Lola T212 brought further success, with wins at Crystal Palace and Nogaro, 3rd at Wunstorf, 4th in the Brands Hatch Martini Trophy, 5th in the Trophee Auvergne at Clermont Ferrand and at Silverstone, and 9th at the Salzburgring. He drove the same car at Le Mans and in the Austrian 1000km, retiring on each occasion. He then went to South Africa at the end of the year and finished 7th in the championship after taking 2nd in the Bulawayo 3 hours and at Pietermaritzburg, 3rd in the Capetown and Lourenco Marques 3 hours and 11th at the Welkom 3 hours. He also shared a Chevron B19 with John Lepp to 10th at Paul Ricard.

1972 Finished 3rd in the European 2-litre Sports Car Championship, with a Barclays-backed Lola T290. He had a class win and 7th overall in the BOAC 1000km, 2nd at Vallelunga and in the Silverstone Martini International, 4th at Enna and 6th at Paul Ricard, won at Snetterton and took 7th in an Interserie race at the Nurburgring. He raced the Lola T290 in South Africa again, finishing 3rd in the Welkom Goldfields 3 hours, 4th in the Lourenco Marques 3 hours and 14th in the Kyalami 9 hours with Paddy Driver. He also began his F5000 career in a McLaren M10B, taking 6th at Brands Hatch and Oulton Park, and 7th at the Oulton Park Gold Cup and at Mondello Park.

1973 Continuing in F5000 with a Lola T330, he had wins at Zandvoort and Brands Hatch, 2nd at Mondello Park, 4th at Mallory Park, 6th at Brands Hatch, 9th at Jyllandsring and 10th at Oulton Park to take 6th in the championship. He also took 5th in the European 2-litre Sports Car Championship with his Lola T290, winning at the Osterreichring and Clermont Ferrand, with 4th at Enna and 7th at Misano.

GRAND PRIX RECORD	
Starts	11
Wins	0
Poles	0
Fastest laps	0
WC points	0
Best finish	7th

1974 Joining the Embassy Hill Lola team for the Grand Prix season, he finished 11th on his debut in Argentina. After retiring in Brazil he failed to qualify in Spain, before finishing 12th in Belgium, 8th in Monaco and 7th in Sweden. His only other classified finish came from 15th in the French. He failed to start the British after a wrist injury in the previous race and failed to qualify for the German. He continued to race in F5000 when circumstances permitted and won at Mallory Park, with 3rd at Zandvoort, 7th at Monza, 9th in the International Trophy and 10th at Thruxton and Brands Hatch in a Lola T332.

1975 There was no Grand Prix drive but with the backing of Encyclopaedia Britannica his Lola finished 3rd in the F5000 Championship. Results included two 2nd places at Mallory Park, 2nd at Snetterton, 3rd at Thruxton, Brands Hatch and Snetterton, 4th at Snetterton, 6th in the Oulton Park Gold Cup, 7th at Brands Hatch and Silverstone and 9th at Zandvoort and Hockenheim. He also raced his Lola T390 in sports cars, finishing 2nd in the Britannic Euro Sports and 3rd at Silverstone.

1976 A return to Grand Prix racing came with Hesketh in Belgium, but he failed to qualify for the race. At the French he was 17th, retired after an accident at the British, finished 15th in the German after stopping to help rescue Lauda, failed to start the Italian and took 20th in Canada. He had occasional outings in an Ultramar-backed Brabham BT42, winning the Oulton Park Gold Cup, with further victory at Thruxton and 5th at Brands Hatch to finish 10th in the F5000 series. He also drove a March sports for the same team.

1977 Finished as runner-up in the Shellsport Group 8 Championship, with a March 751, after two wins a 2nd and a 3rd at Brands Hatch, two wins and a 2nd at Thruxton, a win at Snetterton, 2nd at Oulton Park and 5th at Mallory Park. He was one of many who tried to qualify the woeful BRM P207, but failed to get beyond pre-qualifying at the British. His other results included 13th at the Nurburgring and non-qualification at Vallelunga in an ICI Newsweek Chevron B40. He had a handful of World Sports Car outings with a Lola, netting 6th at the Salzburgring. He retired at Le Mans after sharing a Porsche 935 with Fitzpatrick and Faure and finished 4th in the Spa 600km sharing a Ford Capri with Craft.

1978 Contested the Aurora AFX British F1 Championship, starting with a March 761, before changing to a 781. He won at Oulton Park and Thruxton, with 2nd at Donington Park, 3rd at Mallory Park, 4th at Brands Hatch and 10th at Mallory Park to take 4th in the championship. He also went to Le Mans, retiring the Ibec Hesketh 308LM after engine failure when sharing with Bracey and Grob.

1979 Continued in the Aurora Championship with a Fittipaldi F5A, taking 7th overall and a class win in the Race of Champions. He finished 2nd at Oulton Park and Brands Hatch, 3rd at Mallory Park, 6th at Donington Park, 7th at Zandvoort and 8th at Brands Hatch, for 5th overall in the championship. At Le Mans he shared a BMW M1 with Quester and Grob.

1980 His Fittipaldi started the year with pole at the Newsweek International Trophy at Sandown, finishing 3rd after a spin. In the Aurora Championship he was 3rd overall, after victories at Oulton Park and Snetterton, 2nd at Monza, Mallory Park and Silverstone, 3rd at Thruxton, 4th at Silverstone and Oulton Park and 5th at Brands Hatch. He finished 9th at Le Mans sharing a Porsche 935 with John Paul Jnr and Snr, and took 2nd with a 935 at the Donington Park International Group 5 Race.

1981 Shared a Lola T600 with Villota for most of the year, finishing 8th in the Nurburgring 1000km and 15th at Le Mans. He led the Silverstone 1000km until running out of fuel, and the Watkins Glen race until the car rolled and he was trapped inside.

1982 Drove a Lola T610 in the World Endurance Championship, sharing mainly with Keegan. He was 7th in the Brands Hatch Shell 1000, 16th in the Silverstone 6 hours, excluded on a technicality at Monza, and retired at Spa, Nurburgring and Le Mans.

1983 Finished 5th at Le Mans and retired at Silverstone, sharing a Porsche 956 with Keegan and Henn.

1984 Continued to share a Porsche 956, taking 3rd at Brands Hatch and Silverstone, 11th at the Nurburgring and retiring from Le Mans in a 962.

1985 Finished 4th at Le Mans sharing a Porsche 956 with Hobbs and Gartner, and retired at Silverstone.

1988 After a brief lay-off he returned with a Kaliber-backed Ford Sierra Cosworth in the British Touring Car Championship, finishing 4th in class. He finished 2nd at the British Grand Prix meeting and in a further Silverstone round and 3rd at Brands Hatch, Snetterton and Donington Park (sharing with Dumfries). He added 4th and 5th at Silverstone, 5th at Brands Hatch, 6th at Donington Park (twice) and 11th at Thruxton, plus 6th in the TT sharing with Palmer.

1989 A further year with the Sierra brought considerably less success, with 3rd, 6th and 7th at Silverstone, 4th at Brands Hatch, 7th at Birmingham and 14th at Thruxton, with exclusion from 3rd at Donington Park after illegally changing his co-driver from Dumfries to Percy.

BOB EVANS
Born June 11th 1947

One of a group of talented British drivers who never really got the breaks they deserved. He more than proved himself in Formula 5000, winning the championship in 1974. His dogged perseverance with the uncompetitive BRM in 1975, led to a Lotus contract for the following year and a Grand Prix seat for the first two races. He had an excellent year in the Aurora Championship in 1978, but from thereon he was mainly seen in sports cars until the mid-eighties.

GRAND PRIX RECORD

Starts	10
Wins	0
Poles	0
Fastest laps	0
WC points	0
Best finish	9th

1967 Made his racing debut with a Morris Minor-engined Sprite at Lydden.

1968 Continued racing his Sprite until funds ran out.

1969 Moved into single-seaters with a Formula Ford Merlyn Mk11A, taking a 2nd at Lydden in Formula Ford and a 3rd in Formula Libre.

1970 Won the Brands Hatch Formula Ford Championship in a Palliser, with two wins, three 2nds, four 3rds, a 4th and a 9th. He also won twice at Lydden and had wins at Snetterton and the Osterreichring, with 2nd and 4th at Crystal Palace, 2nd at Silverstone and Lydden (twice), 2nd in the Autosport Formula Ford Trophy and 3rd at Thruxton.

1971 Spent the year with the Alan McKechnie-run Puma in F3, but missed the second half of the season after breaking his neck in an accident at Castle Combe. He had a 3rd at Crystal Palace, 4th and 5th at Brands Hatch and 13th at Silverstone, while in Libre he had a win at Brands Hatch and came 4th in the Rochester Trophy.

1972 Staying in F3 with a March 723 he had a win, two 3rds and a 6th at Brands Hatch. He finished 2nd at Silverstone, 3rd at Zandvoort, 5th at Silverstone, 6th at Chimay, Crystal Palace, Oulton Park and Thruxton, 11th at Rouen, 14th at Monaco, 17th at the British Grand Prix meeting and 18th at Paul Ricard. He also had a run in a Lola T300 Chevrolet at Brands Hatch, and won the Libre race.

1973 A full Formula 5000 campaign with a Trojan brought a win at Snetterton, two 4th places at Oulton Park, including in the Gold Cup, 4th at Mallory Park, 5th at Mondello Park, 8th at Brands Hatch and 13th at Silverstone.

1974 Won the Rothmans F5000 Championship in a McKechnie Lola T332, with wins at Brands Hatch, Mallory Park, Mondello Park and Thruxton. He also took 2nd at Mugello, Zandvoort and Zolder, 3rd and 5th at Mallory Park, 3rd at Thruxton, Brands Hatch and Monza and 6th at Oulton Park (twice). He shared Richard Lloyd's March 74S to 8th in the BOAC 1000 at Brands Hatch, and was the Premier Grovewood Award winner.

Bob Evans in the BRM.

Photo: BRDC Archive.

1975 His Grand Prix debut came with BRM in South Africa, qualifying 24th and finishing 15th. He continued to persevere with the uncompetitive car, and apart from Monaco he always succeeded in making the grid. In Belgium he finished 9th, with 13th in the Swedish and 17th in the French. He also drove the BRM to 5th at the Race of Champions and 10th at the International Trophy. From only five starts he finished 7th in the F5000 Championship, with a Lola T332, taking a win at Snetterton, 3rd at Brands Hatch, 3rd and 10th at Mallory Park and 4th at Silverstone.

1976 A Lotus testing contract led to him starting the season with a Grand Prix seat, but after 10th in South Africa and 9th in the Race of Champions, he failed to qualify at Long Beach and lost the seat. He made one more attempt to get onto the Grand Prix grid at the British, but his RAM Brabham BT44B failed to qualify. His other results included 6th in the Fuji 2-litre Sports Grand Prix in an Alpine Renault and 2nd with a McLaren M25 Chevrolet at Brands Hatch in the Shellsport F5000 Championship.

1977 He contested the first two rounds of the F2 Championship with a Wheatcroft, failing to record a finish. He took 11th in the Race of Champions in a Hexagon Penske and should have raced the ex-Purley Chevron B30 in the Shellsport finale at Brands Hatch, but it failed to last beyond qualifying.

1978 Came into the Aurora AFX series late in the season and was quickly on the pace with John Cooper's Surtees TS19 and Hesketh 308. He won first time out at Zandvoort, had 2nd places at Thruxton (twice) and Brands Hatch, with 3rd at Donington Park, 5th at Oulton Park and 7th at Mallory Park and Snetterton. At Le Mans he shared a Lola T294 with Birrane and Down and finished 14th overall and 2nd in class sharing Richard Lloyd's VW Golf GTi at the TT.

1979 Raced for Dome at Le Mans with Trimmer and had a brief test with the Lotus 80 Grand Prix car.

1980 Raced at Le Mans again sharing a Dome with Craft, but retired.

1981 Retired his Dome at Le Mans sharing with Craft, and contested the Willhire 24 hours at Snetterton with the Morris Stapleton Morgan team.

1982 Became part of the Aston Martin Nimrod team, retiring at Silverstone after sharing with Lees, and at Le Mans with Lees and Needell.

1984 Finished 7th in the Daytona 24 hours with Cooper and Paul Smith in a Nimrod and retired from the Silverstone 6 hours, after sharing a Gebhardt BMW with Jelinski.

1985 Retired from the Silverstone 1000km again after sharing an EMKA Aston Martin with Needell and O'Rourke, and finished 5th at Brands Hatch in Thundersports, sharing a Toj with Sean Walker.

1986 Finished 9th at Brands Hatch in Thundersports, sharing the Toj with Divina Galica.

PETER GETHIN
Born February 21st 1940

Peter Gethin.

Photo: BRDC Archive.

Gethin is best known for his Italian Grand Prix victory for BRM in 1971, which still stands as the closest finish in Grand Prix history. Although he beat Peterson by 0.01s, the whole of the top five was covered by 0.61s. He rose through the ranks of Formula 2 and Formula 5000 and made his Formula 1 debut with McLaren in the 1970 Race of Champions at Brands Hatch. When Bruce McLaren was killed at Goodwood in June, Gethin was promoted into the Grand Prix squad and made his debut in Holland.

Having started the 1971 season with **McLaren**, he switched to BRM and scored the famous victory in Italy. But, after a season plagued with unreliability in 1972 with BRM he returned to Formula 5000, where he excelled on both sides of the Atlantic. He had already won the inaugural European Championship in 1971. He raced in most single-seater categories, plus saloons and sports cars, before retiring at the end of 1977.

1962 Started on pole for his debut race at Brands Hatch in a Lotus 7, but spun out of the lead. He later claimed 2nd in class at Brands Hatch and 3rd in class at Goodwood.

1963 Had a successful year racing a Lotus 23 in national sports car races. At Brands Hatch he had a class win, with two 2nds, he won his class at Goodwood, had two 3rds at Oulton Park and a 3rd at Snetterton. He also won a Brands Hatch sprint in a Lotus 27.

1964 Became Guards Sports Car Champion with his Lotus 23, after class wins at Goodwood (twice), Snetterton, Aintree, Brands Hatch and Mallory Park. He took three 2nds and a 6th at Brands Hatch, 2nd and 3rd at Mallory Park, 2nd and 3rd at Goodwood, 2nd at Crystal Palace and 3rd at Oulton Park.

1965 Moved into F3 driving a Lucas Brabham, with a win and 2nd at Brands Hatch, 3rd at the British Grand Prix meeting, at Oulton Park and Karlskoga, 6th in the Copenhagen Grand Prix and 8th at Oulton Park. He also raced an F3 Lotus 22 winning at Croft, with 2nd at Cadwell Park and Silverstone, 3rd and 5th at Brands Hatch. In Chris Williams' Elva BMW he won a sports car race at Oulton Park, and finished 6th in a Snetterton Libre race with his F3 Brabham.

1966 Continuing with a Brabham, he won the King Hussein Trophy at Ingliston and took wins at Crystal Palace, Mallory Park, Brands Hatch and Oulton Park. He added 2nd at Brands Hatch, Snetterton and Crystal Palace, 3rd at Silverstone, Goodwood, Castle Combe and Crystal Palace and 11th at Monaco to take 6th in the Les Leston Championship. In Libre he won at Oulton Park, with 2nd at Mallory Park in his Brabham and won the SMT Trophy at Ingliston in an F2 Lotus 44. He also raced a Crossle in sports car events, finishing 2nd at Crystal Palace (twice), 2nd at Brands Hatch, 5th at Silverstone and 8th in the TT. He also raced a Chevron to 8th in the Paris 1000km.

1967 A mixed year which included regular outings in an F2 Cooper, taking 2nd at Hockenheim and 14th at the Nurburgring. In F3 he raced a Brabham to victory at Oulton Park, 2nd and 5th at Silverstone, 3rd at Pau and Crystal Palace and 5th at the British Grand Prix meeting, also giving the new Chevron B7 its debut at Brands Hatch with a 4th place. He won Libre races at Oulton Park in a McLaren M2A and a Lola T70, raced a Ford Falcon to 7th in the British Saloon Car Championship race supporting the British Grand Prix and shared a Ford GT40 with Liddell to 12th in the BOAC race at Brands Hatch.

GRAND PRIX RECORD	
Starts	30
Wins	1
Poles	0
Fastest laps	0
WC points	11
Won his 16th Grand Prix	

1968 Began racing an F2 Chevron for Frank Lythgoe, before changing to a Brabham. He finished 2nd at Albi and Ingliston, 3rd at Vallelunga, 4th at Pau, 6th at Monza, 7th at Zolder and 10th in the Race of Champions. In F3 he deputised for Chris Williams at Chevron, winning at Brands Hatch and taking 2nd at Monaco, while in sports cars he finished 3rd in the Guards International at Brands Hatch.

1969 Won the Guards Formula 5000 Championship in a semi-works McLaren M10A, winning at Brands Hatch (twice), Oulton Park and Mallory Park, with 4th at Hockenheim. He raced Formula A in the US and won at Lime Rock.

1970 Finished 6th at the Race of Champions on his F1 debut with McLaren, and following the death of Bruce McLaren he became part of the Grand Prix team. He retired from the Dutch and German races, before taking 10th in Austria. After failing to be classified in the Italian GP, he scored his first World Championship point with 6th in Canada, then ended the season with 14th in the US and retirement in Mexico. He was Guards F5000 Champion again, with wins at Brands Hatch (twice), Zolder, Zandvoort, Castle Combe, Mallory Park, Silverstone and Anderstorp, with 2nd at Oulton Park, Mondello and Thruxton. In CanAm he secured 3rd in the championship for McLaren, with a win at Elkhart Lake, 2nd at Donnybrooke and Edmonton and 7th at Road Atlanta. His other results included 7th at Zolder in an F2 Brabham and victory at the Nurburgring 500 with Redman in a Chevron B16.

1971 Having started the Grand Prix year with McLaren, he recorded 8th in the Spanish and 9th in the French from seven starts, before changing to BRM. After taking 10th on his debut for the team in Austria, he won the record-breaking Italian Grand Prix, took 14th in Canada and 9th in the US. In non-championship races he took 2nd for McLaren at the International Trophy, 2nd at Oulton Park, 8th in the Questor GP and retired from the Rindt Memorial and Race of Champions. With BRM he won the Brands Hatch Victory race that claimed the life of team mate Siffert and retired after an accident in the Oulton Park Gold Cup. He continued to race in F5000 intermittently, taking 2nd at Castle Combe and 6th at Mallory Park in a McLaren M18, and came 2nd in the Interserie Championship with Sid Taylor's McLaren M8E, winning at Zolder, with 2nd at the Norisring and Keimola and 9th at Imola.

1972 Spent another season with BRM but struggled for reliability all year, only making the finish twice from 10 starts with 13th in Austria and 6th in Italy. In the non-championship races however, he finished 4th in the Race of Champions, 5th in the John Player Trophy at Brands Hatch and 6th in the International Trophy, but retired from three other starts. He had little success with Chevron in F2, but did take a victory at Pau and 5th at the Salzburgring. In US F5000 races his best result was 4th at Donnybrooke in a Chevron B24, but in sports cars he won the Pietermaritzburg and Goldfields 3 hours, took 3rd at Lourenco Marques and 5th in the Kyalami 9 hours with Chevron to secure the Springbok title.

1973 His only Grand Prix outing came in Canada, where his BRM retired. Returning to F5000 he won the International Trophy, Oulton Park Gold Cup and at Brands Hatch, with 2nd at Oulton Park and 4th at Mallory Park in a Chevron B24. In the US he finished 4th overall, after taking 2nd at Laguna Seca and 3rd at Michigan and Road Atlanta. He also raced a Chevron B25 in F2, finishing 2nd at Karlskoga and 14th at Albi.

1974 A final Grand Prix appearance came with an Embassy Hill Lola at the British, retiring his ill-fitting car after a tyre deflated. In the Rothmans F5000 Championship he finished as runner-up with his Chevron, with wins in the International Trophy, at Brands Hatch, Zolder, Zandvoort and Monza, with 2nd at Thruxton (twice) and Silverstone, 2nd and 3rd at Mallory Park, and 3rd and 4th at Brands Hatch. He also won the Tasman F5000 title, with wins at Pukekohe and Sandown, 2nd at Surfers Paradise and Adelaide, 3rd in the New Zealand Grand Prix, 4th at Levin and 5th at Teretonga and Oran Park. He continued to race Chevron sports cars and took 4th in the BOAC 1000 and 5th in the Martini Trophy with Redman in a B26.

1975 Finished runner-up in the Shellsport F5000 Championship, taking his VDS Lola to victories at Zolder, Zandvoort and Brands Hatch, 2nd at Snetterton, 2nd and 4th at Silverstone, 4th and 6th at Mallory Park and 4th in the Oulton Park Gold Cup.

1976 Raced for VDS in the US F5000 Championship, finishing 4th at Elkhart Lake, 7th at Mosport, 9th at Pocono, 10th at Riverside and 5th in a non-championship race at Elkhart Lake.

1977 His final year of racing was spent with VDS, finishing runner-up to team mate Brown with a Chevron B37 in the Tasman Series, after taking 2nd in the Australian GP and at Surfers Paradise, and 4th at Adelaide. He also raced a Lola T332C in CanAm, finishing 2nd at Watkins Glen and Sears Point, 3rd at Mosport and Trois Rivieres, 4th at Riverside and 5th at St. Jovite.

BRIAN HENTON
Born September 19th 1946

Brian Henton.

Photo: BRDC Archive.

Henton was a relatively late starter, only beginning his racing career at the age of 24. Despite having Formula Vee, Formula 3 and Formula 2 titles to his credit, breaking into Grand Prix racing proved considerably harder than it should have done. Throughout his career, Henton showed enormous determination and self belief and worked very hard to keep his career going. Early in his career he vowed that he would get into Formula 1 and was noted for racing with the slogan 'Brian Henton racing for Brian Henton' on one of his cars.

Apart from three outings in the uncompetitive works Lotus 72E in 1975, his next attempt was a self funded effort two years later, interspersed with a couple of one-off drives. Having stepped back to Formula 2 and won the European title with Toleman, he finally had a full season with the fledgling Toleman Grand Prix team in 1981. Seventh in the German race that year was to be his best Grand Prix result and after seeing out the following year with Tyrrell, he gave up the struggle and retired from racing.

1970 Began racing with Austin Healey and Marcos sports cars, but quickly moved into Formula Vee with an Austro. Although he didn't win any races, he had three 2nds and a 7th at Thruxton, with further 2nds at Mallory Park and Cadwell to finish 2nd in the championship.

1971 Won the Formula Vee title with wins at Brands Hatch, Lydden, Thruxton, Mallory Park and Llandow, plus 2nd at Brands Hatch. He also had a few Super Vee races, taking victories at Silverstone and Snetterton.

1972 Finished as runner-up in the Formula Super Vee Championship, with two wins at Thruxton, wins at Crystal Palace and Mallory, 2nd at Mallory and 4th at Brands Hatch.

1973 Moved into F3 firstly with an Ensign and then a March. He won at Brands Hatch and took a win, 2nd and 3rd at Mallory Park and a win and 4th at Silverstone.

1974 A double F3 champion, taking both the Lombard North Central and Forward Trust titles with his March 743 in the first season of the new 2-litre Formula 3. He took four wins and a 6th at Oulton Park, two wins at Thruxton, three wins and a 2nd at Silverstone, three wins and a 5th at Brands Hatch, a win and 2nd at Snetterton, a win at Cadwell Park, 3rd at Mallory Park and a heat win in Monaco. He also made his F2 debut at Mugello, finishing 6th in a March 742.

1975 Started the year in F2 with a March 752, with 3rd at Silverstone and Hockenheim and 8th at Thruxton. He joined Lotus for the British Grand Prix, qualifying 21st on his debut and classified 16th in the infamous rainstorm. After failing to start in Austria following an accident in practice, he went to the USGP but was unclassified. He also moved into Formula Atlantic at the end of the season, taking over the Wheatcroft from Richard Morgan to finish 9th and 3rd at Brands Hatch.

1976 Plans to race an Abarth-powered Wheatcroft in F2 fell through after one race, and so his season was restricted to outings in the Shellsport Group 8 Series with an F2 Boxer. At the Oulton Park Gold Cup he qualified 2nd and led half of the race, before finishing second. With a further 3rd place at Brands Hatch, he secured 11th overall in the championship.

1977 He bought a March 761 in partnership with playwright Don Shaw and formed the British Formula One Racing Team. After taking 4th in the Race of Champions, he was called up to deputise in the Rothmans-backed March team at Long Beach, finishing 10th. His three attempts to qualify his own car failed, as did those of rent-a-driver Bernard de Dryver. Henton did get back onto the Grand Prix grid at the Dutch race, with the Boro (nee Ensign) but was disqualified after receiving outside assistance, and failed to qualify the same car at the Italian. In F2 he drove the Boxer to victory at Thruxton, with 5th at Hockenheim and 9th at the Nurburgring and Pau, before guesting in an ICI Newsweek Chevron B40 with 7th at his local Donington Park. He also drove a Penske PC3 to 3rd place at Brands Hatch in the Shellsport Group 8 finale.

1978 A full season in F2 with his own March 782, brought 6th at Enna, 8th at Vallelunga, 11th at Misano and Donington Park, 15th at Mugello and 17th at Hockenheim. He also had a try out with Keegan's works Surtees at the Italian Grand Prix and went to the Temporada F2 Series with Toleman, finishing 6th at Mendoza and retiring from the lead in Buenos Aires.

1979 Another year of F2 with Toleman started with a March 782, before changing to the works Ralt. Victories came at Mugello and Misano, with 2nd at the Nurburgring, 3rd at Silverstone, 4th at Donington Park and Hockenheim and 5th at Zandvoort, only losing out to Surer in the title race after spinning at Donington Park in the final round.

1980 He was almost out of a drive until Stephen South chose CanAm and a McLaren testing contract, in preference to the Toleman Formula 2 team. After early season tests with the Williams Grand Prix team, his Toleman went on to dominate F2, only finishing two races off the podium. He won at Thruxton, Vallelunga and Mugello, with 2nd at Hockenheim, Nurburgring, Zolder, Misano and Enna, 3rd at Pau, 12th at Zandvoort and 5th in the non-championship Monza race, with the title sewn up by the end of August.

1981 Moved into F1 with Toleman and made his first unsuccessful attempt to make the grid at the San Marino Grand Prix. He also failed to qualify at the next eight Grands Prix, before finally making it through to 23rd on the grid for the Italian, where he was classified 10th albeit three laps down.

1982 Having left Toleman he began the year deputising for the injured Surer at Arrows. He failed to qualify in the South African and Brazilian Grands Prix, and retired in Long Beach after an accident. With Surer fit to resume racing, Henton moved to Tyrrell to replace Slim Borgudd. Following retirements in San Marino and Belgium, he took 8th at Monaco, 9th at Detroit, 8th and the fastest lap in the British, 10th in the French, 7th in the German, 11th in the Swiss and 8th at Las Vegas.

GRAND PRIX RECORD

Starts	**19**
Wins	**0**
Poles	**0**
Fastest laps	**1**
WC points	**0**
Best finish	**7th**

1983 Out of a drive at Tyrrell, he hired a Theodore for the Race of Champions and finished 4th before hanging up his helmet for good.

❖

JAMES HUNT
Born August 29th 1947
Died June 15th 1993

An early reputation as an erratic driver during his Formula 3 and 2 career failed to stop Hunt achieving his aim of reaching Grand Prix racing. If he finished a race he was usually well placed, but finishing was sometimes a problem. His nickname of the era was Hunt the Shunt and it was quite an appropriate tag. With a career that could so easily have foundered at this stage, it was his link with the larger than life Lord Hesketh that really turned things around. His partnership with Hesketh took him into F1 within a year of their association, making his Grand Prix debut at Monaco in 1973.

It was the concept of the true British team that won the hearts of the public and Hunt fitted the bill perfectly. They built their own car to take on the world and it proved to be a very fine Grand Prix car. But after collecting a prized victory for Hesketh at the 1975 Dutch Grand Prix, funds ran out and Hunt joined McLaren the following year. In an epic battle with Niki Lauda, Hunt finally clinched the 1976 World Championship in a dramatic rain-soaked final in Japan. Having fought back from dreadful injuries received at the Nurburgring, Lauda pulled out of the Japanese race considering the conditions too bad for racing.

Two further years at McLaren preceded a move to Wolf, but before the season had reached the halfway point he announced his retirement. He soon found a second career as part of the BBC Grand Prix commentary team, until his sudden death in 1993. Throughout his career and in the subsequent years, Hunt continued to be a hugely popular figure with the British public.

1967 Started racing in a Mini, but from three starts he failed to make the finish.

1968 Raced in Formula Ford with an Alexis and then a Merlyn Mk11A. His first win came at Lydden, with 2nd and 5th at Mallory Park, 3rd, 4th and two 6ths at Brands Hatch from 10 starts.

1969 Continued with his Merlyn in Formula Ford, winning at Lydden again, with 2nd at Aspern, 3rd at Zandvoort and Brands Hatch, 4th at Mondello, 5th at Mallory Park, 4th and 7th at Brands Hatch and two crashes at Snetterton. He also raced an F3 Brabham BT21 and March 693 in F3 and Libre, taking wins at Brands Hatch and Mallory Park. He added a 2nd, two 3rds, a 4th and 10th at Brands Hatch, 4th and 6th at Mallory Park, 4th at Cadwell Park and 8th in the Reg Parnell Trophy at Crystal Palace. He took 2nd place in the end of season Grovewood Awards.

1970 With a Lotus 59 in F3 he won at Rouen and Zolder and took 2nd at the Osterreichring, Brands Hatch, Oulton Park, Chimay and Knutsdorp. He was 3rd at Hameenlina, Brands Hatch and at Cadwell Park (twice), 4th at Silverstone and Magny Cours, 6th at Silverstone, 9th at Croft and had accidents at Monaco, Karlskoga and Crystal Palace. He took 5th in the Shell Championship. He also raced in Formula Libre, taking 2nd at Mallory

James Hunt.

Photo: BRDC Archive.

James Hunt in the Hesketh at Silverstone during the International Trophy in April 1975.
Photo: BRDC Archive.

Park and 6th at Oulton Park, and finished 29th in the International Trophy Saloon Car race in a Hillman Imp.

1971 A further year in F3 was littered with more crashes, but in between he won at Monthlery, the Nurburgring, Crystal Palace, Mallory and Brands Hatch. He finished 2nd at Thruxton (twice) and Croft, 3rd at Brands Hatch, Oulton Park and Paul Ricard, 4th at Brands Hatch, 6th at Crystal Palace and 8th at Thruxton, with a March 713 and Brabham BT35. Overall he was 9th in the Shell Championship and 16th in the Lombard. He also had a one-off F2 race at Brands Hatch in a March 712 and finished 12th.

1972 The season began racing a works F3 March 723, before changing to a Hesketh-backed Dastle. He finished 3rd at Mallory Park, 4th and 5th at Brands Hatch, 5th at Chimay, 7th at Silverstone and Rouen, 8th at Snetterton

GRAND PRIX RECORD	
Starts	92
Wins	10
Poles	13
Fastest laps	8
WC points	179
Won his 30th Grand Prix	

and 10th at Mallory Park, but crashed out of four other races. He also graduated into F2 with a March 712, qualifying on the front row of the grid for his debut at the Salzburgring. His best championship result was 5th at Albi, but he later went to Brazil and finished 6th in that series after taking 4th and 5th at Interlagos. Other non-championship F2 outings brought 3rd at Oulton Park, 5th in the Brands Hatch Rothmans 50,000 and 8th at Hockenheim.

1973 His F1 debut came at the Race of Champions in a hired Surtees TS9B, finishing 3rd. A Grand Prix debut soon followed with a March 731 at Monaco, where he was classified 9th after engine problems. His first World Championship point came on his next outing, taking 6th in the French GP. With 4th in the British, 3rd in the Dutch, 7th in the Canadian and an amazing 2nd in the US, he finished 8th in the World Championship. He also raced a Surtees TS15 in F2, taking 10th at Thruxton. He won the inaugural Avon Tour of Britain with Robert Fearnall in a Chevrolet Camaro and drove Alpina BMWs in the European Touring Car Championship to 2nd at Zandvoort and Paul Ricard, sharing with Ickx and Muir.

1974 The year began with a victory at the International Trophy, retirement in Argentina and 9th in Brazil, before forsaking the March for Hesketh's own chassis. After retiring on the car's debut in South Africa, he collected 10th in Spain but soon improved to score 3rd places in the Swedish, Austrian and US races, along with 4th in the Canadian to finish 8th in the World Championship again. His other drives included three USAC outings in an Eagle, with a best finish of 2nd at the Monterrey Grand Prix. He was also 2nd at Laguna Seca in a F5000 Eagle and shared a Gulf Ford with Bell and Schuppan to 4th in the Nurburgring 750km.

1975 Having started the season with 2nd in Argentina and 6th in Brazil, a string of five retirements followed. But form returned dramatically at the Dutch where both driver and constructor collected their maiden victories. With 2nd in France and Austria, 4th in the British and US and 5th in Italy, he secured 4th place in the final World Championship standings. He also finished 7th in the non-championship Swiss Grand Prix.

1976 With Hesketh forced to pull out due to the rising cost of Grand Prix racing, Hunt joined the McLaren Grand Prix team to replace Emerson Fittipaldi. With the already proven M23 he won the Race of Champions and International Trophy and took his first pole in Brazil on his debut for the team. After taking 2nd in South Africa his first victory for the team soon followed in Spain. Further wins in the French, German, Dutch, Canadian and USA East, along with 3rd in Japan, 4th in Austrian and 5th in Sweden clinched the World Championship, despite Lauda's brave comeback in the rain soaked Japanese GP.

1977 Another good start to the year brought three consecutive pole positions, and 2nd place in the Brazilian Grand Prix, 4th in South Africa and 7th in the USA West. The change to the new M26 caused a few hiccups, but

the car came good with victories at the British, USA East and Japanese, which along with 3rd in the French secured 5th in the World Championship.

1978 A poor year with only one podium finish from 3rd place in France. He scored points with 4th in Argentina and 6th in Spain, but left the team at the end of the season. He also went to Australia and won the Rose City 10,000 at Winton in a F5000 Elfin.

1979 Joined the Wolf Grand Prix team but never looked competitive from the start. From seven Grand Prix starts his only finish was 8th in South Africa. A week after the Monaco GP he took part in the Gunnar Nilsson Memorial meeting at Donington Park and he took 2nd place in his Wolf. He then retired from the BMW Procar race on what proved to be his last outing for he announced his retirement shortly afterwards.

James Hunt

❖

James Hunt in the McLaren M23 at Brands Hatch.

50 years of British Grand Prix drivers

Part Three
1970s

CHAPTER 11

RUPERT KEEGAN
Born February 26th 1955

With backing from his father Mike's British Air Ferries aviation company, Keegan's quick but rather unpredictable Formula Ford career launched him towards F3 and a championship title in his second year in the formula. His epic battles with Bruno Giacomelli during the 1976 season culminated in a famous clash at in the final race at Thruxton that left Keegan champion in the BP-backed series.

On the back of that success he made the jump straight into Formula 1 and joined the Hesketh Grand Prix team. But it was a tough season and Keegan struggled all year to make a top ten finish. His best result was 7th in the Austrian GP of that season. After a move to Surtees for 1978, he fared little better and took a year out to race in the Aurora British F1 series in 1979, winning the title. He made brief and not particularly successful returns in 1980 and 1982, before winding up his driving career with a few years in sports cars, racing as late as 1995 in GT events.

1973 Won his debut race in a Ford Escort Mexico and spent the second half of the year racing a Formula Ford Royale RP16, taking a class win at Snetterton in a Formula Libre race on his debut with the car.

1974 Racing a Hawke DL11 in Formula Ford, he won five races, had two 2nds, a 4th, four 5ths, a 6th and lots of incidents.

1975 Moved into F3 with an ex-Henton March 743, taking 6th at Aintree, Oulton Park and Thruxton, 7th at Oulton Park, Silverstone and Thruxton, and 9th at Monaco.

Rupert Keegan (Hesketh 308) at Monaco in 1977.

Photo: BRDC Archive.

GRAND PRIX RECORD	
Starts	25
Wins	0
Poles	0
Fastest laps	0
WC points	0
Best finish	7th

1976 Won the BP Formula 3 Championship and finished runner-up in the Shell Series, after an epic season of battles with Giacomelli. He started the year with the March before changing to a Chevron B34 and scored three wins at Thruxton, two at Silverstone and one each at Zolder, Oulton Park, Mallory Park and Snetterton. He added 2nd and 3rd at Brands Hatch, 2nd at Thruxton and Oulton Park, 3rd, 4th and 6th at Silverstone and 5th at Vallelunga. On his F2 debut for Fred Opert, he crashed a Chevron B35 at Hockenheim, retired from the Macau Grand Prix and finished 2nd in the Grovewood Awards.

1977 The year began with Formula Atlantic in South Africa with a Euroracing March 77B, where he took 6th at Kyalami and Welkom and 7th at Pietermaritzburg. He then joined the Hesketh Grand Prix team and made his debut in Spain, where he qualified 16th, but retired after an accident. From a further 11 starts, his best finish came with 7th at the Austrian, followed by 8th in the USA East, 9th in the Italian, 10th in the French, 12th at Monaco and 13th in the Swedish. He also took the Hesketh to 8th in the Race of Champions at Brands Hatch.

1978 Moved to Surtees and had a disastrous year, with 11th in the Spanish Grand Prix his only classified finish. He never qualified higher than 18th, suffered five retirements and failed to qualify on five other occasions. He did however make it to the finish in 5th place in the International Trophy at Silverstone.

1979 Won the Aurora AFX British F1 Championship with an Arrows, after winning at Mallory Park, Snetterton (twice), Donington Park and Thruxton. He also took 2nd at Silverstone, 11th at Oulton Park after retiring from the lead, and suffered a huge accident on the second visit to Oulton Park. His other results included a win at Mallory Park in the BMW County Championship, 5th in the Gunnar Nilsson Trophy at Donington in his Arrows, retirement at the Macau GP and retirement and non-qualification from F2 outings at Pau and Vallelunga.

1980 Came back to Grand Prix racing with a RAM Williams FW07B, making the grid on four of his seven attempts. He was 9th in the USA East, 11th in the British and Italian, and 15th in the Austrian.

1982 Joined the Rothmans March Team from the German Grand Prix, failing to qualify at his first attempt. He retired from the Austrian and Swiss, failed to qualify in Italy and finished 12th in Las Vegas. He also raced a Lola T610 with Guy Edwards, being excluded from the Monza 1000km, taking 16th at Silverstone and retiring at Le Mans, the Nurburgring and Spa, before taking 7th in the Shell 1000km at Brands Hatch.

1983 Shared a Porsche 956 with Edwards to 5th at Le Mans, but retired from the Silverstone 1000km. He also crashed David Kennedy's Ford C100 during a Thundersports race at Brands Hatch.

1984 Had a full year of sports car racing to finish 12th in the World Endurance Championship in a Porsche 956 and 962. He was 2nd at Mosport with Hobbs, 3rd at Silverstone with Edwards, 3rd at Brands Hatch with Edwards and Boutsen, 8th at Imola with Hobbs and Konrad, 9th at Sandown with Konrad, 11th at the Nurburgring with Edwards and retired at Le Mans and Spa. He also shared a Dome with Aguri Suzuki in the Fuji 1000, retiring after an accident.

1985 A plan to run the Skoal Bandit Lola T900 at the Indy 500 fell through after he was too late to take part in the rookie tests. He did make his Indy Car debut at Laguna Seca in a March 85C, finishing 12th, followed by 10th in Miami and retirement at Mid-Ohio.

1986 Failed to qualify for the Indianapolis 500 in a March Buick.

1990 Raced a Cooper T45 at Brands Hatch and took 4th in a Pre'65 Grand Prix Car race.

1995 Made a brief comeback to share a Lister Storm with Lees and Chappell at Le Mans. He also shared a Porsche 911 BiTurbo with Kaufman to 5th in the Monza Global GT race.

GEOFF LEES
Born May 1st 1951

Geoff Lees.

Photo: BRDC Archive.

A truly talented all-rounder who proved his worth as a triple Formula Ford Champion in 1975. Having run that campaign largely from his own resources, Lees went on up the racing ladder through F3 and F2 before making his Grand Prix debut in Germany in 1979 when he deputised for Jean-Pierre Jarier. His seventh place in that race was to be his best Grand Prix result and a difficult season with Shadow followed in 1980. He stepped back to Formula 2 in 1981 and won the European title with Ralt but only got a couple more Grand Prix chances in 1982.

He then switched his career to Japan and added the Japanese F2 title to his European crown. He has raced sports cars for virtually every major manufacturer, but for some reason his skills were rarely tested in Grand Prix racing. Most of his Grand Prix outings were as an understudy, where he always gave a thoroughly professional and competitive account of himself. From 1983 onwards he was based in Japan and continued to take success after success.

1970 Bought a Lotus 23B but never raced it due to an injury sustained at work.

1971 Made his racing debut in Formula Ford with an Alexis and had a 3rd place at Silverstone.

1972 Finished 5th in the Silverstone-based Formula Ford Championship, with three wins. He also won at Brands Hatch, had a win and 3rd at Mallory Park and 2nd places at Oulton Park and Snetterton.

1973 Continued in Formula Ford with his Alexis, before changing to a Royale RP16, with which he won the John Hamilton Trophy at Mallory Park.

1974 Narrowly missed out on the STP Formula Ford title which was won by Belgian Patrick Neve. His Royale took two wins, four 2nds, a 3rd and a 5th at Silverstone, wins at Mallory Park and Snetterton and a 6th at Brands Hatch.

1975 Scored a famous triple in the major Formula Ford Championships, claiming the Brush Fusegear, National Organs and British Air Ferries title. He took 27 wins in his Royale RP21 and was rarely off the podium. He also won the Snetterton Formula Ford Festival, made his F3 debut at Thruxton with 7th in a Safir and was a Grovewood Award winner.

1976 Moved into F3 with a works Chevron B34 and finished 3rd in both the Shellsport and BP Visco Championships. He had a win, 3rd and 4th at Silverstone, a win and 3rd at Thruxton, 2nd at Snetterton, 3rd at Brands Hatch and Mallory Park, 5th at Oulton Park and 6th in a European round at Vallelunga. He also finished 2nd at Mallory Park behind Stephen South in the Golden Helmet race, and finished 9th overall and 4th in class in a Triumph Dolomite Sprint in a British Saloon Car race at the same circuit.

1977 Finished 4th in the BP F3 Championship in a Chevron B38, with a win, 2nd and 3rd at Thruxton, 2nd at Silverstone, 3rd at Oulton Park and Snetterton, 4th and 7th at Brands Hatch and 6th at Cadwell Park. His other results included 3rd at Silverstone and Brands Hatch in his only outings in the Vandervell F3 Championship, 3rd in a Euro round at Zolder, and 4th in the Thruxton TV race.

1978 Drove an F1 Ensign for Mario Delliotti in the Aurora AFX British F1 Championship, and tried unsuccessfully to qualify the car for the British Grand Prix. He won the Sun Trophy at Mallory Park from the back of the grid, with 2nd at Brands Hatch and 3rd at Snetterton. A change to a March 781 brought retirement at Thruxton, he was 5th at Brands Hatch in a Hesketh and 5th again at Thruxton in a Chevron B42, to finish 6th overall in the championship. In F2 he contested the final five rounds of the year, taking 4th at Misano in a Chevron B42, and 6th at Nogaro. He retired at Donington Park and Hockenheim, and failed to qualify at Enna in a March 782. He also went to the Temporada F2 Series in South America, finishing 5th at Mendoza and 13th at Buenos Aires.

1979 His Grand Prix debut came in Germany as deputy for Jarier in a Tyrrell, qualifying 16th and finishing 7th despite having very little time in the car. In the Australian F5000 series he drove a Wolf and Ensign F1 car. He finished 2nd at Sandown, retired from 2nd place at

Adelaide and non-started at Oran Park after electrical problems on the warm-up lap. He was 3rd with a Wolf WR4 in the final Aurora British F1 race at Silverstone, won the Macau GP in a Ralt RT1 and took a VDS Lola T333 to 3rd place in the CanAm Championship. Results incuded 2nd places at Watkins Glen and Elkhart Lake, 3rd at Mosport, Trois Rivieres and Laguna Seca, 4th at Charlotte and Brainerd and 5th at Mid-Ohio.

1980 A frustrating year was spent trying to get onto the Grand Prix grids. He started with five attempts to qualify a Shadow, only succeeding in South Africa where he finished 13th after suspension failure. At the Dutch Grand Prix he qualified a works Ensign but retired after an accident, he was a non-qualifier in Italy and then moved to a RAM Williams for the USGP, but again failed to qualify. He drove a works Ralt Honda in the last F2 race of the year, retiring at Hockenheim but won the Macau GP again in a Ralt RT4. He also contested two early season Aurora races at Oulton Park and Brands Hatch in a Wolf, but retired from both.

1981 Won the F2 Championship in a Ralt Honda, with wins at Pau, Spa and Donington Park, 2nd at Mugello, Misano and Mantorp Park, 5th at Hockenheim, Vallelunga and the Nurburgring and 7th at Silverstone. A trip to Suzuka brought his Ralt Honda a 4th place, but he retired his RT4 in Macau after an accident.

1982 Once again he was on hand as an F1 deputy. He raced for Theodore in the Canadian Grand Prix, where he was eliminated in an multiple accident at the first start, and in France where he covered for Mansell and brought the Lotus 91 home 12th. In Japan he had a 4th at Suzuka in F2 with a March 822, and raced the Nimrod Aston Martin sports car with Evans and Needell, retiring at Silverstone, Le Mans and Spa. At the Macau GP his Ralt RT4 was classified 15th after retiring when his fuel pump failed.

1983 Became All Japan F2 Champion with a Honda-powered Spirit and March 832. At Suzuka he collected three wins, a 5th, 6th and 7th and also took a win at Fuji. He raced a March 812 Toyota in sports cars, taking 3rd at Atso, but failed to start the Fuji 1000 after his Dome was burnt out in practice.

1984 Finished 9th in the All Japan F2 Championship, taking 4th, 6th and 8th at Suzuka in a March 832 Honda. He was also 7th in Japanese Endurance Championship

GRAND PRIX RECORD

Starts	5
Wins	0
Poles	0
Fastest laps	0
WC points	0
Best finish	7th

and 8th in the Fuji Long Distance Series in a converted March and Porsche 956, with 4th and 6th at Fuji and a win at Suzuka.

1985 Another year in Japanese F2 brought 6th overall with a March 85J Yamaha, after two 3rds and a 6th at Suzuka, and 3rd at Nishi Nippon. He was 4th in the All Japan Endurance Series in a Dome, with a win at Suzuka and 6th at Fuji. He was 6th overall in the Japan Grand Championship, after two 5ths and a 6th at Fuji and 6th at Gotembi. He also shared a Dome with Elgh and Suzuki, retiring at Le Mans and taking 9th in the World Championship round at Fuji.

1986 Continuing in the All Japan F2 Championship, he finished 3rd overall in a March 86J Yamaha with a win and 4th at Fuji, 2nd, 3rd and 4th at Suzuka and 3rd at Nishi Nippon. In Endurance Racing he raced a Dome Toyota, taking 4th at Suzuka, retiring at Le Mans and taking 9th in Fuji World Championship round, but earning the title of Fuji Grand Champion. He also raced at the Macau Grand Prix again in F3, but retired.

1987 Raced a Lola T87/50 in the Japanese Formula 3000 Championship, with a win at Fuji, 2nd at Sugo, 5th at Nishi Nippon, 2nd, 3rd (twice) and 10th at Suzuka. He also drove a Toyota in the All Japan Endurance Series, winning at Fuji with a win and 3rd at Suzuka, to finish 3rd in the championship, and shared a Toyota Supra to 9th at Fuji in the FIA World Touring Car race.

1988 Another year in Japanese F3000 in a March 88B brought a win at Sugo, 4th at Suzuka and Nishi Nippon, and 5th in the championship. He continued to race for Toyota in the All Japan Proto Series, with 6th at Fuji twice, and drove a Supra in the Group A Series, taking 5th at Nishi Nippon and retiring at Fuji. At Le Mans he finished 12th for Toyota and 22nd in the Fuji World Championship round. He also won a Grand Championship race at Suzuka in a March 88GC.

1989 Raced in World Championship Group C with Toyota, sharing 4th at Dijon, 2nd at the Nurburgring, 8th at Spa and 20th at Suzuka with Dumfries. Still racing in the Japanese F3000 Championship with a Reynard 89D, he took 4th at Suzuka and 5th at Sugo. He also raced for Toyota in the Japanese Proto Series, taking 2nd at Suzuka, and 5th and 8th at Fuji, and he won the Grand Championship with victory at Sugo, 2nd and 3rd at Fuji and 4th at Suzuka in his Reynard. At Macau he raced in the Guia Saloon Car race, finishing 6th in a Toyota Supra.

1990 Continued to race in Group C for Toyota, taking 4th at Fuji, 6th at Le Mans, 7th at Montreal and 12th at Silverstone, plus 3rd at Suzuka and 8th at Sugo in the Japanese Series.

1991 Raced a Ralt RT23 in the All Japan F3000 Championship, taking 6th, 8th and 14th at Suzuka, 11th at Mine, 13th at Fuji and 18th at Autopolis. In the All Japan Sports Protos his Toyota took a win and 5th at Sugo, with 3rd, 5th and 6th at Fuji. He also shared a Toyota with Wallace to 6th in the World Championship round at Autopolis.

1992 Finished 5th in the World Sports Car Championship with Toyota, with a win at Monza, 2nd at Suzuka and 3rd at Magny Cours and Donington Park, sharing with Brabham, Ogawa and Lammers. He won the ATMO Class in the Japanese Endurance Championship and won overall at Fuji with Lammers.

1993 Shared a Toyota to 8th at Le Mans with Lammers and Fangio.

1994 Drove for Lister at Le Mans and retired.

1995 Shared a Lister Storm at Le Mans with Keegan and Chappell.

1996 Continued to race for Lister, finishing 19th at Le Mans, but retiring from the Daytona 24 hours after Acheson had a huge accident. He also retired at Suzuka, Brands Hatch and Spa.

1997 Shared a McLaren in the Global GT Championship, taking 7th at Laguna Seca and Donington Park and 8th at Mugello.

1998 Raced a McLaren F1 GTR in the FIA and GTR Series with Tom Bscher, winning at the Hungaroring, Monza and Jarama, with 6th at the A1-Ring and Silverstone, and 7th at Donington Park. He also shared a Toyota at Le Mans, leading the race with Kelleners and Boutsen until transmission failure after 22hrs.

❖

DAMIEN MAGEE
Born November 17th 1945

His 'Mad Dog' image sometimes belied his driving ability, as he moved from one seat to another throughout his career. Having started racing in Ireland in 1967, Magee was one of the first Irish drivers to switch to Formula Ford racing in England. His progress was rapid but punctuated by some large accidents that led to him being the inspiration for the 'Mad Dog' character of the Catchpole cartoons of the era.

Two season in Formula 3 followed and produced some encouraging results. After leaving F3 behind in 1974, he spent most of his time in Formula 5000, finishing as runner-up in the 1976 championship. His only Grand Prix opportunity came with Williams at the 1975 Swedish, where he finished 14th, later failing to qualify a RAM Brabham at the French in 1976. As the offers to drive lessened he had one further year before going into semi-retirement.

GRAND PRIX RECORD	
Starts	1
Wins	0
Poles	0
Fastest laps	0
WC points	0
Best finish	14th

1967 Raced a Lotus XI in Ireland and won a Clubmans heat, final and handicap at Bishopscourt on his race debut. He also campaigned a Cooper in some Formula Libre races.

1968 Finished 2nd at Kirkistown in his Lotus 35 and 3rd with a Merlyn in a handicap race at the same circuit.

1969 Continued to race his Lotus 35 in Irish Formula Libre races, taking two wins and a 2nd at Mondello Park. He also had a 3rd at Mondello and 5th in the Leinster Trophy in his Cooper Ford, with 3rd in a Formula Ford race at Kirkistown in a Crossle 16F.

1970 Won the Scottish Formula Ford Championship, and was runner-up in both the Northern Irish and Eire Championships in his Crossle. He had four wins at Mondello, a win, two 2nds and a 3rd at Kirkistown, four wins and a 2nd at Ingliston, and a win and 2nd at Bishopscourt. He also had a Libre victory at Mondello, 4th at Ingliston and 3rd in a Handicap at the same circuit.

1971 Another year in Formula Ford with a Palliser brought two 2nds, three 3rds and a 6th at Mondello, two wins at Brands Hatch, 2nd at Snetterton, 3rd at Ingliston and Bishopscourt, and 6th at Castle Combe.

1972 Moved into F3 with a Palliser, but also raced a Brabham BT38C. He had two 2nds and a 4th at Brands Hatch, 2nd, 8th and 14th at Oulton Park, 3rd at Thruxton, 4th at Rufforth, 12th at Silverstone and in the Scott-Brown Memorial race at Snetterton.

1973 Continued in F3 with the Palliser and a Brabham BT41. Results included 2nd at Brands Hatch, 3rd at Monaco, 4th at Oulton Park, 5th at Mallory Park and 9th at Zandvoort. He drove won his heat in an F1 Brabham BT37 in the Players No6 Grand Prix at Phoenix Park and made his F5000 debut with 7th at Snetterton.

1974 Campaigned a Lola T330, Trojan 101 and Chevron B24 in the Rothmans F5000 Championship. He finished 2nd and 5th at Brands Hatch, 4th at Oulton Park, 5th at Mondello Park, 9th at Zolder and 11th at Silverstone. He also raced a Palliser in the end of year Formula Libre races at Brands Hatch, taking a 3rd, 4th and 5th place.

1975 His one Grand Prix start came with Williams at the Swedish, qualifying 22nd and finishing 14th. He won the first ever Formula Ford 2000 race for Palliser at Brands Hatch, and with 2nd at Mallory Park, 3rd at Silverstone

Damien Magee.

Photo: BRDC Archive.

and Oulton Park, and 4th at Snetterton, he finished 6th in the Allied Polymer Group FF2000 Championship. He continued to make appearances in F5000 with a Trojan, taking 3rd at Brands Hatch, 6th at Silverstone, 7th at Snetterton and 8th at Mallory Park and raced a Crossle 22F to 5th at Mondello in a Formula Atlantic race. He also raced a Tui in the Canadian Formula Atlantic series.

1976 An attempt to qualify a RAM Brabham BT44C at the French Grand Prix failed by one place, but he tasted long overdue success with a March 75A and Penske PC3 as runner-up in the Shellsport F5000 Championship. He won at Oulton Park and Snetterton, with 2nd at Mallory Park and Thruxton, and 2nd, 3rd and 4th at Brands Hatch, despite changing cars after wrecking the March during qualifying at Brands Hatch for round six. He also raced the RAM Brabham at the International Trophy at Silverstone.

1977 Made a late start in the Shellsport Group 8 Series, after taking over the Len Gibbs-entered Lola from Keith Holland. He had a 2nd at Snetterton and 8th at Brands Hatch, before taking three end of season Formula Libre victories with same car at Brands Hatch.

1979 Raced the Wimshurst FF2000 car to 4th at Snetterton.

1983 Made a brief return to race Hot Rods in an Escort, retiring from his first race and taking 5th in the second.

DAVE MORGAN
Born August 7th 1944

Morgan made his name in the late 1960s as a Mini ace who then switched to single-seaters and enjoyed reasonable success in Formula Ford, Formula 3 and Formula Atlantic. However, he is best known for shocking the establishment with a magnificent F2 victory at Mallory Park in 1972. Pitted against the likes of Lauda, Scheckter and Reutemann, he mastered the conditions on a cold March day to take his privateer Brabham BT35 to a remarkable victory.

However, that performance failed to launch his career beyond more F2 and Formula Atlantic. He was finally given a Grand Prix chance by Surtees at the 1975 British Grand Prix, finishing 18th in the infamous rainstorm. It was to be his only race at the highest level of the sport. After dropping out for a couple of years he returned to race Colts in the British Touring Car Championship. Since 1982 he has been a well-respected race engineer with several teams.

1965 Began racing with a Mini, and had a 3rd in class at Lydden.

1966 Found great success with his Mini, with five wins and 2nds at Lydden, two wins, two 2nds, 3rd and 4th at Brands Hatch, two wins at Croft, a win at Castle Combe,

GRAND PRIX RECORD

Starts	1
Wins	0
Poles	0
Fastest laps	0
WC points	0
Best finish	18th

2nd at Mallory Park and a class win at Snetterton. He also finished 6th in a late season Formula Libre at Brands Hatch in an F3 Cooper BMC.

1967 Became Mini 1000 champion, with four wins, two seconds and six 3rds at Brands Hatch, three seconds at Mallory Park and three 3rds at Oulton Park. He also raced a Brabham BT10 to 4th in an F3 race at Brands Hatch and a 2nd and 3rd in Formula Libre.

1968 Raced a Lola T64 in F3 with little success, apart from 8th at Silverstone and 2nd in a Brands Hatch Formula Libre race.

1969 Moved into Formula Ford with a Merlyn Mk11A and an Alexis, with a win at Brands Hatch, 3rd at Snetterton, 4th at Zandvoort and 13th at Anderstorp.

Dave Morgan.

Photo: BRDC Archive.

1970 Finished 6th in the Forward Trust F3 Championship with a March 703, after two 2nd places at Mallory Park. He added 3rd at Brands Hatch, Thruxton and Crystal Palace, 7th at the International Trophy meeting and Cadwell Park, 10th in the Empire Trophy at Oulton Park and 14th at Monaco. He also had a couple of outings with Alexis in Formula Ford, with a 3rd and 12th each at Brands Hatch.

1971 Moved to Formula Atlantic and finished 6th in the championship with a March 702. He won at Mallory, with 2nd, 4th and 6th at Brands Hatch, 2nd at Castle Combe, 3rd at Snetterton and Castle Combe (twice), 4th at Oulton Park and 10th at the British Grand Prix. At Thruxton he had an F3 win with a Lotus 69, and had an occasional drive in the British Saloon Car Championship.

1972 Drove privateer Brabhams (both a BT35 and a BT38) in F2, with a magnificent victory at Mallory Park, 3rd at the Salzburgring, 4th at Rouen and the Osterreichring and 8th at Hockenheim, to share 5th in the championship with Niki Lauda. In the John Player British Championship he finished 3rd overall, after a 4th and 6th at Oulton Park and victory at Brands Hatch in the Rothmans 1000. At the end of the year he collected the Premier Grovewood Award.

1973 Another year in F2 with a Chevron B25 and Lotus 74, secured 4th at Mallory Park, 5th at Thruxton, 6th at Nivelles, 8th and 14th at Hockenheim and 13th at Enna.

1974 Finished 5th in the Formula Atlantic Championship in a Chevron B25/27, with victories at Thruxton and Phoenix Park, a win, two 2nds and a 3rd at Brands Hatch, 3rd and 12th at Mallory Park, 2nd at Oulton Park and 2nd at Silverstone.

1975 He was finally given a Grand Prix drive by Surtees at the British, qualifying 23rd and being classified 18th in the rainstorm that halted the race. In Atlantic he finished 2nd and 3rd at Silverstone in a Chevron B29 and shared John Lepp's March 75S to 5th at the Osterreichring 1000km and 7th at the Nurburgring 1000km, a class winner on both occasions.

1980 Made a comeback with Colt to race its Hatchback in the British Touring Car Championship, before changing to a Lancer mid-season. It was spectacular to watch but the cars lacked competitiveness, finishing 3rd in class at Brands Hatch and Mallory Park and 4th at Silverstone, Brands Hatch and Thruxton.

1981 Continued with the Colt Lancer and finished 3rd in class in the British Touring Car Championship. He had a 2nd at Thruxton, 2nd and 3rd at Brands Hatch, 3rd at Donington Park, three 4ths at Silverstone, 4th at Thruxton, 6th at Oulton Park. An accident at Mallory Park eliminated Morgan as well as team mate Barrie Williams.

TOM PRYCE
Born June 11th 1949
Killed March 5th 1977

Tom Pryce in March 1975.

Photo: BRDC Archive.

Pryce was undoubtedly a talent lost before his promise was really fulfilled. Only four years after winning a competition in the Daily Express, he was making his Grand Prix debut with the rare Token. His progress through the sport was meteoric and the unassuming Welshman won extensively in Royale sports cars and in Formula Super Vee before arriving in Formula 3 and Formula Atlantic. His prodigious natural talent soon drew the attention of the Grand Prix teams and by 1974 he had made his Grand Prix debut. He won the Monaco F3 race in the same year and shortly afterwards he joined the Shadow team.

The rest of his F1 career was then spent with Shadow and although he finished on the podium twice, his life was lost in a freak accident at the 1977 South African Grand Prix, before he made the top step. His 1975 victory in the Brands Hatch Race of Champions was his only Formula 1 victory, but it was surely only a matter of time before more success followed had he not tragically lost his life.

1970 Began racing with a Lola T100 in Formula Ford, won in a competition run by the Daily Express. He had two wins, a 2nd and a 3rd at Brands Hatch and 2nd at Castle Combe.

1971 Won the Formula F100 Championship in a Royale with a win and 2nd at Mallory Park, four wins and two 2nds at Brands Hatch, two wins at Oulton Park and a win at Snetterton. He drove his Lola to Formula Ford success with a win and two 3rds at Brands Hatch, raced a Formula Super Vee Royale RP9 to 2nd places at Brands Hatch, Castle Combe and Silverstone and finished 6th in the Lydden Challenge Cup F3 race with a Royale RP11.

1972 Won the Formula Super Vee Championship with Royale, with victories at Mallory Park, Brands Hatch and Thruxton, and had a win at Brands Hatch and 3rd at Silverstone in a Formula Atlantic Royale RP12. He missed some races after breaking his arm in the Monaco F3 race, but still took a win and 4th at Brands Hatch, 5th at Snetterton and 9th at Zandvoort in the category.

1973 Continued to race in Formula Atlantic, firstly with Royale and then with Motul. He won at Brands Hatch, Mallory Park and Snetterton, with 2nd and 5th at Mallory Park, 4th at Brands Hatch, 5th at Oulton Park, 6th at Croft and 7th at the British Grand Prix meeting. He also raced for Motul in F2, taking 2nd at the Norisring, 5th at Mantorp Park and 11th at Nivelles, before taking the Premier Grovewood Award at the end of the season.

1974 His F1 debut was made with the Token in the International Trophy at Silverstone, followed shortly afterwards by his Grand Prix debut in Belgium. He qualified 20th but retired after a collision. His entry was then turned down for the Monaco Grand Prix. Rather than be sidelined for the weekend, he chose to contest the supporting F3 race, which he duly won. His long association with the Shadow team started at the Dutch, and after taking 8th at the British he scored his first World Championship point with 6th at the German. From four further outings he had one more classified finish, 10th in the US.

1975 A full season with Shadow brought points finishes with 3rd in the Austrian Grand Prix, 4th in the German, and 6th in the Belgian, Dutch and Italian. He also secured his one and only pole position at the British, having earlier qualified 2nd at Monaco only to retire after hitting the barriers. In the non-championship races he won the Brands Hatch Race of Champions and took 7th in the Swiss Grand Prix.

1976 The season started well with 3rd place for his Shadow in Brazil, but although fairly reliable his car

GRAND PRIX RECORD	
Starts	42
Wins	0
Poles	1
Fastest laps	0
WC points	19
Best finish	3rd

lacked the edge to make it a winner. His only points finishes were 4th in the British and Dutch Grands Prix, but he took 7th in South Africa and Monaco and 8th in the Spanish, French and Italian, only failing to make the finish on four occasions. He also finished 2nd in the Race of Champions, 4th in the International Trophy and crashed a Chevron B35 in a one-off F2 race.

1977 After his Shadow was unclassified in Argentina, he retired in Brazil. He lost his life in a tragic accident at the South African Grand Prix at Kyalami, when he was struck by a fire extinguisher after colliding with a marshal running across the track.

DAVID PURLEY
Born January 26th 1945
Killed July 2nd 1985

Purley's entry into motorsport followed an army career during which he survived a parachuting accident. Most of his racing career was spent working through Formula 3, 2, Atlantic and 5000, recording a hat trick of F3 wins at Chimay and taking the 1976 F5000 title. He first sampled F1 with a hired March 721G in 1972, but made his Grand Prix debut in 1973 backed by his family-owned LEC Refrigeration Company. His last appearance in

Grands Prix put him in the Guinness book of records, after his LEC had the throttle stick open during qualifying at the 1977 British GP at Silverstone, slamming into the barriers to go from 120mph to zero in 26 inches. Despite his heart stopping in the accident and suffering multiple injuries, he returned to racing the following year. Apart from a brief comeback in 1984, he virtually retired from racing at the end of the 1979 season to concentrate on flying. Sadly, he was killed in 1985 when his Pitts Special aerobatic aeroplane crashed into the sea off the South Coast of England.

1968 Raced an AC Cobra, taking a win and 2nd at Lydden before the car was destroyed in an accident at Brands Hatch.

1969 Changed to a Chevron B8, collecting a win at Castle Combe, 2nd at Snetterton, 3rd at Mallory Park and 4th at Thruxton.

1970 Moved into single-seaters with an F3 Brabham BT28. He took a win at Chimay, 2nd in a Castle Combe Formula Libre race, 6th at Snetterton, 7th and 8th at Oulton Park and 8th at Karlskoga and the Flugplatzrennen.

1971 Continued to race in F3 but traded his Brabham for an Ensign. He finished 5th in the Brazilian pre-season series, with 3rd and 4th at Interlagos and 8th at Porto Allegre. He had wins at Chimay, Brands Hatch and Lydden, took 2nd places in Brands Hatch Formula Libre races, 2nd at Crystal Palace and 3rd at Thruxton. Other results included 4th at Castle Combe, 5th at Mallory Park (twice), Brands Hatch, Oulton Park and Croft, 6th at the British Grand Prix meeting, Thruxton and Brands Hatch, 7th at Zandvoort and Silverstone and 10th at Crystal Palace.

David Purley (LEC) at Brands Hatch in 1977.

Photo: BRDC Archive.

GRAND PRIX RECORD

Starts	7
Wins	0
Poles	0
Fastest laps	0
WC points	0
Best finish	9th

1972 A fairly varied year brought him a 3rd successive win at Chimay, with 4th at Snetterton and 5th at Brands Hatch in his F3 Ensign. In F2 he raced a March 722 to 3rd at Pau, 6th at Oulton Park, 8th at Mallory Park and Monza, 12th at the Osterreichring and 13th at Rouen. He then went to Brazil for the Torneio, where he had a 7th at Interlagos. He also sampled F1 by hiring a March 721G from the works for the Rothmans 50,000, which ended with an engine fire. He also drove the one-off Connew which expired on the warm-up lap of the John Player Trophy at Brands Hatch.

1973 With the hired March 731 he made his Grand Prix debut at Monaco, but failed to start on his second outing after an accident during qualifying for the British. At the Dutch he sacrificed his own race in a brave attempt to rescue Roger Williamson from his burning car. Although it proved to be in vain, he was awarded the George Medal for his efforts. His first finish came with 15th in Germany and was followed by 9th in Italy. The rest of the year had been spent in Formula Atlantic, where he finished runner-up in the Yellow Pages Championship and in Formula Libre. Results included three wins and two 2nds at Mallory Park, two wins, a 2nd, 4th and 5th at Brands Hatch, two 3rds at Snetterton, 2nd, 3rd and 4th at Oulton Park, 2nd and 4th at Croft and 5th at the British Grand Prix meeting in his March 722.

1974 A return to F2 brought 5th place in the championship, with 2nd at the Salzburgring, Rouen and Enna, 7th at Pau, 10th at Vallelunga and 2nd in the end of season Macau GP with a Chevron B27. He unsuccessfully attempted to qualify the Token for the British Grand Prix, won the Brighton Speed Trials in a Trojan 101, had a 2nd and 3rd with a Modsports Porsche 911 at Thruxton, and won the Boxing Day Formula Libre race at Brands Hatch in his F2 Chevron.

1975 Finished 5th in the Shellsport F5000 Championship with a Chevron, winning the Oulton Park Gold Cup. He added a further win and 2nd at Brands Hatch, 2nd at Silverstone, 5th at Mallory Park and Thruxton, 6th at Zolder and Snetterton and 11th in the Race of Champions. He also won the Brighton Speed Trials again, this time with his Chevron.

1976 Won the Shellsport F5000 Championship with his Chevron B30, with three wins a 2nd and 8th at Brands Hatch, two wins at Mallory Park, victory at Thruxton, 2nd and 4th at Oulton Park, and 4th and 6th at Snetterton. In

the Brighton Speed Trials he finished 3rd, and drove a Modus at the Macau and Philippine Grands Prix, both races ending in retirement.

1977 Returned to Grand Prix racing with his own LEC chassis, having taken 6th in the Race of Champions. After failing to qualify at the Spanish, he briefly led the Belgian before finishing 13th. In Sweden he was 14th, but crashed at the French after his brakes failed. Then came the British where he survived against all the odds, when his throttle stuck wide open at Becketts during qualifying, leaving him dreadfully injured and fighting for his life.

1978 His return to the track came with two outings in a Porsche 924, followed by 2nd in the Brighton Speed Trials with his LEC F1 car.

1979 After further operations on his damaged legs he had a few races in the Aurora British F1 Series, retiring at Brands Hatch and finishing 10th at Thruxton with his LEC, followed by 4th at Snetterton and 9th at Silverstone in a Shadow DN9B. He also took a class win at a Loton Park Hillclimb in a Porsche 924 and began to compete in aerobatics events with a Pitts Special.

1980 Finished 2nd at Thruxton in Production Saloons with David Yates' Capri, was excluded from the Willhire 24 hours sharing the same car with Yates and Alan Minshaw. He also retired from a Thundersports outing at Brands Hatch sharing Roger Andreason's Chevron B61.

RICHARD ROBARTS
Born September 22nd 1944

Robarts was a Formula 3 Champion in 1973 after starting his single-seater career at the age of 25. After moderate success in Formula Ford, he took Formula 3 by storm in 1973 and shot himself into the limelight.

He then attempted to take the huge leap into Grand Prix racing in one go, with Brabham in 1974, making his debut in Argentina. But after only three early season races his finance ran out and his dream was over. After a only a couple of sports car races in 1975, he returned to race in F2 and the Shellsport Group 8 Series, thereafter only making occasional outings until his retirement in 1978.

Richard Robarts (Brabham BT42) in the Silverstone International Trophy, 1974.

Photo: Ferret Fotographics.

GRAND PRIX RECORD

Starts	3
Wins	0
Poles	0
Fastest laps	0
WC points	0
Best finish	15th

1969 After starting his racing career in a Lagonda, he moved into Formula Ford with a Ginetta.

1970 Continued to race in Formula Ford, but with no notable success.

1971 A further year in Formula Ford with a Palliser, brought three 2nds and a 3rd at Lydden, with 2nd and 5th at Brands Hatch.

1972 Changed to an Elden chassis for his Formula Ford season, taking a win at Oulton Park, two 2nds, a 5th and a 6th at Silverstone, with 3rd and 4th at Brands Hatch.

1973 Graduated to F3 initially with a GRD and later an Ensign. He won the Forward Trust Championship and shared the Lombank North Central title with Tony Brise. Results included a win, 2nd, 4th and 5th at Silverstone, a win and 3rd at Thruxton, a win, 3rd and 9th at Brands Hatch, 2nd at Oulton Park (twice) with 3rd, 6th and 13th at Mallory Park.

1974 Joined the Brabham Grand Prix team and qualified 22nd on his debut in Argentina, retiring with a broken gearbox. In Brazil he was 15th, then 17th in South Africa and 14th in the International Trophy at Silverstone before his money ran out. Later in the year he went to Sweden with the Iso Williams team, qualified 25th but lost the drive in the race to Tom Belso.

1975 Shared a Chevron B23 with Pete Smith to 8th in the Monza 1000km and 10th in the Nurburgring 1000km, and finished 3rd at Thruxton in a Chevron B20 F2.

1976 Raced a March 752 and 762 in F2, taking 14th at Nogaro, 18th at Thruxton and retirement at Hockenheim (twice), Vallelunga, Rouen and Mugello. He used the same car in the British Shellsport Series, taking 2nd and 3rd at Brands Hatch, 8th at Snetterton, 11th at Mallory Park and 9th in the championship.

1977 Raced an Anson in F3 at Thruxton and Zolder, but failed to record a finish. He also had an occasional outing in his March 762 in the Shellsport Series.

1978 Had a one-off outing in the Porsche 924 Challenge, and finished 6th at Thruxton.

JOHN WATSON
Born May 4th 1946

John Watson.

Photo: BRDC Archive.

After starting his racing career at home in Ireland, it was nearly seven years before Watson started to build his reputation in England. He dabbled with Formula 2 for a couple of seasons before mounting a full campaign in 1971. The following year he made his F1 debut, but it was 1974 before he hit the Grand Prix trail regularly with a Brabham run by Hexagon of Highgate. He moved on to further success at Surtees, Penske, Brabham and McLaren, making his final appearance at the 1984 British.

His first Grand Prix win had come in Austria in 1976 for Penske while his most popular victory was with McLaren in the 1981 British at Silverstone. The following season was to be his best in Formula 1 and he challenged for the title before finishing runner-up. Moving into sports cars he drove works Jaguars and Toyota retiring at the end of 1990 to begin a successful commentary career. He was also heavily involved in the development of the racing school at Silverstone through the 1980s and gave his name to the operation for many years.

1963 Began racing in an Austin Healey Sprite.

1964 Won his class at Kirkistown (twice) and Bishopscourt, with 2nd in the Leinster Trophy in his Sprite.

1965 Moved onto a Crossle sports car, winning at Ingliston, with three wins and two 2nds at Kirkistown and four wins at Bishopscourt.

1966 Continued with his Crossle C7S, winning the Ulster Dunboyne Trophy and at Bishopscourt. He added 2nd at Kirkistown (twice) and Oulton Park and 6th at Phoenix Park.

1967 Racing mainly in Formula Libre with a Brabham BT16, he had four wins and a 2nd at Kirkistown, three wins at Bishopscourt, a win at Phoenix Park and 3rd in Mallory Park's Easter Trophy.

1968 Another year in Libre with his Brabham brought a win and 2nd at the inaugural Mondello Park meeting, with two wins and a 2nd at Kirkistown, two wins at Phoenix Park, three 2nds at Bishopscourt and 2nd at Oulton Park.

1969 Most of the year was spent racing a Lola in Irish Formula Libre events. He scored two wins, a 2nd and a 3rd at Mondello Park, a win, a 2nd, three 3rds and a 5th at Kirkistown, a 2nd and a 3rd at Bishopscourt, a win and 2nd at Phoenix Park and 3rd in the Leinster Trophy. He also ventured to Thruxton to race an F2 Lotus 48 but wrote the car off.

1970 Apart from a 2nd and 3rd in a Crossle 17F F3 car at Mondello Park, he had another try at F2 with a Brabham BT30. He had taken 9th at the Nurburgring and Zolder, and 13th at Barcelona and Hockenheim when he broke his ankle, leg and arm during practice at Rouen.

1971 Back in F2 again with his Brabham he was 5th at Mantorp Park and Tulln Langenlebarn, 6th at Vallelunga, 11th at Jarama and 12th at the Nurburgring in championship races. These results were backed up with 5th and 12th at Hockenheim, 8th at Brands Hatch and victories in the Leinster Trophy at Mondello and at Kirkistown.

1972 Another year in F2 racing a Tui, his best results came with 5th at Rouen and 8th at the Osterreichring and Imola. He made his F1 debut with 6th at the Brands Hatch John Player Trophy driving a Hexagon-entered March 721 (formerly the Eifelland). He finished 6th in the Brands Hatch Rothmans 50,000 in a Chevron B20, 4th in the Jarama 2 hours with a Chevron B19 and won a Libre race at Kirkistown in a Brabham BT36. At the end of the year he was awarded 2nd place in the Grovewood Awards.

1973 The season got off to a bad start when he broke his leg in the Race of Champions, when the throttle stuck open on his Brabham BT42. He recovered to make his Grand Prix debut at the British with his Brabham, followed by a further appearance in the US, but both ended in retirement. His other outings brought 3rd in a Brands Hatch F5000 race with a Trojan and 3rd at Mantorp Park

GRAND PRIX RECORD

Starts	152
Wins	5
Poles	2
Fastest laps	5
WC points	169
Won his 41st Grand Prix	

and 10th at Albi in an F2 Chevron B25. He took 4th at the Osterreichring and 5th at Watkins Glen sharing a Gulf sports car with Hailwood along with victory at the Cape 3 hours and 5th in the Kyalami 9 hours sharing a Chevron B26 with Ian Scheckter.

1974 His first full season of Grand Prix racing was undertaken with a Hexagon Brabham BT42 and a BT44. After collecting 12th in Argentina, 11th in Spain and Belgium and retirements in Brazil and South Africa, he won his first World Championship point with 6th at Monaco. He had four further top 10 finishes with 7th in the Dutch and Italian, 5th in the US and 4th in Austria. He also raced a Surtees in F2 taking 2nd at Hockenheim, 9th at the Salzburgring and 11th at Rouen.

1975 Joined the Surtees Grand Prix team but only made the top 10 when he finished 8th in Spain and 10th in both the Brazilian and Belgian races. Although he left the team after taking 11th in the British, he drove a works Lotus in the German and retired, before making a one-off return to Surtees to take 10th in Austria. He ended the

year with Penske, taking 9th in the US Grand Prix. Earlier in the year he had taken 2nd at the Race of Champions, 4th in the International Trophy and 5th in the non-championship Swiss Grand Prix.

1976 Was retained by Penske for the full year, collecting points finishes with 5th in South Africa and 3rd in the French and British, before his maiden victory in the Austrian. His victory led to the team shaving off his beard after a bet with boss Roger Penske. The season ended with 6th in the US and retirement in Japan, before the team withdrew from F1 racing.

1977 Now part of the Martini Brabham team he qualified on the front row of the grid on six occasions, including taking his first pole at Monaco. However there were only five classified finishes, with 2nd in the French Grand Prix after losing the lead when he ran out of fuel on the last lap. The other results were 5th in the Swedish, 6th in the South African, 8th in the Austrian and 12th in USA East. He also took 3rd at the Race of Champions and shared an Alfa Romeo 33T12 with Brambilla at Dijon until the engine failed.

1978 A regular points finisher in his second year with Brabham, taking 5th in the Spanish Grand Prix, 4th in Monaco, the French and Dutch, 3rd in the South African and British and 2nd in the Italian to finish 6th in the World Championship. He was also 3rd overall and the top racing driver in the Donington Rallysprint at the end of the season.

1979 Moved to McLaren to replace Hunt and began the year with his best result, 3rd in Argentina. Although the car was far from competitive, he still managed to accrue points from 4th at Monaco and in the British Grand Prix,

John Watson (Brabham BT45) at Silverstone in 1977.

Photo: BRDC Archive.

5th in the German and 6th in the Belgian, Canadian and USA East to take 9th in the World Championship. He also took 7th in the Donington Rallysprint, 11th in the Gunnar Nilsson Procar race at Donington Park and 4th in the Wynns 1000 at Kyalami sharing a BMW M1 with Mass.

1980 Continued with McLaren but the new M29 proved even less than competitive than the previous year's M28. His only points came from 4th place in the Canadian and US East Grand Prix. He even failed to qualify in Monaco. At the Donington Rallysprint he finished joint 2nd with Alan Jones, took 5th in the SMMT Trophy at Donington Park in a Spice Ford Capri and 8th in the Procars race at Brands Hatch.

1981 Another new season and another new car, the McLaren MP4 showed potential but failed to produce a result better than 7th in Belgium from the first six Grands Prix. But 3rd in Spain, 2nd in the French, victory in the British, 6th in the German and Austrian and 2nd in the Canadian followed, to secure 6th in the World Championship.

1982 A strong start to the Grand Prix year saw his McLaren take victories in the Belgian and US Detroit, with 2nd in Brazil and 6th in the South African and US Long Beach. A string of retirements then dented his championship aspirations, but an end of season 4th in Italy and 2nd at Caesars Palace clinched the runner-up spot in the championship.

1983 His final full year in Grand Prix racing with McLaren brought mixed results. He won at Long Beach, took 3rd in the US Detroit and Dutch, 5th at San Marino and the German and 6th in the Canadian to finish 6th in the World Championship. The low point of the year was failing to qualify in Monaco again, along with team mate Lauda. He also finished 3rd in the Donington Rallysprint.

1984 Having been replaced by Prost at McLaren, he turned to sports cars. He won at Fuji with Bellof and finished 6th with Schuppan at Spa in a Porsche 956. He finished 7th overall in the Japanese Endurance Championship and retired a Jaguar XJR5 at Le Mans, after sharing with Adamowicz and Ballot-Lena.

1985 A one-off return with McLaren at the Brands Hatch European Grand Prix as deputy for Lauda, ended in 7th place. He also went to Le Mans and retired a Porsche 962 after sharing with Holbert and Schuppan. At Donington Park he was 5th in the Rallysprint.

1986 Racing mainly in IMSA he finished 4th at Portland, 6th at Watkins Glen and 7th at Miami with Hobbs in a BMW, and also shared a March to 9th in the Daytona 3 hours.

1987 Finished 2nd overall in the World Sports Car Championship with Jaguar, after winning at Jarama, Fuji and Monza, and taking 2nd at Silverstone and Spa and 3rd at Brands Hatch.

1988 Continuing in both World Sports and IMSA with Jaguar, he finished 2nd at Jerez, Atlanta and San Antonio, with 3rd at Daytona and Jarama. He also shared a Toyota with Boesel and Pescarolo at Le Mans.

1989 Racing sports cars for Toyota, he took 10th at Donington Park and retired at both Brands Hatch and Le Mans.

1990 Shared a Toyota to 7th in Montreal, 12th at Silverstone and 18th at Spa, and went to Le Mans with Giacomelli and Berg, finishing 11th in a Porsche 962.

---------- ❖ ----------

MIKE WILDS
Born January 7th 1946

Mike Wilds.

Photo: BRDC Archive.

GRAND PRIX RECORD

Starts	3
Wins	0
Poles	0
Fastest laps	0
WC points	0
Best finish	14th

There are very few if any categories of racing that Wilds hasn't sampled, after taking the traditional route to Grand Prix racing from F3. After battling against lack of funds for five seasons, he worked his way into Formula 3 and it was in 1973 that he really showed his potential in the famous Dempster Developments-backed March 733. For the following season he tried to make the break into Grand Prix racing.

After struggling to get both the Ensign and privateer March on to the grids in 1974, he made his debut at the 1974 British, followed by two further outings for BRM the following year. But no other opportunities came and Wilds switched his attention to racing a whole raft of different cars. When the equipment was up to it, he was a winner and became one of Britain's most experienced and versatile racers. Despite a very serious accident at the Goodwood Festival of Speed in 1994, he is still a regular race winner today, notably in Richard Budge's historic Chevron sports cars. He has also overseen his son Anthony's entry into the sport.

1965 Finished 7th in the 1172 Championship with a DRW, making his debut at Snetterton. He had a win at Silverstone, 2nd and 3rd at Lydden, 3rd at Snetterton and Castle Combe and a class win at the Woburn Hillclimb.

1966 Put a 2-litre engine in his DRW but had his season cut short by a huge accident at Brands Hatch.

1967 Had a win, two 2nds and a 3rd at Lydden and 2nd at Brands Hatch in his DRW.

1968 Continued to race his DRW, taking two wins and a 2nd at Lydden, with 2nd and 3rd at Brands Hatch. He also had a run in an F4 Vixen and came 3rd in a Lydden Formula Libre race.

1969 Didn't race due to lack of funds.

1970 Raced a Vixen in F4, taking wins at Mallory Park (twice), Oulton Park, Ingliston, Brands Hatch and Snetterton, with 2nd and 3rd at Lydden, but the team withdrew his car before the end of the year. He used the same car in Formula Libre to take a win at Mallory Park, two 2nds at Lydden and two 3rds at Snetterton, and finished 3rd at Mallory Park in F100 with a Royale RP4.

1971 Moved to Formula Ford with a Titan and had a win at Lydden, 3rd at Silverstone and 2nd, 5th and 6th places at Snetterton.

1972 Had his first taste of F3 in a March 713, taking 3rd and 6th at Thruxton, 5th at Snetterton and 10th at Brands Hatch. He also won a Brands Hatch Formula Libre race in a Chevron B8.

1973 Finished 3rd in the Lombard North Central, 6th in the Forward Trust and 9th in the John Player F3 Championships, with a March 733 and an Ensign. He had a win, two 2nds, a 4th and a 7th at Mallory Park, a win at Croft, 2nd, two 5ths, a 6th and a 10th at Brands Hatch, 3rd at Silverstone and Snetterton, and 4th and 8th at Oulton Park.

1974 He attempted to make his Grand Prix debut at the British, with a March 731 supported by long time backers Dempster International, but failed to qualify. For the last four races of the year he joined the Ensign team, missing the cut again in Austria, Italy and Canada. He then qualifyied 22nd in the US, but was unclassified in the race. He also raced a March 74A in F5000, taking a 2nd and two 6ths at Brands Hatch, 2nd at Mallory Park, 4th at Zolder and 6th at Silverstone.

1975 The year started with a works BRM Grand Prix drive, but reliability was questionable and he retired in both Argentina and Brazil before losing the drive. He had occasional outings in Mick Hills's Formula 5000 March 74A, recording 7th in the final round at Mallory Park.

1976 Raced the Team P.R Reilly Shadow DN3 in the Shellsport Group 8 Series and tried unsuccessfully to qualify the car for the British Grand Prix. He also raced an Ensign in the Shellsport Group 8 series, taking 5th in the championship. Results included 2nd at Snetterton, 3rd and 5th at Thruxton, with 4th and 6th at Brands Hatch. He also had a one-off FF2000 race at Cadwell Park in a Ken Hensley-entered Dulon.

1977 A very mixed year in which he finished 6th overall and 2nd in class at Thruxton with a Triumph Dolomite in the British Saloon Car Championship. He took 5th at Brands Hatch in Mick Hill's Beetle Chevrolet, 13th at Thruxton in an FF2000 Osella and 7th in the final Shellsport race at Brands Hatch with the ex-Purley Chevron.

1978 Won the F2 section of the Aurora AFX Championship with Graham Eden's Ralt, after finishing 5th at Snetterton, 6th at Brands Hatch, Zandvoort, Thruxton and Oulton Park, 7th at Brands Hatch, and 7th and 8th at Mallory Park. He also drove a Toyota Celica to 5th in class in the British Saloon Car Championship, with 3rd at Thruxton and 4th at Donington Park.

1979 Spent most of the year driving the Aurora pace car, but did have an outing in Kim Mather's March 772P to finish 12th at Thruxton. He also became Competition Director of the British Racing and Sports Car Club.

1980 Finished 4th at Silverstone in the final Aurora round of the year, driving a Chevron B41. He shared a Porsche 911SC with Adrian Yates-Smith in the Silverstone 6 hours, a Renault Gordini with Neil McGrath at the TT, and deputised for Mark Thatcher in a Formula Talbot race at Oulton Park, which he won.

1981 He was scheduled to race a DB Motors Chevrolet Vega in British Saloons, but it failed to materialise. He did however share Jan Lundgardh's baby Porsche 935 at Le Mans and Silverstone, ending in retirement on both occasions.

1982 Apart from a couple of outings in the CanAm BRM P154, his year was mainly a series of one-offs. At Brands Hatch he finished 2nd in Sports 2000 with a Tiga SC79, failed to record a finish with a de Cadenet Lola at Silverstone and Le Mans, and finished 3rd in a Historic F3 race at Brands Hatch in a Brabham BT21A.

1983 Driving a Williams FW07C he won the British Open race at Oulton Park, and became a regular in Thundersports. At Brands Hatch he shared James Wallis' Chevron B19 to 5th, but retired from the Oulton Park Gold Cup. He was leading the Donington Park round in the Marsh Plant Lola T280 until it caught fire. His other results included 12th in the Silverstone 1000km sharing Ian Harrower's ADA, an HSCC handicap win in Millward's Lola Aston, 2nd in the Bell & Colvill Trophy at Donington Park and 3rd in an Intermarque race at Castle Combe in an AC Cobra. He was also 2nd in the Birkett 6 hour relay at Silverstone in the Lola Aston, 3rd in class at Brands Hatch with a Sports 2000 Tiga and drove a Delta T79 at the Prescott Hillclimb. He left the BRSCC at the end of the season.

1984 Became the Thoroughbred Sports Car Champion with an Aston Martin DB4, after winning at Silverstone, Mallory Park, Thruxton and Donington Park, with 2nd at Silverstone and Oulton Park. He shared the Ecosse with Ray Mallock and David Duffield to 8th at the Monza 1000km on its debut, but retired at Silverstone and Le Mans. He finished 2nd in the HSCC Endurance Challenge sharing Ray Bellm's Chevron B19, took 3rd in class at Prescott with a Delta and 4th in the John Scott Insurance Enduro at Snetterton sharing Keen's Morgan. He was 6th in the Willhire 24 hours at Snetterton sharing a Ford Capri and 7th in class at the TT with Terry Drury in an Alfa Romeo GTV6. He also shared Bellm's Chevron B36 in Thundersports, with victory at Thruxton and two 4th places at Brands Hatch.

1985 Concentrated on racing the Ecosse in World Endurance races, finishing 4th overall in C2 after 6th at Brands Hatch, 8th at Hockenheim, 9th at Silverstone, 10th at Monza and 14th at Spa, sharing with David Leslie and Mallock. He also took a win and 4th with James Wallis' Lola T286 in Brands Hatch Thundersports races and 2nd in the Willhire 24 hours sharing a Mercedes 190.

1986 Won in Thundersports at Oulton Park sharing a Lola T530 with Leslie, and won a GT/Sports Car race at Silverstone with the same car. He continued to drive a Rover MG-powered Ecosse, but retired at both Silverstone and Le Mans.

1987 Finished 5th in C2 with the Ecosse, with 8th overall at Silverstone, 10th at Brands Hatch, 11th at the Nurburgring, 12th at Spa, 13th at Jarama and retirements

at Le Mans and the Norisring. He continued to contest Thundersports races in the Lola T530, sharing with Ian Flux he won at Brands Hatch and Silverstone, with 2nd at Donington Park and Thruxton. He also shared Ian Harrower's ADA at Jerez and finished 10th for Toyota at Fuji in a Japanese Prototype round.

1988 Sharing a works Nissan with Win Percy he finished 14th at Le Mans. He also had two further Thundersports wins at Brands Hatch and Oulton Park, sharing the Lola T530 with John Brindley. He added a 2nd at Brands Hatch sharing Richard Piper's March 847. As deputy for Roger Orgee he had a couple of drives in a March 85/86B finishing 5th overall in the BRSCC Formula Libre Championship.

1989 Finished 6th overall in the British C2 Sports Car Championship sharing Martin Colvill's Ecosse, with 2nd and 6th at Silverstone and 3rd at Donington Park. They shared the same car to a Thundersports win at Oulton Park, and he also shared Mike Smith's Ford Sierra Cosworth in the long distance British Touring Car race at Donington Park.

1990 BRDC C2 Sports Car Champion sharing the Ecosse with Colvill, Leslie and Mallock. They were virtually unbeatable in the class, with 3rd overall twice at Silverstone, 3rd and 4th overall at both Donington Park and Brands Hatch, 5th overall at Thruxton and numerous class wins. He shared a replica Ford GT40 to victory in the Oulton Park Cheshire Cats Trophy, had a win at Mallory Park with an Aston Martin Le Mans replica and 2nd at both Mallory Park and Brands Hatch in a replica Jaguar C-Type. Two end of season outings in an ex-Daly March 811 brought a win at Thruxton and 2nd at Silverstone in Historic F1 races.

1991 Shared Gareth Howell's Ford Sierra Cosworth in the Donington Park 500km and drove a Surtees TS9 in the Donington Park 3-litre Formula 1 Anniversary race. He also won the inaugural RJB Mining Group 6 Invitation race at Donington Park in a Chevron.

1992 RJB Mining Group 6 Sports Car Champion with a Chevron B31/36, winning at Donington Park, Snetterton and Oulton Park, with 2nd at Donington Park. He also raced a Porsche Carrera to 9th overall and 3rd in class in a Silverstone Intermarque race.

1993-1999 Dominated the RJB Mining Historic Sports Car Championship with Richard Budge's Chevrons, taking the overall championship title in 1992, 93, 96 and 98. Continued winning despite a serious accident at the 1994 Goodwood Festival of Speed, when his leg was badly broken after an accident in Nick Mason's ex-Villeneuve Ferrari.

ROGER WILLIAMSON
Born February 2nd 1948
Killed July 29th 1973

Roger Williamson.

Photo: BRDC Archive.

1967 Graduated from karting into a Special Saloon Mini, taking 15 class wins many at his local Mallory Park circuit.

1968 Changed to a Ford Anglia and had a win, two 2nds and a 3rd at Mallory Park. He also tried a Cooper T72 but crashed and destroyed the car at Cadwell Park.

1969 Further success came with the Anglia, winning at Mallory Park (four times) and Thruxton once, plus two 2nds at Brands Hatch, 2nd at Silverstone and 3rd at Snetterton, Castle Combe and Mallory Park.

1970 Became the Hepolite Glacier Special Saloon Car Champion with his Anglia. He had three wins and a 3rd at Oulton Park, two wins at Mallory Park, three wins and a 2nd at Brands Hatch, two wins at Castle Combe, a win and 2nd at Mondello Park and wins at Crystal Palace and Thruxton.

1971 Stepped into F3 with a March 713M and was immediately successful, taking the Lombard Championship and finishing runner-up in the Shell series. He won at Brands Hatch (four times), Crystal Palace, Thruxton, Oulton Park and Crystal Palace. He added four 2nds at Mallory Park, 2nd, 3rd, 5th and 6th at Thruxton, two 2nds, a 3rd and two 5ths at Brands Hatch, 2nd and 5th at Silverstone and 2nd at Croft, Crystal Palace and Snetterton. He finished 3rd at Cadwell Park and in the Empire Trophy, 4th at the British Grand Prix meeting and Paul Ricard and 7th at Monaco. He also partnered Steve Thompson in the British Team to 5th in the F3 European Cup, and had his talent recognised in the Grovewood Awards at the end of the year.

1972 A double F3 Champion in the Forward Trust and Shells Oils Championships, starting the year with his March, before changing to a GRD. He had wins at Oulton Park (twice), Cadwell Park (twice) Thruxton (twice) and at Silverstone, La Chatre, Anderstorp, Clermont Ferrand, Mallory Park, Snetterton and in the British Grand Prix support race. He finished 2nd and 4th at Brands Hatch, took two 4ths at Mallory Park, 3rd and 5th at Silverstone, 2nd at Snetterton and Zandvoort, 4th at Thruxton and 5th at Crystal Palace. His other results included 6th in a Brands Hatch Formula Atlantic race in a GRD, 7th at Oulton Park in F2 with a March 722 and 7th at Oulton Park in F5000 in a Kitchmac.

One of the brightest prospects of the seventies, Williamson quickly rose from karting to Formula 3 via Special Saloons. His speed in a Ford Anglia marked him as a rising star and that was endorsed when he switched to single-seaters. Throughout his career, the patronage of Tom Wheatcroft was a major factor in Williamson's rapid progress. He was a Formula 3 champion in his first season of single-seater racing in 1971 and after moving into Formula 2 with Tom Wheatcroft's backing in 1973, he made his Grand Prix debut at the British in the same year.

He was caught up in the famous startline incident at Silverstone and hoped for better fortunes at the next race, the Dutch GP at Zandvoort. A deflating rear tyre was thought to have caused his March to crash, hitting a barrier and landing upside down in the track on fire. Apart from the bravery of David Purley any help was very slow to arrive and he tragically perished in the flames. It was a shameful waste of life and denied Britain of one of its best hopes for Grand Prix success in the second half of the 1970s.

GRAND PRIX RECORD	
Starts	2
Wins	0
Poles	0
Fastest laps	0
WC points	0
Best finish	DNF

1973 After a few early season F3 races he started racing in F2 with a Wheatcroft-backed GRD 273, before changing to a March 732. He won the Monza Lotteria and took 7th at Pau, 8th at Thruxton, 9th at Mallory Park and 11th at the Nurburgring. An F1 March had also been hired to help acclimatise for the following year and he made his Grand Prix debut with the car in the British GP at Silverstone. After qualifying 22nd he only completed a lap before being caught up in Jody Scheckter's famous crash. Tragically in the next race, the Dutch at Zandvoort, he crashed and died needlessly as the marshals failed to control what started as a minor fire.

50 years of British Grand Prix drivers

Part Four
1980s

CHAPTER 12

KENNETH ACHESON
Born November 27th 1957

A multiple champion in Formula Ford both in his native Ireland and in England, Acheson then stepped up to Formula 3 for two seasons. He was runner-up in the 1980 British F3 Championship, but once he reached F2 his career began to stall. His first break into Grand Prix racing came with RAM in 1983, with a debut in South Africa after a string of non-qualifications. After an aborted attempt to break into Indycars in 1984, he was called back into the RAM Grand Prix team following Winkelhock's death. He started two races with the team but that proved to be the end of his brief time in Grand Prix racing.

He then raced mainly in Japan and the World Sports Car Championship and enjoyed considerable success, including finishing second at Le Mans in 1992. He raced only occasionally then until retiring in 1996 after a huge accident at Daytona in a Lister.

Kenny Acheson in August 1985.
Photo: BRDC Archive.

GRAND PRIX RECORD	
Starts	3
Wins	0
Poles	0
Fastest laps	0
WC points	0
Best finish	12th

1976 Made his racing debut in his father Harry's Crossle 30F at Kirkistown, and won an Invitation race at the same circuit later in the year.

1977 Won the Northern Irish Formula Ford Championship and finished 5th in the Castrol Irish Championship with a Crossle 32F. He had two wins and two 3rds at Kirkistown, two 2nds, a 3rd and two 5ths at Mondello Park and took 5th in the Irish Formula Ford Festival at Mondello Park. His occasional forays to England secured 5th in the RAC Championship, with points scoring finishes at Brands Hatch, Oulton Park, Mallory Park and Silverstone. He also finished 6th in the Brands Hatch Formula Ford Festival at the end of the season.

1978 Switched to England permanently and swept the board in a works Royale RP24, with 29 wins from 56 starts. He won the RAC, Townsend Thoresen and Phillips Car Radio Championship titles, despite three testing crashes and a broken wrist. His main victories were four at Silverstone, four at Oulton Park, five at Snetterton, two at Mallory Park and one each at Lydden, Donington Park, Croft, Thruxton, Brands Hatch and Castle Combe. He added victory in the Irish v English Challenge at Donington Park, along with another eleven 2nd places. He was also honoured in the Grovewood Awards.

1979 Moved into F3 firstly with a Ralt RT1 and then a March 793, to finish 6th in the British Championship. He had two 2nds, an 8th and a 10th at Thruxton, two 3rds, two 6ths and a 10th at Silverstone, 3rd at Oulton Park and Snetterton, 5th and 8th at Brands Hatch and 6th at Donington Park. He won two non-championship races at Donington Park including the Radio Trent Trophy and the Thruxton TV race, and also finished 8th in a BMW County Championship race at Mallory Park.

1980 Finished joint 2nd in the British F3 Championship with Guerrero, driving an RMC backed March 793 and 803B. He had a win, 5th and 9th at Thruxton, two wins, three 2nds, 3rd and 5th at Silverstone and a win and 3rd at Brands Hatch. He added 4th in the Austrian Grand Prix support race, victory in the Howitt Trophy at Donington Park, 9th in the Euro round at Silverstone, and 4th at Monaco after wrecking his original car in qualifying. He was also honoured again in the Grovewood Awards.

1981 Graduated to F2 with Toleman but missed four rounds of the championship after breaking his leg at Pau. He had earlier finished 6th at the Nurburgring, 10th at Vallelunga, 15th at Mugello and 19th at Silverstone, before returning in the finale at Mantorp Park to finish 3rd.

1982 Continued in F2 with a works Ralt Honda, finishing 7th in the championship, with 2nd at Thruxton, 4th at the Nurburgring, 5th at Pau, 6th at Mugello, 10th at Spa and Donington Park, 11th and 13th at Hockenheim and 14th at Vallelunga. He also finished 4th in the JAF Grand Prix at Suzuka.

1983 Started the year with Maurer in F2, taking 2nd at Pau, 8th at Donington Park, 9th at the Nurburgring, 10th at Thruxton and 11th at Vallelunga. He also took 10th at Hockenheim despite blowing four engines in practice and being bitten by a police dog. He also joined the RAM Grand Prix team for the British Grand Prix, but failed to qualify. He tried again in the German, Austrian, Dutch, Italian and European at Brands Hatch, before finally making the grid in South Africa, to finish 12th in the race.

1984 He made his Indycar debut at the Meadowlands Grand Prix in a March 83C, but retired in a 4th lap accident. He also crashed a Forsythe Lola T800 in qualifying at Laguna Seca, missed the race and then spent the rest of the year waiting for a further break, which never came.

1985 He was called back into the RAM Grand Prix team following the death of Manfred Winklehock, retiring from both the Austrian and Italian and failing to qualify for the Dutch. He raced a March Honda 85J in the All Japan F2 Championship, with a win, 3rd and two 4ths at Fuji, 5th and 8th at Suzuka and 6th at Nishi Nippon. He also drove a Porsche 956 in selected races, but failed to start at Le Mans after Dudley Wood crashed the car in practice.

1986 Contested the All Japan Sports Car Championship with Toyota, taking 3rd at Suzuka and 8th at Fuji. But he crashed at 185mph in a further Fuji round after a tyre burst sending the car rolling end over end.

1987 All Japan Sports Car Champion in a Porsche 962, taking two wins, 3rd and 11th at Fuji, and 2nd and 3rd at Suzuka. He also raced a March 87B in the Japanese F3000 Championship to 7th at Fuji and 8th at Suzuka.

1988 He continued to race in the Japanese Sports Proto Series in a Porsche 962, taking 2nd, 3rd and 5th at Fuji. In F3000 he raced a March 88B taking 8th at Suzuka, 9th at Nishi Nippon. In the Japanese Group A Championship he raced a BMW M3, finishing 3rd at Nishi Nippon and Fuji, taking 5th overall in the championship.

1989 Raced for the Sauber Mercedes team with Mauro Baldi in the World Endurance Championship, winning at Brands Hatch and Spa, with 2nd at Suzuka, the Nurburgring and Donington Park, 3rd at Dijon and 5th at Jarama, to finish 4th in the championship.

1990 Moved to Nissan and finished 11th in the World Sports Car Championship, with 3rd at Spa, 4th at Donington Park and Mexico City, 5th at Montreal, 7th at Monza, 9th at the Nurburgring and 21st at Dijon, sharing mainly with Brancatelli. He also shared a Porsche 962C at the West Palm Beach IMSA race and retired.

1991 Finished 3rd at Le Mans in a TWR Jaguar with Wollek and Fabi. He shared a Porsche 962C with Weaver to 6th at Suzuka in a Japanese Championship round and was 9th at Silverstone in the Intercontinental Jaguar race at Silverstone.

1992 Finished 2nd at Le Mans with Sekiya and Raphanel, 11th at Daytona with Wallace and Fangio and retired at Suzuka in a Toyota.

1993 Retired from Daytona in an Eagle-Toyota and from Le Mans in a Toyota.

1995 Drove a SARD at Le Mans and retired.

1996 Racing a Lister Storm at Daytona, he had a huge accident with the car rolling to destruction.

JULIAN BAILEY
Born October 9th 1961

Julian Bailey.

Photo: BRDC Archive.

A serious Formula Ford accident in 1980 could easily have ended Bailey's career before it had really started. But his determination not only got him back racing again, it helped him win both the Formula Ford Festival and Townsend Thoresen Championship two years later. Despite a fairly successful spell in FF2000, he struggled through F3 before leaping straight to F3000 where he had a win at Brands Hatch. After a troublesome debut year with Tyrrell in Grand Prix, he spent two years with Nissan in sports cars, before a handful of Grands Prix with Lotus in 1991.

His best result was 6th at San Marino that season, producing a single World Championship point. But that was not enough to secure his position in the team and his Grand Prix career was over. After that he raced in Touring Cars, before switching to GT racing with the Lister team, winning the 1999 British GT1 title when partnered by Jamie Campbell-Walter.

1978 A frontrunner in the Spanish Junior Karting Championship.

1979 Finished 10th in the Dunlop Star of Tomorrow FF1600 Championship in a Lola T540, after a win at Mallory Park and 6th at Castle Combe. He also had a win at Brands Hatch and 4th in the final Brands Hatch race of the year, after changing to a Rushen Green-entered Royale RP26.

1980 Continued to race a Royale RP26 in Formula Ford, with 4th at Snetterton, 5th at Mallory Park and 6th at Oulton Park. After changing to a Jubilee Racing Crossle 40F he had a huge crash at Snetterton, breaking his left leg and hand and right arm. He just recovered in time to take part in the Formula Ford Festival.

1981 Missed out on the early part of the season in an effort to regain full fitness. After a couple of Spanish Formula Seat races, he returned to Formula Ford and had a win at Brands Hatch in a Jubilee Van Diemen RF81.

1982 Won the Formula Ford Festival and Townsend Thoresen Championship, and finished 2nd in the RAC Championship with a works Lola T640 run by former Grand Prix driver Dave Morgan. He had four wins, 2nd and 3rd at Brands Hatch, a win and two 2nds at Snetterton, two wins at Oulton Park, a win and 3rd at Donington Park, a win and two 2nds at Mallory Park and a win at Thruxton. He was also 2nd in the Grovewood Awards.

1983 Moved into FF2000 with a BP-backed Reynard 83SF and changed to the Rushen Green team mid-season. He was 3rd in the Racing Displays Championship, after a win, two 2nds and three 3rds at Brands Hatch, a win at Snetterton, a win at Thruxton, two 2nds and a 3rd at Silverstone, 3rd at Castle Combe and 5th at Oulton Park. He won the BBC Grandstand FF2000 Trophy, with three wins at Brands Hatch and finished 6th with a BP Ralt on his F3 debut in the Thruxton TV race.

1984 Finished as runner-up in the Racing Displays FF2000 Championship with a BP Reynard 84SF. At Brands Hatch he had three wins, a 3rd and 4th, a win, 2nd and 4th at Silverstone, a win at Cadwell Park, 2nd and 5th at Donington, 2nd, 3rd and 5th at Thruxton, 4th, 5th and 6th twice at Snetterton and 5th at Oulton Park. He was also 3rd in the BBC Grandstand Trophy, after a win, 2nd and 5th at Brands Hatch.

GRAND PRIX RECORD	
Starts	7
Wins	0
Poles	0
Fastest laps	0
WC points	1
Best finish	6th

1985 Started the year in FF2000 again with a Madgwick Reynard 85SF, taking 7th at Silverstone and retiring at Brands Hatch. He moved into F3 mid-season and qualified 7th on his debut at Silverstone in a Dave Price Reynard 853, but retired from further drives at Brands Hatch and Silverstone. He later changed to a Saab-powered Reynard, taking 9th at Oulton Park and 11th at Silverstone.

1986 Finished 5th in the British F3 Championship in a Swallow Racing Ralt RT30, despite missing the opening three rounds. He finished 3rd at Zandvoort, Spa and Zolder, 3rd and 5th at Silverstone, 4th and 5th at Brands Hatch, 6th at Thruxton and 4th in the Cellnet Trophy at Brands Hatch.

1987 Joined the F3000 Championship from the fifth round at Donington Park in a Lola, and took 4th at Enna, a win at Brands Hatch and 6th at Le Mans to finish 7th in the championship. He also returned to F3 to finish 4th in the Macau GP with a Reynard 873.

1988 Made his Grand Prix debut with Tyrrell but failed to qualify at his first attempt in Brazil. In San Marino he retired with a broken gearbox, but nine further attempts ended in non-qualification. He was classified 9th in Detroit, 12th in Italy, 14th in Japan and 16th at the British Grand Prix and retired in Canada.

1989 Drove for Nissan in the World Sports Car Championship, finishing 3rd at Donington Park, Spa and in the Nurburgring Supercup, 8th at Jarama, 12th in Mexico City and 15th at Dijon. He retired at Brands Hatch, Le Mans and the Nurburgring, sharing mainly with Mark Blundell to secure 11th in the championship. He also went to the Macau F3 Grand Prix again and finished 2nd.

1990 Finished 9th in the World Sports Car Championship with Nissan, after taking 2nd at Montreal and Mexico City, 3rd at Dijon and Spa, 6th at Donington Park and 7th at Monza. He also contested the Guia Saloon Car race with a BMW M3 but was disqualified.

1991 Returned to Grand Prix racing with Lotus, but from four attempts to qualify he only succeeded in San Marino, where he finished in a career best 6th place. He was replaced by Herbert from Monaco onwards, but reappeared in the British Touring Car Championship later in the year, finishing 12th at Silverstone and retiring at Donington Park and Thruxton in a Nissan Primera. He also raced a Nissan at the beginning of the year, finishing 2nd at Sebring and retiring at Daytona.

1992 Contested the last four British Touring Car Championship rounds in a works Toyota Carina, taking 9th and 13th at Silverstone, and 16th with a retirement at Brands Hatch.

1993 Raced in the British Touring Car Championship for Toyota. Results included a win and 2nd at Knockhill, 2nd at Snetterton, 4th at Pembrey, 5th at Donington Park and Oulton Park and 6th at Brands Hatch and Silverstone

to finish 5th in the championship. He also went to Monza for the World Cup race, finished 9th in the first heat but retired in the second after a first lap accident.

1994 Finished 11th in the British Touring Car Championship with Toyota, after 5th at Snetterton, two 5ths and a 6th at Silverstone, two 6ths at Donington Park, and 6th at Brands Hatch. He also finished 12th in the World Cup at Donington Park and contested the final rounds of the Asia Pacific Championship, taking 5th and 7th at Wellington.

1995 Continued with Toyota in the British Touring Car Championship and finished 9th overall, after taking 2nd and 6th at Donington, 4th at Oulton Park (twice), 4th and 5th at Silverstone, 6th at Knockhill, Snetterton and Brands Hatch (three times). He also contested the South African Championship in a Toyota Camry, with two 3rds at East London and two 4ths, 5th and 9th at Kyalami. In the Kyalami International his Camry finished 4th and at the Guia Saloon Car race he raced a Toyota Corona to 3rd place.

1996 He began the year as a frontrunner in the New Zealand Championship with a Corona, winning at Teretonga, with further podium finishes at Ruapena. A full year in South Africa with a Camry resulted in a win, 2nd, 3rd, 5th and 6th at Killarney, 4th, two 5ths, two 6ths and 7th at Kyalami and 5th at Goldfields.

1997 Finished 10th at Bathurst sharing a Honda Accord with Warren Luff.

1998 Raced a Lister Storm at Daytona with Needell, and finished 3rd in the British GT1 Championship, after a win and two 2nds at Silverstone, a win at Snetterton, 2nd at Spa, 3rd at Oulton Park and 4th at Donington Park.

1999 Continued to race a Lister Storm in both the FIA and British GT Championships. In the FIA he was 2nd at Donington Park, led until retiring at Silverstone, retired after starting from pole at Zolder and retired at Monza. In the British he shared with Jamie Campbell-Walter and won at Donington Park (twice), Oulton Park, Snetterton, Brands Hatch, Croft and Spa, with two 2nds a 3rd and a 4th at Silverstone. They won the championship and the Tourist Trophy that went with the title.

MARTIN BRUNDLE
Born June 1st 1959

Martin Brundle.

Photo: BRDC Archive.

From a background of grasstrack and hot rod racing, he spent two successful years with a Toyota Celica in the British Saloon Car Championship before embarking on his single-seater career in Formula Ford 2000. He made his F3 debut in 1981 and finished a strong second to Ayrton Senna in the 1983 championship after some memorable battles. Brundle joined the Tyrrell Grand Prix team the following year. He went on to race for Zakspeed, Williams, Brabham, Benetton, Ligier, McLaren and Jordan in Grands Prix and won both Le Mans and the World Sports Car Championship during a long association with Jaguar. He continued to compete at Le Mans with Toyota in 1998 and 99, but retired on each occasion. He also turned his hand to rallying by tackling the Network Q Rally of Great Britain and has become a renowned TV commentator on Grand Prix racing.

1972 Went grasstrack racing with a Ford Anglia at the age of 13.

1973 Changed his grass track Anglia for a Hillman Imp.

1974 Moved into Hot Rods.

1975 Continued to race an Escort in Hot Rods.

1976 Started the year in Hot Rods and progressed to the red top grade, before retiring. He also contested a few end of season Special Saloon races in a Group 1 Toyota Celica.

1977 Raced his Celica in the British Saloon Car Championship and secured pole at Oulton Park in only his 6th ever race. He finished 4th in class in the championship, with a class win at Silverstone, 2nd at Donington Park and Silverstone, 2nd and 3rd at Brands Hatch and 3rd at Oulton Park. He also contested some early season Special Saloon races to gain licence signatures.

1978 Finished 7th overall and 3rd in class in the British Saloon Car Championship with a Celica, after 2nd and 3rd in class at Silverstone, 2nd at Oulton Park, 2nd twice at Thruxton, 2nd twice and 4th at Brands Hatch, 4th twice at Donington Park and 4th at Mallory Park. He also drove a Production Saloon Celica at Snetterton and finished 4th in both parts of the Tricentrol race.

1979 Moved into single-seaters with a Reynard SF79 in FF2000. He won a Challenge race at Snetterton and had a further 5th place finish at the same circuit. A regular in the BMW County Championship, he won at Donington Park and had two 4th places at Mallory Park. He also had a couple of outings in the British Saloon Car Championship with a Celica, taking 3rd in class at Oulton Park and sharing with Win Percy to 6th in the Snetterton night race.

1980 Continued in FF2000 with a Reynard SF80, finishing 5th in the Motorcraft Championship and 7th in the Imperial Leather series. He was 2nd at Snetterton, Castle Combe and Mallory Park, 2nd and 3rd twice at Brands Hatch, and 4th and 8th at Silverstone. He helped Norfolk to the BMW County Championship with two wins, three 2nds, a 3rd and a 6th. Other outings included 4th in class at Brands Hatch with a Celica in the British Saloon Car Championship and he shared a Celica with father John and brother Robin in the Willhire 24 hours race.

1981 Returned full time to the British Saloon Car Championship, partnering Stirling Moss in a pair of Audi 80s. He had two wins at Silverstone, 2nd at Mallory Park

GRAND PRIX RECORD	
Starts	142
Wins	0
Poles	0
Fastest laps	0
WC points	90
Best finish	2nd

Martin Brundle (Ralt RT3) at Silverstone in 1982.

Photo: BRDC Archive.

and Thruxton, 4th at Donington Park and 5th at Thruxton. He was excluded from 2nd at Brands Hatch on technical grounds. Despite his penalty he still finished 7th in class in the championship. He also shared the family Celica to 10th in the Willhire 24 hours and made his F3 debut in the Thruxton TV race, finishing 6th in a Ralt RT3.

1982 Finished 4th in the British F3 Championship with a Ralt, taking wins at Oulton Park and Thruxton, with 2nd, two 3rds, 6th and 7th at Silverstone, two 2nds and a 5th at Brands Hatch, two 4ths at Snetterton and 4th at Cadwell Park. He took pole position for five of the last six rounds and was the Premier Grovewood Award winner.

1983 Moved to Eddie Jordan's team for another season in F3 and had some epic battles with Ayrton Senna. He finished runner-up in the British Championship and 7th in the European, winning at Silverstone (twice), Donington Park (twice), Cadwell Park, Snetterton, Oulton Park and Thruxton. He took ten 2nd places to Senna, five at Silverstone, three at Thruxton and one each at Donington Park and Brands Hatch. With 3rd at Thruxton and Silverstone he was only off the podium once, when Senna crashed over him at Oulton Park! He won the F3 race supporting the Austrian Grand Prix, retired in Monaco and finished 10th at Macau. He also joined the TWR Jaguar team in the European Touring Car Championship, winning at Donington Park and the Osterreichring, with 8th at Zolder. He also drove an MG Metro Turbo in the British Saloon Car Championship finale and finished 4th in class.

1984 Joined the Tyrrell Grand Prix team and finished 5th on his debut in Brazil, followed by a number of minor placings before a huge accident during qualifying in Monaco. He came back to finish 10th in Canada and took a brilliant 2nd in Detroit, before breaking both his ankles in a crash during qualifying at Dallas. The whole season was later erased by a disqualification due to a fuel tank irregularity. He also continued to race TWR Jaguars, taking victory at Enna, 5th at Mugello and 13th at Monza. He made his comeback from injury in the first British Truck race at Donington Park, returning later in the season to take 6th in the Rallysprint.

1985 Began his Grand Prix year with a normally-aspirated Tyrrell, picking up 8th in Brazil, 9th in San Marino, 10th in Monaco and 12th in Canada. After retiring the new turbo-powered car in the French he took 7th in the British, matching the result in the Dutch and South African races to end the season just out of the points. His other results included 5th in the Spa round of the World Endurance Championship in a Jaguar XJR6, 2nd in the Donington Rallysprint and retirement from the Macau F3 race and the Spa 24 hours.

1986 Another year with Tyrrell brought his first points with 5th in the Grand Prix season opener in Brazil. He also took 5th in the British, 6th in the Hungarian, 8th in San Marino and a season's best of 4th in the Australian finale. He finished 4th in the Brands Hatch Rallysprint and continued to drive for Jaguar in World Sports.

1987 Left Tyrrell for Zakspeed and had a disastrous year. 5th in San Marino, 7th in Monaco and 11th in Spain were his only classified finishers. He did taste success however with Jaguar, winning the Brands Hatch and Spa 1000km.

1988 A one-off Grand Prix appearance with Williams as Mansell's deputy brought 7th in the Belgian Grand Prix. He became World Sports Car Champion with Jaguar, winning at Jarama, Monza, Silverstone, Brands Hatch and Fuji, with 2nd at Brno, Spa and the Nurburgring, and 3rd at Sandown. He also raced in IMSA and won the Daytona 24 hours with Boesel and Nielsen and at Del Mar, with 2nd at Miami, Lime Rock, Sears Point and Mid-Ohio, 3rd at Portland and 4th at Road America, to finish 5th in the championship.

1989 A return to Grand Prix racing with Brabham brought 4th on the grid and 6th in the race at Monaco, despite having to pre-qualify. He also finished 6th in the Italian, 8th in the Portuguese and German and 9th in the Mexican, before ending with a season's best 5th in Japan.

1990 Back with TWR Jaguar he won the Le Mans 24 hours with Nielsen and Cobb. He won at Silverstone, and finished 2nd at Daytona, 3rd at Monza and the Nurburgring, 5th at Dijon, 6th at IMSA Heartland and 15th in Montreal, securing 8th in the World Sportscar Championship. He also had a one-off in the British Touring Car Championship, taking a BMW M3 to 9th in class at Brands Hatch.

1991 Rejoined the Brabham Grand Prix team and spent most of the year developing the Yamaha engine. 5th in Japan and 9th in Belgium were his only top ten finishes, and after failing to qualify in Australia he left the team. He also had occasional sportscar outings for Jaguar, sharing a win with Warwick at Monza, finishing 3rd at Silverstone, 4th at IMSA Delmar and retiring at Fuji.

1992 Moved to Benetton to partner Michael Schumacher and began the year with four consecutive retirements. Apart from the Canadian Grand Prix he then finished in the points in every other race. He was 2nd in Italy, 3rd in France, Britain, Japan and Australia, 4th in San Marino, Germany, Belgium and Portugal and 5th in Monaco and Hungary to take 6th overall in the World Championship.

1993 Another move, this time to Ligier began with three retirements before finishing 3rd in San Marino. He went on to finish 5th in the Canadian, French and Hungarian, 6th at Monaco, the Portuguese and Australian, 7th in the Belgian, 8th in the German and 9th in the Japanese to finish 7th in the World Championship.

1994 Another move to McLaren to replace Senna was highlighted by a 2nd place finish at Monaco, one of only two top 10 finishes from the first nine Grands Prix of the year. As the reliability of the Peugeot engines improved, the points began to flow with 4th in Hungary, 5th in Italy, 6th in Portugal and 3rd in Australia, finishing 7th in the World Championship again.

1995 After waiting patiently for Mansell to make his mind up about a McLaren drive, he accepted the offer of a return to Ligier, but only in a shared drive with Suzuki. He finished 9th in the Spanish Grand Prix on his seasonal debut, following up with 3rd in Belgium, 4th in France, 7th in the European at the Nurburgring and 8th in Portugal.

1996 Joined Jordan for his final year in Grand Pix racing and made the finish in nine of his 16 starts, with 4th in the Italian, 5th in the Japanese and 6th in the European, Canadian and British. He also contested the RAC Rally in a Ford Escort Cosworth, crashing out in Wales.

1997 Joined the ITV Grand Prix commentary team.

1998 Raced a Toyota at Le Mans with Collard and Helary, retiring after an accident in the rain.

1999 Secured pole position at Le Mans for Toyota and led the race for a while, before retiring with a tyre blowout. He also retired a Toyota Corolla from the Network Q Rally of Great Britain after hitting a tree stump.

MARTIN DONNELLY
Born March 26th 1964

After an early grounding in Formula Ford in Ireland, two successful years in FF2000 in both the British and European Championships secured an F3 seat for 1986. After finishing 3rd in the F3 Championship for two consecutive years, Donnelly started a third F3 season and was in danger of being passed over for further progression.

A mid-season swap to Eddie Jordan's F3000 team brought immediate success with a debut victory at Brands Hatch. His first Grand Prix came with Arrows in the French Grand Prix in 1989, before plans were laid for a full year with Lotus in 1990. After a fairly tough baptism his season and career ended abruptly with a crash during qualifying for the Spanish Grand Prix, which left Martin fighting for his life when his car disintegrated around him after heavy contact with the barriers. He battled to regain fitness and soon returned to the sport as a successful team owner, running cars in junior British single-seater categories. He still races occasionally in classic and historic events.

12

GRAND PRIX RECORD

Starts	13
Wins	0
Poles	0
Fastest laps	0
WC points	0
Best finish	7th

1981 Began racing in Formula Ford with a Crossle 35F, with a win, 2nd, 3rd, 4th and two 5ths at Kirkistown, 2nd, 3rd, and 10th at Mondello Park and 3rd at Phoenix Park. He also made his FF2000 debut in Harry Johnston's Crossle 41F, finishing 3rd at Kirkistown.

1982 Won the Irish Formula Ford Festival and finished 6th in the Irish Nationwide Building Society and STP Northern Ireland FF1600 Championships in a Van Diemen RF81. He had four 3rds, a 5th and 6th at Kirkistown and journeyed to Brands Hatch collecting a 6th place and reaching the Formula Ford Festival semi-finals. He also had an FF2000 race at Kirkistown again, finishing 3rd.

Martin Donnelly.

Photo: BRDC Archive.

1983 After a double win at Mondello Park in a Crossle 40F, he changed from FF1600 to FF2000 with a Frank Nolan-backed Van Diemen RF83. He had two wins at Kirkistown, two at Mondello Park and one at Cadwell Park before his engine was declared illegal and he lost all his points. Despite starting from scratch he still took the Elf Irish title, after three wins each at Mondello Park and Kirkistown and one at Phoenix Park, plus a further 2nd and 3rd at Mondello Park and 2nd at Kirkistown. He also had a win and 2nd at Donington Park, 2nd at Croix en Ternois, 2nd, 4th and 9th at Brands Hatch and 7th at Oulton Park. In the BBC Grandstand Trophy he had a 3rd and 4th at Brands Hatch and 4th at Thruxton, had a prize drive in F3 with Eddie Jordan at Silverstone and received a Grovewood Commendation.

1984 Finished 3rd in the EFDA Euroseries and 5th in the Racing Displays FF2000 Championships with a Van Diemen RF84. He had a win, 2nd and 6th at Silverstone and wins at the Nurburgring and Kirkistown. He took 2nd at Zolder (twice), 2nd at Zandvoort, 2nd and 4th at Cadwell Park, three 2nds, 3rd and 4th at Brands Hatch, 3rd at Donington Park and Mondello Park, two 4ths at Snetterton, 4th and 7th at Thruxton and 6th at Oulton Park. After changing to a Reynard 84SF he won the BBC Grandstand Trophy, with a win, 2nd, 3rd and 4th at Brands Hatch and a win at Thruxton. He was 3rd in the Brands Hatch World Cup race and won an end of season single-seater race at Kirkistown in a Mondiale M84T.

1985 Runner-up in the British FF2000 Championship and 3rd in the EFDA Euroseries was achieved after starting with a Reynard and then changing to a Van Diemen RF85. He had three wins at Brands Hatch, a win and 2nd at Oulton Park, wins at Donington Park, Zolder and the Nurburgring, two 2nds at Thruxton, 2nd at Castle Combe, 3rd at Mondello Park and Snetterton, plus 3rd and 4th at Silverstone. In the BBC Grandstand Trophy he was 5th overall, with 6th in a Reynard at Brands Hatch and two 3rds in a Swift DB3.

1986 Moved up to F3 with a Swallow Racing Ralt RT30, he won at Donington Park, Oulton Park and Silverstone, with 2nd at Zolder and Donington Park. He took 2nd and 4th at Brands Hatch, 3rd and 7th at Thruxton, 4th at Zandvoort, 7th at Snetterton and two 8ths at Silverstone. He also finished 2nd in the Cellnet Superprix at Brands Hatch.

1987 Continued in F3 and finished 3rd in the championship, with a win at Oulton Park, a win and 3rd at Brands Hatch, 2nd at Zandvoort, 2nd and 4th at Silverstone, 2nd at Snetterton and Spa, and 3rd and 4th at Thruxton. He won the end of season Macau Grand Prix as well as the Knockhill Superprix, with 3rd in the Brands Hatch Superprix and 8th overall in the EFDA Grand Prix to be awarded the Premier Cellnet Award.

1988 Started a third year in F3 and was on the podium for five of the first six rounds, with a win, 2nd and 3rd at Thruxton, a win at Donington Park, 2nd, 3rd and 5th at Silverstone, 7th at Monaco and 4th at Brands Hatch. After taking 3rd at Snetterton he left the series but had amassed enough points to retain 4th in the championship despite missing the last six rounds. He moved on to Eddie

Jordan's F3000 team and made a dream race-winning debut at Brands Hatch, in a race overshadowed by team mate Herbert's horrific accident. He went on to take 2nd at Le Mans and Birmingham, retired at Zolder after starting from pole, and secured a 2nd victory at Dijon to finish an amazing 3rd in the championship from only five starts. He also raced occasionally in sports cars, sharing an RLR Porsche 962 GTi to 7th at the Nurburgring, retiring at Spa in the same car and retiring at Fuji in a SARD Toyota.

1989 Continued to race in F3000 but had to wait until round six to record a finish, and that was a victory at Brands Hatch, after being excluded from a similar success at Vallelunga. He was 3rd at Birmingham, 7th at Le Mans and 17th at Dijon to finish 8th in the championship. His Grand Prix debut came with Arrows in the French, finishing 12th after qualifying 14th and starting from the pitlane. He won a Formula Libre race at Mondello Park in a F3000 Reynard 88D and had a 7th at Sugo and 9th at Suzuka in the Japanese F3000 Series. At Le Mans he shared a Nissan with Bailey and Blundell and finished 6th in the Fuji 1000 sharing a Porsche 962 with Herbert.

1990 Joined the Lotus team for a full Grand Prix campaign, but failed to make the start of the season opener in Phoenix after the ignition failed on the parade lap. After retiring in Brazil he went on to finish 8th in San Marino and Mexico, 12th in the French and Belgian and 7th in the Hungarian. But after retiring in both the Italian and Portuguese, he was critically injured during qualifying for the Spanish and a promising career was brought to a sudden end.

1992 Made his motorsport return in rallycross at Nutts Corner, taking 2nd place in the Nova Challenge. He also raced the car again at the Brands Hatch Grand Prix and finished 6th in his category.

1993 Raced a Lotus Esprit in a GT race at Silverstone.

1995 Contested Tom Wheatcroft's Formula Classic Series and had a win, 2nd and a retirement from three starts at Donington Park.

1998 Had a brief return again at Donington in Paul Whight's CanAm McLaren M8D, but didn't get a race.

1999 Finally got to race the McLaren M8D, spinning off at a wet Donington Park just after taking the lead, followed by a win and 2nd at Silverstone.

JOHNNY DUMFRIES
Born April 26th 1958

Johnny Dumfries.

Photo: BRDC Archive.

With only a couple of intermittent years in Formula Ford behind him and not too much in the way of results, Dumfries undertook a shoestring effort in F3 in 1983, under the wing of former Grand Prix driver Dave Morgan. It was enough however to secure a BP-backed drive the following year and he went on to dominate, winning the British F3 Championship and finishing as runner-up in the European.

In 1985 he tackled some Formula 3000 races and was Ferrari's nominated Grand Prix test driver. His only year in Grand Prix came as partner to Senna at Lotus in 1986, and brought his best Grand Prix finish of fifth in Hungary. No Grand Prix drive was available for the following season but he later raced Jaguar and Toyota sports cars, winning at Le Mans in 1988 with Lammers and Wallace. After retiring from racing the Earl of Dumfries inherited the title of Marquis of Bute.

GRAND PRIX RECORD	
Starts	15
Wins	0
Poles	0
Fastest laps	0
WC points	3
Best finish	5th

1981 Began racing with a Formula Ford Crossle 32F mainly in junior events. His best result was at Croft taking 4th in a non-championship race, he also had a 5th at Lydden and 6th at Cadwell Park.

1982 Finished 5th in the Champion of Brands FF1600 Championship with a Ray 82F, after a win, 2nd, three 3rds, two 4ths and two 5ths. He had a further win at Brands Hatch, 2nd at Snetterton, 4th at Oulton Park, 4th and 5th at Brands Hatch, 4th and 5th at Mallory Park, and was a quarter finalist at the Formula Ford Festival.

1983 Graduated to F3 with Dave Morgan in a Ralt and had five points finishes from a shoestring effort. He took 5th and 7th at Thruxton, two 5ths, two 6ths and a 16th at Silverstone and 8th at Donington, to finish 10th in the championship and 2nd in the Grovewood Awards.

1984 Joined Dave Price's BP-backed Ralt F3 team and dominated the formula. He won the British Championship with 11 wins out of 15 starts, four each at Thruxton and Silverstone, two at Donington Park and one at Snetterton, with 2nd at Zolder, 4th at Silverstone and 7th at Spa plus 10 pole positions. He was also runner-up to Capelli in the European Championship, with wins at Donington Park, Silverstone, the Nurburgring and Jarama, 2nd at Zolder and La Chatre, 4th at Mugello and Nogaro plus eight pole positions. He won his Monaco qualifying heat at Paul Ricard, but retired at Monaco itself. He turned down the chance of a Grand Prix drive with Lotus in Portugal due to a Euro F3 clash, and shared a Porsche 956 with Jack Brabham in the Sandown 1000.

1985 Moved to F3000 with an Onyx March and finished 7th on his debut at Thruxton. He collected a solitary point from 6th at Vallelunga and finished 10th at Dijon after changing to a works Lola T590. The year was also spent as Ferrari's nominated test driver, while other outings included 2nd in a Metro Challenge race at Silverstone. He retired from the Curacao Grand Prix in a March 85B, the Macau GP with a Reynard 853 and the Fuji 1000 when sharing a Porsche 956 with Acheson.

1986 Joined the Lotus Grand Prix team to partner Senna, after the Brazilian blocked Warwick's intended move to the team. He qualified 11th on his debut in Brazil and finished 9th, but retired in both the Spanish and San Marino races and failed to qualify in Monaco. He went on to pick up 7th place in both the Detroit and British races, before scoring his first points with 5th in Hungary. Although retirements continued to outweigh finishes, he did collect 9th in Portugal and 6th in Australia on his final Grand Prix appearance. He also finished 3rd in the Brands Hatch Rallysprint.

1987 Concentrating on sports cars he won at Spa with 2nd at Fuji for Jaguar and won at Road America, with 3rd at Columbus and 10th at San Antonio sharing Cobb's IMSA Porsche 962. He also shared a Porsche 962 GTi to 2nd at Brands Hatch, an Ecosse to 8th at Silverstone and a Sauber to retirement at Le Mans and the Nurburgring. In single-seaters he tested regularly for Benetton's Grand Prix team and finished 9th with a Ralt in the Macau Grand Prix.

1988 Racing almost exclusively for Jaguar, he won at Le Mans with Lammers and Wallace, finished 3rd at Brno and Daytona, 4th at Sandown and 8th at the Nurburgring. He contested the final two F3000 races of the year, retiring at Zolder and finishing 13th at Dijon, and shared Guy Edwards' Kaliber Sierra Cosworth to 3rd at Donington Park in the British Touring Car Championship.

1989 Continued to race sports cars but moved to Toyota, finishing 4th at Dijon, 2nd at the Nurburgring, 8th at Spa, 10th at Donington Park and Jarama, 20th at Suzuka and retired at Le Mans, Brands Hatch and Silverstone.

1990 Another season with Toyota brought 14th in Montreal, 18th at Spa, 20th at Fuji and five retirements, including Monza where he also had a huge accident during qualifying.

1991 Raced a Courage at Le Mans and retired.

JOHNNY HERBERT
Born June 25th 1964

Johnny Herbert.

Photo: BRDC Archive.

As the winner of the Formula Ford Festival Herbert shot to prominence in 1985, before taking the British F3 title two years later. Having tasted success with Eddie Jordan in F3 he graduated to F3000 with the same team and won on his debut at Jerez, but all his hopes came to a sudden end with an horrific crash at Brands Hatch that left him with serious leg injuries. For many it would have spelled the end of their racing career, but determination overcame pain and he started the 1989 season in the Benetton Grand Prix team.

It proved to be too much too soon despite taking 4th place on his debut in Brazil. He was later replaced in the team and went to Japan to rebuild his career. With Peter Collins his former Benetton boss moving to Lotus, the Grand Prix scene beckoned once more as he completed the 1990 season, winning at Le Mans for Mazda the following year. A further four years at Lotus promised much yet delivered little, and so moves first to Ligier and then Benetton were taken. In 1995 he won both the British and Italian Grands Prix, but left the team at the end of the year. Three years with Sauber saw occasional success, but a move to Stewart for '99 brought his third Grand Prix victory in the European race at the Nurburgring.

1975 Started racing karts and finished 6th in his debut race.

1979 Won the British 100cc Junior Kart Championship.

1980 Finished 3rd in the 100c Junior National Kart Championship.

1981 Won the British Junior Kart Championship.

1982 Won the International 135cc Kart Championship.

1983 After another year in karts he made his car debut with a Sparton in the Formula Ford Festival at Brands Hatch. He reached the quarter-final stage after taking 5th in his heat, and returned to finish 5th in the Christmas Bonanza FF1600 race.

1984 Started the year with Valour Racing in his Sparton FF1600 car, but after taking 6th in a BP Superfind round at Brands Hatch, the car was wrecked when he sustained leg injuries in a test crash at Oulton Park. He returned with a Van Diemen RF84 mainly in the Dunlop and BP Junior Championships, collecting a maiden win at Silverstone. He added 3rd and 4th at Oulton Park, 3rd and 5th at Brands Hatch, 3rd at Mallory Park, and 5th at Snetterton and Cadwell Park, to finish 6th overall in the Dunlop Star of Tomorrow Championship and 8th in the BP Superfind sedries. He also contested a couple of Champion of Brands rounds, recording a 4th and 6th place.

1985 Another year in Formula Ford with a Quest FF85 brought 5th in the Esso Championship and 8th in the RAC. He had a win and 2nd at Brands Hatch, four 2nds and a 3rd at Silverstone, two 2nds at Oulton Park, 2nd and 4th at Thruxton and 4th at Castle Combe. He won the Formula Ford Festival at Brands Hatch having famously started his heat from the back of the grid. He also made his FF2000 debut with a Talon in the BBC Grandstand Trophy at Brands Hatch, but retired. At the end of the year he was commended in the Grovewood Awards.

1986 A move up to FF2000 with a Quest 86SF brought little success, apart from a win in the Donington Park Racing Club series. He had a 4th at Snetterton, 5th, 6th and two 10ths at Brands Hatch, 8th at Thruxton, 9th at Cadwell Park and 13th at Silverstone. Occasional outings in the FF1600 Quest resulted in 2nd at Cadwell Park, 4th and 5th at Brands Hatch and 9th at Silverstone. Towards the end of the year he took over Mike Rowe's F3 Ralt from Reima Soderman. On his debut at Donington Park he finished 5th, and went on to take 4th and 5th at Silverstone, 8th at Spa, 10th at Zolder and 3rd in the Brands Hatch Superprix. He also finished 2nd in the end of season Cellnet Awards.

1987 Won the British Formula 3 Championship driving for Eddie Jordan, with two wins and a 3rd at Thruxton, a win, 2nd and 5th at Brands Hatch, two wins, 3rd, 4th and 7th at Silverstone, 2nd at Oulton Park, 3rd at Snetterton, 9th at Zandvoort and 19th at Donington Park. At Monaco he finished 3rd, won the Brands Hatch Superprix and took 3rd in the EFDA F3 Grand Prix. He earned himself a test

Johnny Herbert (Camel Lotus Honda) at Monza.

Photo: BRDC Archive.

drive with Benetton's Grand Prix team and also had an outing in the Metro Challenge, finishing 10th at Silverstone.

1988 A debut win in F3000 with Jordan at Jerez promised much for the coming season. After retiring at Vallelunga and missing the Pau race, he was 7th at Silverstone, 3rd at Monza and retired at Enna, before securing pole at Brands Hatch. His season was brought to an abrupt end, however, when a clash with Gregor Foitek sent his car into an alarming series of rolls. With his legs shattered his future career appeared to be in grave doubt. Earlier in the year he had driven an ADA in the World Sports Car race at Jerez, but retired.

1989 Having fought desperately through the pain barrier he regained fitness and was rewarded with a Grand Prix debut for Benetton. He qualified a magnificent 10th on his debut in Brazil and finished 4th in the race, but despite his undoubted talent the physical pain began to take its toll. 11th in San Marino, 14th in Monaco and 15th in Mexico followed, but after taking 5th in Detroit he failed

to qualify for the Canadian and was replaced by Pirro. He did get two further Grand Prix opportunities with Tyrrell, retiring in Belgium and failing to qualify in Portugal, and shared a Porsche 962 with Donnelly to 6th place in the Fuji 1000.

1990 Most of the year was spent racing in Japan, where he took 5th at Fuji, 6th and 7th at Sugo and 10th at Suzuka in F3000 with a Reynard 90D. He added 2nd and 4th in the All Japan Endurance Championship sharing a Porsche 962 with Rydell. He came back into Grand Prix racing with Lotus, replacing the injured Donnelly in the Japanese and Australian, retiring from both.

1991 The highlight of the season was undoubtedly victory at Le Mans for Mazda with Gachot and Weidler. He contested the All Japan F3000 Championship again in a Ralt RT23 and finished 10th overall, with 2nd at Mine, 5th and 7th at Suzuka, 6th at Fuji and 7th at Autopolis, and had two 4th places at Fuji in the All Japan Endurance Championship with Mazda. From the Canadian Grand Prix onwards he replaced Bailey in the Lotus team, but failed to qualify on his first appearance. His best result was 7th in Belgium, followed by 10th in Mexico and France, 11th in Australia, 14th in the British and retirement in Portugal and Japan.

1992 A full season with Lotus netted five top ten qualifying performances, but only five classified finishes. He was 6th in the South African and French Grands Prix, 7th in Mexico and 13th in Belgium and Australia. He also drove for Mazda in sports cars again, finishing 2nd at Silverstone and 4th at Le Mans.

1993 Continuing with Lotus there was much more promise, with four points finishes punctuating an

GRAND PRIX RECORD	
Starts	143
Wins	3
Poles	0
Fastest laps	0
WC points	98
Won his 71st Grand Prix	

excessive list of retirements. 4th in the Brazilian, Donington Park European and British Grands Prix, plus 5th in the Belgian secured 9th overall in the World Championship. His only other classified finishes were 8th in San Marino, 10th in Canada and Germany and 11th in Japan.

1994 Another Grand Prix year began with Lotus, taking 7th in both Brazilian and Pacific Grands Prix. After taking 10th at San Marino and retiring from both the Monaco and Spanish races, his patience at Lotus was beginning to wear thin. 8th in Canada and 7th in France were his only other top ten finishes with the team and before the end of the year his contract was bought out by Flavio Briatore. He made his debut for Ligier at the European Grand Prix, qualified 7th and finished 8th only to move to Benetton to partner Schumacher for the final two Grands Prix of the year. After qualifying 5th in Japan and 7th in Australia he retired from both races.

1995 Stayed at Benetton to partner Schumacher and soon settled down to become a regular points finisher. After retiring from the Grand Prix opener in Brazil, he was 4th in Argentina, 7th in San Marino, 2nd in Spain and 4th in Monaco. Retirement in Canada and France preceded the highlight of his whole career, victory in the British Grand Prix at Silverstone after Schumacher and Hill collided. A further win at the Italian, along with 3rd in Japan, 4th in Germany and Hungary, 5th in the European and 6th in the Pacific secured 4th in the World Championship.

1996 Joined the Sauber Grand Prix team but failed to start the Australian opener. Apart from 4th place in Monaco he was destined to finish just inside the top ten in all but one of his other eight finishes.

1997 Now with Ferrari power his Sauber recorded six points finishes to secure 11th in the World Championship. His season's best came with 3rd in the Hungarian Grand Prix, closely followed by 4th in Argentina and Belgium, 5th in Spain and Canada and 6th in Japan.

1998 A third and final year with Sauber started with a point for sixth in Australia, but his only other top ten finishes came with 7th in Spain and Monaco, 8th in France and Austria, and 10th in Hungary and Japan.

1999 A move to the Stewart team began with all too familiar bad luck, non-starting in the Australian opener after a fire on the grid. Apart from 5th in Canada the season brought little success, and team mate Barrichello usually outqualified him. But the tide suddenly turned with victory in the European at Nurburgring, 4th in Malaysia and finishing just out of the points with 7th in Japan. For 2000 he stays with the team under the new Jaguar banner.

NIGEL MANSELL
Born August 8th 1953

Nigel Mansell in 1983.

Photo: BRDC Archive.

After six years racing karts, Mansell was a Formula Ford champion in his second year of car racing. But he then struggled to make an impression in either F3 or F2, even though he and his wife Rosanne sold their house to keep his career going. However, his determination to fight back from a broken neck in 1979 brought him to the attention of Colin Chapman, who gave him a Lotus testing contract the following year with a Grand Prix debut in Austria.

It took a move to Williams in 1985 for him to collect a maiden Grand Prix victory, at his 72nd attempt. Further successes soon followed with the runner-up spot in the World Championship claimed in 1986, 87 and 91, before the title itself in 1992. During this period he won the hearts of the British public and became one of the country's best-known sportsmen when Mansell-mania was at its height.

Having won the title in '92, he made a dramatic move to America for 1993 and promptly won the Indycar title with the Newman Haas team. But his defence proved more difficult with only three podium finishes and no victories. From thereafter most of his exploits are best forgotten, a mixture of

GRAND PRIX RECORD

Starts	187
Wins	31
Poles	32
Fastest laps	30
WC points	482
Won his 72nd Grand Prix	

rumours and semi-disasters as an on-off retirement saga ran for several years. Mansell is best remembered for 31 Grand Prix wins and back to back Formula 1 and Indycar titles.

1969-75 Raced karts for Great Britain.

1976 Made his car debut at Mallory Park in Formula Ford with a Hawke DL11, taking five wins from 11 starts. His major results were a win at Castle Combe and the in Oulton Park Gold Cup support race, two 2nd places at Mallory Park, 4th in the Boley Pittard Memorial Trophy at Silverstone, and 6th at Castle Combe.

1977 Won the Brush Fusegear Formula Ford Championship, finished 4th in the RAC Series and 9th in the Townsend Thoresen. He started the year in a Javelin, before moving to a Crossle 25F and then a 32F. He had three wins at Thruxton, three at Donington Park, two at Silverstone, and one each at Snetterton, Oulton Park and Mallory Park. He added three 2nds and a 5th at Silverstone, two 2nds at Donington Park, 2nd at Thruxton, 3rd and 4th at Brands Hatch, and 3rd and 4th at Oulton Park. He made his F3 debut at Donington Park in a Puma, but retired, later taking a works Lola to 4th and 20th at Silverstone, plus 5th and 10th at Thruxton, to earn a Grovewood commendation.

1978 An intermittent year in F3 with a March, brought a 2nd place at Silverstone, 4th at Donington Park and 7th at both Oulton Park and Brands Hatch. He also won a prize drive in an ICI F2 Chevron at Donington Park, but failed to qualify.

1979 Raced in F3 as part of the Unipart March team, he missed a couple of races after crushing his vertebrae in a collision with De Cesaris at Oulton Park. He had a win, two 6ths, 8th and 11th at Silverstone, 2nd, 4th and 8th at Thruxton, 4th and 6th at Brands Hatch, 7th at Donington Park and 8th at Snetterton. He also went to Monaco and finished 11th, took 4th in the Austrian Grand Prix support race and 2nd in the John Player Trophy at Donington Park. He finished 3rd at Mallory Park in the BMW County Championship and 2nd overall with a class win at Donington Park in a Post Historic Jaguar E-Type, and collected 2nd place in the Grovewood Awards.

1980 Started the year with a works March 803, scoring a 4th and two 6ths at Silverstone, 4th and 5th at Thruxton, 4th at Brands Hatch, 6th at Snetterton and 8th at Monaco,

finishing 9th in the BP F3 Championship. He drove a works F2 Ralt Honda in four rounds, taking 2nd at Hockenheim, 5th at Zolder, 11th at Silverstone and retiring at Zolder. He also won BMW County Championship races at Donington Park and Silverstone, with 4th at Castle Combe. The year also brought his Grand Prix debut with Lotus, retiring in the Austrian and Dutch and failing to qualify for the Italian.

1981 As a full member of the Lotus Grand Prix team, he collected his first World Championship points from 3rd in the Belgian, followed by 4th in Las Vegas, 6th in Spain, 7th in France and 11th in Brazil. He also finished 5th in the Donington Park Rallysprint.

1982 Continued with Lotus but struggled for success, 3rd in Brazil and 4th at Monaco were his only points finishes, along with 7th at Long Beach and in the Italian, 8th in the Swiss and 9th in the German. He was 7th in the Donington Park Rallysprint.

1983 Still Lotus mounted and results began to pick-up. Having started the year with 12th places at the Brazilian, Long Beach and San Marino Grands Prix, he went on to 6th at Detroit, 4th in the British, 5th in the Austrian and 8th in the Italian. He then scored a season's best 3rd at the Brands Hatch European GP, along with the fastest lap. He also won the Donington Park Rallysprint.

1984 His final year at Lotus produced only five classified finishes. Results were 3rd in the French and Dutch, 4th in the German and 6th in the Canadian and US at Dallas. He had led in Monaco until hitting the barrier in the rain and finished 2nd in the Donington Park Rallysprint.

1985 Retired on his debut for Williams in Brazil, but soon became a regular points scorer, with 5th in Portugal and San Marino, 6th in Canada, Germany and Holland. He took 2nd in the Belgian and then a crowd-pleasing maiden victory in the European Grand Prix at Brands Hatch. His first pole position came in South Africa, with win number two, to secure 6th in the World Championship. He finished 6th in the Donington Park Rallysprint.

1986 He began the year as a title contender with Williams, but retired from the Brazilian opener after a first lap clash with Senna. 2nd in the Spanish was followed by 4th at Monaco, before the first win of the season in Belgium. Pole and a victory followed in Canada, and after 5th at Detroit he was the victor in the French, British and Portuguese, with 2nd in Italy, 3rd in Germany and Hungary and 5th in Mexico and Detroit. The title slipped from his grasp in Australia when a tyre exploded, losing out to Prost by two points.

1987 Took eight pole positions along with victories at the San Marino Grand Prix, the French, British, Austrian, Spanish and Mexican races. He added 3rd in the Italian, 5th in the US Detroit and 6th in Brazil, but still lost out in the title race to Williams team mate Piquet. He missed the last two races of the year after injuring his back during qualifying in Japan.

1988 A Change from Honda turbo power to a Judd V8 brought 12 retirements and only two classified finishes, albeit 2nd in both the British and Spanish Grands Prix.

1989 A move to Ferrari started with a dream debut of victory in the Brazilian Grand Prix. Four consecutive retirements and disqualification in Canada followed before the points began to flow again. He was on the podium for the next five Grands Prix, with 2nd in the Canadian and British, 3rd in the German and Belgian and a victory in Hungary to secure 4th in the championship.

1990 Another up and down season with Ferrari brought his first threat of retirement. He had a win in Portugal, 2nd in Mexico, Spain and Australia, 3rd in Canada and 4th in Brazil and Italy to finish 4th in the championship, before bidding farewell to Maranello.

1991 A return to Williams now with Renault power started with three retirements. From there on he dominated the championship, with wins in the French, British, German, Italian and Spanish races, 2nd at Monaco, the Mexican, Hungarian and Australian and 6th in Canada, but was still pipped to the title by Senna.

1992 Pole position in all but two of the Grands Prix and a dream start of successive wins in South Africa, Mexico, Brazil, Spain and San Marino showed the domination of the Williams Renault. Ignoring his four retirements, he never finished lower than 2nd, with further victories in the French, British, German and Portuguese to become World Champion.

1993 Turned his back on Grand Prix racing and took the Indycar world by storm, winning the title in a Newman-Haas Lola. He took six pole positions, and won at Surfers Paradise, Milwaukee, Michigan, New Hampshire and Nazareth. He added 2nd at Portland and Road America, 3rd at Long Beach and Cleveland, 6th at Vancouver, 12th at Mid-Ohio and had accidents at Phoenix, Detroit and Laguna Seca. He also took 3rd in the Indy 500. He returned victorious to the Donington Park Touring Car Shoot-Out, where he was hospitalised after crashing his Ford Mondeo into Starkeys Bridge.

1994 He defended his Indycar title with less success, finishing 2nd at Long Beach and Cleveland. He was 3rd at Phoenix, 5th at Milwaukee and Portland, 7th at Mid-Ohio, 8th at Laguna Seca, 9th at Surfers Paradise, 10th at Vancouver, 13th at Elkhart Lake, crashed in the Indy 500 and finished 8th in the championship. He turned out for Williams in four Grands Prix following Senna's death. He qualified 2nd in the French and 3rd in the European at Jerez, retiring on each occasion, before taking 4th in Japan and both pole and the victory in Australia.

1995 He signed for McLaren for the Grand Prix season, before the on-off saga of whether he could fit in the car. He made his first appearance in San Marino and struggled home 10th, before surrendering at the Spanish and handing the car back to Blundell.

1996 Tested for Jordan and began rumours of a comeback.

1997 Contested the Chamonix Ice races with Vatanen in an Escort Cosworth.

1998 Had occasional outings in the British Touring Car Championship with a Ford Mondeo, Retiring and taking 5th at Donington Park, after leading for a while in the pouring rain. He retired in both races at Brands Hatch, and finally took 14th and 11th at Silverstone in the final races of a remarkable career.

❖

TIFF NEEDELL
Born October 29th 1951

Tiff Needell.

Photo: BRDC Archive.

A Formula Ford Lotus won in an Autosport Competition launched his career in 1971. He soon showed promise and graduated through FF2000, F3, Aurora British F1 and F2 to a solitary Grand Prix start with Ensign in 1980. From there on he has raced in almost every category around the world, achieving considerable success and proving himself a highly versatile racer who has sampled just about every branch of the sport. But he is now best known as a successful TV presenter, which started with a chance visit to the commentary box at Brands Hatch.

GRAND PRIX RECORD	
Starts	1
Wins	0
Poles	0
Fastest laps	0
WC points	0
Best finish	DNF

1971 Had 25 races in Formula Ford with his Lotus 69, despite a few weeks out after a huge crash. Among his best results were a 3rd and 4th at Mallory Park.

1972 Continued to race his Formula Ford Lotus, taking a victory at Thruxton, 2nd, two 3rds and a 9th at Brands Hatch, 2nd at Cadwell Park and Mondello Park, and 3rd and 5th at Castle Combe.

1973 His Lotus was finally pensioned off after 82 races and three wins, to be replaced with an Elden. He had a win at Cadwell Park, 2nd and two 3rds at Mallory Park, three 3rds, a 4th and a 5th at Brands Hatch, 4th at Thruxton, and 5th and 6th at Oulton Park.

1974 Finished 2nd in the BARC Wella Formula Ford Championship with his Elden. Results included a win at Llandow, a win, 2nd and three 3rds at Thruxton, 2nd at Mallory Park, 3rd at Oulton Park, 2nd at Cadwell Park, two 3rds and a 4th at Brands Hatch. He also finished 8th in the Snetterton Formula Ford Festival.

1975 Starting the year in a works Elden, he changed to a Crossle 25F and had an immediate change in fortunes. He won the Townsend Thoresen Brands Hatch Formula Ford Championship and was 5th in the Brush Fusegear series with 12 wins. Seven victories came at Brands Hatch, two at Silverstone, and one each at Mallory Park, Oulton Park and Thruxton. An end of year change to FF2000 brought him 4th in the Allied Polymer Group Championship in a Hawke, with four wins from five starts. He also took a Christmas victory at Brands Hatch and earned a Grovewood Commendation.

1976 Finished runner-up in the APG FF2000 Championship in his Hawke DL14, with five wins, seven 2nds and 10 pole positions, winning at Brands Hatch, Oulton Park, Cadwell and Silverstone. Occasional trips into Europe brought him a win and 3rd at Zandvoort, plus 2nd at Hockenheim. He also debuted in F3 at Oulton Park with a Safir, finishing 4th, and followed up with 2nd and 6th at Thruxton and 5th and 6th at Brands Hatch, to finish 7th in the BP Championship and earn the Premier Grovewood Award.

1977 Moved into F3 with a Unipart March 773, finishing 9th in the BP Championship and 11th in the Vandervell series. He was 2nd at Thruxton, 4th at Snetterton and 4th and 6th at Silverstone. He also finished 10th in the European F3 round at Donington Park and made his F2 debut at the same circuit, as a last minute stand in for Fred Opert's team, taking 10th in a Chevron.

1978 Another year in F3 netted 4th in the BP Championship and 6th in the Vandervell series. He had a 2nd at Cadwell Park, 2nd at Thruxton, 4th at Oulton Park, 4th and two 5ths at Brands Hatch, 4th at Silverstone and 5th at Donington Park. He came close to a maiden F3 win in the Austrian Grand Prix support race and also took 11th at Dijon and 14th in Donington Park's Euro round. A late season F2 outing in a Toleman March 782 at Hockenheim ended in retirement.

1979 His Grand Prix aspirations with Ensign were quashed by licence problems, but he did get to race the F1 Durex Chevron B41 in the Aurora Championship. He finished 10th overall in the championship after taking 2nd at Zolder, 6th at Mallory Park and Silverstone and 8th at Zandvoort. A one-off race with an Ensign ended in retirement at Nogaro. He got another F2 outing at Donington Park, taking the Toleman March 782 to 8th. He went to Suzuka and finished 4th in F2 with a March 792, shared Stuart Graham's Capri to 4th at the TT, finished 11th in the BMW Procar race at Silverstone and raced a March 76B in the Atlantic races at Macau and Selangor. He also became a regular in the BMW County Championship, taking 3rd at Oulton Park, 4th at Castle Combe and Thruxton and 5th at Brands Hatch.

1980 Finally got his Grand Prix chance with Ensign, retiring on his debut in the Belgian and failing to qualify at Monaco before losing the drive. A couple of trips to Suzuka brought 4th and retirement in a March 792 and 782. He shared the Ibec in the Silverstone 6 hours and a Rover at the TT, retiring from both. He finished 2nd from pole with a March 79B at Selangor and finished 3rd at Silverstone, 5th at Castle Combe and at 6th Thruxton in the BMW County Championship.

1981 He deputised for Richard Dallest at Donington Park in the F2 AGS and finished 11th. He shared the Ibec at Silverstone and Le Mans, retiring from both, and took 3rd in the Kyalami 2 hours sharing a Mazda Capella.

1982 Raced the works Aston Martin Nimrod at Le Mans and crashed at 210mph after a puncture, and retired again at Spa. A one-off F3 return at Silverstone brought 11th in an Anson, he was 10th at the Macau GP in a Ralt RT4 and contested the Willhire 24 hours at Snetterton in an Opel Monza, with Steve Soper, John Cleland and Tony Lanfranchi.

1983 Finished 3rd in the Willhire 24 hours sharing Colin Blower's Porsche 911SC. He was 14th at Macau in a Ralt RT3, 17th at Le Mans in the EMKA Aston Martin and 6th in the Monza 1000km with Lammers and Lloyd in the Canon Porsche 956. He also drove a Fittipaldi F1 in the British Open, a March 83G in IMSA and a Dome at the Fuji 1000.

1984 Drove a Ralt Honda to 6th and 8th at Suzuka in the All Japan F2 Series, took 9th at Le Mans in a Porsche 956, and shared Richard Piper's Chevron B26/36 in Thundersports to two 2nd places at Brands Hatch and one at Thruxton. He also raced a Dome in Japanese Endurance races and shared Blower's Mitsubishi Starion to 13th in the Willhire 24 hours.

1985 He went to India with a Chevron B42 and won the Bangalore Grand Prix, but retired from both legs in Madras. He finished 3rd, 5th and 10th at Fuji in the Japanese Endurance Series, sharing a Dome with Weaver, and had a Thundersports win with Piper's Chevron B36 at Brands Hatch. He shared Blower's Mitsubishi Starion to 18th in the Willhire 24 hours, and drove the Aston Martin powered EMKA and Cheetah in the World Endurance Series without recording a finish.

1986 Further Thundersports outings with Piper's Chevron B36 brought 2nd and 3rd at Brands Hatch. He shared a Porsche 962C with Jo Gartner to 3rd in the Silverstone 1000km and shared a March 84G with Costas Los to 9th in the Brands Hatch Shell 1000 and at Jerez, and 10th at Spa. He was 5th in the Southern Sun 500 at Kyalami in a Lamborghini Countach, won a Production Porsche race at Donington Park, shared Blower's Starion to 22nd in the Willhire 24 hours, and was 5th in the Saab Challenge.

1987 Shared Piper's March 847 in Thundersports to victory at Thruxton, and finished 4th in class in the British Touring Car Championship with a Toyota Corolla, after taking 4th in class at the British Grand Prix meeting and 3rd at Oulton Park. Another year in the Saab Challenge brought 3rd overall with a win and 2nd at Oulton Park, two wins at Donington Park, a win and 3rd at Thruxton, 2nd at Mallory Park and Snetterton and 4th at Silverstone. He retired a Toyota at Le Mans and the ADA at the Brands Hatch 1000km, shared Blower's Starion to retirement in the Willhire in the Snetterton 24 hours and 2nd at Brands Hatch, and finished 2nd at Snetterton with Bill Taylor's Porsche Carrera RS.

1988 Finished 5th at Suzuka, 10th at Fuji and 24th at Le Mans in a Toyota and took a class win in the TT with Dowsett in a Corolla. He also contested the Porsche Challenge in a 944 and finished 4th in his class, after a win and 2nd at Oulton Park, wins at Brands Hatch,

Zandvoort and Silverstone, with 3rd and 4th at Snetterton.

1989 He won the British Touring Car Enduro at Donington Park sharing Laurence Bristow's Sierra, and shared a Porsche 962 GTi in World Sports Cars, taking 2nd in the Silverstone Supercup, 4th in Mexico City, 5th at Dijon, 11th at Donington Park, 15th at the Nurburgring and 19th in Suzuka.

1990 Finished 3rd at Le Mans in a Porsche 962 with David Sears and Anthony Reid. He also shared a 962 in the World Sports Car Championship to 8th at Fuji and Monza, and in the Japanese Championship to 5th and 10th at Fuji and 8th at Suzuka.

1991 Had a 7th and 8th at Fuji in the Japanese Endurance Championship, sharing a 962 with Reid and retired a similar car at both Daytona and Le Mans. He also contested the Intercontinental Jaguar Challenge, taking 6th at Silverstone and 7th at Monaco.

1992 Finished 7th in his class with a Ford Sapphire Cosworth on the RAC Rally, took 10th in the British Touring Car finale at Silverstone in a Nissan Primera and had a 2nd at Castle Combe in an RML GT40 replica. At Le Mans he shared a Porsche 962 with Derek and Justin Bell to 12th place.

1993 Made occasional appearances in the British Touring Car Championship with an Ecurie Ecosse Vauxhall Cavalier and a works Nissan Primera. He finished 10th at Brands Hatch, 12th at the British Grand Prix meeting, 12th at Oulton Park, 12th and 13th at Knockhill and 19th at Pembrey. He was 6th in the TOCA Shoot-Out with a Cavalier, and shared Andy Middlehurst's Nissan Sunny GTi to 3rd in class in Donington Park's Production Saloon Enduro.

1994 Raced for Nissan in the British Touring Car Championship, taking 9th, 17th and 18th at Brands Hatch, 10th and 16th at Knockhill, 13th and 17th at Oulton Park, 14th, 15th and 18th at Silverstone, 15th twice at Donington and 12th in the TOCA Shoot-Out. He also went to Kyalami to finish 3rd in the International Challenge with a Nissan Sentra.

1995 Drove a Lister Storm and a Jaguar XJ220 in sports car racing, retiring at Daytona and Le Mans. He also took 6th at Donington Park in the Maserati Ghibli Cup.

1996 Shared a Lister Storm at Daytona until the car was destroyed in an accident, finished 19th at Le Mans and retired at Suzuka, Spa and Brands Hatch. He also had a 3rd place driving an Ascari in the British GT at Silverstone, and 4th in a TVR Tuscan race at Croft.

1997 Apart from a few one-off drives it was a quiet year.

1998 Finished 5th in the British GT1 Championship sharing a Lister Storm with Julian Bailey, after wins at

Snetterton and Silverstone, 2nd at Silverstone, 3rd at Oulton Park and 4th at Donington Park. He also drove a Nissan Primera at Brands Hatch in British Touring Cars, finishing 12th and 15th, and took 6th in the inaugural MGF race at Silverstone.

1999 Shared the Lister Storm with Bailey and Verdon-Roe in FIA GT rounds at Monza and Silverstone, retiring from both after showing the car's potential.

❖

JONATHAN PALMER
Born November 7th 1956

Jonathan Palmer in May 1984.
Photo: BRDC Archive.

With an early racing career restricted while he qualified as a doctor, it was during his seventh season of racing in 1981 that it really began to take off. Although previously a podium finisher in Formula Ford, his domination of the British F3 Championship led to F2, where he won the European Championship, and a Grand Prix debut with Williams in the 1983 European Grand Prix at Brands Hatch. He went on to drive for RAM, Zakspeed and Tyrrell in Grands Prix, as well as carving out a successful sports car career. His best Grand Prix result was fourth in the 1987 Australian race.

After racing a BMW in the 1991 British Touring Car Championship, he retired from racing and joined the BBC Grand Prix commentary team. In 1998 he realised another dream with the launch of his Formula Palmer Audi single-seater category in Britain.

1975 Had six races in a self prepared Austin Healey Sprite that he shared with David Mercer, and took three class wins, a 2nd and 3rd racing mainly at Brands Hatch.

1976 Won his class in the BARC Modsports Championships with a Marcos. He took a debut win with the car at Thruxton and another four wins included Llandow and Castle Combe, 2nd and 3rd at Mallory Park and 3rd at Brands Hatch.

1977 Won his class again with the Marcos in the STS Modsports Championships and finished second overall, with four wins at Brands Hatch and one each at Thruxton, Mallory Park and Donington Park. He added class wins at Silverstone, Cadwell Park, Brands Hatch and Mallory Park and took 2nd in class at Snetterton.

1978 Moved into Formula Ford with a Hawke DL20, becoming a works driver from mid-season. He finished 12th in a Silverstone consolation race on his debut, had a further 3rd, 5th and 6th at Thruxton, two 5ths and a 6th at Mallory Park, 3rd at Donington Park, 4th at Silverstone, 6th at Brands Hatch and a non-championship win at Brands Hatch. He also finished 9th overall in the Phillips BARC Championship.

1979 Another season in Formula Ford with a Van Diemen RF79, finishing 3rd overall in the Townsend Thoresen and P&O Ferries Championships. He had wins at Snetterton, Mallory Park and Cadwell Park, despite missing some later races after breaking his arm at Oulton Park.

1980 Began the year with a works Royale RP26 in Formula Ford, until he lost the drive mid-season and changed to a West Surrey Racing Van Diemen RF80. He finished 3rd in the Townsend Thoresen and 4th in the P&O Ferries Championships, with wins at Snetterton (twice) and Thruxton. He was also 4th in the Formula Ford Festival and came third in the Grovewood Awards.

1981 Won the British F3 Championship in a WSR Ralt RT3 (Johansson's championship winning car from 1980). The season started with consecutive wins at Silverstone, Thruxton, Silverstone again and Mallory Park. Those

GRAND PRIX RECORD

Starts	83
Wins	0
Poles	0
Fastest laps	1
WC points	14
Best finish	4th

were followed by further victories at Cadwell Park, Silverstone, Oulton Park and Snetterton. He turned down the chance of a British Grand Prix drive in a March 811, but did finish 7th with a class win sharing Richard Lloyd's Audi 80 in the TT.

1982 Moved up to F2 and finished 9th in the championship in a works Ralt Honda, taking 3rd at Donington Park, 5th at Mugello and Vallelunga, 6th at Pau and Spa, 11th at Thruxton, 14th at the Nurburgring and 15th at Thruxton, but was hospitalised after rolling at Mantorp Park. He had two F2 outings at Suzuka finishing 3rd and 8th and joined the Williams Grand Prix team as test driver. In sports cars he shared a Ford C100 with Desiree Wilson to 4th in the Shell 1000km at Brands Hatch, and Lloyd's Porsche 924 Carrera to a class win and 15th overall in the Spa 1000km and retirement at Monza.

1983 Won the F2 Championship with a Ralt Honda, only missing the podium on two occasions. He won at Hockenheim, Donington Park, Misano, Enna, Zolder and Mugello, with 2nd at Vallelunga, 3rd at Thruxton, Pau and Jarama and 4th at the Nurburgring. Having spent a further year as the Williams test driver, he was rewarded with his Grand debut in the European at Brands Hatch, finishing 13th. He also had a successful year in sports cars with 3rd at Mugello and in the Nurburgring 1000km, 4th in the Imola 1000km, 5th at Kyalami, 8th at Le Mans, 9th at the Brands Hatch 1000km and 18th in the Daytona 24 hours, driving Canon Porsches. Sharing a BMW 635 CSi with Weaver he was 2nd in the TT, and drove the same car to 5th in the final round of the British Touring Car Championship. He took Peter Millward's Lola Aston Martin to an Historic GT win at Silverstone, and had end of season tests in an ATS Grand Prix car and a March 84C Indycar.

1984 Spent his first full Grand Prix season with the RAM Skoal Bandit team, where despite never qualifying in the top 20, he managed to bring the uncompetitive car home 8th in the Brazilian and 9th in the San Marino, Austrian and Dutch. He continued to race a Canon Porsche 956 with Lammers, to finish 6th in the World Endurance Championship, winning at Brands Hatch, with 2nd at Imola, 3rd at Monza and Sandown, 4th at the Nurburgring, 5th at Silverstone and 9th at Fuji. He also raced solo at the Norisring and finished 2nd. He was 7th in the Atlantic Computer Leasing Historic GT Championship with the Lola Aston, and finished 3rd at Brands Hatch in a one-off European Renault 5 Elf Turbo Cup outing.

1985 Began the Grand Prix year without a drive, but joined Zakspeed from the Portuguese. From eight attempts he only made the finish on one occasion, 11th in Monaco. At Le Mans he finished 2nd with Weaver and Lloyd in the Canon Porsche 956, with 5th at Monza, Silverstone and Hockenheim to finish 12th in the Endurance Championship. He also won a Renault 5 Elf Turbo UK Cup race at Thruxton and had further outings in the Lola Aston and an Arundel Ford.

1986 Continued with Zakspeed with little reward. He was classified as a finisher on seven occasions with 8th at Detroit, 9th at the British and Australian, 10th in Hungary and Mexico and 12th in Portugal and Monaco.

1987 Moved to Tyrrell but his normally aspirated car was no match for the turbo cars. He won the Jim Clark Trophy for non-turbocharged cars, but still managed to collect World Championship points from 5th in Monaco and Germany, and a career best 4th in the Australian finale. He had seven further top 10 finishes and only retired on two occasions. A return to sports cars saw him paired with Baldi in a Brun-entered Porsche 962, winning at the Norisring.

1988 A further year with the normally-aspirated Tyrrell brought 5th in Monaco and Detroit and 6th in Canada, with the low point being at the Italian where he failed to qualify. He also shared a Ford Sierra Cosworth with Guy Edwards, to 6th in the TT.

1989 A final year with Tyrrell started with 7th in the Brazilian Grand Prix, 6th in San Marino and 9th in Monaco, before the results took a dive. Apart from 6th in Portugal it became a struggle to break into the top 10.

1990 Became test driver for the McLaren Grand Prix team, and raced in sports cars with a Joest Porsche 962C, taking 5th in Mexico City, 8th at Dijon, Monza and Montreal, 10th at Donington Park and 11th at Fuji.

1991 His last season of racing was spent with a Prodrive BMW M3 in the British Touring Car Championship, finishing 7th overall. He had a 2nd and 6th at Thruxton, 3rd and 4th at Donington Park, 5th at Oulton Park, 5th and 7th, at Silverstone, two 6ths and a 7th at Brands Hatch and 7th at Snetterton. He also shared a Porsche 962 with Lammers at Sugo in the Japanese Championship, finishing 8th.

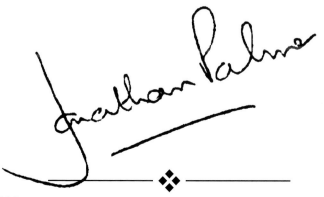

DEREK WARWICK
Born August 27th 1954

Derek Warwick.

Photo: BRDC Archive.

A quick acclimatisation from World Championship Stock Cars, brought him to the forefront of Formula Ford racing within a year. Warwick was a Champion in Formula Ford and F3 before moving into F2 with Toleman to finish as runner-up to team mate Brian Henton in 1980. After a year's perseverance and a list of non-qualifications, he made his Grand Prix debut at Las Vegas in 1981. He later moved on to drive for Renault, Brabham, Arrows/Footwork and Lotus.

He won Le Mans and the Sports Car World Championship with Peugeot in 1992 during a tremendous spell in sports cars, but was never able to claim an elusive Grand Prix victory. His final years of racing were spent in Touring Cars, where his determination often outweighed his competitiveness, but did bring a race win at Knockhill with Vauxhall. However, his racing was tinged with great sadness when his younger brother Paul was killed in a Formula 3000 race at Oulton Park. It was an awful blow to Derek, who later turned his energies to the subject of circuit safety. He also developed a team management role with the Triple 8 touring car team.

1971 British Champion in Stock Cars.

1972 English Superstocks Champion.

1973 World Champion in Superstox.

1974 3rd in World Superstox.

1975 Made his Formula Ford debut at Thruxton in a Hawke DL12 and finished 2nd in the Christmas race at Brands Hatch, he also took a 4th at Silverstone, 5th at Mallory Park and Brands Hatch and 6th at Castle Combe and Silverstone.

1976 Drove a works Formula Ford Hawke to 31 wins, 18 2nds, 7 3rds, 27 fastest laps, 28 poles and only 3 retirements from 63 starts. He was the European Champion, came 2nd in the DJM and RAC Series, 3rd in the Brush Fusegear, 5th in the Townsend Thoresen and 8th in the TEAC Championship. He also finished 2nd in the Formula Ford Festival and 3rd in the Grovewood Awards.

1977 Moved into F3 with a Chevron B38 and later a Ralt RT1. He was 3rd in the Vandervell Championship and 4th in the BP series. Results included two 2nds at Thruxton, 2nd, 3rd and 5th at Brands Hatch, 2nd, 5th and 6th at Donington Park, 2nd and 4th at Silverstone, 2nd at Oulton Park and Mallory Park, 4th at Cadwell Park and 6th at Zolder.

1978 Won the Vandervell F3 Championship and came 2nd in the BP Series to Nelson Piquet. He won at Brands Hatch, Donington Park (twice), Thruxton (twice), Silverstone and Mallory Park. He was also 6th in the European Championship after a win at Donington Park and 3rd at Jarama, won the Thruxton TV race and made his F2 debut at Suzuka with 6th place in a Theodore Racing March 782.

1979 Moved into F2 with a BP-backed March 792, and took 5th at Mugello, 9th at Pau, 10th at Donington Park and 11th at Vallelunga. He also took part in non-clashing Aurora AFX rounds and finished 2nd at Mallory Park and 13th at Thruxton, along with a 6th place in the BMW County Championship at Thruxton.

1980 Joined the Toleman F2 team and took seven podium finishes from 11 starts, to finish runner-up behind team mate Henton in the championship. He had wins at

GRAND PRIX RECORD	
Starts	147
Wins	0
Poles	0
Fastest laps	2
WC points	71
Best finish	2nd

Silverstone and the non-championship Monza race, 2nd at Thruxton, Mugello and Zandvoort and 3rd at the Nurburgring, Vallelunga and Misano.

1981 Moved into Grand Prix racing with Toleman, failing to qualify on his debut at San Marino and at every other Grand Prix until the final round at Las Vegas, where he qualified 22nd and retired with a broken gearbox.

1982 Stayed with Toleman and failed to qualify again for three of the first six Grands Prix. His first classified finish came with 15th in the French and was followed by 10th at the German and another string of retirements, but he did record the fastest lap during the Dutch race.

1983 A third and final year with Toleman began with 8th in Brazil, but from his next 10 starts he recorded only 7th in Belgium. The tide suddenly turned and his first World Championship points were claimed with 4th in the Dutch, followed by 6th in the Italian, 5th in the Brands Hatch European GP and 4th in the South African. He also began to race in sports cars, winning the Brands Hatch 1000km with Fitzpatrick in a Porsche 956, but retired at both Le Mans and Spa. He was also 8th in the Donington Park Rallysprint.

1984 Joined Renault and qualified 3rd in the Brazilian Grand Prix on his debut for the team, before retiring from the race lead when his suspension broke. In South Africa he was 3rd, with 2nd in Belgium and 4th at San Marino, before another string of five retirements. Form and reliability later returned to collect 2nd in the British and

3rd in the German to finish 7th in the World Championship.

1985 After rejecting an offer from Williams he stayed with Renault for a second year. He recorded points finishes with 5th at Monaco and in the British Grand Prix and 6th in the Belgian, followed by 7th in the Portuguese and French and 10th in Brazil and San Marino.

1986 With Renault pulling out and Senna blocking a move to Lotus, he was out of a Grand Prix drive until Brabham signed him following De Angelis' death. From 10 starts he finished 7th in the German Grand Prix, 8th in the British, 9th in the French and 10th in the US Detroit. In sports cars he was 3rd in the Daytona 24 hours in a Porsche 962 and after joining Jaguar he won the Silverstone 1000km. He added 2nd at Spa, 3rd at the Norisring, Fuji and Jerez and 4th in the Shell Gemini 1000 at Brands Hatch in an XJR6, to finish 3rd in the World Championship. He also finished 6th in the Brands Hatch Rallysprint.

1987 Joined Arrows for the Grand Prix season, finishing 5th in the British, 6th in the Hungarian, 10th in the Spanish and Japanese, 11th in San Marino and 13th in the Portuguese.

1988 Another year with Arrows brought a regular flow of points finishes, with 4th in Brazil, Monaco, Italy and Portugal, 5th in Mexico and Belgium and 6th in the British. He also finished 7th in Canada and Germany and 9th in San Marino to finish 7th in the World Championship.

Derek Warwick (Renault RE60) in 1985.

Photo: BRDC Archive.

1989 A third year with Arrows started with 5th place in both the Brazilian and San Marino Grands Prix, further points came from 6th in Germany, Belgium and Japan, and he also took 9th in the British and Spanish and 10th in the Hungarian.

1990 Moved on to the Camel Lotus Grand Prix team and finished in the points with 5th in Hungary and 6th in Canada, along with 7th at San Marino, 8th in Germany, 10th in Mexico and 11th in France and Belgium. He failed to record a finish in any of the last five races, but hit the headlines with a huge crash at the Parabolica during the Italian Grand Prix. He crawled out of his wrecked car to sprint back to the pits for the restart. He also raced in the Honda CRX Challenge at Donington Park finishing 5th, and drove a works Subaru on the RAC Rally, retiring on the 25th stage after leaving the road in Kielder Forest when in contention for a top 10 finish.

1991 Raced a TWR Jaguar in the World Sports Championship, winning at Monza with Brundle, Silverstone with Fabi and the Nurburgring with Brabham. He added 2nd at Autopolis, 4th at Le Mans, 5th at Magny Cours and 6th in Mexico City, to secure 2nd in the Championship. He also won the Monaco round of the Jaguar Intercontinental Challenge.

1992 Joined Peugeot for a World Sports Car campaign, winning the Le Mans 24 hours and sharing the title with Dalmas. He won at Silverstone and Suzuka, with 2nd at Donington Park and Monza and 5th at Magny Cours.

1993 Made a Grand Prix return with Footwork, collecting 4th in Hungary, 6th in the British, 7th in the South African, 9th in the Brazilian and 10th in the Australian in his final Grand Prix. He also contested the TOCA Touring Car Shoot-Out at Donington Park in a Toyota Carina.

1995 Raced for Alfa Romeo in the British Touring Car Championship, taking 8th places at Brands Hatch (twice), Silverstone and Oulton Park.

1996 Finished 13th at Le Mans sharing a Courage-Porsche with Lammers and Mario Andretti.

1997 Raced a Triple Eight-entered Vauxhall Vectra in the British Touring Car Championship, and finished 14th overall. Best results were 5th places at Silverstone and Oulton Park. He also shared a Vectra with Peter Brock to 6th at Bathurst.

1998 A second year racing the Vectra brought a victory at Knockhill, 3rd at Donington Park, 4th at Silverstone and 5th at Thruxton and Oulton Park, to finish 9th in the championship. At Bathurst he shared a Vectra with John Cleland to 5th place.

❖

50 years of British Grand Prix drivers

Part Five
1990s

CHAPTER 13

MARK BLUNDELL
Born April 8th 1966

After competing on motorbikes as a teenager, Blundell made a successful start in FF1600 and FF2000. That led to a jump straight into F3000 for the 1987 season, taking a magnificent second at Spa. When commitments allowed he stepped back for the occasional F3 foray, but tended to concentrate on F3000 until the end of 1989, never managing to improve on that earlier second place. Having been part of the Nissan sports car team in 1989, he resigned for the team the following year and became the Williams Grand Prix test driver.

After making his Grand Prix debut with Brabham in 1991, his Grand Prix career became very on-off, driving for Ligier, Tyrrell and McLaren and collecting three podium finishes. His first third place was for Ligier in the 1993 South African race. His sports car career was highlighted by victory at Le Mans with

Peugeot in 1992, but after continuing to battle for a Grand Prix seat, he joined the PacWest Indy Car team for the 1996 season. He collected three wins in his second year and, despite a couple of major accidents, continues to race for the team.

1984 Began racing in Formula Ford with a Lola T644E before changing to a Van Diemen RF84. His maiden win came at Snetterton, but he went on to take victory in 25 of his 70 races, ten at Snetterton, four at Oulton Park, three at Mallory Park, two at Brands Hatch, and one each at Lydden, Silverstone and Cadwell Park. He won the Champion of Snetterton title, and was runner-up in both the Dunlop Star of Tomorrow and BP Superfind Championships and earned a Grovewood Award. He also took 3rd in the BARC P&O series and 8th in the RAC. At the end of the year he made his FF2000 debut with 8th in the World Cup race at Brands Hatch in a Van Diemen RF84, and contested the BBC Grandstand Trophy taking 9th at Brands Hatch and two 10ths at Thruxton before changing to a Reynard for 10th in the Brands Hatch finale.

1985 Another year concentrating on FF1600 brought the Esso title and runner-up spot in the RAC Championship, with a Van Diemen RF85. He had three wins, two 3rds, 4th and 6th at Silverstone, three wins, 2nd and 4th at Brands Hatch, a win and 2nd at Donington Park, two wins and 2nd at Oulton Park, 3rd at Thruxton and 6th at Snetterton. He was 4th in a Euro round at Brands Hatch and 4th in the Formula Ford Festival, before

Mark Blundell in a Formula 3000 Reynard at Brands in August 1989.
Photo: Peter Scherer.

```
GRAND PRIX RECORD

Starts           61
Wins             0
Poles            0
Fastest laps     0
WC points        32
Best finish      3rd
```

contesting the BBC Grandstand Trophy FF2000 again in an Anglo European Reynard 84SF. He had two wins, a 2nd, 3rd and 4th at Brands Hatch to win the title.

1986 A full year in FF2000 with a Reynard 86SF saw him crowned as the EFDA European Champion and runner-up in the British based championship. In Europe he won at Zolder, Zeltweg and Zandvoort, with 2nd at Hockenheim, 3rd at Jyllandsringen and Mondello Park and a further 3rd and 4th at Zolder. His home wins were at Cadwell Park (twice), Oulton Park, Brands Hatch and Donington Park, with two 2nds and 4th at Brands Hatch, 2nd at Snetterton, 2nd and 5th at Thruxton, 2nd at Silverstone and 6th at Oulton Park.

1987 Made a huge jump straight into F3000, taking 6th in the second round at Vallelunga before going to Spa to finish an excellent 2nd. He went on to take 9th at Donington Park and Enna, 6th at Brands Hatch, but failed to qualify at Birmingham. His season ended with 6th at Jarama, and his occasional runs in F3 netted 2nd and 8th at Donington Park, 7th at Oulton Park and 10th at Silverstone.

1988 Finished 5th in the F3000 Championship with a works Lola, having started well with 2nd in the season opener at Jerez. He also took 2nd at Zolder, 3rd at Brands Hatch, 5th at Vallelunga, 7th at Le Mans and 9th at Silverstone.

1989 Another year in F3000 with Middlebridge brought only four finishes, but all in the points with 3rd at Silverstone, 5th at Birmingham and 6th at Pau and Le Mans. He also finished 9th in the World Sports Car Championship with Nissan, after 3rd at Donington Park and Spa, 8th at Jarama, 12th in Mexico City and 15th at Dijon with Bailey.

1990 Having joined Williams Grand Prix as a test driver, most of his racing was restricted to the Nissan sports car team. He finished 10th in the championship after taking 2nd in Montreal and Mexico City, 3rd at Dijon, 5th at the Nurburgring, 6th at Donington Park and 10th at Spa, sharing with Bailey again.

1991 Joined the Brabham Grand Prix team with Brundle and began his campaign with retirement in Phoenix and Brazil. After taking 8th at San Marino he posted four further retirements and a non-qualification in

Monaco, before coming home 12th in the German. Apart from scoring his first World Championship point with 6th in Belgium, the rest of the year became more and more of a struggle, failing to even pre-qualify in Japan.

1992 Rather than chase an uncompetitive drive, he joined McLaren as test driver, but went to Le Mans as part of the works Peugeot team and won with Derek Warwick and Yannick Dalmas.

1993 Teamed up with Brundle again in the Ligier Grand Prix team, and started the year in great form with 3rd in South Africa and 5th in Brazil. He was 3rd again in Germany, with 7th in the Spanish, British, Hungarian and Japanese, and 9th in Australia. Eight retirements, all either spins or accidents prevented him finishing higher than 10th in the final World Championship standings.

1994 Moved to Tyrrell for the season's Grand Prix racing and accumulated points from 3rd in the Spanish and 5th in the Belgian and Hungarian. He had three further finishes just inside the top ten, but overall it was a disappointing year, with only a 13th place in Japan to show for his last five outings.

1995 The season began as test driver with McLaren again, before waiting patiently in the wings for Mansell's decision on whether to drive or not to drive. In the Brazilian Grand Prix he qualified 9th and finished 6th, but after retiring in Argentina he was back on the sidelines as Mansell took over for San Marino and the Spanish. In Monaco he was back in the cockpit for good finishing 5th, with further points from 4th in Australia and Italy, and 5th at the British and Belgian to secure 10th in the final World Championship standings. He also raced a McLaren at Le Mans and finished 4th with Ray Bellm and Maurizio Sandro-Sala.

1996 Having turned his back on the Grand Prix scene he headed for the US Indycar Championship to race a PacWest Reynard 961. After finishing 17th on his debut at Homestead, he crashed at 195mph during practice in Rio and was out of action for two months with a broken foot. He returned with 5th at Michigan and Detroit, 8th at Portland, 11th at Cleveland and Toronto, 6th at Michigan, 10th at Mid-Ohio and 12th at Vancouver.

1997 His year in a PacWest Reynard brought 6th overall in the championship, with a maiden victory at Portland in the closest finish in the championship's history. He also won at Toronto and Fontana, with 2nd at Michigan and Laguna Seca, 7th at Vancouver, 8th at Rio and Surfers Paradise, 9th at Cleveland and 13th at Long Beach.

1998 Continuing with PacWest he had a disappointing year, finishing only 17th in the final standings. He finished 6th at Fontana, 7th at Long Beach and Elkhart Lake, 10th at Gateway, Motegi and Cleveland, 11th at Surfers Paradise and Rio, 12th at Homestead, Vancouver and Milwaukee, 14th at Houston and 17th at Michigan, and was hospitalised for a while after hitting the wall at Nazareth.

1999 His fourth year with a PacWest Reynard began with 8th at Homestead, retirement at Motegi, 13th at Long Beach and 17th at Nazareth, before a 170mph crash practicing at Gateway. After several months out of racing with neck injuries, he returned with 10th at Detroit and 13th in Mid-Ohio, before posting a string of retirements.

DAVID COULTHARD
Born March 27th 1971

It was obvious from the start that this multiple kart champion was aiming for the top, proving virtually unbeatable in his first season in cars in 1989. He won both Junior Formula Ford Championships and was snapped up by Paul Stewart for the following year. However a broken leg put paid to his title hopes in both the British and European Formula Vauxhall Championship. He stepped up with the team to Formula 3 and was runner-up to Rubens Barrichello in the 1991 British Championship, but did win the prestigious Marlboro Masters and Macau Grand Prix. He stayed with Stewart's for his first year in F3000, although he had one podium finish, overall it was a disappointing year.

In 1993 he was in line for the F3000 title, but lost out to Panis and Lamy at the final stage. He had started another year in the formula when Senna's death launched his Grand Prix career. His maturity under enormous pressure was rewarded with a fine second place in his season's finale in Portugal and eventually earned him the drive for the following year. Previously, lack of confirmation of the Williams drive almost led Coulthard to join McLaren for the 1995 season. After a succession of podium finishes he took his maiden win in Portugal, moving to McLaren in 1996 since when his fluctuating form has generally seen him overshadowed by team mate Hakkinen.

1989 After great success in karting, he began his car racing career in a Van Diemen RF89 run by David Leslie Snr and won both the Dunlop Star of Tomorrow and P&O Junior FF1600 Championships. He had wins at Thruxton (twice), Brands Hatch (twice), Silverstone (twice), Mallory Park (four times), Castle Combe (twice), Cadwell Park (twice), Snetterton (three times) and at Donington Park, Oulton Park and at Knockhill. On his occasional senior outings he was equally successful and with 3rd in the Formula Ford Festival, he became the McLaren/Autosport Young Driver Award winner.

1990 Moved into Formula Vauxhall with Paul Stewart Racing, finishing 4th in the British Championship, after wins at Silverstone and Brands Hatch. In the Euroseries he took 5th after a win at Knutsdorp, 3rd and 4th at Hockenheim, 4th at Donington Park, 5th at Estoril, 6th at Paul Ricard and Zandvoort and 9th at Imola. A broken leg at Spa dashed his title aspirations in both series, but he also took 2nd in a non-championship race at Zolder, 4th in a German round at Hockenheim and 3rd in the individual with 9th in the team standings at the Spa Nations Cup, partnering Nicky Hart. At Brands Hatch he had a one-off British Touring Car race, taking a Vauxhall Cavalier to 13th.

1991 Stepped up to F3 with Paul Stewart Racing and finished 4th on his debut at Silverstone. Wins at Donington Park, Brands Hatch, Silverstone, Snetterton and Brands Hatch again, brought him head to head with Barrichello for the title. However, a disastrous end to the year saw no points from the rounds at Silverstone and Thruxton, leaving him as the reluctant runner-up. He had

David Coulthard.

Photo: Peter Scherer.

David Coulthard in the Williams FW16.

Photo: BRDC Archive.

also taken 2nd at Brands Hatch and 3rd at Thruxton and Silverstone, and won both the Marlboro Masters at Zandvoort and the Macau Grand Prix, with 2nd at Fuji.

1992 Continuing with PSR he stepped up to F3000, and although a regular top ten finisher he had to wait until round seven at Spa before taking his first points with 4th place. With 3rd at Nogaro and Magny Cours he secured 9th in the championship, his other results being 7th at Albacete, Silverstone and the Nurburgring and 8th at Barcelona. He stepped back into F3 at the end of the year, retiring at Macau and taking 8th at Fuji.

1993 Joined Pacific for another year in F3000 and despite only finishing 13th in the opening round at Donington Park, he soon became a title contender. He won at Enna with 2nd at Silverstone and Pau, but apart from 3rd at Spa and 7th at Nurburgring he failed to record another finish. Both Panis and Lamy overhauled his points and he was left with only third in the championship. He also spent the year as Williams Grand Prix test driver and shared a class win in a Jaguar XJ220C at Le Mans, only to be excluded on a technicality.

1994 The year began in F3000 again with 2nd at Silverstone, but Senna's death plunged him straight into the Williams Grand Prix team. On his debut in Canada he qualified 9th but retired with electrical problems, and followed up with 5th in both the Canadian and British Grands Prix. He quickly settled into the Grand Prix scene and picked up further points from 4th in Belgium and 2nd in Portugal to finish 8th in the World Championship.

GRAND PRIX RECORD

Starts	90
Wins	6
Poles	8
Fastest laps	12
WC points	221
Won his 21st Grand Prix	

1995 He had almost joined McLaren when Williams finally exercised its option. His first pole position was gained in Argentina and he only qualified outside the top three on three occasions. A maiden victory came towards the end of the year in Portugal, after losing out to a late stop go penalty at the British. He also claimed 2nd in Brazil, Germany, Hungary and the Pacific, 3rd in the French, British and European and 4th in San Marino to take 3rd in the World Championship.

1996 Moved on to McLaren but completed the season without a win. He was a points scorer on six occasions, with 2nd at Monaco, 3rd in the European, 4th in the Spanish, 5th in the British and German and 6th in the French, to finish 7th in the Championship.

1997 His second year at McLaren began with victory in Australia. Winning again in Italy, along with 2nd in the Austrian and European, 4th in the British and 6th in the Spanish, brought joint 4th in the World Championship with Alesi. Seven retirements during the year had however cost him dearly.

1998 Another year at McLaren began with controversy, after he allowed team mate Hakkinen through to win in Australia. From thereon he always seemed to be playing back-up to Hakkinen's title campaign. Following his 2nd place in Australia, he took 2nd in Brazil, 6th in Argentina after taking pole, took victory from pole in San Marino, 2nd again in Spain, Austria, Germany and Hungary, 3rd in Luxembourg and Japan, 6th in France and 7th in Belgium to take 3rd in the championship.

1999 The season began with retirement in Australia and Brazil, preceding 2nd places in San Marino and Spain. His greatest success came with victory at the British, followed later in the year by another win in Belgium. Further podium finishes were taken with 2nd in Austria and Hungary, and points from 5th in Germany and Italy saw him take 4th overall in the championship. For 2000 he remains with McLaren as Hakkinen's partner.

--- ❖ ---

DAMON HILL
Born September 17th 1960

As the son of a double World Champion the pressure to succeed was never far away, but rather than cars it was bikes that brought Damon to the racing circuits. After reasonable success at club level, he made his car racing debut at Brands Hatch in late 1983, before mixing the two disciplines during the next season. His patience brought rewards in his second year of FF1600 and led to his graduation into F3, where he became a regular podium finisher during his three years in the category. Three seasons in F3000 with intermittent glimpses of his true promise led to a Williams testing contract in 1992 and a Grand Prix debut with Brabham at the British in the same year. The following year he joined Prost in the Williams Grand Prix team and was an immediate contender for victory. He collected his first win in Hungary the same year and continued to go from strength to strength, finishing third and twice runner-up in the World Championship, before taking the title himself in 1996.

A move to Arrows the following year brought a magnificent second place in Hungary, after leading for almost the entire race, before moving onto Jordan for 1998. He gave the team its maiden victory in the '98 Belgium, but was unable to produce the same form in '99 as talk of his impending retirement overshadowed his driving. His final Grand Prix was the 1999 Japanese which brought to a close a career marked by sportsmanship, honour and great affection from the British public.

GRAND PRIX RECORD	
Starts	116
Wins	22
Poles	20
Fastest laps	19
WC points	360
Won his 13th Grand Prix	

1983 After racing motorbikes all year he made his car debut with an Argo JM14 in the BBC Grandstand Formula Ford 2000 Trophy race at Brands Hatch.

1984 Until August he continued to race bikes exclusively and won the 350cc Champion of Brands title. Having kept his four-wheeled hand in with a couple of Ford Escort Celebrity race wins, he began racing a Ricoh-backed Van Diemen RF84 in Formula Ford 1600. He had a win, two 5ths, 7th and 9th at Brands Hatch, 3rd and 4th at Snetterton and 4th at Thruxton, taking 10th overall in the BP Superfind Championship. At the Formula Ford Festival he finished 5th in the final, with 6th in the FF2000 World Cup at Brands Hatch in an Argo, plus two 8ths and a 9th at Brands Hatch and 8th at Thruxton in the BBC

Grandstand Trophy to receive a Grovewood commendation.

1985 A further year in FF1600 with a Ricoh Van Diemen RF85 brought 3rd in the Esso Championship and 5th in the RAC. He had three wins and a 2nd at Silverstone, a win at Donington Park, 2nd at Thruxton, a 2nd and two 3rds at Brands Hatch and a 2nd at Cadwell Park. He took 9th in the Euro Final at Zolder and 3rd in the Formula Ford Festival. He was also placed 3rd in the Grovewood Awards.

1986 Moved into F3 with a Murray Taylor-run Ralt RT30, finishing 9th in the championship. He was 2nd at Snetterton, 4th at Oulton Park, 5th at Donington Park and Zandvoort, 6th at Silverstone, 6th at Brands Hatch, 8th at Thruxton and 15th in the Brands Hatch Cellnet Superprix. He also won the Brands Hatch Rallysprint.

1987 Spent another year in F3 but with the Cellnet Intersport team in a Ralt RT32, finishing 5th in the championship. He won both the overseas rounds at Zandvoort and Spa, and had a 2nd, 4th and two 5ths at Silverstone, 2nd and 3rd at Brands Hatch, 3rd at Oulton Park and 5th at Thruxton. He also raced in the Maestro Challenge at Silverstone, finishing 3rd and won a Saab Challenge race at Brands Hatch.

1988 Finished 3rd in the British F3 Championship with his Cellnet Ralt, after winning the Grand Prix support race at Silverstone. He added a 3rd and 6th at the same circuit, a win and two 3rds at Thruxton, 2nd at Brands Hatch (twice), 3rd at Oulton Park, 4th at Donington Park (twice) and 4th at Spa. He also contested the Macau and Monaco F3 races, taking 2nd and 6th and also the final F3000 races of the year, retiring at Zolder and finishing 8th at Dijon.

1989 Joined the Footwork F3000 team and made the finish in three of his six starts, 14th at Spa, 15th at Dijon and 16th Le Mans. He also shared a Ford Sierra Cosworth with Sean Walker at Donington Park, taking 4th in the British Touring Car Championship Enduro, finished 3rd at Oulton Park and 6th at Brands Hatch in British F3000 and shared a Porsche 962 with Hobbs at Le Mans.

1990 Signed for Middlebridge Racing for another F3000 campaign, but failed to qualify for the opening round at Donington Park. After retiring at Silverstone and Pau, his first finish came from 7th at Jerez. He took three consecutive pole positions at Monza, Enna and Hockenheim, but despite taking two fastest laps, he only made the finish with 11th at Monza. His best result came with 2nd at Brands Hatch, before the ending the season with 10th at Nogaro.

1991 Another year in F3000, but his Lola was never able to match the Reynards for pace. He picked up points from 6th at Brands Hatch, 4th at Vallelunga and Le Mans, but saved his best for the season's finale at Nogaro where he finished 3rd. His other results included 8th at Jerez and 11th at Enna.

Damon Hill in the Jordan, testing at Silverstone in June 1999.

Photo: Bury Mason.

1992 Joined Williams on a testing contract, but had his first attempt at a Grand Prix debut with Brabham in Spain. After failing to make the grid in his first five attempts, he secured the final place on the grid for the British and survived to finish 16th. He failed to qualify again in Germany, but went to Hungary and finished 11th.

1993 Became a fully fledged member of the Williams Grand Prix team, partnering Alain Prost. He never qualified lower than sixth all year and secured his first pole position for the French. After retiring in the South African opener, he was 2nd in the Brazilian, the Donington Park European, in Monaco and the French. He then took his maiden victory in Hungary, and following it with further consecutive wins in Belgium and Italy. With 3rd in Canada, Portugal and Australian and 4th in Japan, he finished 3rd in the World Championship behind Prost and Senna.

1994 Started the year as Williams number two again to new team mate Senna, finishing 2nd in Brazil and retiring from the Pacific Grand Prix. His 6th at San Marino was all the more creditable as the race had claimed the life of his new team mate, and he suddenly become team leader. He quickly rose to the enormous task and took victories at the Spanish, British, Belgian (after Schumacher's disqualification), Italian, Portuguese and Japanese, with 2nd in the Canadian, French, Hungarian and Jerez European. His season-long battle for the title with Schumacher ended with their infamous collision in Australia, leaving Hill second in the World Championship.

1995 Another year with Williams heralded the continuation of his battle with Schumacher's Benetton. After retiring from a strong drive in the Brazilian Grand Prix when his suspension broke, he won in both Argentina and San Marino. He continued to pick up points from 4th in Spain and 2nd in Monaco and France, but as Schumacher edged away, win number three came in Hungary. Despite collecting 2nd in Belgium, 3rd in Portugal and the Pacific and another win in Australia, he was runner-up again to Schumacher.

1996 Joined at Williams by Jacques Villeneuve, he started the season on tremendous form, with successive wins in Australia, Brazil and Argentina, with 4th in the Nurburgring European GP preceding a further win at San Marino. Having taken nine poles, further wins came in Canada, France and Germany, before taking win number eight in Japan, to clinch the World title over Villeneuve.

1997 Released by Williams he moved to Arrows where the season started disastrously, as he failed to even start the Australian Grand Prix. After taking 17th in Brazil, he had to wait a further five races before recording another finish with 9th in Canada. After 12th in France he picked up a hard-earned point from 6th in the British and followed it up with 8th in Germany. The new found reliability almost brought a victory in Hungary, only for the car to become stuck in gear after dominating the race, but he still limped home 2nd. He recorded further top ten finishes with 7th at the Austrian and 8th at Luxembourg GP, but left the team after one season.

1998 Joined Jordan and began the year with 8th in Australia, Argentina and Monaco, but after spinning off at the British the season turned for the better. 7th in Austria was followed by 4th in Germany and Hungary and victory in Belgium. His run of 6th in Italy, 9th at the Luxembourg GP and 4th in Japan secured him 6th in the World Championship.

1999 Spent a second year with Jordan, but after 4th in San Marino the rumours of his retirement gained momentum and doubts over his participation in the British Grand Prix grew. He raced and finished 5th but the doubts remained as to whether he would complete the season. 6th in Hungary and Belgium were his only other points finishes and his season fizzled out with retirements in the final three races of the year as his Grand Prix career came to an end.

EDDIE IRVINE
Born November 10th 1965

Five years in Formula Ford, firstly in Ireland and then in Britain, culminated in a double championship win and Formula Ford Festival crown in 1987. After one season as a regular podium finisher in F3, he stepped up to F3000 where he finished third in the championship in his second year. With no obvious chance of advancement, he went off to Japan where his F3000 campaigns were supported by occasional sports car outings.

In 1993 he came within a whisker of claiming the All Japan F3000 title and was called on by Eddie Jordan to replace Thierry Boutsen in the final two Grands Prix of the year, finishing 6th in Japan on his debut. After two more years with Jordan he had already re-signed for 1996 when Ferrari invited him to partner Schumacher. With two years spent as the dutiful number two, he collected his first victory in the 1999 season opener in Australia and became team leader after Schumacher broke his leg at Silverstone. Three further wins brought him desperately close to pipping Hakkinen to the World title. But Hakkinen's dominant victory in Japan settled the matter and left Irvine as runner-up after his best season of racing.

Eddie Irvine.

Photo: Peter Scherer.

1983 Raced Formula Ford in Ireland with a Crossle 50F, including taking a 3rd place at Kirkistown.

1984 Began the year racing his Crossle in Ireland, before changing to a Mondiale M84S with immediate success. He had a 2nd and 4th at Kirkistown, three 2nds and a 5th at Mondello Park and 7th in Formula Ford Festival at Brands Hatch. He stayed on at Brands Hatch for the final Champion of Brands rounds, collecting a win and 2nd, and ended his year 4th in a single-seater race and 3rd in a handicap at Kirkistown.

1985 Moved to the British FF1600 scene with a Murray Taylor-run Mondiale M85S, but later changed to a Quest FF85. He finished 10th overall in the Esso Championship, with a 3rd, two 4ths and two 5ths at Silverstone. He had a further 5th at Mondello Park in a Mondiale M84S and made his FF2000 debut in the BBC Grandstand Trophy with a Mondiale, taking 15th at Brands Hatch.

1986 Drove a Mondiale in some early season Irish FF1600 races, before returning to England with a Van Diemen RF85. He had a 3rd at Cadwell Park, 4th at Thruxton, 7th at Brands Hatch, 6th at Silverstone and Snetterton and 8th in the Formula Ford Festival. In the BBC Grandstand Trophy FF2000 Series he raced a Talon, taking 6th in one of the Brands Hatch rounds.

1987 At the wheel of the works Duckhams-backed Van Diemen, he won the Formula Ford Festival and both the RAC and Esso Championships, with 14 wins in total. He had wins at Oulton Park, Silverstone (four times), Thruxton (twice), Brands Hatch (three times), Donington Park (twice) and Kirkistown. With a works FF2000 Van Diemen he also finished 2nd in the BBC Grandstand

Trophy, with two wins and a 2nd at Brands Hatch.

1988 His graduation into F3 came with West Surrey Racing, but while overall victories eluded him he became a regular podium finisher, and took 5th in the championship. He had three 2nds and a 3rd at Silverstone, 2nd and 3rd at Donington Park, 2nd at Brands Hatch, 3rd at Spa and 4th at Oulton Park and Thruxton. He also went to Macau where he won the first heat of the F3 race.

1989 His F3000 baptism with Pacific Racing started with four consecutive non-finishes. After taking 3rd at Enna he collected further points from 4th at Le Mans and Dijon and 6th at Birmingham, to finish 9th in the championship.

1990 A second year in F3000 brought 3rd in the championship behind Erik Comas, after moving to the Jordan team. Although he only recorded six finishes, they were all in the points, with a maiden victory at Hockenheim, 2nd at Monza, 3rd at Brands Hatch and Le Mans, 4th at Enna and 6th at Silverstone. He also contested the Macau and Fuji F3 races finishing 3rd in both.

1991 Moved to Japan to contest F3000 in a Lola T90/50, taking 7th in the championship. He won at Mine, with 4th and 8th at Suzuka, 5th at Autopolis, 7th at Sugo and 9th at Fuji.

1992 Finished 8th in the All Japan F3000 Championship with a Lola. He won at Mine, with 4th and

GRAND PRIX RECORD	
Starts	97
Wins	4
Poles	0
Fastest laps	1
WC points	173
Won his 82nd Grand Prix	

8th at Suzuka and 4th, 5th, 7th and 11th at Fuji. He also raced for Toyota in the Japanese Prototype Series and finished 4th at Fuji with Elgh and Ratzenberger.

1993 A third year in Japanese F3000 saw his Lola just pipped to the title by Hoshino. At Suzuka he had a win, 2nd, 3rd and 4th, with 2nd, 3rd and 6th at Fuji. At Le Mans he shared a Toyota with Suzuki and Sekiya to 4th place and made his Grand Prix debut for Jordan in Japan with a fine 6th place finish. He also raced in the Australian Grand Prix, but retired after damaging his suspension.

1994 A full Grand Prix season with Jordan started with a multiple crash in Brazil. He was given a one-race ban, appealed against the decision and promptly had his penalty trebled. On his return he took 6th in the Spanish GP before accumulating a string of retirements. Reliability returned towards the end of the year, when he collected 7th in Portugal, 4th in the Jerez European GP and 5th in Japan, before spinning out of the Australian finale. He also went to Le Mans again with Toyota, finishing 2nd with Krosnoff and Martini.

1995 With Jordan having exchanged Hart power for Peugeot, his early season qualifying form showed great potential. Mechanical failures forced retirement in both Argentina and Brazil, before his first finish of the year came with 8th in San Marino. 5th in Spain soon followed before his first podium finish came with 3rd in Canada. He went on to score further points from 6th in the Nurburgring European GP and 4th in Japan, finishing 12th in the year's standings.

1996 Jordan agreed to release him after an offer to join Ferrari as Schumacher's number two. He started the year with 3rd in Australia, followed by 7th in Brazil and 5th in Argentina. After retiring from the Nurburgring European GP, he was 4th in San Marino and 7th in Monaco, but from the next 10 starts a 5th place in Portugal was his only finish. He finished 10th in the World Championship.

1997 His second year with Ferrari brought three podium finishes from his first five Grands Prix, with 2nd in Argentina and 3rd in San Marino and Monaco. Apart from 3rd in the French, the rest of the season provided few results, apart from 3rd in Japan when he surrendered a huge lead to boost Schumacher's title charge, and 5th in the European. He was 8th in the World Championship.

1998 Despite numerous rumours, he remained at Ferrari for a third year as Schumacher's number two. He was 2nd in France, Italy and Japan, 3rd in Argentina, San Marino, Monaco, Canada and the British, 4th in Australia, Austria and Luxembourg, and 8th in Brazil and Germany, to finish a strong 4th in the World Championship.

1999 Right from the start of the year he was on peak form, with his maiden victory in the season's opener in Australia. With 2nd at Monaco, 3rd in Canada, 4th in Spain, 5th in Brazil, 6th in France and an engine failure in San Marino, he was an aspiring champion. When Schumacher broke his leg in an accident in the British GP at Silverstone, Irvine was suddenly Ferrari's number one. After 2nd at the British he scored consecutive wins in the

Austrian and German races. He continued to collect points with 3rd in Hungary, 4th in Belgium and 6th in Italy, but after only 7th in the European the odds began to turn against him. Schumacher's return aided a win in Malaysia, despite the threat of a technical exclusion. But despite heading for the Japanese finale with a four point lead over Hakkinen, third place saw him lose out on the title by two points. For 2000 he moves to the Jaguar team to partner Herbert.

Part Six

STATISTICS

CHAPTER 14

THE NON-STARTERS

So near and yet so far..... Thirteen British drivers got as far as qualifying for a World Championship Grand Prix, but never made the start of the race.

Lotus supremo **Colin Chapman** had a one and only opportunity with Vanwall at the 1956 French Grand Prix, qualified in 5th but damaged the car and was unable to start.

Bernie Ecclestone attempted to race in Grands Prix before he ran the whole show, but his Connaught missed the cut at the 1958 Monaco and British.

Former Olympic skier **Divina Galica** had hoped to become only the third woman to race in a World Championship Grand Prix. Her first attempt at the 1976 British was with a Surtees TS16 used more successfully in the Shellsport Group 8 Series. She joined Hesketh the following year, but after finishing last during qualifying in Argentina and Brazil, she moved on.

Brian Gubby raced his Lotus 24 in domestic F1 races in the early sixties, but tried just once to make a Grand Prix start at the 1965 British.

For most of 1992 **Perry McCarthy** was nominated to drive for the Andrea Moda team, one of his main reasons for not qualifying was that he rarely drove the car. At San Marino and the British he failed to progress beyond pre-qualifying, he was excluded from last in Germany and did actually set a time in Belgium but still missed a grid slot by three places. At four other Grands Prix he never got out of the pitlane.

Bill Moss took his F2 Cooper to Aintree for the British Grand Prix in 1959, intending to contest the concurrent F2 class.

The lack of a correct licence stopped **Ken Richardson** from starting the 1951 Italian in a BRM V16, even though he had qualified 10th and was the test and development driver for the car.

Former F5000 and F2 frontrunner **Alan Rollinson** did compete in non-championship F1 races, but his only attempt to start a World Championship race failed when his Gerard Cooper Ford missed the cut at the 1965 British.

Stephen South had a bright future ahead of him when he signed for McLaren in 1980, but after non-qualifying his M29 at Long Beach, he had a serious accident racing in CanAm which ended his career.

Andy Sutcliffe was one of many drivers to try his luck with the RAM team, but failed to get beyond pre-qualifying with a March 761 at the 1977 British.

Dennis Taylor was another driver who aimed to contest the F2 class at the 1959 British Grand Prix, but like Bill Moss his Lotus 12 failed to make it. Three years later he was killed during a Formula Junior race at Monaco.

A former Monaco F3 winner and British F1 Champion, **Tony Trimmer** never got the break into Grand Prix racing that his talents deserved. Driving for Maki he went to the 1975 German, Austrian and Italian, and the 1976 Japanese. He also tried again with his Melchester Racing Surtees TS19 and McLaren M23 at the 1977 and 78 British, without success.

Finally **Ted Whiteway** was mainly a national racer, but he went to Monaco in 1955 to try and get a start in his HWM Alta.

British World Champions

Mike Hawthorn	1958		
Graham Hill	1962	1968	
Jim Clark	1963	1965	
John Surtees	1964		
Jackie Stewart	1969	1971	1973
James Hunt	1976		
Nigel Mansell	1992		
Damon Hill	1996		

British runners-up in the World Championship

Mike Hawthorn	1954			
Stirling Moss	1955	1956	1957	1958
Tony Brooks	1959			
Jim Clark	1962			
Graham Hill	1963	1964	1965	
John Surtees	1966			
Jackie Stewart	1968	1972		
Nigel Mansell	1986	1987	1991	
Damon Hill	1994	1995		
Eddie Irvine	1999			

The following statistics are for the 50 years of the Formula 1 World Championship and cover only British drivers. The top 10 are listed in each of the categories.

Greatest number of Grand Prix starts

1	Nigel Mansell	187
2	Graham Hill	176
3	Martin Brundle	158
4	John Watson	152
5	Derek Warwick	147
6	Johnny Herbert	143
7	Damon Hill	116
8	John Surtees	111
9	Jackie Stewart	99
10	Eddie Irvine	97

Greatest number of fastest laps

1	Nigel Mansell	30
2	Jim Clark	28
3	Damon Hill	19
	Stirling Moss	19
5	Jackie Stewart	15
6	David Coulthard	12
7	John Surtees	11
8	Graham Hill	10
9	James Hunt	8
10	Mike Hawthorn	6

Greatest number of Grand Prix wins

1	Nigel Mansell	31
2	Jackie Stewart	27
3	Jim Clark	25
4	Damon Hill	22
5	Stirling Moss	16
6	Graham Hill	14
7	James Hunt	10
8	Tony Brooks	6
	David Coulthard	6
	John Surtees	6

Greatest number of pole positions

1	Jim Clark	33
2	Nigel Mansell	32
3	Damon Hill	20
4	Jackie Stewart	17
5	Stirling Moss	16
6	James Hunt	14
7	Graham Hill	13
8	David Coulthard	8
	John Surtees	8
10	Mike Hawthorn	4

Greatest number of World Championship points

1	Nigel Mansell	482
2	Damon Hill	360
	Jackie Stewart	360
4	Graham Hill	289
5	Jim Clark	274
6	David Coulthard	221
7	Stirling Moss	186.64
8	John Surtees	180
9	James Hunt	179
10	Eddie Irvine	173

Highest number of wins per race start

1	Jim Clark	1 in 2.88
2	Jackie Stewart	1 in 3.66
3	Stirling Moss	1 in 4.12
4	Damon Hill	1 in 5.27
5	Nigel Mansell	1 in 6.03
6	Tony Brooks	1 in 6.33
7	James Hunt	1 in 9.20
8	Peter Collins	1 in 10.66
9	Graham Hill	1 in 12.57
10	David Coulthard	1 in 15
	Mike Hawthorn	1 in 15

Whatever happened to .....?

It is a question often asked about former racing drivers and many of the surviving members of this elite club of 137 men have been contacted during the author's research. Analysis of the fate of the 137 makes a chilling statement about the dangers of the sport through the 1950s and 1960s in particular.

However, the bare statistics are that 23 of these men died of old age and/or natural causes, while 19 of them perished in racing cars. Five died in aviation accidents and three in road accidents. Three will continue to compete in Grands Prix in 2000 and ten others are still active racers. Another 17 continue to be directly involved in the sport. The remaining 57 are either retired, working outside motorsport or, in the case of John Barber, untraceable.

❖

50 years of British Grand Prix drivers
ALPHABETIC INDEX

50 years of British Grand Prix drivers

Chris Irwin, 125

John James, 48

Leslie Johnson, 49

Rupert Keegan, 179

Chris Lawrence, 126

Geoff Lees, 181

Les Leston, 51

Jack Lewis, 128

Stuart Lewis-Evans, 53

Ken McAlpine, 55

Mike MacDowel, 56

Lance Macklin, 57

Damien Magee, 183

Nigel Mansell, 209

Leslie Marr, 59

Tony Marsh, 59

John Miles, 128

Robin Montgomerie-Charrington, 62

Dave Morgan, 184

Stirling Moss, 62

David Murray, 66

Brian Naylor, 67

Tiff Needell, 211

Rodney Nuckey, 69

Jackie Oliver, 130

Arthur Owen, 132

Jonathan Palmer, 214

Mike Parkes, 133

Reg Parnell, 70

Tim Parnell, 135

David Piper, 72

Dennis Poore, 74

David Prophet, 136

Tom Pryce, 186

David Purley, 187

Ian Raby, 137

Brian Redman, 139

Alan Rees, 143

John Rhodes, 144

John Riseley-Prichard, 76

Richard Robarts, 188

Tony Rolt, 76

Roy Salvadori, 78

Archie Scott-Brown, 81

Brian Shawe-Taylor, 83

Mike Spence, 146

Alan Stacey, 84

Ian Stewart, 85

Jackie Stewart, 148

Jimmy Stewart, 87

John Surtees, 150

Henry Taylor, 88

John Taylor, 152

Mike Taylor, 90

Trevor Taylor, 154

Eric Thompson, 91

Leslie Thorne, 92

Desmond Titterington, 92

Peter Walker, 93

Derek Warwick, 216

John Watson, 190

Peter Westbury, 156

Ken Wharton, 94

Graham Whitehead, 97

Peter Whitehead, 98

Bill Whitehouse, 100

Robin Widdows, 157

Mike Wilds, 192

Jonathan Williams, 158

Roger Williamson, 195

Vic Wilson, 159